Divided Sisters

Divided Sisters

Bridging the Gap Between
Black Women and
White Women

Midge Wilson and Kathy Russell

Anchor Books
Doubleday
New York
London
Toronto
Sydney
Auckland

AN ANCHOR BOOK
PUBLISHED BY DOUBLEDAY
a division of Bantam Doubleday Dell Publishing Group, Inc.
1540 Broadway, New York, New York 10036

ANCHOR BOOKS, DOUBLEDAY and the portrayal of an anchor are
trademarks of Doubleday, a division of Bantam Doubleday Dell
Publishing Group, Inc.

The names of some of the people who appear in this book, along with details of their lives,
have been changed to protect their privacy.

The authors gratefully acknowledge permission to reprint the following:

Page 37 from "Nikki-Rosa" by Nikki Giovanni. From *Black Feeling, Black Talk, Black
Judgment* by Nikki Giovanni. Copyright © 1973 by Nikki Giovanni. Reprinted by
permission of Broadside Press.

Page 107–8 from "In Magazines (I Found Specimens of the Beautiful)" by Ekua Omosupe.
Copyright © 1990 by Ekua Omosupe. From *Making Face, Making Soul/Haciendo Caras:
Creative and Critical Perspectives by Feminists of Color*. Copyright © 1990 by Gloria
Anzaldúa. Reprinted by permission of Aunt Lute Books.

Page 109 from "Barbie Doll" by Marge Piercy. From *Circles on the Water* by Marge Piercy.
Copyright © 1982 by Marge Piercy. Reprinted by permission of Alfred A. Knopf, Inc.

Page 111 from "I Have Been Hungry" by Carolyn M. Rodgers. From *How I Got Ovah:
New and Selected Poems* by Carolyn M. Rodgers. Copyright © 1976 by Doubleday, a division
of Bantam Doubleday Dell Publishing Group, Inc. Reprinted by permission of Doubleday.

Page 132–33 from "does it matter if she's white?" by Dajenya Kafle. Copyright © 1993 by
Dajenya Kafle. From *Sister/Stranger: Lesbians Loving Across the Lines,* edited by Jan Hardy
(Sidewalk Revolution Press, 1993). Reprinted by permission of the author.

Page 197–98 from "Among Things That Use to Be" by Willie M. Coleman. From *Home
Girls: A Black Feminist Anthology,* edited by Barbara Smith. Reprinted by permission of the
author and of Kitchen Table: Women of Color Press, Box 40-4920, Brooklyn, NY 11240.

Page 201–2 from "Who Said It Was Simple" by Audre Lorde. From *From a Land Where
Other People Live* by Audre Lorde. Copyright © 1973 by Audre Lorde. Reprinted by
permission of Broadside Press.

Page 210–11 from "In Answer to the Question: Have You Ever Considered Suicide?" by
Kate Rushin. Copyright © 1990 by Kate Rushin. From *The Black Women's Health Book:
Speaking for Ourselves,* edited by Evelyn C. White. Reprinted by permission of the Seal Press.

The Library of Congress has cataloged the Anchor hardcover edition as follows:
Wilson, Midge
    Divided sisters : bridging the gap between black women and white
women / by Midge Wilson and Kathy Russell.
        p.   cm.
    Includes index.
    1. Afro-American women—Social conditions. 2. White women—United
States—Social conditions. 3. Racism—United States. 4. United States—
Race relations. I. Russell, Kathy. II. Title.
E185.86.W555   1996
305.4'0973—dc20   95-8966
                                                             CIP

ISBN 0-385-47362-1
Copyright © 1996 by Midge Wilson and Kathy Russell

All Rights Reserved
Printed in the United States of America
First Anchor Books Trade Paperback Edition: February 1997
10   9   8   7   6   5   4   3   2

This book is dedicated to our mothers,
Marjorie Nock Wilson
and
Dorothy Clarese Russell,
the primary
women in our lives.

Acknowledgments

We would like to express enormous thanks to our editor at Anchor/Double-day, Roger Scholl, whose early faith in and enthusiasm for our project helped to make this book a reality. And although we had to explain to him what "house music" is, Roger was very knowledgeable on a wide range of issues about women and race. We would also like to thank his assistant, Papatya Bucak, for her careful attention to detail throughout publication.

Individually, Midge Wilson would like to express her appreciation to the following: First of all, to literary agent Suzanne Gluck at International Creative Management for her support and friendship. Best of luck with your new son, Nicholas. One of the people who helped to make the mountain of work manageable is Sandra Trafalis, my graduate research assistant, whose sleuth-like talent for tracking down obscure references and cheerful demeanor helped to keep the book on course. I would like to thank my co-author and friend Kathy Russell, the diva of excellent book ideas, and DePaul University's library staff for their assistance in finding books and journal and newspaper articles. I would also like to give a special, loving thanks to my husband, Shaun Reynolds, for his sweet understanding of my variable moods during the long two years it took to complete this project. I extend my love and appreciation to my family, especially my mom and dad, for being so proud of me. Finally, I would like to give a special thanks to the birthday club women, Claire Dishman, Sandi Belushi, and Toy Suddeth, for keeping me laughing.

Kathy Russell would like to thank the following:
First, I would like to thank God for making it all possible. I would also

like to thank my mom, Dorothy, for her love, inspiration, and friendship; my father, Will R. Russell, for his artistic genes (you are the real writer, Dad!); my literary agent, Matt Bialer, at the William Morris Agency, for his professional support and belief in me; my manager girlfriend Allison Jordan for her longtime friendship (I love you Allie); my friend Shannon Marie, who forever encourages me and who is always there for me no matter when I call or where I may be; my friend and protector, Al, for being there for me all those years (you are so dear to me); my co-author, Midge Wilson, whom I admire, whom I've learned so much from, and whose friendship and partnership I will forever cherish. And I would like to give a special thanks to all the brave, bold, beautiful, wise, and wonderful women of this world who have inspired me and continue to fill me with the pride and wisdom of their womanhood, so that I may continue to realize my own potential and special place as a female in this universe.

Contents

Introduction

White women are so nosy. They are always asking a bunch of questions, trying to find out things that are none of their business.

—*Hillari, a thirtysomething
Black secretary*

It's so hard to establish trust with African American women. Even when you work closely with them on a political campaign, like I have, they always seem to hold something back.

—*Helen, a fortysomething
White woman in public relations*

These two comments represent the mere tip of the iceberg in the Arctic Ocean of tension that too commonly exists between African American women and White women. Why, after more than three decades of Civil Rights legislation, school desegregation, and widely integrated work environments, are so many White women and Black women still at odds with one another? While men have fared no better, and arguably race relations between men have been worse, somehow it seems that women, who have fought so hard to overcome inequality in the workplace and the stigma of second-class citizenship, would have formed friendships and alliances through their common cause. For over twenty years, feminists have been proclaiming that all women are "sisters beneath the skin." But it turns out that the appeals for sisterly solidarity during the first two decades of the modern feminist movement were issued largely by White women, rather than White women and Black women together. These women, their Black counterparts have proclaimed, were ignorant and insensitive to the harsher realities of racism experienced by Blacks. In turn, White women, to their frustration, have felt that Black women resisted change and sisterhood, focusing exclusively on the concerns and agendas of Black males, continually placing the issue of race and the needs of the men in the Black community before their own, often separate issues.

The fact is that few White women or Black women as adults have close friendships with women from different racial backgrounds. As we rapidly approach the turn of another century, it would seem the time has come to examine the many reasons for women's continuing racial coldness, indifference, and more than occasional anger toward one another. We fastened on the title *Divided Sisters* because, despite "sisterhood," the reality is that the overwhelming majority of White women and Black women dwell in separate cultures. As Sharon A., an African American high school circulation librarian, described it, "In the faculty lunchroom, there are the White tables and the Black tables. You might acknowledge women at the 'other' table, but never would you sit with them." White women are often hurt and confused by Black women's preference for separating themselves. White women also underestimate just how different the two cultures can be. When Candy, a White college student from Arlington, Virginia, first discovered that her freshman roommate was Black, she thought, "Okay, this will be fun." But by the end of the year, Candy had this to say:

Rosemary, my roommate, played different kinds of music than I was used to, and filled the room with strange-smelling perfume and hair products that I was unaccustomed to. She even ate certain types of food than I had never seen before. I mean I liked Rosemary fine—and I think that she liked me, too—but we mutually decided to call it quits. For our sophomore year, we both chose roommates who were of the same race.

While schools and workplaces may be officially integrated, most dormitories, neighborhoods, churches, and nightclubs are decidedly not. And it is there, within these social milieus, where true friendships develop and endure.

In a more positive vein, we subtitled our book *Bridging the Gap Between Black Women and White Women.* We believe that despite, or perhaps because of, women's lesser political power, it is they, rather than men, who hold the key to improving race relations in this country. By now, it is clear that as long as women of different races remain at odds, traditional, White-male-dominated corporations and institutions will change only incrementally, if at all. Conversely, society will transform itself only when women decide together to fight social inequality in all its various forms, whether based on race, gender, or class.

Certainly women of Latino culture, and those of Asian, Middle Eastern, and Native American descent, are part of this engine of change. We hope that they will read and learn from this book as well, and not feel left out of the discussion. The fact is, however, that tackling the relationships between women of two racial backgrounds and cultures is itself an ambitious and challenging focus for a book, and the relationship between Black women and White women in our culture is, because of the far-reaching economic effects of slavery and century-long legal constraints of segregation, by far the association with the oldest and fullest history. It is our hope that by addressing the obstacles to better relations between White women, who help to make up the "dominant" culture, and African American women, who make up the "dominant" racial subculture, we can also improve relations between women of other races.

A book of this nature should address, and diffuse as well, some of the controversy behind the meaning of race. Increasingly, scientists say that race has no basis in biology. While this may be true when it comes to genetics, on a more practical level race continues to have enormous sociopolitical meaning in this country. Race has something to do with skin color, but it is defined by much more than that. Having white skin generally, but not always, means that you are White. Nonetheless, many Latinos have white skin, yet they are not considered White in this culture. And there are some Blacks with lighter skin than many Whites, yet they are not considered White, either. The reason for the apparent contradictions goes back to the one-drop rule of racial identity. During the Colonial era, persons who were racially mixed and free were legally declared to be Black, even if they had but one drop of African blood, as a means of restricting this growing population and limiting their rights. More than three hundred years later, this "rule" still permeates our cultures and dictates the identities of most African Americans. Those who attempt to claim multiple racial identities are often met with strong resistance, from White supremacists, but also from Blacks who fear the weakening of their political base if the Black community starts to splinter. Thus, whether biologically based or not, persons of European ancestry in the United States are assumed to be White and are raised and treated as such, while those of mixed or pure African ancestry are assumed to be Black.

Another issue we grappled with is terminology. In the past few years, the term for those of African descent living in the United States has changed from Black to African American. The newer label is preferred by many because it places emphasis on the cultural aspects of racial identity, as opposed to just skin color. We debated long and hard about the use of "Black" versus "African American," especially in the subtitle. In the end, we decided that *Bridging the Gap Between African American Women and White Women* was awkward and unbalanced, while *Women of African and European Descent* reeked of political correctness or academic jargon. We settled on *Black Women and White Women,* in large part because it was the easiest to say. For now, at least, the terms Black and African American remain interchangeable, especially in casual conversation.

And finally, we needed to take into the account the issue of class in discussions of race. Whenever anyone attempts to make generalizations about one group compared with another, as in "White women are this way and Black women are that way," they risk gross racial stereotyping. This is particularly true when one attempts to discuss people who come from widely disparate educational and economic backgrounds. Distinguishing between differences of class and differences of race is a constant struggle, and we have tried to acknowledge the continual interplay of race and class. At the same time, in a racist country like ours, perceptions often outweigh realities; Oprah Winfrey or Whitney Houston, among the wealthiest people in all of show business, can still be passed over by a cab driver in favor of a White passenger. Snap judgments are made all the time on the basis of skin color. The sad truth is that racial stereotypes of women, whether we dare to name them or not, exist in the day-to-day world.

Throughout *Divided Sisters,* several themes emerge to define and shape women's cross-race relations. The first is the issue of power and privilege. As far back as the Colonial era, White women enjoyed an unequal position of power in their relations with women who are Black. On plantations in the antebellum South and throughout a good part of the twentieth century, many White middle-class and upper-class families across America could count on the services of Black women to cook their food, clean their homes, and raise their children. Rarely have African American women had the luxury, or even the desire, to hire White women to do the same for them. And to this day, in female-dominated pink-collar occupations, where as many as 70 percent of women are employed, far more White women supervise Black women than vice versa.

Issues of privilege also affect relations between White women and Black women. Regardless of economic circumstance, White women can count on skin color privilege, that invisible package of benefits that comes from simply being White in a primarily White society, especially one that has historically discriminated against Blacks. For most White women, racism is not a factor in their lives. They don't even think about it. This was recently driven home to us when we were on a plane traveling to Omaha, Nebraska. When she was serving refreshments, the White female flight attendant skipped over the row we occupied. Midge interpreted the woman's behavior as mere oversight, but Kathy, who had noticed that she was the only African American person on board the flight, could not help considering the possibility that the attendant's actions were racially motivated. In some instances, the behavior of the offending person is racially motivated; but even when it's not, the effect of race discrimination and inequality in our society raises questions about individual and corporate motivation, questions that do not arise for White women.

A more controversial theme we explore in the book is that of competition. Whether at school, at work, or in politics, African American women and White women have often assumed a competitive stance, vying with one another for a limited number of scholarships, promotions, or elected positions at the top. While sex discrimination has much to do with this, rarely have Black women and White women recognized the divisive effect of such competition. As a result, more often than not, Black women and White women view one another as major obstacles to their own advancement. This is exactly what happened to an African American woman named Sandrya and a White woman named Rebecca, both of whom were up for partnership in the same year at a prestigious, primarily White male law firm. Sandrya was convinced the firm would deny a partnership to a woman of color; Rebecca was certain that the firm, intent on becoming more racially diverse, would opt for a woman who was Black.

A more subtle issue has to do with standards of beauty and femininity. In a culture that narrowly defines the ideal feminine beauty as White, anorexically slim, and preferably blond, tensions among women of the two races are bound to run high. So vast is the subject of beauty that it spills over to affect girls' friendships from childhood to college, women's political alliances, and their images in the media. Ultimately, questions of beauty exacerbate differences between "mainstream" American culture, as seen in the pages of *Vogue, Cosmopolitan,* and other publications, and African American culture.

There is perhaps no more divisive or potentially explosive issue between White women and Black women than interracial sex, dating, and marriage. For reasons that are both historical and contemporary, sexual jealousy continues to plague women's cross-race relations. As an African American woman named Missy from the East Coast complained:

> When I was a junior in college, I had a White roommate who was very pretty and dated a lot. I used to get pissed off because it was mostly Black guys, the cute popular ones or the basketball stars, who came by to see her. Here I am, an attractive Black girl, and it's my White roommate who had all the Black guys coming to see her, not me.

For Black women, such jealousies are partly fueled by the shortage of marriageable Black men—among Blacks, there are seven men for every ten women, while among Whites, there are ten men to nine women—and the tendency among successful and celebrated Black men, including O. J. Simpson and Michael Jackson, to take White women as wives because of their perceived higher status in society. Ironically, most White women who date interracially tend to see their behavior as proof that they are not racially prejudiced. They can't understand why Black women don't see such dating in the same light. This gap in understanding and interpretation of interracial sex only sets the stage for more conflicts between Black and White women.

Beneath the surface of relations lie often unspoken feelings of guilt and resentment. Such destructive feelings pervade nearly every aspect of Black and White women's lives together, from love affairs to work relationships.

Feelings of guilt permeate women's social relations as well. A White woman named Cheryl remembers one night when a homeless Black man was spotted by party guests in the alley below. The White hostess, apparently fearing that the only African American woman present might think her racist, invited the man upstairs. Unwittingly, the hostess ended up angering the woman, who deeply resented that she was being equated with a homeless man simply because she and he were both Black.

If guilt proves divisive for White women in their relations with African American women, resentment often divides Black women from White. African American women are bitter that even the poorest White women seem to have a better chance of experiencing upward social mobility than many middle-class Black women. They also resent that standards of beauty and desirability are slanted against them. Even as minor a matter as hair texture and hair style, in this atmosphere, can be a source of intense irritation, if not rage. A Black lawyer named Cassandra said, "One of the big reasons why I can hardly stomach White women is because of their hair."

White women, too, harbor feelings of resentment. Affirmative-action programs may grant advantages to Black women in the workplace or in gaining entrance to college over equally qualified or needy White women. Such negative feelings can begin as early as adolescence. We spoke to Patty, a White high school cheerleader, who took exception to the presence of a Black cheerleader, Michelle, on the varsity squad. Patty believed that Michelle was picked only because she was Black, even though some of the White girls who were not selected had better skills.

Despite these different concerns, increasing numbers of women of both races are forming lasting interracial relationships. The most powerful expression of this intimacy is manifested in the interracial relationships of White and Black lesbians, but many heterosexual women are also coming to value deeply their friendships with women of the other race. Still, these friendships are viewed differently by women of the two races. Black women rarely want to gloss over the racial differences, whereas White women often do. Deanna, a White woman, learned the hard way not to "whiteface" her Black girlfriend, Temple, when she expressed her feelings of fondness for her by saying "Your blackness doesn't faze me. I see you as my best friend, as a person with no color." To Deanna's surprise, Temple shot back, "A major part of who I am is that I'm a Black woman. For you not to see me as Black really hurts." Despite such occasional flare-ups, Deanna and Temple have successfully learned to negotiate the sometimes treacherous but ultimately rewarding waters of an interracial friendship. As an African American journalist named Audrey Edwards wrote, about a White girlfriend with whom she had been tracking birthdays for twenty-five years, "Race, in some ways, has mattered the least in our friendship, [but] in other ways, it has mattered most." Or, as another light-skinned African American woman, Stephanie, put it, summarizing why her friendship with a White woman, "We know that we are divided by our race, but we also know that we are bound by our gender. And what is common between us—that we both are women—is as strong as the race that divides us."

Perhaps this bridge of affection between Black women and White women is best seen in racially mixed families, such as those in which the father is Black and the mother is White. Among the Black and biracial women celebrities from these families are actresses Jasmine Guy and Halle Berry, singers Mariah Carey and Paula Abdul, and *Village Voice* columnist Lisa Jones; each gives credit to her White mother for raising her well. And in other racially mixed families, where a White mother adopts a Black daughter, there is no question that the maternal bond is secure. As Mary Brown, a White California foster mother who has been trying to adopt the biracial girl she took in more than three years ago, put it, "You don't spell love C-O-L-O-R."

A spirit of cooperation and hope for social change has similarly marked the relations of Black and White women activists throughout history, from the nineteenth century, when the Grimké sisters and Sojourner Truth joined forces to help bring an end to slavery and win female suffrage, to the present. But for women's status in society to be truly advanced, everyday women, not just feminists and those on the front line, must begin to work together. A house divided will never stand. It is our intent in *Divided Sisters* to open doors between women of different races, to provoke discussion, and to expose to the sunlight and open air some of the issues that distinguish and too often divide American women of European and African descent. To some extent, the interracial experiences that inspired us to undertake this book are further reflections of the spirit of unity and hope among growing numbers of White and Black women today. We believe a book like this is long overdue.

Chapter One

History

The Divisions Begin

There is no slave, after all, like a wife . . . Poor women, poor slaves
. . . All married women, all children and girls who live in their fathers'
house are slaves.

—*Mary Boykin Chesnut*
A Diary from Dixie, *1861*

Moreover, my mistress, like many others, seemed to think that slaves had
no right to any family ties of their own; that they were created merely to
wait upon the family of the mistress.

—*Harriet Jacobs*
Incidents in the Life of a Slave Girl, *1861*

Departing from separate, distant shores, European and African women first sailed into American history together at Jamestown in 1619. The White women came as part of a plan to ensure the continuing success of the first permanent English settlement in the New World. Those in charge of the new colony feared that if "maydens" were not sent soon, the tiny settlement would fail. In contrast, the first African women who disembarked at Jamestown that same year were rather less expected, although perhaps no less welcome. They were among a small group of mostly male African slaves on board a Spanish slave vessel en route to the West Indies when it was pirated at sea by a "Dutch man of War" ship. After finding his way to Virginia, the ship's captain, in need of food, offered his human bounty in exchange for more substantial supplies. Thus it was that, as casualties of imperialism, the first women of European and African descent stepped ashore in America.

Nearly four hundred years later, we can only speculate how these women, whose appearance and culture varied sharply, reacted when they set eyes on each other. History has traditionally been written from the male perspective, but in this chapter, our nation's past will be framed by the unique experiences of White women and Black women. They were not always in conflict. Initially, in fact, they likely shared an intense desire not to be in this strange land. But as the scattered settlements grew, and most particularly as slavery was institutionalized and race mixing banned, their experiences diverged along lines of color, class, and freedom. Even when slavery ended, relations between Black women and White women were so damaged that the women were unable to form an effective alliance to win their suffrage. Exploring Black and White women's history together can help us better understand why so many tensions still linger between them.

Early Relationships

For the most part, White women did not want to come to the New World; they were bribed, captured, and banished here as punishment. Nonetheless, some American history books continue to romanticize the arrival of the first White women—portraying them in pictures as fashionably dressed, carrying parasols, and strolling down gangplanks to a crowd of eagerly awaiting courtly gentlemen. The stark reality was that most of the women were

....

prostitutes and waifs, ne'er-do-wells and religious dissidents, rounded up off the streets of London and rudely informed that their punishment was shipment abroad. A more accurate scenario is that of downtrodden females dressed in filthy rags, staggering off rat-infested ships, sick and demoralized, albeit grateful to be on land again. Once they disembarked, these White women, like many of those who followed, were treated like chattel, sold as indentured servants to the highest bidder. Indeed, it is estimated that up to 80 percent of all female English immigrants to arrive in the colonies during the 1600s paid for their voyage with four to seven years of hard labor.

The first Negro women who came to America were similarly sold as indentured servants. As good Christians, the colonists were morally opposed to slavery, so all servants were set free following some specified period of servitude. Originally, the darker-skinned women and men came not directly from Africa, but from the West Indies, where slavery had been in practice since the early 1500s. Some of them were educated, and a few had already converted to Christianity. In general, the colonial landowners who purchased servants of African descent viewed them as good workers, stronger than most Whites, and less inclined to escape into the wilderness like the Indians. The demand for their labor grew. A 1625 census indicated that there were only twenty-three Blacks, of whom ten were female, but by 1649, there was an estimated three to five hundred Negro servants. Even then, the majority of bound servants who came to the colonies were English.

For White and Black female indentured servants alike, life was physically demanding, with no guarantee of survival. Along with the men, they were sent to the fields to clear the undergrowth and plant the crops. In the evenings, the women were also expected to cook, clean, garden, and sew. And if they disobeyed, they were flogged at the whipping post. Female servants faced the additional hazard of being sexually assaulted by unscrupulous masters who stood to benefit economically from their misconduct. Colonial law was such that an indentured servant who became pregnant during her servitude was required to serve her master an additional two years. In 1662, this outrageous law was only slightly modified, so that a servant who became pregnant still had to serve an extra two years, but under a different master.

Before the mid-seventeenth century, far more men than women had made the journey to America, in part because landowners preferred male to female laborers. Among the Africans there were at least three men for every two women, and among the Europeans there were as many as three to four men for every woman. The resulting imbalance had a number of curious social effects. For one, there was a fairly high rate of interracial marriage, especially between White men and Black women. In the wilderness no one seemed to care much, and mulatto children were a common sight. Second, the scarcity of females meant that a woman of either race who started life in America as an indentured servant could greatly improve her social and economic standing in the community by marrying someone with land, perhaps even her former owner. And if she was then lucky enough to outlive her husband, or if she inherited land from her father, she might become a landowner herself. The shortage of women probably helped women of both races get along better. Instead of being fierce adversaries in a tight marriage market, they could relax and be friends; for once there were plenty of good men to go around.

Slavery

By the second half of the seventeenth century, life for colonial Black women changed dramatically for the worse. As the demand for a cheap, permanent labor force rose, Christian concerns about the morality of slavery ebbed. Up and down the Atlantic Coast, colonies passed laws that rendered Negro indentured servants ineligible for freedom. It was also during this time that the demand for African women grew, as slave traffickers and local buyers realized the profit of exploiting slave women as both workers and breeders. The rights of landowning African men were gradually taken away, and African women's opportunities for marrying up were further reduced when interracial relationships were outlawed.

With the institutionalization of slavery, the growing population of free mulattoes in the colonies came to be viewed as a threat to society. What was the status of those who were half Black and half White in a land where race dictated who lived free and who was enslaved? In 1662, the same year that the Virginia Assembly modified its statute governing the servitude of pregnant women, colonial legislators declared that offspring rights in America would follow those of the mother, not the father. The immediate effect of the statute was to dash the hopes of slave women that their children sired by free Black men and by White men would live free. Even worse, the law encouraged White masters to exploit their female slaves sexually in order to increase the number of slaves they owned.

By the beginning of the eighteenth century, slavery was an established fact of life. For every new indentured servant imported from England, three to four slaves were imported from Africa. The slave trade continued to flourish at this rate until 1807, when it was finally abolished. By then, close to a million slaves of African descent had been brought to America, and many others were being born daily in the New World.

During the 1700s, women's lives divided strictly along lines of color. Tensions between women of the two races mounted as White women vacillated between relishing their higher status and relative power over Black women, and feeling sympathetic toward those less fortunate than themselves. On an individual basis, how Black and White women treated each other depended on such factors as personality, religious and political affiliation, and geography—whether they lived in the North or South, in rural or urban areas.

Before the American Revolution, most female slaves in the North worked as domestics in urban settings in groups of one to three. Male slaves tended to remain in the country, where they were needed to work the land. This was the pattern until some time after the Revolution, when the political climate began to change. The fight for national independence inspired many Northerners to liberate their slaves, and some joined the abolitionist movement. With an influx of White ethnic immigrants willing to work cheaply, the economic benefits of owning slaves also lessened. By the end of the eighteenth century, most states above the Mason-Dixon Line had voted to bring an end to slavery.

Quaker women were especially vocal in their opposition. Throughout the eighteenth century, they began offering freedom to their female house slaves, and others soon followed suit. Most White women, particularly wealthy ones charged with running large households, needed the domestic help, though, and did not wish to terminate relationships with their slaves. With their husbands' permission, they offered the former slaves a pittance to be paid servants instead, so even after freedom was granted, most Negro women remained in the homes of White women and were dependent on White women to treat them with kindness.

Northern White women varied in their treatment of Black women, both as slaves and as domestic servants. While many Whites were abusive, some nurtured their female African house slaves and supported their education. When John and Susannah Wheatley in 1761 purchased a slender girl of seven or eight, shivering on a Boston dock, they could have denied her an education and allowed her to pass into obscurity like so many African women who came to America. Instead, Mrs. Wheatley taught the girl they named Phillis to read and write, and gave her free access to the family's library. Mrs. Wheatley, by encouraging her slave to write poetry, helped Phillis Wheatley become this country's first published author of African descent. Sadly, when her White patron died, Phillis Wheatley found her life take a dramatic turn for the worse. Legally she was free, but poetry has never paid well. She ended up marrying a man who alienated her White friends, and she lost important literary contacts. Eventually she succumbed to poverty and disease in a boarding house in 1784.

In the predominantly rural South reliance on and defense of slavery grew after America's independence. During the eighteenth and early nineteenth centuries, White women and Black women viewed each other across a line of freedom, where their lives often touched and overlapped. While the majority of slaves in the rural South worked alongside poor White wives doing backbreaking fieldwork and domestic chores, less is known about these women than about those who worked on the larger plantations. And even among the slaves on the wealthier estates, less is known about the 95 percent of females who worked the fields every day than about the handful who came inside. Much of what we do know about all women of the antebellum South comes from the diaries of White mistresses, as they were called, who wrote about their house slaves, and from the journals of former house slaves who were educated enough to leave records of their own. Female field slaves and mistresses rarely interacted, nor did many free Black women and White women, rich or poor.

Well-to-do Southern White women were expected to do their part to uphold the plantation image, subservient to an all-powerful husband and mistress of a "family of contented slaves." As historian Anne Firor Scott put it, "Women, like slaves, were an intrinsic part of the patriarchal dream." The true Southern lady was at all times virtuous and self-sacrificing, and the wives of yeoman farmers and others on the social scale sought to attain her charming ways and perfect decorum. Ironically, even free mulatto women in cities like Charleston and New Orleans imitated the affectations of White mistresses, carrying parasols and feigning weakness when it came to doors that needed opening.

The women of both races interacted according to these unwritten rules. White women were expected to be passive because they were ladies, and Black women were expected to be submissive because they were slaves. Not surprisingly, their feelings toward each other ran the gamut. Undoubtedly, female slaves envied mistresses for being free, and especially for knowing that their children would never be sold. Yet some White women also saw advantages in how Black men treated Black women, more as equals than as subordinates.

To keep the plantation household running smoothly, mistresses and female slaves alike worked hard. Before sunrise, house hands were expected to be at the "big house," where they cooked, cleaned, washed, mended, ironed, and made clothes. They also milked the cows, fed the chickens, and kept a watchful eye on the White children. Like their Black female slaves, White mistresses faced a mountain of chores every day. During a visit to America, Harriet Martineau, commenting on the workload of the Southern plantation wife, said that she "is forever superintending, and trying to keep things straight, without the slightest hope of attaining anything like leisure and comfort." Even slaves verified that their mistresses toiled endlessly. Polly Colbert recalled that "Miss Betsey cut out all de clothes and helped wid de sewing . . . She learnt all her women to sew . . . She done all the sewing for de children." In addition to overseeing all the cooking, cleaning, and sewing, plantation ladies were also expected to be perfect hostesses, regularly entertaining their husband and his friends. As one mistress confessed, "I have almost gotten thro' Christmas. What a slave a holiday makes of a mistress! Indeed, she is always a slave, but doubly and trebly so at such times."

Although wealthy plantation wives, including Mary Boykin Chesnut, whose diary entry opens this chapter, frequently mentioned working as hard as their slaves, few of them actually understood or identified with the condition of slavery. In reality, most mistresses saw themselves more as martyrs than as oppressed sisters in their dealings with female slaves. White Southern ladies may have complained about having to manage their house slaves, but they nonetheless believed that slavery was essential to their privileged position as plantation mistresses. In fact, the more slaves a mistress had, the greater her status as a Southern lady.

Southern White men were, of course, highly invested in making sure that White women in Southern society thought the same way they did on the subject of slavery. Virginia planter and proslavery philosopher George Fitzhugh, convinced that slavery helped preserve the natural softness of White Southern women, claimed that women of the North were hardened by having been "thrown into the arena of industrial war." Author Thomas

Dew suggested that class slavery was at least better than gender slavery, because having slaves rescued White women from various kinds of labor that they might otherwise have had to do themselves. And William Drayton similarly detailed the ways in which White women benefited from the institution of slavery:

> Her faculties are developed, her gentle and softening influences is seen and felt; she assumes the high stations for which nature designed her; and happy in the hollowed affections of her own bosom, unwearily exerts those powers so well adapted to the task of humanizing and blessing others.

For the most part, White women were convinced of the necessity of owning slaves. They drew the line, however, at female slaves serving as prostitutes. The argument that sex with slaves was advantageous to the plantation owner, as he could simultaneously satisfy his sexual needs and increase his slave property, was an affront to most White women. Although some may have privately believed, as did their husbands, that Black women were by nature more promiscuous than themselves, they nonetheless saw few advantages in having a spouse spend his spare time in the slave cabins.

Among the slaves, few girls could hope to reach the age of sixteen without being sexually assaulted. At any time, anywhere, a master, his son, the overseer, or a neighbor might suddenly decide to have his way with her. In addition to the physical and psychological pain of such attacks, the women often had to contend with pregnancy and venereal disease. Worse, these women were blamed for their own rape, unfairly characterized as Jezebels constantly tempting good White men. Although occasionally a female slave did actively seek the affections of a master in the hope that he would grant her special favors and privileges, such women were typically scorned by the other slaves.

While White mistresses were spared the physical trauma of rape, they too suffered from their husbands' constant infidelities. One North Carolina planter rudely informed his wife that his favorite slave was now in charge of all domestic duties. This "gentleman" then proceeded to sleep with his concubine in his wife's bedroom. An Alabama woman finally left her husband and went to live with her parents when he abandoned her for one of his slaves. Some White wives simply resigned themselves to the fact that their husbands were sexually promiscuous; others comforted themselves with the delusion that their husbands' sexual commerce with slaves was better than adultery with other White women. Most Southern White women, however, learned to perfect the psychological defense of denial, a strategy apparent in an entry from Mary Chesnut's diary:

> Like the patriarchs of old our men live all in one house with their wives and their concubines, and the mulattoes one sees in every family exactly resemble the white children—and every lady tells you who is the father of all the mulatto children in everybody's household, but those in her own she seems to think drop from the clouds, or pretends so to think.

No other issue so divided mistresses and house slaves as deeply as plantation rape. Sometimes when wives could no longer handle their husbands' infidelities, they vented their frustrations on female house slaves. One mistress, suspecting that her husband was molesting a thirteen-year-old house slave, severely beat and whipped the girl, then locked her in the smokehouse for two weeks. Fearing that she might eventually kill the slave, the mistress finally ordered her son to sell the girl.

Light-skinned mulatto women were particularly vulnerable to the sexual advances of White men, and unfortunately they were the ones most frequently chosen as house servants. According to the "mulatto hypothesis," slaves with an infusion of White blood were more intelligent than those who were pure African. Consequently, it was erroneously believed that mulatto women made the finest house slaves, best able to learn the nuances of European customs, and slave jobs were frequently assigned on the basis of color, with darker-skinned women working the fields and lighter-skinned women inside.

Not all dealings between mistresses and slave women centered on rape. Nor were all Black-White female relationships filled with conflict. When women work closely together on a daily basis, as mistresses and house servants did, great bonds of friendship can form. One Southern gentleman, reflecting back on the relationship between his mother and a female slave, wrote of "an affectionate friendship that was to last for more than sixty years." Some mistresses looked on favorite female slaves as members of the extended family. They bought them presents and handed down to them the previous season's clothes. Because of this, house slaves were sometimes more fashionably dressed than the White wives of local farmers, much to the resentment of the latter.

An indication of the affection mistresses felt for house slaves was evident when they died. White women mourned long and hard when a favorite slave passed away, particularly if they believed that there was something they could have done to prevent her death. In several entries of an 1834 diary, the mistress, Sarah Gayle, severely berated herself for failing to notice that her favorite slave, Rose, was limping from a wound that eventually caused her to die of lockjaw. She declared "that color made no difference, but that her life would have been as precious, if I could have saved it, as if she had been white as snow." Slave women remained more skeptical, however, about the sincerity of "Miss Anne's" grieving. As one house servant cynically put it, "Huh crying because she didn't have nobody to whip no more."

Working in close confines could also breed intense hostility, especially when the relationship was one of such unequal power. House slaves expected to work hard, but greatly resented mistresses who placed unreasonable demands on their precious free time. Slaves also took exception to the wrath of Miss Anne when her negligence caused them to get in trouble for damage done to a precious family heirloom, for example. Sometimes tensions became so great between mistresses and female house slaves that physical violence erupted. In *We Are Your Sisters,* Dorothy Sterling cites the following story of one such slave:

> One day my Mistress Lydia called for me to come in the house, but no, I wouldn't go. She walks out and says she is gwine make me go. So she takes and drags me in the house. Then I grabs that white woman and shook er until she begged for mercy. When the master comes in, I wuz given a terrible beating but I didn't care for I give the mistress a good un too.

Despite their many differences, women of both races typically shared one thing—the desire to fall in love and get married. In the antebellum South, the wedding of a slave woman as well as that of a free woman was cause for great celebration. Even though slave marriages were not recognized as legal, they were sometimes encouraged by the masters, who believed such unions enhanced stability in the slave cabins and produced more property for them in the form of children. With an eye toward breeding, some masters even attempted to have particular slaves mate with each other, although their contrived efforts usually failed. The majority of slave marriages took place out of real affection. Ironically, compared with most White marriages, in which wealth, position, and class played a strong part, slave marriages were oftentimes more romantic. When slave men and women fell in love, together they would "jump the broom" and enter a slave cabin as true partners.

White mistresses may have coveted the slave women's more romantic relationships as well as their greater freedom not to marry. White girls faced being stigmatized if they remained single beyond a certain age, and many were pressed to accept even loveless proposals to avoid "old maid" status. Young White women could also be "ruined" by even a hint of premarital sexual activity, while slave women appeared to enjoy much greater sexual freedom. Mary Chesnut commented on this with more than a hint of envy when she wrote, "The Negro woman have a chance here that women have nowhere else. They can redeem themselves—the impropers can. They can marry decently and nothing is remembered against these colored ladies." Feminist scholar and women's studies professor bell hooks disagrees with this characterization of slave women, however, claiming that there is no evidence in slave narratives or diaries that female slaves were in any way more sexually liberated than their White counterparts.

Beyond the slaves' more romantic feelings for each other, their marital relationships also appeared to be more equal. Blacks' notions of equality apparently derived from a number of sources. Any woman who worked as hard as a man in the fields deserved his respect, and usually got it. Being at the bottom of the pecking order also served as a great equalizer; enslaved husbands could hardly claim privilege based on property, voting, or income. But there was another factor, too. African culture genuinely valued and respected women more than European culture did, particularly for their sacred role as mothers, though even in Africa women rarely assumed positions of political leadership, and the gender roles of women in "the Motherland" were in many ways just as traditional as they were in Europe. Unfortunately, the relationships of free Black men and women living in the antebellum South more closely resembled Whites' unequal marital relationships than those of Blacks who were slaves.

Pregnancy and childbirth were viewed as frightening, life-threatening events by White and Black women alike. Without proper medical care, women frequently died from such complications as ectopic or tubal pregnancies, breech positioning of the baby, failure to expel the placenta, and hemorrhaging.

Among slave women, ambivalence about having children ran high. On the positive side, women of African descent genuinely valued motherhood, perhaps even more than marriage, at least according to White historian Elizabeth Fox-Genovese. It was also considered a plus among the slaves that a woman who was pregnant could look forward to a few months' relief from the more arduous chores. As she neared delivery, a slave woman sat with the older slaves and children, doing the plantation's weaving and spinning. Some slave women apparently regularly faked pregnancy and other illnesses to do just that, although it was hardly the case that pregnant slaves were pampered.

On the other hand, slave women could hardly feel joy at bringing a child into a life of slavery. Many of them resented that they were helping to increase a master's slave holdings. They also worried that the children, once they were old enough, might at any time be sold away from them. Slave women were also reluctant to have a child because of the sheer exhaustion of taking care of it. Even while nursing, they were expected to work in the fields. At lunchtime, young mothers could be seen trudging miles back home to feed their hungry babies, and then heading back into the hot sun for the afternoon shift. Other slave women opted to carry their newborns with them, strapping them onto their chests as they swung their scythes and picked the cotton.

White plantation mistresses reacted with similar mixed feelings to multiple pregnancies, but they enjoyed a distinct advantage when it came to child care; they had the luxury of turning to a slave woman to help watch over their young. The house slave who assumed primary child care duties around the plantation was traditionally called Mammy. Perhaps because she was selected by the mistress, the Mammy was usually an older and larger woman than some of the attractive house slaves picked by the master.

While much has been made of Mammy's responsibilities in caring for the White plantation children, less has been said of the White woman's role in supervising and caring for the slave children. Yet the mistress often attended to sick slave children, and it was she who was called in the middle of the night when a Black child required emergency attention. Beyond basic medical care, the White woman also did her part to make sure that slave girls were properly socialized. One slave woman, Ester King Casey, remembered that when she was young her mistress once whipped her for playing with the jailer's children, because, Miss Susan said, those poor White trash kids "told lies and talked bad." Another female slave, Frankie Goole, claimed that her mistress gave her advice any mother might give a daughter, saying "ter alluz be a good girl, en don't let a man er boy trip me." Clearly there was honest affection between some mistresses and the slave children who worked in their homes. A slave named Dora Franks recalled that when she arrived in the big house, the mistress's own children had already grown and gone. Franks believes that her mistress was sweet and attentive to her because she missed having her children to care for.

Social Reform Movements

For Black and White women, the antebellum South was a darkly mysterious and contradictory place, where they shared a sense of gnawing helplessness, mutual respect, seething resentment, and occasional love. By the mid-nineteenth century, the plantation slave system was on the verge of collapse. As the winds of change blew from the North, women of the South reacted differently to the shifting political milieu. Female slaves were cheered by word of the abolitionist activities of their free sisters to the North, and perhaps heartened to learn about the antislavery work of White women there. A growing number of Southern White women, too, began expressing antislavery sentiments in their personal documents, as reflected in the following passage written by a Southern White woman shortly before the Civil War began:

> I cannot, nor will not, spend all these precious days of my life following after and watching Negroes. It is a terrible life . . . They are a source of more trouble to housewives than all other things, vexing them and causing much sin . . . When we change our residence, I cast my vote for a free state.

Women in the South who held such views tended to be closet abolitionists, though, as it was considered unladylike for them to express their political views in public.

In the North, women's political activities probably began with participation in the moral reform groups that sprang up at the turn of the nineteenth century. Benevolent societies, as they were also called, took on a number of

social issues, including temperance, hunger, public education, and reform of
our nation's prisons and mental institutions. While females were still considered intellectually inferior to men and not qualified to enter public life, they
were thought to be well suited to perform high-minded charitable work. It
was an important development. Those women who wished to do something
outside the domestic sphere were for the first time granted an acceptable
outlet for their energies.

Throughout the first half of the nineteenth century, White and Black
women of the urban North formed and joined their own benevolent societies. White women's groups were mostly populated by those who were financially well off, because poor women, without domestic help of their own,
were too busy taking care of their families or earning a living. These
wealthy women were for the most part well meaning in their social reform
efforts, but they attempted to distinguish between the poor who were worthy and deserving of help and those who were not.

In contrast, Black moral reform groups made no such distinction in their
charitable activities. From the beginning, when the free Black women of
Salem, Massachusetts, in 1818 founded the Colored Female Religious and
Moral Society, the primary goal was to offer assistance to one another. As
those who had had intimate experience with poverty and racial prejudice,
these women knew all too well that at any time they could just as easily be
on the receiving end of their group's mission. Thus, even very busy poor
Black women somehow managed to find time to devote to charitable societies.

Perhaps because of their greater identification with those whom they
were helping, Black women led the way in making reform groups more
explicitly political. As early as 1832, the determined Black women of Salem
established this country's first women's abolitionist group, the Female Anti-
Slavery Society. Politically minded White women were quick to follow. One
year later, Lucretia Mott, who is credited, along with Elizabeth Cady Stanton, for founding this country's women's movement, established an identi-
cally named group in Philadelphia. Quaker women who joined Mott's
group stressed the importance of everyday interactions with Negroes, and
among its charter members were four Black women. Later that year, when a
group of White women from Boston formed a female antislavery society,
they too invited Black women to join them.

When the Black members of the Philadelphia and Boston groups attended their first national female antislavery convention in New York, in

1837, however, they were shocked to learn that one of the first items on the agenda was whether or not they should be received. As African American historian Rosalyn Terborg-Penn noted, "Abhorrence of slavery was no guarantee that White reformers would accept the Afro-American on equal terms." Predictably, lighter-skinned Afro-American women had a much easier time joining White women's groups than did their darker-skinned sisters. That White women attending abolitionist conventions would generally discriminate against Black female delegates is ironic, especially since Black men, including the famous abolitionist Frederick Douglass, were often welcomed at these meetings.

In retrospect, the fact that more White women didn't embrace Black women into their antislavery groups was a missed opportunity. Beyond the obvious racial issues of their behavior, there was much that White women of the times could have learned from Black women, most of whom were not hindered by European notions of femininity and passivity. Black women often lived on their own, and therefore were more confident in their abilities and opinions. As a group, Black women held few illusions about the promise and value of marriage; some even viewed the institution as burdensome. Finally, through working more closely with Black women in the abolitionist movement, White women would have come into contact with such powerful role models as the gifted and humorous orator Sojourner Truth and the courageous Harriet Tubman, who personally freed more than three hundred slaves on the Underground Railroad. Later, both of these Black women also became strong advocates of women's rights.

In the South, White women were much slower to react to the social reform movement of the early nineteenth century. One obstacle was that they were more spread out geographically, and it was harder for them to get together on a regular basis. In addition, Southern women were typically overwhelmed by the responsibilities of running their plantation households and farms, and didn't have the time to commit to outside activities. But the main reason that so few Southern women joined social reform groups was slavery; it had a chilling effect on all moral reform efforts. Even though some Southern White women did quietly oppose slavery, the majority remained content with the status quo.

Two women from South Carolina, however, proved to be major exceptions. Sarah and Angelina Grimké were born in Charleston in 1792 and 1805. Their father was a slave-owning judge, and in most ways they were no different from other Southern belles of that era. But when Sarah visited

Philadelphia as a young woman, she came under the influence of antislavery
Quakers and was awakened to the evils of slavery. When she returned
home, she recruited Angelina to the cause but ran into trouble with other
family members and friends. In 1821, Sarah left the South for Philadelphia,
and eight years later, Angelina followed.

Angelina became just as active as her sister in the abolitionist movement.
In 1835, she wrote a strongly worded antislavery letter to William Lloyd
Garrison, publisher of the abolitionist newspaper *The Liberator*. The following year, she drafted a thirty-six-page letter, "An Appeal to the Christian
Women of the South," on why White Southern women in particular needed
to speak out against slavery. That same year, Sarah made a similar plea to
religious leaders when she wrote "An Epistle to the Clergy of the Southern
States." Few Whites in the South were ready to hear what the Grimké
women had to say, though, and most dismissed the sisters as unfortunates,
influenced by Northern politics.

The Grimkés were actually far more progressive than most women living
above the Mason-Dixon Line. In fact, Sarah was among the first to specify
how traditional male-female relations paralleled those of masters and slaves.
To the annoyance of many, she asserted that slaves and women were similar
in that both were expected to be passive, cooperative, and obedient to their
master-husbands.

It seems obvious that in working for social reform, women were bound to
begin fighting for their own rights, too. In 1840, Lucretia Mott and Elizabeth Cady Stanton became committed to women's rights issues while attending an international antislavery convention in London. Despite their
considerable effort and expense to get there, the two distinguished women
were denied delegate status, and had to sit in the balcony because they were
female. When they returned to America, they put their considerable organizational skills to work to fight for women's rights. By then, other women
active in female societies had begun to share with one another—for the first
time, away from the influence of disapproving fathers and husbands—accounts of their oppressive experiences. Thus, while it was indeed true that in
working for the rights of slaves, White and Black women were made more
aware of their own lack of rights, other factors, including the education that
took place in social reform groups, made conditions ripe for the emergence
of a woman's movement.

In 1848, Mott and Stanton hosted the first Women's Rights Convention,
in Seneca Falls, New York, on July 19 and 20. In attendance were approxi-

mately 250 women and forty men, including Frederick Douglass, who passionately argued that women needed their political rights as much as Black men.

From the beginning, Black female abolitionists like Truth and Tubman were active in the women's rights movement. While many White women, including Mott, Stanton, and the Grimkés, welcomed Blacks to their cause, there were many other White women who shunned them. Still, Black women continued to insist that their demands be heard. Sojourner Truth officially began her participation in the women's movement in 1848, when she spoke at a small convention for women in Worcester, Massachusetts. At the second national Woman's Right Convention, in Akron, Ohio, in 1851, she made another statement, although she was almost denied the right to speak by a small but noisy contingent of racist White women who wanted her silenced. Apparently, they feared that Truth would damage their cause by giving the public the impression that women's rights were somehow "mixed with abolition and niggers." Her longtime supporters barely managed to hold off these detractors, and it was amid boos and hisses that Sojourner Truth took to the podium to deliver her infamous "Ar'n't (or Ain't) I A Woman" speech. Outraged by what had just happened, she drew brilliantly on her experiences as a former slave to mock the logic on which sex discrimination was based:

> Dat man ober dar say dat woman needs to be lifted ober ditches, and to have de best place everywhar. Nobody eber helped me into carriages, or ober mud puddles, or give me any best place, and ar'n't I a woman? Look at me! Look at my arm! I have plowed, and planted, and gathered into barns, and no man could head me—and ar'n't I a woman? I could work as much and eat as much as a man (when I could get it), and bear de lash as well—and ar'n't I a woman? I have borne thirteen chilern and seen em mos'all sold off into slavery, and when I cried out with a mother's grief, none but Jesus heard—and ar'n't I a woman?

Unfortunately, Sojourner Truth and other Black female activists continued to face racism at many women's right meetings, as well as sexism and racism at some abolitionist meetings.

By the end of the 1850s, women's rights had assumed all the elements of yet another social reform movement. Those involved met regularly on the local level, held annual national conventions, and formulated plans of action, but the movement ground to a halt when debates about slavery and state rights finally erupted into war in 1861.

Although the American Civil War, like every war, was waged largely by men, it undeniably altered the lives of the women left behind. In the North, female factory workers were promoted to supervisory positions, jobs previously denied them but now vacated by the men joining the Union forces. In both parts of the country, heretofore exclusively male colleges and universities began to admit women for the first time as their pool of male applicants dried up. And in the South, many wives discovered that they could do just as good a job as their husbands in running family farms and large plantations.

By the time General Robert E. Lee surrendered, in April 1865, the country was in a state of near political ruin. Reconstruction, a difficult time, was especially hard on women. In both regions of the country, White women who had discovered their strength and independence in wartime were now being told to return to their roles as wives and mothers. Those who could go back to their old lives were considered the lucky ones. Tens of thousands of White women were widowed by the war, and found themselves struggling mightily, in the absence of fair wages for females, to make it on their own.

In the South, former slaves, many of whom were uneducated, similarly faced a life of poverty. They faced something else as well: White do-gooders from the North who invaded the South during Reconstruction. Black women, who had enjoyed fairly equal marital relationships under slavery, were suddenly being told by White missionaries and members of the Freedmen's Bureau that they were supposed to obey their husbands without question. Even Black preachers began to emphasize the necessity of conforming to traditional sex roles, drawing on the biblical injunction "Wives, submit yourselves to your husbands." Meanwhile, Black men were told that it was their responsibility to be the family's sole provider. Wives were to stay home and take care of the house and children. Denied the option to do just that for so long, many former slave women were happy to oblige. But they discovered that when they did stay home, they were called lazy, not only by their husbands, but by White men whose own wives did the same without condemnation.

Those Black men able to earn enough money to support their families took great pride in providing fashionable dresses, pretty hats, and delicate parasols for their wives to wear in public. It is said that so many Black women began carrying parasols at that time that White women abandoned the custom. During Reconstruction, racist White men harassed well-dressed Black women who walked down the street. They were particularly vicious in their treatment of light-skinned women—many of whom came from families that had been free for generations before Emancipation—perhaps because their physical appearance and cultural manner most closely resembled those of White Southern "ladies."

Suffrage

Amidst the emerging social order, Black women were confused about what their new rights and roles should be, especially since everyone kept telling them they should put men's interests ahead of their own. They were particularly unclear about their right to vote.

During Reconstruction, suffrage was a subject on everybody's mind, and in 1866, Congress passed the Fourteenth Amendment, which guaranteed full citizenship to former slaves and free Blacks. The amendment also introduced the word *male* into the Constitution, giving states the right to determine who among its male citizens of twenty-one years and over could vote. Alarmed by this development, female suffragists worried about the implications and disagreed about how to respond to the proposed Fifteenth Amendment, which, even more strongly than the Fourteenth, stated that citizens of the United States could not be denied the right to vote on the basis of their race, color, or previous condition of servitude. The suffragists wanted sex to be included as a protected category, along with race and color, but when it became clear that that wasn't to happen, they divided on whether to accept or reject the amendment as it was. Some suffragists believed that campaigning against the amendment would be a betrayal of their abolitionist friends, because a better law might not be forthcoming. Others, including Susan B. Anthony and her colleague Stanton, feared that if women did not win their rights at this juncture, the opportunity would not present itself again for a long, long time.

Stanton and Anthony had already butted heads with their old friend Frederick Douglass at an 1866 meeting of the American Equal Rights Association. Their former ally appeared to back down from his earlier commitment to female suffrage, and was now saying that, while the ballot was "desirable" for women, it was "vital" for Black men. In response, Anthony declared, "I will cut off this right arm of mine before I will ever work or demand the ballot for the Negro and not the woman." White and Black women fought among and between themselves over the best course of action.

Sojourner Truth remained unwavering in her support of women's rights. In her inimitable way, Truth commented on the issue in 1867, when female suffrage was still very much being debated:

> I feel that I have right to have just as much a man. There is a great stir about colored men getting their rights, but not a word about the colored women; and if colored men get their rights, and colored women not theirs, the colored men will be masters over the women, and it will be just as bad as it was before. So I am for keeping the thing going while things are stirring; because if we wait till it is still, it will take a great deal to get it going again. White women are a great deal smarter, and know more than colored women, while colored do not know scarcely anything. They go out washing, which is about as high as a colored woman gets, and their men go about idle, strutting up and down; and when the women come home, they ask for their money and take it all, and then scold her because there is not food. I want you to consider on that, chil'n.

Truth surely did not believe that White women were by nature smarter than Black women—perhaps more educated, but never more intelligent. She was savvy enough, however, to recognize the political advantages of such a comment, because her White activist friends were outraged at the prospect of illiterate former slaves getting the vote ahead of White women, many of whom were far more educated. For the most part, these women did not wish to deny Black men their franchise, but, understandably, they felt qualified to vote, and were angry at being denied the right simply because they were female.

In 1870, the Fifteenth Amendment passed without reference to sex as a protected category. Battered and embittered from the debate, members of the American Equal Rights Association split into two separate factions, the National Woman Suffrage Association (NWSA) and the American Woman Suffrage Association (AWSA).

The vast majority of American women, Black and White, did not belong to either organization. In the decades following the Civil War, they seemed inclined to accept society's claim that they were by nature apolitical beings and, as such, belonged not in the voting booth, but at home, taking care of their families. Some housewives even denounced female suffrage, claiming that if women were to vote differently from their husbands, domestic unrest would surely follow.

During the last quarter of the nineteenth century, White and Black women, however, did return in droves to their pre–Civil War role as social reformers. And once again the majority of women's clubs were split along racial lines. While Black women sometimes preferred segregated groups because they were more comfortable in them and could more easily assume positions of leadership, it was also the case that Black women were often denied membership in White women's clubs.

The largest and best known of the social reform groups of this era was the Woman's Christian Temperance Union (WCTU), founded in 1874. Temperance was considered a particularly appropriate cause for women because alcohol abuse was so disruptive of family life. From the beginning, WCTU policies encouraged separate Black and White unions, but at least one White woman, Amelia Bloomer, campaigned against racism within the movement, and some African American women did rise to positions of prominence within the WCTU. Frances Harper, for one, was most effective in recruiting Black women to the cause and was eventually appointed to the national office. Even so, she was plagued by issues of race, and once commented that "some of the members of different unions have met the question in a liberal and Christian manner, others have not seemed . . . to make the distinction between Christian affiliation and social equality."

Another African American woman highly active in social reform work was Josephine St. Pierre Ruffin. Initially, she was admitted to the 1900 conference of the General Federation of Women's Clubs because her skin color was so fair that the White delegates who registered her didn't know that she was Black. When they discovered the truth, Ruffin was banned from speaking, and an attempt was made to remove her from the convention. The White Woman's Era Club then issued an official statement, saying "that colored women should confine themselves to their clubs and the large field of work open to them there."

Not all Southern White women were racist. Some worked alongside Black women in various social reform groups, and many joined in the campaign to fight against the lynchings of Black men. In 1902, the White

women's societies of the Southern Methodist Church openly criticized
Southern racial attitudes contributing to such lynchings, and a year later, a
White woman named Jessie Daniel Ames founded the fully integrated Association of Southern Women for the Prevention of Lynching. At its peak, the
group had over forty thousand members.

At the turn of the century, thousands of Black women also joined in the
campaign for female suffrage, which had once again gathered steam during
the 1890s. Among Black women who were staunch suffragists was Anna
Julia Cooper, best known for the statement: "Only the BLACK WOMAN can say
when and where I enter in the quiet undisputed dignity of my womanhood,
without violence or special patronage; then and there the whole Negro race
enters with me." Cooper was particularly effective in emphasizing to Black
women that they required the ballot to counter the belief that "Black men's"
experiences and needs were the same as theirs. (Even today, ask anyone
when Blacks first got the right to vote, and most will tell you "after the Civil
War"—and in so doing, fail to acknowledge that only Black men were
enfranchised at that time.)

Unfortunately, not all African American men supported female suffrage.
Many believed, as did their White conservative counterparts, that women
belonged in the home. The opposition of Black men did not stop Black
female suffragists from speaking up about their rights, though. In a 1912
article for *The Crisis,* Mary Church Terrell wrote:

> If I were a colored man, and were unfortunate enough not to grasp
> the absurdity of opposing suffrage because of the sex of a human be-
> ing, I should at least be consistent enough to never to raise my voice
> against those who have disenfranchised my brothers and myself on ac-
> count of race.

There also remained a significant number of Black women opposed to
female suffrage. Some took that stand for no other reason than that their
husbands did, and others simply distrusted anything that White women
were fighting so hard to get. Even many Black women who supported the
ballot recognized the expediency with which some White female suffragists
treated Blacks. Antilynching crusader and journalist Ida B. Wells-Barnett
reacted strongly to evidence of racism, and was not afraid to call White
suffragists on their often hypocritical behavior. Others were more diplo-
matic in their response to White women. For example, when Susan B.

Anthony attended the 1903 NWSA national convention in New Orleans, she was invited to visit the all-Black Phillis Wheatley Club. While she was there, the club president, Sylvamie Williams, informed Anthony that Black women were painfully aware of their inferior position among the White suffragists, but added:

> When women like you, Miss Anthony, come to see us and speak to us it helps us believe in the Fatherhood of God and the brotherhood of Man, and at least for the time being in the sympathy of women.

It didn't seem to matter how Black women responded; they were being ignored. As late as 1919, it was clear that a growing number of White women were ready to settle for an amendment that would give them, but not Black women, the ballot. Even Alice Paul, White president of the radical National Women's Party (NWP), whose extreme suffragists experienced picketing, imprisonment, and a hunger strike, appeared willing to write off suffrage for Black women. She is alleged to have told one audience of Southern Whites "that all of this talk of Negro women voting in South Carolina was nonsense." White men, particularly those in the South, were convinced that Black women would turn out in greater numbers to vote than White women, which would upset their White advantage at the polling place.

In 1920, the Nineteenth Amendment, guaranteeing women the right to vote, was finally ratified, without any reference to race. As it turned out, White women's concerns about the South hardly mattered. The amendment passed without the support of Virginia, Maryland, North Carolina, South Carolina, Georgia, Alabama, Louisiana, Florida, and Mississippi. In fact, the only Southern states to ratify it were Tennessee, Kentucky, Texas, and Arkansas.

White women could not have predicted this course of events, though. In a lingering era of lynchings and Jim Crow laws, any move to double the enfranchisement of the American population was perceived as having potentially volatile racial implications, and nowhere was this more so than in the South. For White women, the issue was a double-edged sword. On the one hand, had more of them visibly aligned themselves with Black women, the passage of the suffrage amendment most certainly would have been delayed by racist White men threatened by the new alliance. On the other hand, had White women fully embraced Black women into their suffragist cause, there would have been more good will between them. Ironically, some historians believe that American women would have soon gained the right to vote anyhow, as most other Western nations were moving in the direction of enfranchising their female citizens. Again, though, White women didn't know this at the time, and they used "whatever means necessary" to get the suffrage amendment ratified.

When Black and White women did vote in their first federal election, in 1920, they learned that enfranchisement had been oversold; White men remained in control of federal, state, and local governing bodies. Women of both races discovered that their influence in politics was hardly felt.

Following passage of the suffrage amendment, younger women failed to keep the feminist bandwagon rolling. Despite their short skirts, cigarette smoking, and bobbed hair, the women of the Roaring Twenties and Harlem Renaissance were basically apolitical. They were out to have fun. While women may have flirted with independence, their primary goal in life was to marry well and have children.

Even the formally activist NWSA lost its political edge when it designated as its successor organization the conservative nonpartisan League of Women Voters. During the twenties, the LWV opposed the equal rights amendment (ERA), first introduced by Alice Paul and her National Women's Party. Even though the NWP pledged to work for all women's equality, it remained a racially segregated group. Debates on the ERA, even then, were carried out mostly by middle- and upper-class White women.

For the most part, attempts at Black-White female cooperation failed during the first half of the twentieth century. One effort included the Council for Interracial Cooperation (CIC), founded in Atlanta in 1920, and another was the Young Women's Christian Association (YWCA), which similarly sought to develop an interracial alliance. But as the lynchings of Black men continued, Black women activists turned away from White women, forming their own groups, such as the National Association of Colored Women and the National Federation of Afro-American Women, and establishing coalitions with Black men to address more pressing matters of racial discrimination and hatred. As early as 1924, Black activist Nannie Burroughs observed that White women were overlooking and undervaluing Black women as a political force. She repeatedly warned that White women should tap the voting potential of the Black female electorate before White men denied it, but her advice went unheeded. Throughout the South, the disenfranchisement of Blacks spread, through exorbitant poll taxes and demanding literary competency tests. Although Black women were disappointed, they were hardly surprised when their former White suffragist friends failed to stop this development.

During the long depression that followed, voting must have seemed the least of Black women's problems. They continued to face severe poverty and wage discrimination. By one estimate, 80 percent of Black women in 1920 were employed as menial workers, such as farm laborers, cooks, or domestic servants. Even during the Second World War, when Blacks and Whites were both hired to do so-called men's factory work, Black women continued to be paid less than White women for doing the exact same job. By 1945, the situation was not much better, as Black women continued to hold the lowest rank in the economic scale among men and women, Blacks and Whites.

Historians Lois Scharf and Joan Jensen have described the period from the 1920s to the 1940s as the "decades of discontent" in the women's movement because so little happened. White and Black women still interacted, but primarily as domestic servants and employees in the homes of Whites, or as co-workers in factories and offices. Politically, they did not come back together until the late fifties and early sixties, when a handful of Northern White women headed South to help in the drive to register Blacks. By the end of the sixties, White and Black women again joined forces for this country's second wave of feminism. It was time for a new generation of White and Black women to learn the painful lessons of social activism and political cooperation.

Chapter Two

Childhood:

From Schoolgirls to Homegirls

childhood remembrances are always a drag
if you're Black
. . .
and I really hope no white person ever has cause
to write about me
because they never understand
Black love is Black wealth and they'll
probably talk about my hard childhood
and never understand that
all the while I was quite happy

—Nikki Giovanni
"Nikki-Rosa," 1973

There are good things about Bonna Willis and there are bad things about Bonna Willis, and right now I shouldn't be caring about any of them because right now we hate each other's guts and I don't guess that is going to change this June the way it usually does when school is out. Now that we're older you can bet all of that's over. I already know she won't be caught dead talking to no honky bitch this year, and the same goes for her from me only backwards using the word I won't say.

—Lynda Barry
The Good Times Are Killing Me, *1988*

A brief conversation with a six-year-old White girl named Justine reveals just how early guilt can intrude on children's interracial friendships. At first, Justine happily chattered away about Alison, a new Black girlfriend in her kindergarten class. "She's fun. We play together. I just like her." But when asked if she planned on making any other friends who were Black, Justine suddenly grew serious and eventually confided, "I'm afraid they won't like me." When asked why not, she said, "You know about slavery, right? I just learned about it in school. We were taught that some Whites were really mean to Black people. So I'm afraid that those Black girls who don't know me will think I'm going to be mean to them like those other Whites were."

Generations earlier, another White first-grader named Jane, who grew up in a small liberal college town in the North, responded far more naïvely when she first encountered a Black schoolmate in the first-grade girls' bathroom. Jane innocently asked the girl, "What does it feel like inside black skin?" To her horror, the girl burst out crying and went running out of the room to tell the teacher.

Across the country and for much of our nation's history, girls have struggled to understand the meaning of race. That girls of different racial backgrounds might actually become friends is a relatively recent development, though, by and large. With the exception of a few White girls in the antebellum South who sometimes played with the Black daughters of house slaves and, after abolition, with the daughters of house servants, and a few Northern girls like Jane who lived in one of the few integrated communities that existed, most White girls and Black girls in this country did not expect to become friends. In fact, most women over the age of forty never had much contact as children with girls of the other race. Such women were the last generation to come of age largely before Civil Rights, school desegregation, and multicultural curricular initiatives. Today, more girls like Justine and Alison are not only interacting, but are doing so with far greater knowledge of societal racial issues than girls of years past.

In this chapter we want to look at the ways young girls move from simple expressions of curiosity about each other's race and skin color to a sophisticated awareness of race and racism in America. More specifically, what is the role of gender in shaping children's cross-race friendships? Among the factors we explore are neighborhood and school integration, prejudice, physical attractiveness, and skin color.

....

Early Childhood

Infants lying next to each other in the hospital nursery are unaware of race. It will be months before they have even the slightest clue that they have any identity apart from their mothers. Exactly how children come to acquire a sense of self, and gain an understanding of how that self fits into the larger social order, is a remarkable process that has been the subject of much psychological research. We now know that children begin to understand both their racial and sexual identities during their first few years of life. Black children tend to establish a sense of racial identity ahead of White children, perhaps because our society is so aware of race, and girls tend to be attuned to the nuances of their social identities slightly ahead of boys.

After gaining a sense of their own identities, children next learn how to classify others socially. Marguerite Alejandro-Wright, one of the psychologists who have studied the unfolding of a child's racial awareness, sees the process as a multistage development that begins with the child's recognition of simple physical differences. She asked thirty-two Black girls from three different age groupings—three- to four-year-olds, five- to six-year-olds, and eight- to ten-year-olds—to respond to a set of photographs of children with different skin colors. The girls were given cut-out figures with various hair styles and facial features, and then asked to manipulate these items in response to a series of questions and tasks regarding issues of race. For example, one activity required that all the photos that looked as if they went together be grouped together.

Alejandro-Wright found, as have other researchers, that children as young as three can sort photos on the basis of skin color and hair texture. She termed this level of racial awareness idiosyncratic, because children this young do not employ or really understand commonly accepted race terms. Instead, they prefer their own. One biracial girl referred to her White mother as pink, and described another African American child as gray. Other popular race adjectives used by three- to four-year-old children included tan, coffee, and beige. Ironically, the one term most rejected by children at this stage was black.

According to developmental psychologist Jean Piaget, children at this age are too concrete in their thinking to regard the word *black* as anything but a color. To three-year-olds, calling someone Black, when visually that person is not, makes no sense. Christine Kerwin, a school psychologist in Peekskill, New York, concurs on the basis of her own research. "These kids simply call it what it is in the absence of racial prejudice."

One look at nursery school children of different races climbing all over each other further supports such observations. At this point in their lives, they are old enough to recognize rudimentary physical differences between races, but too young to infer personality traits based on them. In other words, the ugly business of racial stereotyping has not yet begun.

But by the age of four or five, children enter another phase in their understanding of racial classification, a stage Alejandro-Wright calls "subliminal awareness." At this age, children are capable of using conventional labels to sort others by race, but they don't realize that membership in any one racial grouping is exclusive and permanent. According to Piaget, children at this age lack the understanding that the race that they (and others) are at this time is the race that they (and others) will always be. Thus, a four-year-old White girl may insist that she can become Black by getting a dark tan, while a Black girl of the same age may feel that by donning a blond wig, she can become White like the rock star Madonna.

Such talk can be either amusing or alarming to parents. Brooke L., a White college student in her twenties, remembered that, when she was young, she was convinced that she was Black. She was taken care of by a friend of her mother's, an African American woman named Mrs. Richie, and all of Brooke's dolls were Black, the hand-me-downs from Mrs. Richie's children. On Sundays, Brooke used to accompany Mrs. Richie to her all-Black Baptist church. But when she told her mother that she was Black, her mother laughed and said, "No, honey, you're not Black; you're White." Brooke burst out crying and begged, "Please, please, please, aren't I Black even a little?" provoking more laughter from her mom.

For African American parents, however, confusion in their young children about wanting to be White can raise concerns about self-hatred. Ever since the 1930s, when psychologists Kenneth and Mamie Clark first conducted their doll preference studies, psychologists have known that children as young as three will often reject playing with Black dolls in favor of White-looking dolls. Researchers since then have found that the phenomenon is both short-lived and easy to manipulate. In 1975, psychologists Albert Roberts, Kathleen Mosley, and Maureen Chamberlain found that, while 40 percent of the three- to four-year-old Black girls thought that the blue-eyed

White doll was "prettiest," by ages six and seven, only 23 percent did. And in 1988, psychologist Darlene Powell-Hopson and her husband, Derek Hopson, reported that preference rates for Black dolls could be dramatically increased by repeatedly pairing positive words, such as *pretty* and *nice,* with Black dolls rather than White dolls. The fact is that before the age of four or five, most children are blissfully unaware of racial stereotyping or prejudices.

Once they start preschool, however, children begin to grasp the larger social implications of race in America. When that happens, the relative innocence of earlier cross-race friendships begins to fade. By the time they are five, many of today's children have watched enough television to become attuned to its stereotypes, overheard enough adult conversation to know what members of their families think about "those others," and learned enough at school—in the classroom and on the playground—to realize "that some Whites were really mean to Black people," as Justine put it. Unfortunately, as awareness about various racial stereotypes grows, so does the use of racist slurs. Certain race-related terms are not just descriptive of physical difference; they have the power to belittle, hurt, and enrage.

A White woman named Alana, now in her twenties, recalls that she was six when she first gained awareness of the social importance of race. The year before, her family had moved to a small town in the Midwest, and Alana quickly became friends with Nina, a Black girl who lived on their block. All summer the two girls played without incident. But one day after school began, Alana returned home to discover that the furniture on her front porch was gone. As she stood there pondering the empty space, a neighbor came by to offer his opinion on the matter. "Some niggers probably took it," he said. Alana, never having heard the word *niggers,* assumed that it meant something like *bandits,* used in the Frito Bandito commercials that were popular at that time. Later that evening, when her mother came home, Alana announced, without guile, "Some niggers took our porch furniture." Without questioning why her daughter assumed this, Alana's mother flew across the room, grabbed her arm, and shook her, exclaiming, "Don't you ever use that word again!" Alana was confused about exactly what she had done to make her mother react so violently. It wasn't until her mother let her go, and more calmly stated, "We use the word *Black* in this household," that Alana realized what *nigger* meant. She also instinctively knew, by her mother's response, that she now had in her possession a weapon she could use against her girlfriend Nina. Although Alana claims never to have used the *n* word, just knowing that she could somehow shifted the power in her favor in future dealings with Nina.

The Middle Years

By the time children are in second and third grade, their understanding of race undergoes its final transition. By now they know that race is based not just on physical difference, but embraces a host of other factors, such as style of dress, speech patterns, culinary tastes, musical preferences, socioeconomic status, lifestyles, history, and ancestry, that set Whites and Blacks apart. When asked how you could tell if someone was Black, one ten-year-old Black girl from Alejandro-Wright's study replied, " 'Cause you were born that way." But if the person's skin color was actually White? She then said, "For real, they would still be Black if they were born that way." Such seemingly complex contradictions in racial classification are not possible in younger children. By the age of seven or eight, children deliver race-inspired compliments and insults, such as "you jump rope like a Black girl" and "you talk like a White girl," with increasing frequency.

Because White children tend to lag in their awareness of race, most of the research on racial identity is conducted on Black children. There is also a growing recognition that Whites are able to choose whether or not to have a racial identity. That is, for many Whites, *race* is something that only Blacks have. While there is much for Blacks and other races to celebrate about racial or ethnic identity in terms of culture, food, language, and music, there is also a stigma attached to being different. Children who do not fit in are always vulnerable to taunting by those who do. And it can be especially painful for Black girls, because so much of each girl's identity has to do with her appearance.

At birth, children are defined only by their biological distinction, but very quickly their sexual identity begins to take on cultural overtones. The process is helped along by both family members and friends, who typically describe female newborns as pretty and sweet, while describing male newborns of the same size and appearance as big and strong. Gender-role messages are further reinforced by children's books, toys, television, and films. The result is that, by the time they are three, children have figured out not only that there are two sexes in the world, but also that they have a well-defined role to play as a boy or as a girl. This is true despite more than two decades of challenges to traditional child-rearing practices.

As a result of the differences, each has clear preferences in toys and styles of play. In general, boys prefer larger, more organized group activities, like playing with balls and toy guns. Girls tend to gravitate toward smaller, more intimate groups of two or three, with whom they play dolls, comb hair, and jump rope. Such activities for girls, in particular, turn out to greatly affect the quality and chances for developing friendships with girls from other racial backgrounds.

Playing with dolls is an enormously popular activity for girls of both races. Historically, with the exception of novelty mammy-style dolls, nearly all the dolls available for parents to buy used to be White, with long—usually blond—hair and blue eyes. Before the nineteen-sixties, major toy companies never made dolls with African American features; studies indicated that even most Black girls rejected dolls that looked like themselves. Following the activist era of the sixties, with its powerful messages of Black pride, however, a growing number of Black parents began to question the possibly damaging effect on their daughters' identity and self-esteem from playing with White-looking dolls. In response to growing demands for dolls with more Black-looking features, toy companies finally began to manufacture Black dolls, beginning in 1968 with Mattel's Christie.

How is girls' cross-race play affected by dolls that are White instead of Black? The meager evidence suggests that there are wide variations. For some Black girls, having only a White doll to play with can produce strong feelings of resentment. In her novel *The Bluest Eye,* African American novelist Toni Morrison captures the kind of explosive anger that can develop. A young Black girl named Claudia opens a gift on Christmas, to find a blond, blue-eyed doll staring back at her. The rage she feels is palpable.

> I destroy white baby dolls . . . But the dismembering of dolls was not the true horror. The true horrifying thing was the transference of the same impulses to little white girls. The indifference with which I could have axed them was shaken only by my desire to do so. To discover what eluded me: the secret of the magic they weaved on others. What made people look at them and say, "Awwwww," but not for me?

For other Black girls, having a White doll to play with, along with Black dolls, may afford the opportunity to role-play an interracial friendship.

Psychologists Joseph Hraba and Geoffrey Grant found evidence that four- to eight-year-old Black girls who enjoyed friendships of both races were, in fact, more likely to prefer playing with Black dolls than were Black girls whose friends were exclusively Black. These findings suggest that having a White girlfriend is not only *not* damaging to a Black girl's racial identity and pride, but may be racially affirming.

In a related study, psychologist Margaret Spencer found that Black children who are taught by their mothers about civil rights, racial discrimination, and Black history get along better with White children than do Black children who are ignorant of their own history. In other words, a strong racial identity may facilitate rather than detract from a young African American girl's desire to form friendships with children of another race.

White girls, too, benefit from playing with dolls that are Black. We discovered from our interviews for this book that a growing number of White mothers are now buying their daughters Black dolls along with White dolls. One White mother, a professional in her thirties named Sara, from New York City, explained her decision this way:

> I originally bought the Black Barbie for Jennifer when she was about four because I thought that it was the right thing to do. I knew that she was going to be attending kindergarten soon with Black children, and I wanted her not to be afraid of them. It's funny, but that Black doll has turned out to be one of Jennifer's favorites. And I don't know if there is any connection, but at age seven, she gets along really well with the Black girls in her class.

Because boys rarely play with dolls, girls appear to have an advantage in exploring, through their dolls, their feelings about children of the other race. On the other hand, because much of the play associated with dolls, especially Barbie, has to do with how she looks, how pretty her hair and how sexy her wardrobe, doll-playing may also encourage in girls a preoccupation with appearance. For African American girls, in particular, a doll's long silky hair may serve as a painful reminder that they lack certain idealized feminine features.

Another form of play that is uniquely feminine is hair grooming. A surprising number of women of both races have strong childhood memories of playing with the hair of other girls of both races. Throughout elementary school, both Black and White girls want to stroke, comb, and pull the hair of others and explore the many fascinating hair styles worn by girls of different races. One Black woman, now in her thirties, remembers that at the pajama parties she used to attend with her White girlfriends, the main activity was playing with each other's hair. At the time, she was wearing hers in Afro puffs—a popular style in which the hair is parted in the center and then puffed out on either side to form two mini Afros. "The White girls used to just love to make my 'puffs' stick straight up. They thought it was the neatest thing in the world that my hair would stay where they put it. There was nothing mean-spirited or embarrassing about the activity. We were just being girls." And she used to enjoy combing the long straight hair of the White girls. A White woman named Kara, now in her twenties, used to love to braid the hair of her best girlfriend in elementary school, who was Black. "You could braid it all the way down to the end and it would stay put without a rubber band!" Kara used to wear her own long hair down, but her friend was not able to do the same because her mother said that her hair "was too pouffy." And another White woman named Nana, now in her thirties, remembers that one of her first memories of a Black girl at school had to do with hair. When Nana was just starting first grade, she stood in line in front of a Black girl whom she did not know. Suddenly, Nana became aware that her hair was being touched by the Black girl, who stroked it, repeating, "Soft, soft. You have the softest, prettiest hair." By the end of the school year, the same girl viciously yanked Nana's hair whenever she could. Issues of hair, and how that feature can divide White women from Black women, is explored more fully in our chapter on beauty.

Another common play activity of young girls is jumping rope. But unlike playing with dolls or grooming hair, it is an activity in which African American girls often seem to excel. More important, it has nothing to do with looks, which are subjective and based in culture, and everything to do with individual athletic coordination and skill. In particular, Black girls excel at a style of jump roping known as double-dutch, in which two ropes are swung together but in opposite directions. Every year Black girls dominate the national double-dutch contest, and those who are proficient at double-dutch see themselves as special, with a skill that distinguishes them from White girls. As Mattie, now aged fifteen, admitted:

In grammar school, I lived for recess, when a crowd of White girls would just stare at me and my girlfriends jumping rope. It made me feel so good—like I was good at something that they could only dream about.

This common playground activity can also bring Black and White girls together, creating an atmosphere of mutual respect. Annie, a White woman now in her thirties, recalls attending a racially mixed inner city school as a young girl.

I was really good at double dutch jumping—never as great as the Black girls, of course—but still pretty good. I would say that it definitely helped me gain respect from the Black girls at school. I hung in there with them and tried to do all the new moves that they were learning. So, yes, I got along better with Black girls, much more so than my White girlfriends, who didn't even try to double-dutch jump rope.

Doll playing, hair grooming, and rope jumping take place at a time in a young girl's life when segregation by sex is far more prevalent than segregation by race. In her book *Gender Play,* sociologist Barrie Thorne observes that elementary school children "generally separate first by gender and then, if at all, by race or ethnicity." According to Thorne, the natural tendency for children to split into groups while playing is reinforced in the classroom, where children are often lined up by sex. The same teachers would never ask children to separate out by race. As a result, during the grammar school years, Black girls and White girls may be more likely to be friends with one another than with boys of the same race.

Of course, there are many other factors that affect the likelihood of girls developing cross-race friendships. The most important is whether the neighborhood they live in and the school they attend are racially segregated or racially mixed. According to social psychologists, the single most important factor affecting friendship is proximity. Conversely, the biggest obstacle is distance. The implications of this are enormous, because the majority of neighborhoods in this country are still segregated by race. For White children who live in middle-class, primarily White suburban areas, and for those who reside in vast stretches of the rural Midwest, the chances of having a Black friend are highly diminished. The same can be said for many

Black children who live in the central city, as well as those who dwell in remote rural areas of the deep South.

The extent of neighborhood segregation in America was documented in the 1987 book *Divided Neighborhoods,* edited by Gary A. Tobin. In the introduction, Tobin refutes several myths, including the one that segregation has been significantly reduced since the 1960s. He also corrects the misconception that where racial segregation does still exist, it is because minorities are poor (that is, since housing markets are formed by income, segregation is merely a reflection of that economic reality). In fact, the overwhelming evidence indicates that "poor whites are no more likely to live with poor blacks than upper-middle-class-income blacks are to live with upper-middle-income whites." He also helps to overturn the myth that minorities cluster together because they prefer living among their own kind. While some certainly do, strong evidence suggests that it is mostly Whites who, in the words of Tobin, "prefer not to live with blacks." Sociologist John Farley, one of the book's contributors, presents census data showing that from 1970 to 1980, the percentage of Blacks still living in neighborhood tracts where the population is at least 80 to 95 percent Black is holding steady, at around 70 percent. Although the percentage of Whites living in neighborhoods where the population is less than 1 percent Black has dropped during this same period—from 70 percent in 1970 to about 52 percent in 1980—Farley predicts that segregation levels will not decline much further. His research indicates that most Whites, whether urban or suburban, want to live in primarily White neighborhoods. When a neighborhood starts to become "too racially mixed," other Whites stop moving in. And once that happens, the neighborhood starts to destabilize and ultimately turns Black.

A fictional example of how a destabilized neighborhood fosters cross-race friendships can be found in the cartoonist Lynda Barry's semi-autobiographical book *The Good Times Are Killing Me.* The protagonist, Edna Arkins, is a young White girl who lives in a neighborhood that used to be predominantly White, but over the years has become racially mixed, as Chinese, Black, Japanese, and Filipino families have moved in. Edna's parents, scared of the neighborhood's changing demographics, have forbidden Edna to have any Black children over to play. One day, however, a Black girl named Bonna Willis comes to visit because word has gotten out among the neighborhood children that Edna has turned her parents' basement into the Record Player Night Club. Although Edna is concerned about Bonna's presence, she has no White girlfriends and desperately wants a friend.

That night I imagine me and Bonna becoming best friends," says Edna. "I imagined naming the Record Player Night Club 'Edna and Bonna's Record Player Night Club at Edna's.' "

Edna's dream comes true—she and Bonna do become best friends, at least for a while.

Neighborhood segregation in particular limits the opportunities for young girls to form cross-race friendships. Parents, regardless of race, are more protective of daughters than of sons in setting boundaries for how far they can roam from home. And as we shall discuss later, boys have more competitive sporting events that help to pull them out of their immediate communities to meet boys of another race. But the chances are that most girls, unless they happen to live within easy walking distance of girls of different races, will grow up without a true cross-race friendship.

Children who live in segregated neighborhoods but attend racially integrated schools are also unlikely to develop close interracial friendships. To thrive, a close friendship needs long stretches of unstructured play time, the kind not offered in classrooms. An African American actress named Tracey recalled the way she became friends with a White girl in the fourth grade, after her family moved from an all-Black city neighborhood in Chicago to a racially mixed suburb on Chicago's South Side. In her old neighborhood, Tracey had not known any White children. On the second day of class at her new school, she struck up a conversation with a White girl named Rachel, who was sitting next to her and who also wore glasses. But it wasn't until later, when they discovered that they lived on the same street, that their friendship was cemented.

A small percentage of Black girls dwell in neighborhoods and attend schools that are primarily White. The effects on their self-esteem are varied. Some thrive, especially in terms of school achievement and later career success. Lynn, an African American woman who is now thirty and a successful business executive, recalls:

My early years were spent in a town in Nebraska, so you know that my girlfriends growing up were all White. But because of that, I believe that I now have an advantage in the workplace, compared to Black women who did not know any White girls when young.

Other Black girls, who go from living in a predominantly Black neighborhood to one that is predominantly White, may find the adjustment psychologically difficult. In her popular children's book series, *The Baby Sitters Club,* Ann M. Martin, through the story of twelve-year-old Jessica, touches on the pain this can cause. As the only Black girl in "the club," Jessica reflects:

> Our old neighborhood was mixed black and white, and so was my ballet school and my regular school. But believe it or not, we are one of the few black families in all of Stoneybrook. In fact, I'm the only black student in my whole grade. When we first moved here, some people weren't very nice to us. Some were even mean. But things have settled down and are getting better.

In other cases, growing up among only Whites can damage a young Black girl's self-esteem. Sheronda (not her real name) reveals but one kind of psychological harm that can occur to a young Black girl growing up in an all-White neighborhood, in this case in Phoenix. Two years ago, when Sheronda was four, she made her first visit to see Aunt Deborah in Chicago. One evening Sheronda, her aunt, and her grandmother, Deborah's mother, were watching Black Entertainment Television. The two women were casually commenting on which of the entertainers they thought especially good-looking, when suddenly Sheronda announced, somewhat angrily, "In order to be beautiful or handsome, you have to have blond hair and blue eyes." Mistaking her aunt's and grandmother's looks of surprise for one of misunderstanding, Sheronda ran over to some nearby magazines and said, "Here, I'll show you." She rapidly flipped through the pages, skipping over even the brunette White models, to point only to those men and women who had blond hair and light eyes. Alarmed, Deborah asked Sheronda, "Is your mother beautiful?" "No," replied the girl. "Well, is your father handsome?" Again, Sheronda's reply was an emphatic *no*. Very gently, Deborah then asked, "Are you beautiful?" In exasperation, Sheronda retorted, "No, because my hair is not blond and my eyes are dark." Deborah called Sheronda's mother in Arizona to express her concern. Later that year, Sheronda's mother took her daughter to an African American arts festival on the campus of Arizona State University. For the first time, Sheronda got to play with other Black children; she joined them in a dance, singing, "I'm happy 'cause I'm nappy." The festival seemed to have a big impact on Sheronda. Shortly afterward, she started attending school with some other Black girls, and two years later, when Sheronda returned to Chicago for a visit, Aunt Deborah was pleased with the change in her niece's attitude toward herself. On the first morning there, Sheronda woke up with her hair sticking out all over the place, and when Deborah offered to comb it, much to her surprise and delight Sheronda responded, "I'm happy to be nappy."

Of course, for children who do not live in racially diverse neighborhoods, school is often their first exposure to children of another race. Research shows that even children who live in segregated neighborhoods, but attend nearby integrated schools, are more accepting of each other than of those who are bussed in. In other words, children know which kids belong at their school and which do not. Studies also indicate that when the balance of children of both races is nearly equal, more children will cross the race line to become friends than when the class population is tilted in one direction or the other. Thus, the more racially balanced the school, the easier it is for children to treat each other equally and the less likely it is for them to treat members of a different race as "those others."

These findings are corroborated by the racial attitudes of two White sisters we interviewed, Megan, nine, and Shawn, seven, who live in a racially diverse neighborhood and attend a school that is roughly one-third White, one-third Hispanic, and one-third Black. When asked whether they had any close friends who were Black, Megan and Shawn both said yes. When asked if they ever had problems getting along with Black girlfriends because of their racial differences, Megan and Shawn just looked at each other and, in a somewhat perplexed tone, replied, "No." After all, why would they be friends if they didn't get along? Clearly, for Megan and Shawn, close friends were made on the basis of their being fun.

When the race ratio at school is way out of kilter, however, it is harder on girls than boys. Psychologist Janet Kistner has found in her classroom observations that young Black girls in mostly White classes, and White girls in predominantly Black classrooms, experience more social rejection than boys in comparable situations. She blames this difference on the fact that girls tend to play in small groups of one to three best friends, while boys are more likely to participate in team sports, which may encourage racial mixing, if only to reach the necessary numbers to play.

As in most neighborhoods, when schools are either predominantly one race or another, differences in social or economic class are also evident. Because White communities, on the whole, statistically are wealthier than most Black communities, everything from the physical facilities and the quality of the instruction to the availability of classroom supplies may be better at a school that has more White students than Black students. That means that the experiences of a White girl attending a mostly Black grammar school, compared with those of a Black girl attending a mostly White grammar school, may be very different in ways that go beyond race. A White girl in a predominantly Black school may need to act tough in order to survive psychologically, especially if the school is a poor inner-city school. A Black girl in a predominantly White school, on the other hand, may become quiet and withdrawn, especially if the school is an exclusive preparatory school. These are two examples at the extremes, but other patterns of solo racial status also exist.

Jacqueline Woodson's 1994 novel *I Hadn't Meant to Tell You This* offers a fictional example of a grammar school in which the usual relations between race and class are reversed. Her story takes place in Chauncey, Ohio, where the majority African American students are prosperous and the minority White students are poor. The book centers on the friendship between a well-to-do Black girl named Marie and a impoverished White girl named Lena, who is also an incest survivor. In one scene, after Lena expresses doubt that she will ever get to go to college, Marie reflects on her own advantages in life:

> For the first time I began to understand the privilege I had. My father was a college professor. I never had to worry about money or the future. There was money waiting for me when I turned twenty-one.

There are many other factors that influence whether a child will form an interracial friendship. One is certainly racial prejudice. Even children from the same neighborhood vary tremendously in their racial attitudes. Those who grow up in households, either White or Black, where strong hatred for members of the other racial group is frequently expressed are less likely to be open to cross-race friendships than those who grow up in homes where parental messages, as well as toys, books, films, and television, stress respect for racial diversity. A White college student named Lydia, from Richmond, Virginia, commented:

In our house, Dad was king, and I know that his racist views influenced mine. I was so mean to the Black girls in grade school. I called them ugly names right to their face, and you can bet whenever I told Dad about it, he was proud. It wasn't until I went away to school, and took some classes from African American professors, that I began to rethink and develop my own views about racial matters. Now, I deeply regret all those terrible things that I did and said to those Black girls in my elementary school.

But even when parents make a concerted effort to educate their children in positive ways about race, many children still harbor misconceptions. For example, some White children assume, perhaps from watching television, that all Black children are poor and come from single-parent homes. And some Black girls believe that all White girls are "spoiled," and that everything they need or want will be provided for them. Any kind of racial stereotype can erase the individuality of others and hinder the development of interracial friendships.

Skin color, too, can have an impact on cross-race relations. As one six-year-old White girl put it, "I like two of the tan girls in my class, but I am not friends with any of the girls who are really, really black. I'm afraid of them." Skin-color prejudice is the subject of our first book (written with Ronald Hall), *The Color Complex: The Politics of Skin Color Among African Americans.* There, we traced the rise of colorism, as it has come to be called, and documented scientific research demonstrating a pattern of color classism in America. Within the African American community, for example, one's skin color can affect earning potential, career advancement, and dating popularity. Many, if not most, Whites are only vaguely aware of the issue. How, then, would a young White girl like the one quoted above pick up such negative attitudes about dark skin color? Quite possibly, it starts with children's fairy tales and folklore. The evil witches who populate children's literature are both hideously scary and always dressed in black. The symbolism of color abounds in Saturday morning cartoon shows and reruns of old Westerns, where the bad guys always dress in black, and the good guys—the sheriffs, the fairy princesses, the virtuous brides, and angels—wear white and usually *are* White. Prolonged exposure to such color stereotyping reinforces the belief that White means good and Black means bad.

Young girls in particular are highly attuned to the nuances of physical attractiveness. Compared with boys, they are much more sensitive to the social importance of good looks, including skin color. According to research by social psychologists on physical attractiveness and discrimination, girls of both races by the age of three are capable of ranking others by prettiness in ways that are consistent with adult judgments. Girls of similar physical attractiveness seek each other out by nursery school. It seems that pretty White girls who reject dark-skinned Black girls may be doing so for reasons having to do with their perceived social desirability. An attractive White accountant named Becky, now in her late twenties, admitted to us:

> I never wanted to make friends with girls, either White or Black, who I thought were too ugly or too fat. Even in elementary school, I remember that the Black girls who got along best with White girls like me were the prettier ones, those who had light skin color and nice long hair. The darker-skinned girls hung out mostly with themselves, or sometimes with the ugliest White girl in class.

Social rejection based on physical appearance is painful at any age, but is especially hard on young dark-skinned Black girls because of negative stereotyping. Many endure a stage in which they feel not only ugly, but also inadequate. Nobel Prize winner Toni Morrison wrote about such anguish in *The Bluest Eye,* and Maya Angelou addressed the issue in her semiautobiographical work *I Know Why the Caged Bird Sings*. We will examine how differences in skin color, hair, and features affect relationships between White and Black girls and women further in the chapter on beauty and style.

The greater willingness of White girls to befriend Black girls with light skin may also be driven by the perception that such girls are "Whiter" and therefore less different. In some cases, when the light-skinned Black girl is biracial, the physical differences between them may in fact be very slight. Biracial children vary widely in skin color, but on average they have lighter skin than children of two African American parents, although they too can range from dark to extremely light because of ancestral race mixing. And as discussed in *The Color Complex,* extremely light-skinned African American children may sometimes be rejected by other darker-skinned African American children, who tease them for "looking and acting too White." When this happens, a very light-skinned Black or biracial girl may have to turn to White girls, because they're the only ones who will be friends with her. This is what happened to Jerrilyn, a biracial girl with near-White skin, light-colored eyes, and long wavy hair. Now in her late thirties, Jerrilyn can still recall the constant teasing from other Black children because she looked White. The White girls, on the other hand, accepted her without problem.

Some biracial children feel that they serve as bridges between the two racial communities, moving easily from one racial group to the other. The ease with which biracial girls are able to do this may depend, in part, on whether their mothers are Black or White. Girls with White mothers and Black fathers—the more common pattern among interracial relationships and marriages in this country—have an easier time approaching and be-friending White girls than do girls who have Black mothers and White fathers. This makes sense, when one considers that, with a White mother in their life, they already have a presumably loving cross-race female relation-ship.

A Black or biracial girl who is adopted by White parents has a similar advantage. Growing up in a White household gives such girls a greater sense of ease in the presence of other Whites. And if they are very light-skinned, and not particularly self-identified as Black, White girlfriends may not view or treat them as Black. So it was with Katie, a light-skinned biracial girl who was adopted during the early sixties by a White family that lived in a predominantly White town in Minnesota. Not wanting to risk social rejection, and perhaps not fully understanding that she was racially mixed, Katie simply let her friends assume that she was White. She became what is sometimes called an inadvertent passer, although Katie does remem-ber several instances that suggest her White friends had an inkling that she was different from them. In third grade, a popular number for sing-along was an old slave tune called "Cotton Needs Pickin (So Bad)." Whenever her classmates requested this bizarre little ditty, which to Katie's dismay seemed to be every day, they would gather around her and pick at her nappy hair as though it were cotton. Although the teacher reprimanded the children for doing this, Katie would weakly protest, saying, "It's okay. I don't mind." Katie also remembers that her White girlfriends used to call her "noseflat."

Because of the potential for alienating experiences like Katie's, in 1972 the National Association of Black Social Workers took a stand officially oppos-ing the adoption by White families of Black children, even biracial ones like Katie. This policy has been in effect in most states since then. Harvard University law professor Elizabeth Bartholet claims, however, that "there is not a shred of evidence to support that kids do better on racial identity if they are raised in a same-race home." She is among a growing number of professionals challenging the NABSW policy, which she feels harms Black children who are languishing in foster homes when they could be adopted by loving White parents. While research on the racial identity of trans-racially adopted Black children indicates that it does often take a little longer for racial identity to develop—age four instead of age three—once it does, these children usually do fine. This is especially true of those Black children whose White parents provide them with lots of opportunities to explore their racial heritage. The issue is discussed at greater length later in this book.

The Teen Years

Depending on a girl's racial makeup, her physical attractiveness, her family's circumstances, and whether or not she grew up in a racially mixed neigh-borhood or attended an integrated or segregated school, interracial friend-ships of girls in their middle childhood years clearly can and often do blossom. However, as the girls approach puberty, social groups that were once based primarily on gender begin to be shaped by other factors, includ-ing those which are strictly racial. The result is a dramatic drop in the number of same-sex interracial friendships.

The decline in cross-race relations as children become older has been documented by psychologist Steve Asher. He found that 24 percent of White third-graders named a Black student as a best friend, while 37 per-cent of Black children named a White student as a best friend. By high school, these percentages were considerably reduced. Asher found that among White tenth-graders, only 8 percent named a Black student as a best friend; among Black tenth-graders, a mere 4 percent named a White student as a best friend.

These figures are discouragingly low, although it should be pointed out that they represent "best friend" status only. Certainly, there are many other kinds of cross-race friendships and informal relationships in junior high and high school that don't fit into this category. Still, the evidence is incontro-vertible: during adolescence, interracial friendships suffer a huge decline.

Perhaps this is not so surprising. After all, someone of this age wearing the wrong brand of jeans can become a social outcast. Issues of race are bound to come into play as both White and Black teens forge new identities for themselves. But for teenage girls in particular, same-sex friendships are intense, and sudden shifts in social relations can be confusing and painful. As one fifteen-year-old Black girl told us, "I could be friends with this White girl as long as we were girls first, and Black or White second. But as soon as I began to get older and realized I was a *Black* girl, and she a *White* girl, our relationship changed." Or, as Lynda Barry's fictional Edna laments in regard to her best Black girlfriend, Bonna, "Now that we're older you can bet all of that's over."

Claudia, a White college freshman, remembers the exact moment in high school when her Black girlfriend Lichelle turned on her. It was in the ninth grade. Claudia spotted Lichelle during lunchtime sitting at a table with some other Black girls. As usual, Claudia headed over to join Lichelle, but as she approached, Lichelle abruptly turned around and told Claudia that she had to sit elsewhere. For a second, Claudia just stood there with her tray, hardly able to believe that she was being rejected. For those White and Black girls who attempt to maintain cross-race friendships in the face of growing opposition from peers, even the potential for violence exists. New York's *Newsday* reported the story of two fourteen-year-old girlfriends in Brooklyn in 1992, one White and one Black, walking home from school together and being attacked by a group of about fifty Black teenagers. As the Black girl was being grabbed and robbed of her earrings, her attackers demanded to know, "What are you doing with the white bitch?"

Physical assaults like this are rare: verbal threats and name-calling are usually enough to drive or keep apart most teenage girls of different races. After all, what Black teenage girl wants to risk being called an UT, or Uncle Tom, because she hangs out with White girls, and what White teenage girl wants to risk being called a "nigger lover" or "wigger"—a pejorative term for Whites who act Black? At some schools, there are groups who keep other members of their race in line. Among Blacks, it is the Soul Patrollers who warn Black girls against being too studious, well spoken, or polite if they want to avoid being called "White." Among Whites, it is the Race Monitors, who warn White girls against acting too sexy, loud, cocky, or uninhibited if they want to avoid being called "Black." The result is that the majority of White girls and Black girls who may have been friends at an earlier time eventually reach a point in adolescence when they turn away from each other.

This pressure to segregate by race is fueled by a number of factors, including differences in maturation rates, in academic achievement, and in self-esteem. Even gender differences in sports participation can play a part. But the biggest reason for the split between Black teenage girls and White teenage girls, as we shall see, has to do with concerns fostered by sexual competition.

Puberty is the time when the body makes its biological transition from childhood to the adult, with the ability to reproduce. Exactly what triggers the maturation process is not fully understood, but biologists do know that, all other things being equal, a girl who weighs more will mature sexually earlier than a girl who weighs less. This has enormous racial implications, because on average Black girls weigh more than White girls. In fact, by the age of nine, more Black than White girls suffer from obesity, high blood pressure, and even lower levels of good cholesterol. Explanations for the observed race differences range from genetics to social attitudes about the value of being large, a topic examined further in the chapter on beauty and style. Whatever the reason, it is clear that early discrepancies in size between White and Black girls take on larger social meaning when it comes to the menarche, the first menstrual period.

A recent study by the American Academy of Pediatrics confirms that there is a biosocial gap in the development of White girls and Black girls. More than five thousand girls of three to twelve were examined by physicians in twenty-four different states. Findings showed that, while the age of maturation is dropping for girls of both races, Black girls are maturing even earlier than White girls. By the age of eight, only a sixth of White girls but almost half of Black girls already have begun some breast or pubic hair development. Two years later, almost all the Black girls, but only two thirds of the White girls show these same signs of physical maturity. And predictably, the Black girls on average begin to menstruate ahead of White girls.

This difference in physical maturation is one reason that children's interracial friendships are strained by puberty. A White college student, Meredith, recalled what happened to her:

> My best friend growing up was Tonette, a Black girl. She lived down the street and we were together every day. Then, around fifth or sixth grade, she began to get breasts and to get bigger and taller than me. She was ready to move on and find out what boys were all about, while I still looked and probably acted like a little kid. That pretty much marked the end of our friendship.

It would seem that even biology conspires to keep White and Black teenage girls apart.

Early sexual maturity is also linked to poor academic achievement, although for reasons that have nothing to do with hormones and everything to do with the exaggerated reactions of adolescent boys to girls with breasts. Given the biosocial gap in development, this means that more Black teenage girls than White teenage girls are vulnerable to academic derailment from their sudden sexual metamorphosis.

There are other reasons, unrelated to biology or boys, affecting the divergence in school academic performance between White girls and Black girls during their teens. For many White girls, good grades are equated with being "good," something that will help them be accepted, both at school and, later, in White society. But for adolescent Black girls, being labeled "smart" can lead to reprimands from the Soul Patrollers, and may thus be the cause of anxiety. While certainly not all White teenage girls strive to excel academically, nor do all Black teenage girls avoid academic success, there is again a race difference in the proportions of those who opt to become "schoolgirls" and those who aim to be "homegirls."

The study of what actually happens to girls as they make the difficult transition into womanhood was long ignored in the male-dominated field of psychology. But in 1992, the special nature of girls' adolescent development was finally addressed in *Meeting at the Crossroads: Women's Psychology and Girls' Development,* by Harvard psychologists Lyn Mikel Brown and Carol Gilligan. Their research took them to the Laurel School, a private day school for predominantly White middle- and upper-class girls in Cleveland, Ohio. For five years, Brown and Gilligan had observed and interviewed girls from seven and eight years of age up to fifteen and sixteen about their changing attitudes on sexual morality, politics, and violence. Among the major findings were that the confidence and moral clarity exhibited by girls during middle to late childhood gave way to a chorus of "I don't knows" by the time these girls hit adolescence. It was as though the confidence and integrity the girls established naturally when they were younger had to be compromised as they became older in order to preserve their relationships with others. Sadly, Brown and Gilligan noted, it was often the adult women in these girls' lives who served as role models for this journey into silence, as they subtly instructed the girls on the value of being passive and pleasing, behavior that reinforces and maintains traditional male hierarchy and dominance in society at large.

However, the loss of voice observed by Brown and Gilligan at the Laurel School appears to reflect a uniquely White middle-class notion of femininity —one that dates back at least as far as Victorian England. As journalist Peggy Orenstein states in her book *SchoolGirls,* "the model of European femininity, grounded as it is in delicacy, innocence, and an idealized help-lessness—has largely been unavailable to Black women."

The reason European femininity has been largely unavailable to Black women has much to do with confounding issues of class. Economically disadvantaged Black girls are not raised with the expectation that one day their Prince Charming will come and rescue them. In fact, according to 1992 U.S. census data, 54 percent of all Black children under the age of eighteen live with mothers only, compared with 18 percent of comparably aged White children. While there are many reasons for concern about the lack of stable two-parent families on children's development, one positive conse-quence for daughters raised by single mothers is that they are more likely to be told to be self-reliant than are the daughters of more middle-class fami-lies with wage-earning fathers present.

A report entitled "Shortchanging Girls, Shortchanging America," re-leased in 1991 by the American Association of University Women, provides empirical evidence that Black teenage girls do often feel better about them-selves than White teenage girls. Approximately three thousand girls and boys, ages nine to fifteen, across the country were interviewed for the impact of gender and race on self-confidence, academic interest, and career goals. Among the study's major findings were that the self-esteem level of most girls is significantly lower than that of most boys, that the self-esteem of girls steadily declines as they move through the educational system, and that the self-esteem of White girls relative to Black girls drops even faster. At the elementary school level, only 55 percent of the White girls and 65 percent of Black girls report being happy with themselves. By high school, a mere 22 percent of the White girls, but 58 percent of Black girls, continue to be happy with the way they are. According to Dr. Janie Victoria Ward, a leading authority on African American girls and a consultant to the project, "There is high self-esteem among black girls because black culture empha-sizes independence and assertiveness. But academic self-esteem is low. There's a decline in academic pride. Black girls are not relying on schools to give them positive images of themselves."

For some adolescent Black girls, doing well in school can actually make them feel worse about themselves. Signithia Fordham, a Rutgers

University professor, has been exploring the ways academic achievement can threaten a Black girl's sense of self, both culturally and sexually. Fordham believes that smart Black girls are forced to adopt one of two demeanors at school: they can become silent, in effect acting like those docile White girls whom the teachers seem to adore, or they can become one of "those loud Black girls," as Fordham calls them, who always mouth off, crack jokes, and disrupt class. While the first strategy allows a Black girl to pursue academic excellence, she does so at the risk of social rejection and hostile accusations from other Black students that she is "acting White." The second strategy thus holds much appeal for a smart Black girl, as she is better able to preserve her popularity with her Black peers, albeit at the risk of getting poorer grades, being suspended, or even dropping out. But by becoming one of "those loud Black girls," she can avoid, in Fordham's words, "the perceived 'nothingness' of White middle-class notions of womanhood and femininity."

Among the smart but "loud" Black girls Fordham observed and inter-viewed at a high school in Washington, D.C., was Rita. Because she scored well on her Practice Scholastic Achievement Tests (PSATs), Rita's teachers encouraged her to write a strong, upbeat essay to send with her college applications. Most of the female students who had similarly earned high PSAT scores complied with this request, but Rita resisted. To the shock and disappointment of her teachers, she wrote a rather morbid essay about the value of death and dying. In analyzing Rita's behavior, Fordham notes "The 'slam dunking' part of her persona that propels her to the margins of good behavior, without actually forcing her into the realm of bad behavior, makes 'shrinking lilies' out of most adults who interact with her or, alternatively, motivates them to avoid contact with her, if that is an option." For Rita, however, the strategy worked. She got into the college of her choice and did so without provoking accusations of "acting White."

The bold and brassy behavior of some adolescent Black girls is in sharp contrast to the obedient and restrained demeanor of the mostly middle-class White students Brown and Gilligan observed. When Peggy Orenstein com-pared the classroom behavior of girls at a predominantly White middle-class school outside San Francisco with that of girls in a predominantly Black working-class school in Northern California, she too noticed a distinct dif-ference. Becca, a White girl with curved shoulders, thin legs, and home-streaked Sun-In hair, and April, a Black girl with a broad build, dark skin, and reddish, straightened hair, showed some of the differences in personality and style. When she was interviewed by Orenstein, Becca admitted that she would never speak up in class "unless I'm really, really sure of an answer, and sometimes not even then," while April was observed to raise her hand frequently and shout out answers to questions, even though she was nearly always wrong.

Unfortunately, one consequence of the greater confidence of many smart Black girls is that their "bossiness" may get them into trouble with teachers and school authorities, and even cause them to drop out of school. A study conducted by New York's Education Department confirms that African American teenage girls get suspended at a rate three times that of White girls. And another study, conducted in Chicago, found that 44 percent of Black girls dropped out of high school, compared with only 16 percent of White girls. While prejudice toward African Americans is certainly a contributing factor to these race differences in suspension and dropout rates, attitudes toward the value of education also play a role.

By senior year, the cumulative effects of some of these cultural differences take their toll. White girls significantly outperform Black girls on their Scholastic Achievement Tests (SATs). Of a possible top score of 800 on each of the two sections, White girls in 1994 earned an average of 441 on the verbal component and 475 on the math, while Black girls earned an average of 354 on the verbal and 381 on the math. Since SAT scores are supposed to correlate with grades and be predictive of classroom performance, one would think that White girls could claim greater confidence in school than Black girls. However, again the evidence suggests otherwise. Black females' confidence in school is closer to that of White males than it is to that of White females.

That Black girls act more confident in school than White girls, when it is White girls who academically outperform Black girls, would be expected to create a strange dynamic between them. But in fact it rarely does, because White girls and Black girls do not compare themselves with one another. Instead, White girls compare themselves with White boys, whose academic achievement starts to soar in high school. As a result, White girls end up concluding that they aren't as smart. They know that White boys typically outscore them on both sections of the SATs and that a great deal of emphasis is placed on SAT scores as an indicator of raw intelligence. In contrast, Black girls compare their academic accomplishments with those of Black boys, and therefore may conclude that they are just as smart, if not smarter, than the guys. Black teenage girls on average outscore Black teenage boys on the verbal, if not the math, SAT: the combined score for Black boys is only eighteen points higher than it is for Black girls.

Cultural differences, too, can affect self-esteem. White parents expect more academically from sons than from daughters—after all, White boys are future members of the highest paid subgroup in America. In contrast, African American parents expect roughly the same, if not more, from daughters as from sons.

Another reason for the observed lack of self-esteem among middle-class White girls has to do with negative attitudes about such girls boasting of their accomplishments. But working-class Black girls are often encouraged to do just that. Also, African American teenage girls view criticism not as stemming from personal shortcomings but as evidence of racism, so such criticism is likely to be dismissed. White girls lack this buffer, and conclude that any shortcomings in their academic performance are theirs and theirs alone.

The issue of self-esteem can be a source of conflict between White girls and Black girls, especially at private preparatory schools. At Wexler, for example, a school in the North for academically accelerated sixth- to twelfth-graders, Black girls complained that the White girls acted conceited about their school work and sometimes flaunted their grades as a way to humiliate the Black students. Social psychologist Janet Schofield, who interviewed students at Wexler Middle School, found that levels of conflict were higher between the girls than between the boys at the school. The teaching staff agreed. A White teacher, Ms. Engle, said, "I think the boys react better than the girls. Girls can be very catty and they want to have their own friends and that's it . . . The girls seem to stick to themselves [within each racial group] more." A Black teacher, Ms. Partridge, noted, "Girls are more clannish than boys and they tend to hold on to their own little groups . . . It's kind of hard to break into a circle that's been going on for a year [or more]." She added, "Boys discuss sports and they tend to have more to talk about [cross-racially] than we [females] do."

The mention of sports is significant. Just as at the elementary school level, teenage boys and girls who participate in sports have an advantage over others in establishing and maintaining interracial relationships. During adolescence, however, far more boys than girls continue in sports. The results of a recent major survey sponsored by Wilson Sporting Goods showed that 87 percent of seven- to ten-year-old girls were involved in some form of athletic activity. In fact, roughly half of all girls report that they were tomboys when growing up, suggesting that this is a fairly "normal" phase of girls' development. But athleticism in girls dramatically declines after puberty. Among fifteen- to eighteen-year-old girls, 75 percent in the Wilson survey stated that they no longer participated in sports of any kind. Furthermore, the survey found that Black girls drop out of sports even faster than White girls.

A number of factors contribute to this. One is the cultural attitudes toward what the boys think. Compared with White girls, Black girls in the Wilson survey were twice as likely to say that "boys make fun of girls who play sports." Another factor is financial. Sports activities are expensive, and while economically disadvantaged parents may be willing to invest their dollars in athletics for their sons in the hope of athletic scholarships or a professional sports career, they are far less likely to spend money on an equally gifted daughter. After all, her chances of becoming a well-paid professional are slim to none. Transportation is also a hindrance. Mothers who are poor and without a car are not available to chauffeur a child to and from the many practices and meets that are scheduled. Again, sacrifices are less likely to be made for a daughter. Thus, issues of demographics and sexual inequality combine to make Black girls less active in sports than White girls.

Even when Black girls and White girls are involved in sports, there are differences in which sports they choose. As Willye White, a five-time Olympian and 1956 long-jump silver medalist and consultant on the Wilson survey, notes, "You take poorer kids, they'll tend to excel in poverty sports—volleyball, basketball, track and field. But the suburban black kid will have the same interest in the same sports as white kids." Since more White families than Black families live in the suburbs, they have greater exposure to tennis, swimming, soccer, ice skating, and gymnastics. More important, even when Black and White teenage girls participate in the same sports, the effect of the activity on interracial friendships is not the same as it is for boys. Boys are encouraged to be athletic and strong, and they may come to admire each other for these very qualities. But in junior high and high school, girls gain status from their looks and social popularity, not from their ability to shoot hoops or serve an ace in tennis. As Thorne notes in *Gender Play:*

> Athletics provides a continuous arena where at least some boys can perform and gain status as they move from primary through secondary schooling. But for many girls, appearance and relationships with boys begin to take primacy over other activities.

But the major reason that White and Black teenage girls begin to part ways during junior high and high school has less to do with differences in academic achievement, self-esteem, or sports participation than with the growing competition to attract boys. This point is also made by Shirley Abbott in her autobiography, *Womenfolks,* which recounts what it was like to grow up as a White woman in the South during the sixties. After acknowledging the advantage that boys enjoyed in cross-race relations from playing sports together, Abbott writes:

> But, for girls of either race, high school is the time to forget other kinds of achievement and start competing for boys. What matters is getting elected homecoming queen or being invited to the parties, buying pretty clothes. Obviously, in all such endeavors, the white girls were ahead of the blacks. They were more likely to be categorized as pretty, to have money for clothes and jewelry and hairdos, to have pleasant homes and parents who could afford to give them cars, more likely to have their families behind them with the effort it takes to get elected homecoming queen or chief cheerleaders and to have the money for uniforms and long dresses and out-of-town trips . . . The black girls, though the teachers didn't say so, were simply being outgunned in the belle department.

While Abbott's comments relate to a particular time and place, little seems to have changed in high schools across America since then. In particular, the two annual competitive traditions mentioned by Abbott—the selection of members of the homecoming court and the cheerleading squad, based largely on considerations of beauty—still exacerbate White and Black teenage girls' insecurities everywhere.

Because judgments of beauty are so subjective, accusations of racism over the election of homecoming queen and her court are perhaps inevitable. Tensions at some schools have run so high that policies have had to be implemented to ease them. At Hahnville High School, in Louisiana, a quota of three Black girls and seven White girls has been in effect for members of the homecoming court since 1975. These numbers reflect the ratios in the student body, which is approximately 70 percent White and 30 percent Black; the policy was originally established to ensure the representative presence of at least some Black girls on the court. Recently, though, Black students have become aware that the policy sometimes works against them.

In 1986, Black students and parents filed a complaint after discovering that several Black girls had been denied a place on the court, even though they had received more votes than some of the White girls who did make it.

Another high school, in Brownsville, Tennessee, following a court-ordered merger in 1970 of two segregated schools, also established a policy for electing homecoming queen. Concerned that a Black girl, in the face of stiff competition from White girls, might never be selected queen at the newly merged school, administrators announced the title would alternate from year to year between a Black girl and a White girl. Although the rule was originally designed as a measure of fairness for Black girls, it has become apparent that during the "off" years, Black girls are receiving more votes but having to settle for the court's maid of honor. (The school's principal and the county superintendent maintain that their method must be working, because there have been no race riots over the issue.)

While rigid policies like these are far from widespread, they say much about issues of competition—and the institutionalization of female beauty in high school. Similar policies have not been enacted for the annual election of class president, editor of the school paper, or captain of any of the varsity sports teams. But one can argue that these positions are presumably based more on ability than on subjective considerations like beauty.

Racial tensions similarly run high over the annual selection of cheerleaders. While the ability to jump, dance, and sing is important, a girl must also be deemed pretty. Appearance matters in another way, as well. At many racially integrated schools, even schools that are largely White, most of the boys on the two big varsity teams, basketball and football, are Black. Should the cheerleading squad reflect the racial makeup of the school as a whole or of the team for which the girls are cheering? Is it "right" for a group of White girls to be cheering on to victory a group of Black boys? Hanley J. Norment, the vice president for programs of Washington State's Montgomery County NAACP, believes that the way in which high schools in his county select members of the cheerleading squad is unfair to some of the Black girls who try out. He suspects that hair texture has something to do with this. If a Black girl's hair doesn't swing about like the White girls' hair, her chances of being selected are considerably reduced.

At the same time, some White cheerleaders resent what they call "affirmative action" positions on cheerleading squads. At schools where a certain number of Black girls, regardless of talent, have to be on the squad, White girls who are technically better may be sometimes left off. Patty, the White captain of a cheerleading squad at a largely White school in the South, complained:

> We had one Black girl named Michele on our cheerleading squad, but she was the worst. But, of course, she made the squad every year, just because she was Black, and we couldn't all be White.

Of course, not all of today's teenage girls want to try out for the cheerleading squad. Many, White and Black, invest themselves and their identities in academics or various social activities. One way that teens create a sense of identity is through fashion. In the early sixties and seventies, the height of fashion was the hippie look; today it is the "in" thing to be a hiphopper.

Hip-hop has it origins in urban Black rap music, but has since come to embrace a way of dressing—baggy clothes, gold jewelry, and hats turned backward—a way of greeting—"Yo, homegirl, what's happening?"—as well as styles of hair (for boys, razor cuts and short dreads; for girls, tiny braids covering the head). While imitation may be the highest form of flattery, African American teens often do not appreciate the sight of White teens appropriating Black culture. Once again, the element of competition may drive Black and White teens apart. White girls who adopt hip-hop fashion have been known to incite violence from Black girls, who feel their very identity and culture are being stolen. At North Newton Junior-Senior High in Indiana, thirteen-year-old Michelle Kegley was punched in the face by a Black student in 1993 because she wore baggy hip-hop clothes and styled her hair in tiny braids. Another White student, Andrea Van Winkle, dressed similarly and was harassed for "acting Black"; she was called a "wigger." Although in both cases the physical attacks were made by Black boys, the Black girls did nothing to defend the two girls and, in fact, egged the boys on.

Such extreme negative reactions to their way of dressing and wearing their hair are confusing to White girls, who think they deserve credit, not blame, for dressing in race-friendly ways. Other White girls don't feel that Blacks are justified in claiming cultural property rights to a particular fashion. As Melissa from Detroit put it:

> I get so tired of Black girls accusing me of acting Black. Yeah, I wear gold hoop earrings. I wear oversized clothes. I can even dance.

But it's more about being urban than Black. It's the whole MTV
thing.

And still others question why the Black kids assume that the White girls are
"trying to act Black" because they choose hip-hop fashions. A girl, named
Canan, argued, "I say I don't act Black; I act myself. I'm different from
Black people. I'm different from White people . . . I just want to show
people I can go both ways."

This jealousy over perceived encroachments is but one example of how
Black and White girls end up in competition, exacerbating the division
between them. There is also an element of sexual jealousy in the anger felt
toward White girls for dressing "Black." While some Black girls feel that in
such traditional endeavors as running for homecoming queen, they may
well be, in Abbott's words, "outgunned in the belle department," no Black
girl wants to be "outgunned" when it comes to hip-hop styles. They may
perceive such White girls as trying to steal away Black guys. This fear is
clear in the comment of a New Jersey Black teen named Tara:

> Every time a White girl either starts hanging around Black girls or
> *dating a Black boy,* all of a sudden she's Black. She starts trying to talk
> "Black." She even dresses like a Black girl by wearing large gold ear-
> rings 'n' stuff. I hate that.

In fairness, not all Black teenage girls feel threatened. In fact, one strikingly attractive African American college student, Donna B., from Chicago,
pointed out that her best friend in high school was a White girl named
Sharon who dressed in hip-hop fashions. "Sharon was totally cool and into
Black culture," remarked Donna.

But for many African American teenage girls, the threat of White girls
stealing the affections of Black boys is an ever-present danger. Conditioned
by our cultural definitions of feminine beauty, it isn't surprising that Black
teenage boys are attracted to White girls to some degree. In fact, for some
Black boys, it is a rite of passage to see how far they can get with a White
girl. But to Black teenage girls witnessing such cross-race flirtations, it is a
painful reminder that White girls have the looks that our larger society says
are beautiful. Instead of getting angry at the guys, though, most African
American teenage girls take it out on White girls, especially the prettiest
ones. After all, less attractive White girls are less of a threat.

When we asked a group of Black teenage girls at a middle school in Joliet, Illinois, what they thought of White girls, one, named Renee, said, "I can't stand them 'cause they're always flinging their damn hair all over the place, thinking their shit don't stink. I wanna walk up to them and slap their little pug noses off." Her friends agreed, offering such comments as: "They always want to date Black guys, especially the basketball players," and "They think they are so much prettier than Black girls," and "They think they can get anything they want because their Daddy will give it to them."

When we asked the White girls at the same school what they thought of Black girls, we heard fear. A seventh-grader named Jennifer whispered, "I'm scared to death of them! Black girls are so tomboyish and are always picking a fight with me. I don't know why they want to be so mean all the time." Another admitted to trying to become teacher's pet for protection. When the Black girls were told what the White girls had said, they acted pleased. "Just drop Miss Priss off in my neighborhood," Renee said. "She'll see why we're so mean." Her friends added, "We'll put the fear in her that her mamma never did."

While by no means universal, the deep-seated rage of some Black teenage girls clearly produces intense anxiety in many White girls, some of whom devise strategies to protect themselves. One strategy is to exchange academic assistance for physical protection. A White girl named Sally at the Wexler School explained, "You get exposed to a lot of black people who are trying to act tough. You have to know a lot of people. You have to get yourself a black friend. You just have to be nice and show you care a lot. You also have to take your time to help them."

But the most common strategy seems to be avoidance. This was employed by a White teenager, Tru Love, when she attended a predominantly Black school in Detroit. In an article for *Ebony* magazine, Love noted that the Black boys at school were often protective of her, but when it came to the Black girls, she tried to hide from them. This wasn't always possible, though. Love admitted that she was

> deathly afraid of going into the bathroom . . . There was always a gang of unfriendly girls hanging out. They used to say thing like, 'What are you looking at, White girl? Why don't you go back where you came from?' I thought for sure they were going to jump me and

pound my skinny butt. There were some things the guys couldn't help me with. In the bathroom, I was on my own.

Another woman, Lana, a White student at a predominantly Black inner-city Northern school during the late sixties, remembers being very careful not to get to school too early, lest she get beaten up by Black girls. One day she got caught.

I was coming up the school steps, and there, waiting for me, was a gang of Black girls. I started yelling, 'I don't wanna fight. Leave me alone,' but they shoved and pulled my hair anyway. But I'm not racist, and I never had any problems with the Black guys. In fact, I loved to dance with them at parties.

Sandra T., who grew up in the North but moved to Florida during the early seventies, recalled how she learned the hard way to avoid Black girls. Sandra remembers a day when she was walking home from eighth grade and suddenly heard a Black girl taunting her: "You're an ugly White bitch. You think you're something special, but you're just an ugly White bitch." Sandra flipped the girl the bird, and the next thing she knew her hair was being pulled and she was socked hard in the stomach. Sandra said, "She didn't stop beating me until I started screaming 'I give up, I give up.' " She added:

After that, I became so frightened of Black girls that I actually developed an intense phobia of them. I became afraid to go outside for fear one might be around. I never feared the Black boys, though, because they all thought that I was cute.

Ironically, in seeking to prove that they are not racist and therefore do not deserve Black girls' rage, many White girls, including some of those quoted here, unwittingly threaten Black girls by seeking the protection and friendship of Black boys. This results in sexual jealousy, of course, which only divides Black girls and White even further. Nor are all White teenage girls unaware of the rage their flirtations with Black boys can inspire in Black girls. A teenager from Little Rock, named Addie, asked whether she had ever been the target of Black teenage girls' rage, responded:

Black girls hate me because Black guys ask me out. It's funny, because I hear them say they don't know why a Black guy would want a pale White girl anyway. Well, if they don't get it, then why do they try so hard to look like White girls? I grew up in a very mixed neighborhood, so I know about Black girls wearing fake hair and blue contacts. They're all a bunch of hypocrites. I don't think I could ever really get along with Black girls.

Such intense feelings of antagonism, of course, do not characterize all cross-race relations. Obviously, many teenage girls do manage to resist pressures to segregate, and instead become good friends. However, for too many others, the teen years represent a low point in interracial relations.

Clearly, new ways must be found to ease tensions between Black and White teenage girls. The most obvious way is through education. If first-graders like Justine and Alison can be taught about slavery, then surely junior high and high school girls can learn how the combined effects of racism and sexual inequality work to their mutual disadvantage. The bridge of friendship among younger Black and White girls must be kept open. As we shall see, it is during adolescence that so many of the seeds of women's conflicts are first planted.

Chapter Three

Surface Divisions:

Issues of Beauty and Style

Silky, long hair automatically inspires a cluster of preoccupied gestures
that are considered sublimely feminine because they are sensuously self-
involved: an absent-minded twisting of a stray curl, the freeing of loose
ends that get caught under a coat collar, a dramatic toss of the entire
mane, a brushing aside of the tendrils that fall so fetchingly across the
forehead and into the eyes.

—*Susan Brownmiller*
"Hair," Femininity, *1984*

I grew up believing that grease grew hair and if I could just find the
magic brand I'd be Rapunzel's twin sister.

—*Lonnice Brittenum Bonner*
Good Hair: For Colored Girls Who've Considered Weaves
When the Chemicals Became Too Ruff, *1991*

When we were on tour promoting our first book, *The Color Complex,* we made some startling discoveries about each other's cosmetic practices and beauty concerns. The revelations began on a cold February night, in an overheated motel room in Omaha, when Kathy asked Midge whether she had any skin lotion she could use. As Kathy rubbed some of the lotion into her skin, she casually commented, "White women are so lucky their skin doesn't ash in winter." "What do you mean?" asked Midge. She raised her pants leg to show Kathy her own dry, chapped skin, and Kathy leaned back in surprise. "It never occurred to me that White women's skin could get like that." Nor did it occur to Midge that dry skin was a problem for African American women. She simply assumed that all Black women had skin as smooth and glistening as that of African American models.

As the tour continued, Midge was surprised to learn that Kathy could go up to a week without washing her hair. Midge watched curiously as Kathy wrapped her processed hair in a scarf every night. To Midge, it seemed a real time-saver, especially in the morning. Kathy, on the other hand, believed it was easier to have short, straight hair like Midge's, but she had never before seen how much time it took to wash and blow-dry even short hair every morning. At times, even their choice of what to wear for a particular occasion seemed shaped by different cultural norms. The more Kathy and Midge observed each other preparing to face the world every day, the more they realized how dissimilar were the private cosmetic practices of Black women and White women.

Shared concerns over beauty and style both unite Black women and White women—if only because they commonly live in a society that defines and even restricts them according to their looks—and divide them. Most White women and Black women, of course, look very different. Without some understanding of the historical, cultural, and social forces that shape and influence each other's beauty and fashion choices, women are at risk of alienating one another, passing unfair criticism, and judging one another on the basis of stereotypes. These judgments are further confounded by race and class, thus giving appearance a political charge, as well. Issues of beauty and style undermine women's interracial relationships in ways that never apply to men and their cross-race relations. As poet and feminist Adrienne Rich once observed, "Black women and white move as myths through each other's fantasies," myths that include perverse ideas of beauty created by White society at large.

Skin Color

Within this mythology, the most obvious physical difference between women of European descent and women of African descent is skin color. Throughout history, the relative lightness and darkness of skin color has affected the status of women of both races. Until this century, women with lighter skin tones were generally more revered in terms of status and beauty. This was true even in regions of Africa and South America, where indigenous populations are fairly dark-skinned. The preference for lighter-skinned women was strongest in agricultural societies, though. Daughters of the wealthiest families were typically spared from doing outdoor labor. Their skin, being shielded from the sun, was therefore paler; the skin of poor women who worked the fields was darkened by the sun. In that way, the relative lightness and darkness of a woman's skin came to play directly into perceptions of her wealth, class, and marriageability. Eventually, light skin also came to be associated with femininity, youth, and even virginity.

In America, too, White women with the palest, creamiest skin were usually praised as the most beautiful. It was not until the arrival of the jet age, when only the well-to-do could afford to travel to sunny climes in winter, that the desirability of pale skin began to lessen. The glow of a healthy tan, especially during the winter months, came to symbolize wealth and luxury—the luxury of having nothing better to do all day than lie about in the hot sun. Concurrently, less privileged women left the farms to work indoors in factories, offices, and the homes of others, and they began to look pale, even in summer. The result was a 180–degree shift in attitude. Pale skin became undesirable, something to avoid. And while dark tans are currently undergoing re-evaluation by health-conscious White Americans, most Whites in this country still associate "having some color" in their skin as a plus. After a day in the sun, a young White girl is often affectionately told that she looks "as brown as a berry." In contrast, a young Black girl who spends too much time in the sun may hear, "You're as black as a skillet."

To understand why such cultural differences exist in this country it is necessary to return to the antebellum South. As we more fully discussed in *The Color Complex,* the origins of colorism can be traced to that era. On the large plantations, slave owners accepted what is called the "mulatto hypothesis"—that an infusion of White blood would lift Negroes out of their base inferiority. As a result, they began selecting lighter-skinned female slaves, some of whom were their own offspring, for the high-status household jobs of nanny, cook, and seamstress. Owners further believed that slaves with darker skin were stronger and better suited to tolerate the hot sun, so those who were racially pure were sent to the fields to perform the most physically demanding jobs, such as plowing, planting, and harvesting. In essence, White slave holders equated lighter skin with intelligence and darker skin with strength, and their attitudes became adopted by the slaves themselves. Light-skinned slaves, returning from the "big house," started to imitate the genteel ways of the White families, believing themselves superior to their dark brothers and sisters.

Light-skinned slave women were particularly valued for their exotic beauty, in part because of the high prices they could command when sold. White owners and traffickers began specifically to breed "quadroon" (one-fourth Black) and "octoroon" (one-eighth Black) slave women as concubines to be auctioned off at special balls held in New Orleans and other cities throughout the South. Although they were still slaves, these women were valued because of their lighter skin and mix of Caucasian features.

Light-skinned Negroes, both men and women, had other advantages as well. Before Emancipation, many light-skinned Negroes lived free. When the Civil War ended, the mulatto elite, as they called themselves, sought to maintain their status by doing business only with each other and establishing preparatory schools and colleges that denied admission to applicants who were dark. They even restricted their marital choices to those who were light-skinned; the goal was always to lighten the line, never darken it.

But it was African American women who were the most negatively affected by the preoccupation with skin color. It was much harder for them than for Black men to improve their social standing, unless they were born into the mulatto elite. A Black man, no matter how dark his skin, could find a way to earn money and improve his lot in life. He could also marry someone much lighter than himself, thereby "improving" the skin color of his offspring. But no such opportunities existed for women. A woman's social worth was determined solely by her marriageability, and if she was very dark, her prospects were poor. In a society controlled and dominated by

White men, dark-skinned Black women found themselves at the bottom of a cruel color caste hierarchy.

To deal with this, many dark-skinned Black women did what women everywhere have done—they attempted to change their looks. In their efforts to become lighter, nineteenth-century Negro women rubbed lye and other acidic products, used to remove dirt from floors, directly on their skin. Homemade blends of lemon juice, bleach, and urine were smeared on faces and limbs; some women swallowed arsenic wafers, and others took bleach baths, all in the pursuit of making their dark skin turn light.

Fortunately, within today's African American community, negative attitude toward dark-skinned women have lessened. Following the Black Pride Movement of the sixties, women of all shades began to be appreciated for their ethnic beauty. However, it would be misleading to conclude that the chant of "Black is Beautiful" completely eliminated the long-standing preference even in the African American community for lighter-skinned women. Recent surveys indicate that a majority of African American men still prefer to marry a woman as light as, or lighter than, themselves. This is particularly true among those who are successful. One look at the wives and girlfriends of the most visible, powerful Black men in this country, be they politicians, businessmen, athletes, or entertainers, confirms that lighter-skinned Black women or, in some cases, White women are preferred.

Culturally based differences in the value of light or dark skin color is a potential source of conflict for Black and White women, particularly when it comes to getting a tan. White women, ignorant of their skin color privilege, may unknowingly insult a brown-skinned African American woman by saying something like "You're lucky. You never have to worry about getting a tan." Of course, many African American women are quick to dismiss White women's reasons for wanting to stay out in the sun all summer, and especially for paying to go to tanning salons in winter. Ironically, if the two groups of women were better informed of each other's beauty issues, they would realize that their seemingly contradictory attitudes about tan skin were actually driven by the same underlying concern: improved social status.

Another beauty issue related to social status is that of dry skin. As Kathy and Midge discovered, Black and White women alike suffer from dry skin in winter, but there are important race-related differences in attitude. Because the white residue of dry skin is far more evident on dark skin than light, the condition among African American women is vaguely linked with concerns about color and class. By elementary school, most Black girls are well aware of the need to cover themselves with Vaseline or another lubricant to avoid ashy-looking skin. Kathy recalls that, when she was young, her grandmother used to smear Vaseline over her legs, which would make her tights stick and cling uncomfortably. Kathy envied the White girls at school for not having to contend with this problem.

Among White women who are aware of attitudes about dry skin in the African American community, some report that they learned of such concerns from reading African American novels and books of nonfiction. For example, in *The Bluest Eye,* Toni Morrison makes several references to the need to be vigilant about dry skin. One passage is:

> In winter his mother put Jergens Lotion on his face to keep the skin from becoming ashen. Even though he was light-skinned, it was possible to ash. The line between colored and nigger was not always clear; subtle and telltale signs threatened to erode it, and the watch had to be constant.

In *The Company of My Sisters,* Julia Boyd discusses the possible damage to a Black girl's self-esteem from constantly having to smear her skin with Vaseline. A friend named Vy says:

> To this very day, I hate the feel of Vaseline on my skin. Mama used to grease us from head to foot in her never-ending battle to keep us from looking ashy. It was like it's okay to be black, but don't be ashy black, be shiny black, 'cause white folks don't understand ashy black. I always wanted to ask, What's the difference, Mama? 'cause I would see white folks treat ashy black folks the same way they treated shiny black folks.

White women may be spared concerns about their skin when young, but not when they get older. Skin ages differently in Black women and in White women. As Liza, a White middle-aged housewife from Atlanta, pointed out, "Black women don't seem to wrinkle as quickly as White women. Look at Lena Horne, Tina Turner, and Diahann Carroll. Beautiful." White novelist Connie May Fowler, in *Sugar Cane,* makes a similar observation through the description of an elderly White woman, seen through the eyes of her Black domestic servant:

Now this was an old white woman, and white women tend to show their age. Mrs. Barthaleme Finster was no exception. Wealthy. Widowed. A string of pearls around her neck. A white-powdered face dotted with vermilion rouge. And an absolute fascination of lines colliding, splitting off, and colliding again, beneath that carefully applied cloud of expensive, smelly, desperate dust.

Why does the skin of Black women seem more resistant to aging? Ironically, melanin, the very substance that gives skin its color and has been the source of indictment of countless African American women, accounts for the advantage. According to Carla Herriford, co-director of the Institute of Aesthetic and Cosmetic Dermatology, the greater presence of melanin in Black women protects the skin from the damaging effects of ultraviolet rays. The result is that dark skin stays pliant and youthful-looking longer than skin with relatively little melanin. African American plastic surgeon Dr. Pearlman Hicks similarly observes, "My Black patients who come for face lifts are ten to fifteen years older than my White ones; they don't seem to age as quickly." Or, in the words of African American actress L. Scott Caldwell, "Black don't crack!" Differences in how dark and light skins age may account in part for the recent research findings of Mimi Nichter and Sheila Parker, anthropologists at the University of Arizona. When they asked White and Black junior high and high school girls to describe women as they get older, 65 percent of the African American girls said women get more beautiful with age, often citing their mothers as examples. White girls thought that their mothers may once have been beautiful but no longer were.

Compared with Black women's hair, White women's hair turns gray earlier. On average, White women start to become noticeably gray around the age of thirty-four, but the hair of African American women doesn't gray, on average, until the age of forty-four. As a result, more White women than Black women use hair-coloring products to hide the gray. Observed race differences in the aging process like those above do not necessarily create conflict between African American and White women. Who could blame Black women for pointing proudly to the fact that they age more slowly than White women? At the same time, a preoccupation with aging on the part of so many Black and White women distracts them from what should be a larger common endeavor: challenging the double standard in society whereby men who grow old are distinguished and respected, while women who grow old turn ugly and invisible. No woman, regardless of race, should have to hide the natural effects of aging on her body.

Hair Texture and Styles

A far more divisive issue concerns racial differences in hair texture. The hair follicles of women of African descent emerge from a slanted or oval shaft, which causes the hair to fold over and curl into a tight or loose spiral as it grows out. In most Caucasian women, however, the hair follicles emerge from a rounded shaft, growing flat or straight against the scalp. Although some White women have hair that is just as tightly curled as that of any woman from Africa, and many African American women, particularly those of mixed White or Native American ancestry, have hair as straight as any White woman's, there remain fundamental differences in the texture of hair of most White and Black women in this country. Unfortunately, in a society with a strong history of racial prejudice, such differences are not without social and even economic consequences.

Historically, within the African American community, hair texture was very much linked to the concerns about skin color. According to the standards of beauty set by the mulatto elite, who were in turn influenced by White society, a Black woman with straight or wavy hair was considered more attractive than a woman of the same color whose hair was tightly coiled, nappy, or kinky. Straight hair was declared "good"; nappy hair was deemed "bad."

As a result, hair products and techniques were developed to "fix bad hair." Even during slavery, women used to put hog lard on their tightly curled hair to make it lie flat like "Miss Anne's." Later, hot combs were invented, and various formulas, including that of Mme. C. J. Walker, were concocted to help tight curls relax. Until the sixties, it was assumed that any Black woman whose hair was "bad" would have to perm it straight. The Afro was the first natural hair style for Black women, but it was just a fad, and by the mid-seventies most women returned to routine processing of their hair.

White women's notions of good and bad hair have never been as clear cut, nor the consequences of "good hair" as important. To White women, good hair means hair that is thick (but not too thick), shiny, rich in color, long or short, but bad hair is either too thin or too thick, too curly, dull, and mousy brown in color. Good hair can also be naturally wavy or bone straight, depending on the style. Within the White community, however, hair is generally not categorized as "good" or "bad." Many White women may have "bad hair" days, but they do not have "bad hair" lives.

For most Black females, concerns about hair begin early. By the age of four or five, a Black girl typically knows how her hair is going to be. If she is "unfortunate" enough to be cursed with "bad hair," she learns what she must do. A Black girl also knows that her mother will strictly oversee what she does with her hair. Whether it's nappy or not, she will usually be allowed to grow her hair long. Black mothers almost never cut a daughter's hair short. Still, conflicts over hair style are common between Black mothers and their daughters. An African American woman named Dorothy recalls the hair battles she had with her daughter Lynn, now twenty-eight years old.

> Every day, I had to get my eight-year-old daughter up half an hour earlier for school just so I could plait her hair. Then Lynn wanted to sign up for a swimming class, but there was no way I could deal with her hair being wet every day. I had to tell her she couldn't swim because I didn't have the time to keep washing, drying, and pressing her hair all the time. I thought Lynn would never forgive me for that. When she turned ten, I allowed Lynn to get her hair permed so that it would be easier for both her and me. That was eighteen years ago, and Lynn still perms her hair today, as do I. Lynn also just learned how to swim, something I never did.

It is sad to realize that Black girls may have their activities and their free time curtailed simply because of their hair.

Today a growing number of African American mothers are determined to raise their daughters with a sense of pride in the texture of their hair. But even with the generally more positive messages about nappy hair currently circulating in the Black community, many girls with such hair still go through at least a phase when they secretly long to have hair that is straight and flowing, like the hair of models in beauty magazines.

For most Black girls, the fantasies begin when they see what the hot comb can do to flatten out their curls. Hot combing can hurt, leaving painful burn marks on ears, foreheads, and especially along the nape of the neck, known as "the kitchen." But the desire to have straight hair is so strong, and the pressure to conform to the White ideal so effective, that most Black girls learn to put up with the discomfort and inconvenience of hot combing. They know that having straight hair requires discipline. By the time she is seven or eight, the Black girl is ready for her first hair-straightening perm; it is a big event, a day that will mark her entry into the world of adult women. The perm holds the promise of turning the young nappy-headed girl from what she considers an ugly duckling into a beautiful swan. As Caroline, a Black woman we interviewed for *The Color Complex,* recalled of her first perm, "It changed my whole life."

In order to maintain a perm's soft curl, every night the girl's hair must be put in rollers or wrapped around her head with a scarf. Also, once a girl gets a perm, it is hard to go back. Each six to eight weeks she will need a touch-up to avoid having her hair begin to break at the point where the permed hair and new hair growth meet. Sadly, the end result of all this attention to hair maintenance is the girls do not feel good about their hair. As Black feminist bell hooks notes, "Most of us were not raised in environments where we learned to regard our hair as sensual or beautiful in an un-processed state."

In contrast, a White girl is exposed to very different lessons about her hair. She learns that a girl's hair is something to fuss over—certainly more than if she were a boy—but whether it's straight or naturally curly, most girls enjoy playing with it, wearing it long and down, in ponytails or braids, or held back with barrettes, headbands, or bows. In the White community, where there is no history of class difference linked to hair texture, mothers tend to give their daughters more leeway in how they wear their hair. And for White females, a perm usually means adding curls, rather than straight-ening hair, and it is something that can be done, or not done, at any point in their lives.

Unless they happen to have an interracial childhood friendship, White girls generally do not know that the feelings they have about their hair are any different from those experienced by Black girls. For Hillary, a White woman, it took having her hair braided by her best Black girlfriend's mom to realize the difference.

There I was, clutched on the floor between this woman's thunder thighs. She had a big green Afro comb. She would grab my hair and part my scalp, then pull relentlessly on my hair as she twisted it into braids, all the while complaining about how stringy my White hair was. When I would move, she would slap the top of my head with that green Afro comb and tell me to be still, or she would never be done. She finally finished over an hour later, and the braids were so tight that my eyebrows were at the top of my head, and for days I had the worst headache. I knew then that I was very happy to have White hair, because I had no hair discipline.

But for most White girls, a lack of understanding about issues of hair texture, particularly its relationship to class and status, may lead them to seem patronizing, insensitive, and insincere when they comment on a Black girl's hair. Theresa, a White junior high school student with shoulder-length blond hair, was surprised and hurt to discover that she had angered some Black teenage girls by the following comment:

You know, I don't get it. The whole thing with Black girls and their hair. I think their hair is wonderful. It's thick. It holds curls. It holds any hair style you put it in. And you don't have to wash it every day. I'd trade hair with a Black girl in a minute.

Of course, when it comes to "tress stress," the teen years are hard on every girl, White or Black. Perhaps the anxieties about being different, about having one's body grow in unpredictable ways, get focused on one of the few body parts—hair—over which some degree of control can be exercised. Or perhaps it is the sudden pressure to appear attractive to boys, in which one's hair seems to play a large part. For whatever reason, hair becomes such a major preoccupation for adolescent girls of both races that their self-esteem can actually rise and fall with every glance in the mirror.

It is during the teen years that race differences in hair texture and style also turn political. Among White girls, seemingly every major hair decision —whether to perm, dye, or cut—requires constant feedback and reassurance from closest friends. An unwritten social rule in the White community seems to be that whatever a White girlfriend does to her hair, however it may look, it is essential to tell her, "It looks great!" Privately, one may think the friend is vain, insecure, or silly for experimenting the way she does, but one must never question her decisions or motives. Among Black teenage girls, however, hair decisions are subject to more critical feedback from friends, because hair styles are laden with political overtones. Anxiety about differences in choice of style may cause rifts in friendship. One thirteen-year-old Black girl, Janie, described her experiences this way:

> I have a best friend who sometimes wears braids and sometimes she doesn't, but she never gets her hair pressed. Her Mom won't let her. I do press my hair, and she says that it is because I wanna be like a White girl. But I like my hair like this. I think it's pretty. The other way hurt too much when my Mom used to comb it.

When an African American girl straightens her hair, as Janie did, the Black girls who don't may accuse her of being a White "wannabe." But if she leaves her hair natural, she risks having the girls with "good hair" call her "jigaboo" or worse. So common are tensions between African American women regarding differences in their hair that it became the topic of a musical number in Spike Lee's 1988 film *School Daze,* set on a Black college campus. While in real life, such conflicts are hardly as vicious or intense as Lee portrayed on the screen, hair nonetheless remains a painful divide among many young Black women today.

Hair also has the power to create conflict between Black and White women. When Eurocentric standards emphasizing long, flowing hair are the cultural norm, it is difficult for African American women with short and nappy hair not to feel resentful. Some, not surprisingly, lash out against White women whose hair does fit the norm. They may feel that White women who wear their hair that way do so just to flaunt it. But most White women who keep their hair long do it because of the high sexual appeal placed on long, flowing, disheveled hair *à la* Farrah Fawcett in the seventies or Cindy Crawford in the nineties. White feminist author Susan Brownmiller mentions the "long hair mystique" in the epigraph to this chapter.

Actually, the constant hair stroking and head tossing of those whose hair is long annoys many women, White and Black alike. Columnist and author Erma Bombeck is among those who poke fun at women who can't keep their hands out of their hair. Secretly admitting to fantasies of wanting to do the same, Bombeck fears, after watching supermodels Cindy Crawford and Christie Brinkley push what appear to be pounds of hair off their face over and over again, that if she did have long hair, there would be no time to do anything else. She quips, "These people can't carry a package, eat hot dogs, wave, or shake hands. Every second of their lives is consumed with raking their fingers through their hair and getting their sight back." African American poet Gwendolyn Brooks similarly derides White women for not being able to "keep their hands out of their hair."

It especially bothers African American women, though, to see other Black women fall prey to the "long hair mystique," especially when they seek it artificially, with a weave or a wig. Whenever a "sister" is spotted in public with unusually long hair, she is scrutinized. If there is evidence that her hair is not natural, those around her may make derisive comments, such as, "That bitch has a weave." White women who get weaves—and more of them are opting to do just that—are never held politically accountable for the decision. However, for many African American women, it is a badge of honor not to attempt anything so obvious in pursuit of White society's ideal. Unfortunately, this leaves a Black woman whose own hair is short and nappy in somewhat of a dilemma. On the one hand, she knows that long hair in today's society has undeniable feminine appeal, but if she uses a weave or wig, she may suffer accusations of "selling out."

African American stand-up comedian Rhonda Hansome, better known to her fans as Passion, describes the complex psychology behind her own recent decision to "go long." Rhonda grew up with a light-skinned cousin who was constantly praised for having "good" hair and being pretty, while Rhonda, who had darker skin, was said to have "bad" hair. She was considered smart, but no one ever told Rhonda she was pretty. Rhonda was able to use her considerable talents and quick wit to make a successful career on stage and television, and, in doing so, turned her "bad" hair into a signature trademark—short, spiked, multicolored hair that sat on her head like a satellite dish. Then one day, to the enormous disappointment of her friends, fans, and family members, Rhonda abruptly switched from that distinctive style to hair that was long and straight, with bangs. She explained what had happened.

I was in L.A. and it rained. It ruined my hairdo, so I went to a store and tried on a wig. Then I decided to buy it, because I loved the way it made me feel. I felt so sexy and glamorous.

Eventually Rhonda replaced the wig with a long-hair weave. In wearing her hair long, Rhonda has finally been able to work through the resentment she harbored toward White women for possessing this one beauty attribute denied to her. She now says:

Whenever I see the ideal White woman with long blond hair and blue eyes, I acknowledge her beauty. And I say I am her equal and perhaps more extraordinary. I would say she is the prize, but I am the treasure.

Ironically, Rhonda also claims that wearing a weave is "the last stop before dreadlocks."

Today, a growing number of African American women are deciding to throw away their wigs and weaves, and no longer manipulate their hair with chemicals or heat. It can be a big, even a traumatic, step, although the majority of African American women who do decide to go natural wonder why they hadn't done it sooner. African American author Lonnice Brittenum Bonner, in her book *Good Hair: For Colored Girls Who've Considered Weaves When Chemicals Became Too Ruff,* encourages Black women to move beyond attitudes about "good" and "bad" hair, and replace them with notions of "healthy" and "unhealthy" hair. Once the chemicals are out, Black women have the choice of keeping their hair short, usually in a short natural, or growing it long, either braided or in dreadlocks.

Short hair on women has a long history of being shunned, in large part because such styles were viewed as powerful political statements of defiance against accepted feminine appearance and behavior. Perhaps that's why some African American and White activists who have short hair are more inclined to feel unified by their shared style than divided by their different hair texture. It is curious to note, however, that many of today's leading White feminists, including Gloria Steinem, Germaine Greer, Betty Friedan, Andrea Dworkin, Catharine MacKinnon, Susan Faludi, and Naomi Wolf, choose to keep their hair long. Perhaps they do so purely out of personal choice, or, perhaps consciously, they realize that having long hair makes their radical words somehow more palatable to the mainstream society they knew they must impress.

Today, most women who keep their hair short do it more for convenience and fashion than for politics or homosexuality. Diana, a Black woman, confessed there were times when she had to sit for four hours just to get her hair "fixed." Now she proudly proclaims, "It takes me exactly five minutes to brush and lightly spray my short Afro with an oil sheen. I wouldn't change my new style for the world." Still, some women, Black and White, who keep their hair very short may have their sexuality called into question or find themselves perceived as trying to make some kind of radical statement when they are not. Jean Norris and Renée Neufville of the soul duo Zhane love their short hair, but complain that others often try to read something into it. Jean explains, "We just like short hair—it's easy to take care of on the road." And Renée adds, "As African American women in this society, we're told we need long hair to be beautiful. It's when we cut our hair, though, that you can really see our full lips, the strong cheekbones, features we were taught are so ugly." Interestingly, Susan Brownmiller also had a small revelation when she finally cut her long hair. She proclaimed, "It looks smashing! I now realize I've been a fool not to have it this short for the last decade. The heck with what men think."

Of course, it is much easier for White women to say "The heck with what men think" than it is for Black women to say "The heck with what all of White culture thinks." This is particularly true when it comes to some of the longer natural Black hair styles like dreadlocks and braids.

Traditionally, dreadlocks are associated with the Rastafarians of Jamaica, and for that reason alone have been viewed as vaguely dangerous by White culture. Because few White women know an African American woman with dreadlocks, most are too embarrassed or intimidated to ask how the style is created and maintained. White women can be kept at a distance by their ignorance or unease, but there is nothing inherently threatening or mysterious about hair fashioned in dreadlocks. Tightly curled hair naturally "locks" if it is left uncombed. It is washed just like other hair, only the dreadlocks do not come "unlocked" when wet. It doesn't smell any more than other hair. One common question is, How do you change the style if you tire of it? Usually the hair has to be cut off and grown anew.

Dreadlocks have become more acceptable in recent years as a growing number of African American celebrities have allowed their hair to grow that way, people like actress Whoopi Goldberg, singer Tracy Chapman, author Alice Walker, and former talk show host Bertice Berry. For many with dreadlocks, the experience is joyful and even spiritual, as Alice Walker wrote in her essay "Oppressed Hair Puts a Ceiling on the Brain." Walker confessed that for years she and her hair were not friends. Finally, she realized that the problem lay not with her hair, but with the way she was relating to it. She began to see that her hair was blocking her path to inner peace:

> If my spirit had been a balloon eager to savor away and merge with the infinite, my hair would be the rock that anchored it to Earth. I

realized that there was no hope of future growth of my soul . . . if I
still remained chained to thoughts about my hair.

It is hard to imagine White women talking about their hair in such spiritual
and liberating terms, but, then, they do not have to traverse a mental mine
field of negative attitudes about its texture and quality.

The other popular choice for Black women who wish to keep their hair
both long and natural is braids. Elaborate braiding originated in Africa, but
the style is now very much "in" as part of American hip-hop culture. One of
the most popular looks today is long hair, or short hair made long with
extensions, plaited into as many as fifty to four hundred tiny braids all over
the head. Ever since Bo Derek wore her hair that way in the 1980 film *10*,
even some White women have embraced cornrows and multiple braids, a
fact that, not surprisingly, annoys many Black women. But on the whole,
African American women view braiding as a positive reflection of their
African heritage, and are glad to see the style gaining acceptance. The braids
are easy to maintain and, according to the women who have them, just plain
fun to wear. This is especially true for Black women who use extensions, of
real hair or synthetics, to make their braids longer. Extensions for braiding
are far more accepted by the Black community than extensions for making
hair unnaturally long and straight.

One White woman who recently decided to take the plunge was Siobhan
R., a thirty-one-year-old woman of Irish descent with naturally wavy, long,
auburn-colored hair, working in the music promotion business. For about a
year and a half, Siobhan wanted to get multiple braids, but family members
and friends kept talking her out of it. Finally, she went to the home of two
African women and over the course of five hours had her hair carefully
braided.

Siobhan experienced varying reactions to her new look. Some of her
White friends liked it, but most were puzzled that she wanted to do something so extreme to what they thought was beautiful long hair. Siobhan
found herself a conduit for White women's curiosity about Black women's
hair styles. Strangers would walk up to her and ask personal questions about
the maintenance of her hair. Among African American women, the reactions to Siobhan's braids varied. Some Black women, particularly those who
had, or had once had, their hair in braids, respected Siobhan for having such
"hair discipline." They knew how long it took to have one's hair fashioned

that way. Siobhan also experienced some not quite so friendly looks from mostly young Black women, although no one was openly hostile to her.

Siobhan did find, though, that the new style was not appreciated at work, but for entirely different reasons. Although she was involved in promoting African American musical acts on tour, Siobhan had to meet occasionally with White executives to convince them to sponsor a certain concert event. In the weeks following her braiding, it dawned on Siobhan that she was no longer being introduced to the "stiff shirts," and was, in fact, being actively excluded from meetings that earlier she would probably have attended.

After about six weeks, Siobhan took out her braids, partly because the style was wreaking havoc with her hair. And once her braids were removed, Siobhan discovered the true extent of her all-White supervisors' disapproval. In retrospect, Siobhan realizes that she was naïve to think that her employers wouldn't react politically to an ethnic hair style. But at least she did not get fired for it, something that has happened to some African American women who dared to show up at work with their hair in braids or other styles deemed "too ethnic."

Within the last few years, there has been a flurry of lawsuits against major corporations for hair policies that discriminate against African American female employees. In order to conform to corporate definitions of appropriate grooming, a Black woman must typically perm her hair straight, an expensive and time-consuming process for which she is not compensated. To keep the perm looking good, she must pay anywhere from $40 to $100 every six to eight weeks for a touch-up. In comparison, White women spend roughly half that much to maintain their hair. Given a choice, many Black women would prefer to wear more natural hair styles, like dreadlocks and braids, but in today's climate, their jobs could be at jeopardy.

In 1987, an African American woman named Cheryl Tatum (now Tatum-Tandia) worked as a cashier at the Hyatt Regency outside of Washington, D.C. After she showed up for work with neat cornrows, her immediate supervisor, a White woman who did not understand that cornrows are intended to last several months, asked Cheryl to take out the braids before work the next day. When Cheryl refused, she was told she was in violation of the corporate hair code, and was forced to resign.

The following year, another African American woman, Pamela Mitchell, was asked to leave her job as a reservation agent with the Marriott hotel chain in Washington, D.C., for refusing to remove her braids. And in 1988, a nineteen-year-old African American woman named Renee Randall was fired from Morrison's Cafeteria, in Annapolis, for wearing a long multicolored braided ponytail. Randall's ponytail was said to be extreme; she, however, claimed that no customer had ever complained about her hair, and that she should not have to change her looks to satisfy a White employer ignorant of her culture.

These are only a few of the cases in which African American women have been either harassed or fired because of their "offensive hair." Fortunately, because of the lawsuits they and other Black women brought against companies, many major corporations have since modified their grooming codes to allow cornrows and braids at work—as long as they are "neat and professional-looking." It is hoped that this trend will continue, and that White women, especially those in executive and managerial positions, will support African American women who seek greater tolerance, recognition, and understanding of Black hair styles, fashion, and culture in the workplace.

Most African American women at the executive level would not dare to wear long natural hair, though. In the conservative world of business, it is widely believed that such a style would threaten a Black woman's job security or hinder her chances for promotion. An article in the *Wall Street Journal*, "Braided Hair Collides with Office Norms," confirms that only 1 percent of Black women managers currently wear their hair in braids. According to White journalist Patricia McLaughlin, braids have an "in-your-face" quality, in effect saying to Whites, "This is the kind of hair I have. Get used to it." It is exactly the sort of message that strikes fear into the hearts of many White managers, male and female, who would rather see ethnic differences in the workplace muted or glossed over.

In some fields, such as journalism and academia, where the expression of personal freedom is valued, attitudes toward natural hair styles, including braids and dreadlocks, have become far more tolerant. But as recently as the early eighties, when bell hooks was preparing for a job interview at Yale, she recalled a White female adviser suggesting that she take out her braids. The message was clear: her ethnic appearance was not appropriate for an Ivy League university. Fortunately, hooks did not take out her braids and did get the job. Today, in fact, ethnic styles like braids, dreadlocks, and short naturals are practically *de rigueur* for radically chic African American female college professors, especially those teaching Black or women's studies. Ironically, it is White feminists who sometimes erroneously believe that African

American women who don't wear a natural style are somehow lacking in Black consciousness. Pamela, an African American psychology professor at a large urban university, after cutting her shoulder-length, processed hair and getting a short, natural "finger wave" style, recalls just such a comment from a women's studies colleague:

> This White woman, who had never before commented on my appearance, told me I looked like an African goddess with my new hair style. She went on and on about how I finally seemed to be at peace with my new style. It was embarrassing. To me, it was just a change, and I have not ruled out going back to processing my hair. However, this White woman made me feel that would be a big mistake.

But in reality most White women don't take much notice of what African American women do to their hair. Rae, a forty-three-old White salesclerk, sums up the feelings of many when she states, "I couldn't care less what Black women do to their hair. It doesn't affect me in any way." This applies even to the most obvious imitation of European standards of beauty—African American women dyeing their hair blond. White women may be curious about what drives a Black woman to do this, but they don't, as a rule, feel threatened or bothered by the practice. Lynette, a White actress from New York, had a typical response to the phenomenon:

> I have yet to see a Black woman who I would say really had blond hair. It always seems more gold. Next to dark skin, real light hair takes on another look. It's not really blond, though. So if two women walk in a room, one Black and the other White, and they both have "blond" hair I don't see that as any real competition. So-called blond hair just doesn't create the same effect for Black women as it does for White women. I think it looks rather weird. I really wonder why they do it.

African American women dye their hair blond for the same reasons that White women with brown or black hair do it—the exaggerated aesthetic value of blond hair in our culture. The rise in popularity of blond hair had its "dark roots" in burlesque, when Lydia Thompson brought her troupe of peroxided erotic dancers to America from England in 1869. Before then,

White women with blond locks were thought to be pretty but bland in personality; it was the dark-haired woman who inspired great passion. The burlesque troupe changed the appeal of the blond woman forever, transforming her into someone sexy and simmering. Later, Hollywood did its part to fuel the fantasy with such blond bombshells as Mary Pickford, Jean Harlow, and, later, Marilyn Monroe, Jayne Mansfield, and a dozen imitators. But it was the brilliant slogan "Blondes have more fun," part of the marketing campaign of Clairol hair products during the sixties, that forever cemented the image of the blonde as a superior, fun-loving kind of gal.

Social-psychological research on how White women are stereotyped by their hair color reveals that, while brunettes are seen as more intelligent, ambitious, and sincere by men and women, blondes are thought to be more beautiful, delicate, dangerous, and unpredictable. Blondes are also thought to be dumber, a stereotype buttressed by the recent rash of "dumb blond" jokes. Cultural critic Camille Paglia believes that the enormous popularity of these jokes can be understood as a political effort to rectify the many social advantages and privileges conferred on the blond-haired woman today.

Not all White women who go blond do so to attract men, though. Hair experts believe that blond hair softens the face of White women, thereby reducing the aging effects of fine lines, small wrinkles, and slight complexion flaws. Thus, many White women begin to dye or streak their hair lighter as they get older, at a time when they first feel the need to mitigate the effects of aging. Older women with blond hair are rarely accused of cashing in on the privilege of youth, though. In fact, a White woman today can generally dye her hair whatever color she wants, and few will question it. Such is not the case for the African American woman who dares to color her hair lighter; her motives are nearly always suspect. Predictably, the main accusation hurled at a Black woman who dares to dye her hair blond is that she is trying to be White. Erica, an African American art student at a Chicago suburban community college, lamented after she went blond:

> The Black community is not very accepting of change. If you change your eye color or your hair color, it always means you are trying to deny who you are. But I'm not. This is just about fun, about fantasy. I know that dyeing your hair blond is not embraced by my community, and that other Black women look at me and sneer or make snide remarks, but it's my hair and I like it. That's really all that matters to me.

African American author Wendy Chapkis was similarly surprised at the extent to which others reacted negatively to her streaking a few strands of hair. In her book *Beauty Secrets,* Chapkis describes the experience and the sarcasm she used to counter the criticism:

> I recently bleached a few strands of my hair reddish-brown, and the comments I got! "I never thought that you, as a Black woman, would dye your hair blond." Now, in the first place, I never thought of it as blond and, secondly, it is only a couple of pieces of hair. I did it in a crazy mood for fun. The reaction irritates me so much I've started to answer, "Yes, I've decided to integrate myself in White society and thought I'd start with a couple of pieces of white hair."

To better understand the standard "denial of heritage" accusation that is leveled at Black women, it is helpful to look at hair dyeing from a personal and a sociological perspective. On a personal level, individual African American women choose to dye their hair "just for the fun of it." No one in his or her right mind could believe that blond hair on black skin represents a serious attempt to pass as White. But, on a larger sociological level, in a country where the prevailing standard for beautiful hair is long, blond, and free-flowing, the practice of dyeing hair light smacks of White assimilationism to many in the Black community. That is, few women with naturally blond hair ever streak or dye their hair darker "just for the fun of it." Whether women admit it or not, European standards of beauty are in place. Only when White women and Black women lighten and darken their hair in equal numbers will hair coloring be free of political overtones. Erica confessed to wanting to dye her hair blond because "White girls shouldn't have all the fun." Considered from this vantage point, Erica's unconscious motive for wanting blond hair is indeed culturally driven.

Certainly not all the African American women who dye their hair blond cite such obvious reasons as Erica. Nor do all Black women with blond hair project the same sort of image. An African American furniture designer, Cheryl Riley of San Francisco, readily admits to dyeing her very short natural hair blond for the "vanity" and "drama" of it, but she defends her choice by pointing to the ancient practice by African women of manipulating their hair color with ocher and wax. Cheryl views her near-platinum hair, which she pays $65 twice a month to maintain, as a positive expression of her ethnic pride. Mentioning Africa is, of course, a common means for some Black women in this country to counter the "wannabe" accusation. But whether Cheryl's real reason for going blond is ethnic pride or not, there is no denying that she looks striking. Had her hair been long, and especially if it had been processed, the blond effect would have been entirely different.

Negative attitudes about long blond hair on African American women stem in large part from the association with prostitution. It used to be that a Black woman standing on a corner with a big, blond wig was selling but one thing: her body. Even today, one of the hazards for African American women who dye their hair blond is that they may be propositioned while just walking down the street.

Insulated from the hazards of the street, African American celebrities are better able to "get away" with having long blond hair, even weaves and wigs. The practice became popular during the seventies, when top recording artists, including Aretha Franklin, Donna Summer, and Tina Turner, began wearing blond wigs on stage. Selling sex appeal is a far more legitimate enterprise than selling sex, and a blond wig has come to be viewed as just another playful accessory for Black female entertainers. The blond wig may even enhance their crossover appeal for White audiences. For whatever reason, the trend remains. Among the current generation of African American celebrities who have, or have had, long blond hair are rapper Yo-Yo, actress Toukie Smith (from the sitcom "227"), and supermodels Naomi Campbell and Shari Belafonte.

Why do so many women of European and African descent continue to dye or perm their hair? The answer is that we are a hair-obsessed society, and the way a woman wears her hair says a great deal about who she is and what she believes in. Women are bombarded with commercials and print ads that not only prey on their insecurities about their hair, but also promise "good things to come" if only their hair looks better. These campaigns are highly effective. In 1991 alone, Americans spent more than $16 billion on hair products and at beauty parlors. It is estimated that Black women spend as much as three times as much as White women on their hair care.

The politics of beauty for White and Black women hardly end with skin color and hair care. In a country where "blond hair and blue eyes" go together like salt and pepper or bacon and eggs, eye color assumes almost as much importance as hair color in judgments of beauty. Not surprisingly, the ideal is tilted in favor of women of European descent whose eye color ranges from blue to brown. Since the vast majority of African American women have eyes that are brown in color, they are somewhat at a disadvantage. Of course, with the invention of tinted lenses, eye color too can be changed for a fee. And once again, because women of both races are more likely to replace dark eyes with light ones, this unidirectional preference is fraught with social and political implications. This is especially true for Black women. As Elsie B. Washington, senior editor of *Essence,* notes in a 1988 essay, "The wish to acquire what we were not born with, to adopt the coloring that has for centuries been touted as prettier, finer, better, carries with it the old baggage of racial inferiority and/or superiority based simply, and simplistically, on physical traits."

Knowing that they will be accused of wanting to be White, it is often with mixed feelings that African American women pop blue or green contact lenses in their eyes. Even those Black women whose eyes are naturally light in color can find themselves being chastised by the cultural police. Yet, as hurtful as such accusations may be, the practice of wearing tinted lenses continues within the African American community, both for prescriptive lenses and for cosmetic lenses.

For the most part, White women don't worry about what others may think about their eye color, even if it varies from one day to the next. Nor are other cultures necessarily restricted. When figure skater Kristi Yamaguchi, a brown-eyed woman of Japanese descent, proclaimed in a national television spot for DuraSoft tinted contact lenses that she enjoyed changing her eye color "just for the fun of it," she suffered no political condemnation by Asian Americans for doing so. But the general feeling is that if an African American female celebrity were to participate in such an advertising campaign—and it is hard to imagine anyone who might—she would never hear the end of it from her community. Taken together, the politically charged, often status-driven, beauty concerns of skin, hair, and eye color create a great deal of tension between White and Black women in this country.

Although hair styles and eye color still clearly shade toward Eurocentric standards, there is one positive facial feature that is found more often among women of African than of European descent: full lips. Larger lips have not always been valued. While growing up in the seventies, Kathy Russell remembers how much she hated the size of her lips. She attended a predominantly White grade school, and the other girls considered lips that were more petite than hers to be beautiful. Kathy recalls trying to hold her lips tight together to create the illusion of thinner lips. It was not until she attended a predominantly Black high school that she began to re-evaluate the appearance of her lips and come to think of them as beautiful. Society later caught up, when thin lips came to be viewed as a sign that a woman was uptight and sexually aloof, and a woman with fuller lips was seen as more seductive and desirable.

In fact, it has been rumored that actresses like Cher, Barbara Hershey, and Michelle Pfeiffer have had their lips given a more pouty look through the surgical technique of collagen injection. In recent years, many less famous White women have also undergone the procedure. But collagen treatments cost anywhere from $700 to $1000, last on average only about three months, and carry with them the risk of autoimmune disorders, such as lupus.

African American women have varying reactions to White women enlarging their lips. While some Black women are proud to see their culture affecting notions of beauty, others are suspicious of the practice, and even a bit annoyed. There is also a double standard in the way full lips are described. On Black women, full lips are "big and thick," but on White women, the same size lips, whether natural or augmented by collagen, are "pouty, sexy, and voluptuous." African American print model Tammi expressed genuine resentment at what she saw as the appropriation of Black features by White women for cosmetic purposes.

> White people are culture vultures, especially White women. They pick us apart, piece by piece. They steal and exploit our looks, make them their own, throw them away when they're through, and then move on to some other feature, whether it's our hair, skin color, or lips. As a Black woman and model, I have to live with this skin, this hair, these lips, this nose, and these buttocks. I don't have the luxury of declaring that my features are now "in," only to later declare them "out."

But in reaction to Tammi's angry tirade, Sheila, a White actress from Los Angeles, responded:

> Black people aren't the only ones with full lips. Many White women also come by them naturally—just look at comedienne Sandra Bern-

hard or actress Kim Basinger. Believe me, the White woman who gets collagen injections to make her lips larger is not trying to look Black. Besides, don't Black women hate it when others accuse them of wanting to be White just because they wear blue contact lenses or perm their hair straight? It's the same ridiculous thing, only in reverse.

However fair or unfair, there are substantial differences when women of the prevailing culture imitate the looks of those in a minority, and when women of a minority culture imitate the looks of those in the majority. In the case of the former, the imitation often has the quality of a fad, and seems to be done primarily for fun and fashion. A common result is that women in the minority end up feeling robbed of their singularity. However, when minority women emulate the appearance of those in the majority, it is typically done for more serious purposes, such as improving their economic and social standing, or better "fitting in" with dominant societal standards. But their attempt to do just that may threaten the identity of others in the community who are committed to preserving their culture and racial distinctions.

The recent popularity of ear, nose, nipple, and other body piercings can similarly cause consternation among some African American women, who view these practices as yet another appropriation of their Black culture. The first examples of ear piercing are seen in artifacts from the twelfth century B.C., showing African women with ears pierced for purposes of decoration. More than a thousand years later, the practice was brought to America by African slave women. Poking holes in one's skin was originally viewed by White women as vaguely primitive and certainly "lower class."

Attitudes toward ear piercing changed dramatically during the sixties, however. Hordes of young middle-class White women suddenly began clamoring to get their ears pierced, despite their mothers' resistance. Natalie, a White woman from Delaware now in her early forties, remembers her own battle to get permission. Her mother categorically refused, claiming that pierced ears would turn gangrenous. The mother would intone, "Our poor maid once tried to pierce her ears and ended up with only half an ear left. You want that to happen to you?" Natalie couldn't have cared less; she just wanted her ears pierced like everyone else at school. She finally had it done when she went off to college, in 1970. Ironically, about five years later, her mother also had her ears pierced, admitting that it was much easier and less painful than wearing "those damn clip-on" earrings. Comfort and convenience are two factors that will override resistance to the cosmetic practices of those with "lesser status."

While pierced ears today are common among both White and Black women, there remain certain cultural differences associated with the practice. The average age for getting their ears pierced is younger among Black girls than White girls, although this too appears to have class implications. Middle-class Black girls are often forced to wait, like the majority of White girls, until they are near adolescence; poorer Black girls and White girls may get their ears pierced earlier. Another difference is that an African American woman is more likely to point to her heritage as a primary motive for piercing her ear multiple times. White women do it for fashion purposes, simply because "it looks cool." Finally, when it comes to getting other parts of the body pierced, White women seem to be taking the lead.

While piercing noses, navels, tongues, cheeks, and nipples is gaining in popularity among an urban subculture of middle-class White women (as well as some Black teenage men who are into rap and hip-hop culture), middle-class Black women remain hesitant about embracing this particular fashion trend. When Yvette, who was considering getting her navel pierced, told a Black girlfriend, her friend dismissed Yvette's suggestion with the comment: "Girl, that's for White women."

On a recent "Day One" (ABC magazine show) feature about the phenomenon of body piercing and tattooing in today's youth culture, all the women except one were White. The only African American on the show was a young woman about to pay a surgeon a lot of money to have her tattoo removed. She warned, "I wouldn't advise anybody to get a tattoo. I got one when I was eighteen and now I'm twenty-four, and it has been an embarrassment ever since." While those interviewed on a TV magazine show can hardly be assumed to be representative, her comment raises interesting questions. Do middle-class, college-educated White women, with multiple ear piercings and tattoos, worry less about how their unconventional appearance may affect job prospects than middle-class Black women? Is the freedom to experiment with one's body and appearance greater for White women than for Black women? It is certainly a possibility, and if it is true, is yet another wedge between Black women and White women—even those from the same economic background.

Body Size

Difference in body size is another beauty issue that can divide White women from Black women. In a 1994 survey of over six hundred college students, African American women were found to weigh ten pounds more than White women of the same height. The same study also found that significantly more Black women than White women are satisfied with their body image. And in 1995, anthropologists Mimi Nichter and Sheila Parker interviewed teenagers in focus groups to find that 90 percent of White girls are dissatisfied with their bodies, while 70 percent of Black teenage girls are proud of the way they look. Black teenage girls also overwhelmingly agreed that it was better to be little overweight than underweight, but the White girls believed the exact opposite. There is also evidence that White women get many more liposuctions and undergo more potentially dangerous cosmetic operations, like breast augmentation or reduction, to alter their natural shape. An African American psychologist, Roy Allen Roberts, analyzing the ads and articles in White and Black women's magazines, found that publications aimed for the Black market (for example, *Essence*) contained significantly fewer articles and advertisements dealing with weight loss than similar publications aimed at White women (such as *Vogue* and *Cosmopolitan*). And Carolyn West, another African American psychologist, reported that Black women's magazines are more likely to include ads for "butt pads" and actual weight-gain products to help "get rid of those skinny legs"; such type ads were quite rare in primarily White magazines. In presenting her findings at the 1993 American Women in Psychology conference, West noted, "White people are hard on their large women."

Why is there greater acceptance of large women in the African American community? Certainly one explanation is that in traditional African societies, full-figured bodies were valued as symbols of health, wealth, desire, prosperity, and fertility. This cultural ideal was brought to America by the slaves, and may continue to influence standards of attractiveness among Black women in America today. The slave planation system, too, encouraged Black women to be large, to help better in the field, and perhaps in the home to present less of a temptation for the male planation owner.

On the other hand, according to prevailing White Victorian standards of attractiveness, the ideal woman was delicate, with an abnormally small waist tightly corseted to keep its shape. Her thinness and frailty were considered essential to her femininity, potent reminders of a woman's constant need of masculine protection. The value of thinness is reflected in a saying commonly heard in the White community, "You can never be too rich or too thin."

Despite the dominant society's ideal of thinness, many Blacks retain negative attitudes toward women who are too skinny. This is reflected in a saying popular in the Black community, "Don't nobody want a bone but a dog." Madeleine Nelson, an African American woman from Virginia, has experienced the cultural disparity in her modeling work and participation in beauty pageants. "When I competed in black pageants in D.C., I never won a swimsuit competition . . . I was told by Black-owned companies that I was too skinny. But in competitions with white women, I did very well. I either won or got first runner-up." Nelson further observed, "Black women don't strive to be very thin. And black men don't want their women too thin. Even with black men who date white women, you'll notice that the white women tend to be more voluptuous." A White woman named Yvonne Neil-Powell noted, "If you are white and weigh 105 or 110, you've got the perfect shape. If you are black and weigh that much, you're too skinny."

Cultural differences in body size can make it difficult for White women and Black women to feel comfortable in each other's presence. A White woman of normal weight, used to complaining to her White women friends about how fat she is, may suddenly feel self-conscious in front of African American women, who possess the very body type she disparages. Of greater concern, some African American women, previously content with their substantial size, may, following exposure to White women's ideals of thinness, start to question their attractiveness. The reflections of one thirty-four-year-old Black woman are quite telling:

> At work, where there are only a few of us Black women, I feel pretty fat. At home, with my friends, I don't think about it hardly at all. I guess it's because I'm closer to the middle [of my Black friends' weight range].

Black girls and women who live in predominantly White middle-class neighborhoods, or attend predominantly Whites schools, may similarly have their self-image changed. An African American woman named Jesse Putnam recalls how, as a teenager growing up amidst friends who were White and extremely thin, she used to sit on the floor because someone once told her that doing so would help make her butt flat. Said Putnam, now at peace with her 36–25–38 shape, "It wasn't until my mom held me and told me that I was blessed with the body that I have, that I began to feel good about myself."

Like the emphasis on straight hair and light skin, the preference for a slender body has class connotations. Jocelyn, a Black woman, recalls that when she was younger, signs of her working-class family's doing well included serving big meals, having chubby children, and keeping plenty of food in the house. As they started to "move on up," however, these values changed. According to Jocelyn, "When my father's business began to bloom and my father was interacting more with white businessmen and seeing how they did business, suddenly thin became important. If you were a truly well-to-do family, then your family was slim and elegant."

Kim Chernin, author of *The Obsession: Reflections on the Tyranny of Slenderness,* draws an important distinction between fears about being fat and fears about being perceived as lower class. Chernin, who is White, grew up in a predominantly Black neighborhood in Los Angeles during the 1950s, a time when women's bodies tended to be larger on the whole than they are today. She was comfortable with her breasts and hips, curves and softness, until she left that community at the age of seventeen. In White society, Chernin began to think of herself as overweight and, in a desperate attempt to make herself thinner, ended up anorexic. After recovering and becoming a counselor for others suffering from eating disorders, Chernin realized the extent to which negative images of fat women underlie racial hatred and negative stereotyping. In an article in *Essence* magazine, she commented:

A lot of the imagery of disgust has to do with body disgust. They— whoever "they" are—smell, they're dirty, they're lazy and self-indulgent. This culture feels the same way about large women. Poor people are seen that way by those on an aristocratic level.

What is interesting is that standards of thinness have become stricter since the 1950s. By today's standards, even Marilyn Monroe looks a bit on the fleshy side. A study of the body measurements of Miss America contestants and *Playboy* centerfold models confirms that the ideal size for women has literally narrowed since the 1960s. Even the Barbie doll is more slender today than she was in 1959, when she was introduced. Now, the new ultra-thin ideal lives on in the fashion pages of our magazines, as seen in an extreme form in Kate Moss. Through her blank gaze and childlike de-meanor, Moss is the ultimate backlash mascot. She informs women that, to be sexually desirable, they must be vulnerable and passive, nonthreatening, and stripped of all experience. Suzanne Henrick, a registered dietician and counselor at the Wilkins Center for Eating Disorders in Greenwich, reports that a lot of White female anorexics bring Moss's picture to the center as their ideal body type. Even some Black women succumb to the fantasy. In the premier issue of *Tell,* a new magazine for African Americans, Robinne Lee describes her gnawing preoccupation with Moss:

> There it is again. That bus! Seven images of Kate Moss in all her waifish glory flash by as I innocently try to cross the street. I didn't eat today. Instead, I did two hours of high impact aerobics . . . 900 sit-ups. So that I can have a body like Kate's . . . In my dreams, I am Kate Moss. She stares at me from all corners of my apartment. I have tacked her image to my refrigerator door, my mirror, my bathroom wall. My waif. My hero. It doesn't matter that she's white and I'm black. It's the essence of Kate. I have fallen for her. How can I get her out of my mind if I can't get her out of my face? My parents have always taught me that . . . beauty is only skin deep. But my parents did not grow up in the age of MTV. They don't understand why I would want to be 5'9" and a size four; they think I'm perfect at 5'4" and a size six. And I am, according to statistical height/weight charts. But obviously the people who design those charts have never met Kate Moss.

Concurrent with the growth of the Black middle class in this country has been a steady rise in the number of young African American women suffer-ing from bulimia and anorexia, eating disorders that were previously associ-ated almost exclusively with achievement-oriented middle-class White teen-age women. A 1993 *Essence* survey of its readers found that 54 percent were at "high risk" for an eating disorder, 71.5 percent admitted to being preoc-cupied with the desire to be thinner, and the same percentage were terrified of being overweight. Of course, *Essence* readers are hardly a representative sample of women in the African American community at large. They tend to be fairly upscale and success-oriented, exactly the type that is most vulnerable to eating disorders. Despite this recent rise in eating disorders among young Black women, far more White women than Black women develop anorexia and bulimia. According to the National Association of Anorexia and Associated Disorders, an estimated eight million women in this country, most of them White, suffer from these dangerous diseases.

At the other end of the spectrum, obesity affects twice as many Black women as it does White women. An estimated 35 percent of Black women between the ages of twenty-two and forty, and nearly 60 percent of those over forty, are obese. The pattern is most common among poor, working, single Black mothers. For many, the stress of trying to live and cope in neighborhoods that are often crime-ridden is enough to trigger compulsive eating behaviors. Food becomes the drug of choice; it is cheap and does not cause a hangover.

In addition to the obvious medical risks associated with being overweight, such as diabetes and hypertension, obese women suffer from a reduction in their earning potential. A recent study in the *New England Journal of Medicine* documents the social and economic consequences of obesity. For the years between 1981 and 1988, a team of researchers tracked a representative sample of 10,039 young adults, including 145 White women (of whom 44 percent were overweight), and 42 Black women (of whom 67 percent were overweight). They found that weight alone has the power to adversely affect the quality of a woman's life. Compared with women who were of normal weight, those most overweight completed four months less of school, had household incomes averaging $6710 less, were 20 percent less likely to be married, and had rates of poverty 10 percent higher. These differences held even when the social and economic backgrounds of the overweight and normal weight cohorts were the same. Contrary to prevailing assumptions—that socioeconomic status influences rates of obesity—these findings indicate that being overweight by itself can lower the socioeconomic status. This is of special concern to Black women, given their already high rate of obesity and low earning potential.

Instead of judging themselves, and especially each other, on matters of weight, White and Black women would do better to spend their energy fighting fat prejudice in society. Women of both races should challenge the use of unnaturally tall and slender women as fashion models, and the insulting advertising campaigns for weight-control products and programs that equate being obese with being unloved.

Body Hair

Another potentially alienating difference between Black and White women has to do with body hair. Psychologist Susan Basow found that among White women, close to 80 percent regularly shave their legs, but only half of Black women do. White women's reactions to Black women's hairier legs can range from indifference and puzzlement to curiosity and even disgust. The comments of a thirty-four-year-old White businesswoman named Linda are typical:

> At my office, there is a Black woman who always dresses to the nines, expensive-looking suits, nice dresses with matching accessories and shoes—you name it, she puts a lot of time and money into her appearance. But one thing I always notice is that she doesn't shave her legs. Here she is all dressed up, and this leg hair is smashed flat under her stockings. To me, that is gross, and completely ruins the effect of being dressed up. Now mind you, I hate shaving, and in winter, especially, you're just as likely to find beneath my nice pair of pants some very hairy legs. However, the one time that I will drag a razor across them is when I have to wear stockings and heels. There is definitely something going on here that I don't understand regarding Black women and their leg hair.

Part of the difference in women's body hair may stem from the fact that Black men are more likely than White men to appreciate body hair on their women. This strikes White women, particularly those who are feminists, as the height of irony. During the sixties, refusing to shave one's legs and underarms was something of a feminist litmus test—a measure of how far a (White) woman was willing to go *not* to please her man. But that era passed, and now most women shave their body hair less because of personal preference than because of the dictates of their immediate culture. This increases the chances of women of the two races feeling uncomfortable and even disrespectful of each other's decisions.

Clothes

Cultural differences in the clothes that White and Black women wear is
another potential source of conflict. While similarities in dress codes and
style are certainly far greater than differences, women of both races agree
that they don't always like the same fashions. In recognition of these differences, Spiegel recently joined with *Ebony* magazine to create E Style, a new
mail-order catalogue specifically designed to reflect the fashion tastes and
trends of Black women. E Style fashions tend to be brighter in color than
similarly priced items and styles in catalogues marketed more for White
women (such as Tweeds and J. Crew). The oranges, reds, purples, and
fuchsias of E Style fashions better complement the darker skin tones of
many African American women; many of the earth tones so popular today
tend to look better on lighter-skinned women, both European American
and African American. The size charts also reflect race differences in average body size. Not all Black women are pleased by the development of E
Style. Linda Williams protests, "I feel kind of insulted that they would have
to segregate me." But another African American, named Paula Raspberry,
said: "Why do they have to come up with clothing just for us? We're being
labeled again. But as I thought about it more, we are different. We do have
different tastes and we like different colors."

Many of the fashion preferences of White women and Black women may
reflect class differences rather than racial or cultural differences, although
these factors are never easy to disentangle. For example, one stereotype is
that Black women dress more flashily than White women. But is this really
a difference characterizing the clothes of women who are poor—proportionately more of whom are Black—as compared with those who are well-to-do
—proportionately more of whom are White? Possibly. Nonetheless, it also
seems that even at formal events like weddings and "black tie" fund raisers
attended by solidly middle- and upper-class Black women, the women get
more "dolled up" than White women of comparable backgrounds. This
cultural difference seemed particularly evident to us when we attended the
1994 Chicago Ebony Fashion Show. The Black women arrived in big fur
and leather coats, and many wore sequined dresses and fancy outfits of gold
lamé. Others wore elaborate accessories—big hats, colorful scarfs, and large
pieces of jewelry—complemented by what looked to be expensive but rather

impractical shoes for a cold winter's night. Most of the White women in attendance wore far fewer accessories, and some even wore pantsuits instead of dresses. Also, many of the White women wore comfortable flat shoes that better enabled them to negotiate the snow outside. At times, different cultural norms appear to shape what is deemed appropriate for White and Black women, and this difference is bound to lead women of the two races to question who is overdressed or underdressed.

Why are middle-class African Americans more inclined to dress up than middle-class White women? One reason may be a response to race. Black women in expensive clothing are able to communicate effectively to others that just because they are Black does not mean they are poor. This is why African American women are typically more dressed up than White women when they go shopping in upscale department stores, like Bloomingdale's, Saks, and Neiman-Marcus. Because of prejudice, Black women know that unless they look tastefully and expensively attired, their credit may be questioned and the service they receive may be poor. White women, even those who walk into such stores in torn jeans and baggy T-shirts, can still expect to be politely waited upon by most salesclerks, White and Black.

There is feeling among some in White society that Black women have less of a sense of "boundaries" or appropriateness of attire for specific situations. This can be a problem in the workplace, as reflected in the following comments by a White bank teller named Crystal about the attire of another teller, who is Black:

> We have very important customers that bank with us and we are on the front lines. We are the first thing they see when they enter the front door. I work with a Black woman who dresses more like she is going out for an evening on the town than coming to work nine to five. Her makeup is always on the heavy side, she has long multicolored nails sprinkled with glitter, and sometimes her hair has glitter in it, too. She wears five earrings in one ear that spell her name, in addition to the two long gold and crystal earrings that hang to her shoulders. Once, she even came to work wearing tight leather pants with a red bodysuit. No White woman would be caught dead in this type of attire.

Crystal was quick to add that she had other Black colleagues who didn't dress in this flashy way, but some in White society do make blanket assumptions. The issues in such cases appear to be those of economic class and education, not race, however. Both lower-class Blacks and Whites often lack understanding of the "proper" way to present themselves in more formal work situations. Unfortunately, their inappropriate appearance may keep them from getting promoted or, in many cases, getting hired in the first place.

College-educated Black women are well aware of the stereotypes drawn about the dress of members of their race, and properly resent the assumption that they don't know how to dress correctly. Sondra, an attractive young African American woman, recalled an experience with this kind of subtle race prejudice in an early job interview.

I remember going for an interview for a marketing job and the interviewer kept saying, "You look great today, but we do have a professional dress code that's enforced daily"—as if I was just dressing this way to get the job, but after that, I was going back to my 'ghetto garb.' It really infuriated me.

Negative stereotypes about the "looseness" of Black women's sexuality can pose another fashion concern, particularly, again, for those who are middle class or are college educated. To forestall sexual comments of this type, some African American women feel they have to be even more conservative and conscientious than White women about what they wear. This can create feelings of resentment in some Black women who go to school and work with White women. After all, having to worry about what message an outfit sends can stifle a young Black woman's fashion sense. Author Wendy Chapkis says:

I choose my clothing with some care not to appear sexually provocative. As a Black woman you are seen as something of a whore to begin with and I just refuse to play to that stereotype . . . Since eleven I have been aware of how White men look at Black women—the sex object . . . always available.

A Los Angeles Black publicist named Alice adds, "White girls have the sexual liberty to dress in those cheap dresses with the plunging necklines because they have never been stereotyped as whores. White female privilege allows them to wear what they want."

Yet many White women are shy about wearing clothes that might create undesirable sexual stereotypes about them. Ellen, a White woman from a Southern socialite family, recalls that when she was growing up in the seventies, her mother absolutely refused to let her wear anything that was form-fitting. To Ellen's mother, tight clothing meant one thing—you were advertising to men that you were sexually available. Today, in her thirties, Ellen has a slender body, but still struggles to feel comfortable wearing stretch pants, a popular look in the nineties. She explains why.

> I know that I have nice hips and legs, but for me to wear anything that would so boldly show off my body feels wrong, wrong, totally wrong. When I finally broke down and bought my first pair of stretch pants, I found that I can only wear them with a big, baggy sweater coming down to my knees. I am amazed and even envious of some of the Black women I've seen—with these enormous butts and thighs—who look totally comfortable in these stretch pants and short tops. I honestly don't think I'll ever be able to do that.

Nonetheless, there are differences in the kinds of sexually revealing outfits that some Black and White women do feel comfortable wearing. For example, Ellen and many other White women report feeling more at ease wearing plunging necklines than do many African American women, while African American women seem to be comfortable wearing tight stretch pants. These preferences may reflect differences in dressing for Black and White men's sexual desires. A popular stereotype is that White men love cleavage, but Black men love buttocks.

The fashion preferences of White and Black female activists is another area where the casual observer is apt to find difference as well as tension. During the sixties, when activist White women traded in their feminine dresses and high heels for more comfortable androgynous clothes, African American women took to the streets wearing dashikis and other fashion items inspired by African culture. Today, White women continue to fight for the right to wear pants and flat shoes in the workplace, while a growing number of Black women are once again embracing an Afrocentric look. At academic conferences and political rallies, Black female scholars and activists are apt to be dressed in beanie hats, draped scarves, and wide woven belts of green, black, gold, and red—the colors of Black liberation. Curiously, those who don't wear such attire report that it is "politically correct" White women who put the most pressure on them to conform to the exotic image of the "radical woman of color." One possible reason for this is that other African American women are more understanding of the various practical factors, such as job security and housing concerns, that a Black woman may have to take into account before adopting such a radical look.

Clearly, appearances are heavy with political meaning, but issues of beauty are so subjective that they are extremely hard to address and change. While legislation can be passed to help ensure that White and Black women are paid equally for the same work, reactions to attractiveness and presentation cannot be legislated. Marcia Gillespie, a former editor of *Essence* and current editor of *Ms.,* states that as long as the ideal beauty image in Western society remains Eurocentrically biased, Black women, as well as other minorities, will "bear a greater burden than their White counterparts as lookism combines with sexism and racism to stigmatize them as unattractive."

Unfortunately, this extra burden sometimes means being used as the yardstick by which ugliness is gauged. Nationally acclaimed poet Maya Angelou once found herself the reluctant savior of a White girl simply because the latter found Angelou "uglier" than she. But what is astounding is that African American women still manage to feel more positive about their looks than most White women, according to numerous polls and studies. It may be that Black women are so far from the White communities' ideal that it is easier for them to summarily reject society's judgment. Increasingly, Black women proclaim, "I know that I'm beautiful." In some cases, the statement may smack of defensiveness, but by and large African American women seem to mean it. The following poem by Ekua Omosupe describes the journey of one African American woman in accepting her physical appearance:

IN MAGAZINES (I FOUND SPECIMENS OF THE BEAUTIFUL)

Once
I looked for myself
between the covers of
Seventeen
Vogue
Cosmopolitan
among blues eyes, blonde hair, white skin thin bodies
this is beauty

I hated this shroud of
Blackness
that makes me invisible
a negative print
some other one's
nightmare.

In a store front window
against a white backdrop
I saw a queenly head of nappy hair
and met this chiseled face
wide wondering eyes,
honey colored, bronzed skin
a mouth with thick lips
bowed painted red
smiled purple gums and shining pearls
I turned to leave
but this body of
curvaceous hips
strong thighs
broad ass
long legs
called me back to look again at likenesses of
African Queens, Dahomey Warriors, statuesque Goddesses.
I stand outside those covers meet
Face to Face
Myself
I am the Beautiful

In contrast, a White woman rarely says, "I am beautiful." If she did, others would laugh at her (because she obviously wasn't pretty) or think her incredibly arrogant (because she *was* pretty). After all, only a few White women actually measure up to what is supposed to be beautiful in this culture. Perhaps because more White women feel they are generally "in the ball park" of the ideal, they keep measuring themselves against it, and try to conform to the ideal through one cosmetic operation and diet after another. The following poem by Marge Piercy reflects the tragic consequences of one White girl's effort to become beautiful:

BARBIE DOLL

This girlchild was born as usual
and presented dolls that did pee-pee
and miniature GE stoves and irons
and wee lipsticks the color of cherry candy.
Then in the magic of puberty, a classmate said:
You have a great big nose and fat legs.

She was healthy, tested intelligent,
possessed strong arms and back,
abundant sexual drive and manual dexterity.
She went to and fro apologizing.
Everyone saw a fat nose on thick legs.

She was advised to play coy,
exhorted to come on hearty,
exercise, diet, smile and wheedle.
Her good nature wore out
like a fan belt.
So she cut off her nose and her legs
and offered them up.

In the casket displayed on satin she lay
with the undertaker's cosmetics painted on,
a turned-up putty nose,
dressed in a pink and white nightie.
Doesn't she look pretty? everyone said.
Consummation at last.
To every woman a happy ending.

At first glance, issues of beauty and fashion may seem superficial, but much of the tension between White women and African American women begins at this level. Our physical differences keep us apart. Perhaps it's only natural that birds of a feather flock together, but the plumage of others should not be judged so harshly. African American feminist scholar Patricia Hill Collins maintains that traditional male aesthetics foster such us-them thinking, and must be rejected by the women of both races. It does no good to proclaim all Black women "beautiful" and all White women "ugly," because that merely replaces one set of controlling images with another. Instead, Collins advocates creating an alternative feminist aesthetic that would defy "existing standards of ornamental beauty that objectify women and judge us by our physical appearance."

People will always respond to others in terms of their physical appearance. That, too, is perhaps natural. But it is also important that, as a society, we expand notions of what we call attractive, especially for women. In some ways, the process has already begun. Compared to only a few years ago, there are significantly more women of color gracing the covers of fashion magazines and walking the runways of fashion shows. The expansion continues through the power of single individuals. Certainly Barbra Streisand and Whoopi Goldberg are not traditionally beautiful, yet each has successfully managed, through her inner beauty and personality, to enlarge ideas of attractiveness in ways previously not thought possible. Beauty may be in the eye of the beholder, but it is also in the psychology of the beheld. Still, there is much work to be done in the area of beauty, and in stopping the damage that restricted definitions do to individual girls and women and their relations with others. No child should have to endure a phase of growing up during which she feels ugly; no teenager should have to starve herself because she believes herself unacceptably large; and no break-down in communication between Black women and White women should have to occur simply because we don't understand each other's beauty practices and fashion concerns.

Chapter Four

Sexual Tensions

and you white girl
shall I call you sister now?
Can we share any secrets of sameness,
any singularity of goals . . .

you white girl
i am yet suspicious of/
for deep inside of me
there is the still belief that
i am
a road
you would travel
to my man.

—*Carolyn M. Rodgers*
"I Have Been Hungry," 1976

I was made to feel that I had committed some sort of unspoken crime
against the black community, particularly black women.

—*Gail Mathabane, White co-author*
(with Black husband, Mark Mathabane)
of Love in Black and White:
The Triumph of Love Over Prejudice and Taboo, *1993*

A few years ago, Jackie, an attractive, light-skinned African American woman from Chicago, and her Black boyfriend, Kevin, traveled together to Atlanta to visit his relatives and friends. Having lived all her life in the North, Jackie found the South an unwelcome and even frightening place. "The farther south we went," she said, "the more hostility I encountered." Ironically, the hostility she felt came not from Southern Whites, but from other Black women. Jackie's skin is so fair and her features are so Caucasian-looking that others—often other Blacks—don't immediately recognize her racial identity. Jackie found herself accused of being White and "stealing" an available Black man. Although she had encountered this kind of reaction before, never had it been manifested with such intensity and rage. On more than one occasion Kevin had to come to her rescue, telling the others, "Be cool, now. She's a sister like you." As the two headed back home, Jackie told her boyfriend, "You know, Kevin, if looks could kill, I would be long gone."

Interracial sexual jealousy remains a flashpoint between women of African and European descent in this country. Fueled by a history of racial antagonism, especially in the South, and sustained by the current shortage of Black men, it is a jealousy so intense that it can destroy women's natural alliances. Women would rather blame each other for their sexual abuse than confront the men of their own race who date and marry interracially.

Yet, paradoxically, interracial sexual relationships are also a tremendous source of connection between women of the two races. Heterosexual women who love men of another race may develop strong attachments with their companions' mothers, sisters, and female friends. Among White and Black lesbians who cross the color line, especially intense bonds of love and companionship are frequently formed. Regardless of sexual orientation, interracial love can be a bridge between women of different races.

In this chapter we look at the ways in which matters of the heart and flesh define White and Black women's interpersonal relationships. We begin by identifying various racial myths regarding Black and White women's sexuality and how these myths serve White and Black men. From there, we look at new research on women's sexuality, and how findings, particularly among adolescents, are often distorted by class bias. Next, the floodgate of raw emotions surrounding interracial sexual relationships is opened. Finally, we turn to the role race plays in women's sexual abuse and exploitation, from rape to pornography.

....

Myths and Realities

One myth regarding female sexuality has to do with African women's "animalistic sexuality," a myth created to rationalize the breeding and selling of slaves for profit and to justify the sexual exploitation of female slaves. The myth made it easier for White owners to think of their slaves as animals, rather than as human beings with family ties and the capacity to love.

Another source of myth about African American women's sexuality was White reaction to Black women's more rhythmic bodily movements. African women, even when strolling casually from one place to another, often had a way of gently swaying their hips. In Europe, good Christian women were carefully taught not to swivel their hips or in any way emphasize their sexuality. Within Christian cultures in general, rhythmic body movements of any sort were associated with sex, and thus ultimately linked to sin. But in Africa, rhythm and dance were, and continue to be, central to expressions of spirituality and freedom.

White European-based society found it difficult to accept that other cultures might have standards of behavior different from their own. In Europe, women's breasts were carefully concealed and far more sexualized than in Africa. To African women, exposing one's breasts was natural. Not only was it easier for them to feed their children, but it was also more comfortable in hot weather. Thus, to African men, nude breasts were simply part of the cultural landscape, more functional than erotic. But to White men, unaccustomed to such casual nudity, bare-breasted women were a sign of heightened sexuality, and imaginations ran wild.

Even the differences in the body shape and size between European women and African American women were used to divide them. Between 1810 and 1815, preoccupation with the perceived differences in buttock size reached a nadir when the naked body of a Black South African woman named Saartjie (known as Sarah Bartmann) was put on display in London and Paris naked, like an animal. She was called "the Hottentot Venus," and her protruding buttocks and "unique" genitalia were exhibited as proof that Black women were more primitive and animalistic in their sexuality than White women. Scientists of the era pointed to evolution to account for this so-called structural difference, claiming that African women's buttocks were protectively raised higher and angled forward as an effective way to keep their genitalia above and away from the high grasses through which they ran. In looking back on the misguided and racist notions from an earlier century, however, it's important to note that differences between two groups are rarely equal, but instead become proof of one's racial superiority or inferiority.

These damaging myths of centuries past persist to this day. For African American women whose ancestors were psychologically scarred and physically terrorized, there is a collective consciousness of shared survival around issues of their sexuality. White women in this country, obviously, do not share this history. This is not to say, however, that they too weren't harmed by the myth-making of an earlier time.

When America was first settled, European culture in general, and Christianity in particular, severely penalized and repressed female expressions of sexuality. According to the dictates of Victorian morality, White women were expected to feign a total lack of interest in matters of the flesh, except as a means to have children. In polite society, White women were never free to be seductive or to act passionate with the men they loved. That a Black woman could, at least in theory, caused White women alternately to envy and to feel threatened by her. In the end, these sexual myths, perpetuated and abetted by White men, had the effect of driving apart the women of the two races. Instead of confronting the men who had sexual relations with their slave women, Southern White women found it more expedient to blame "hypersexual" Black women for seducing "innocent" White men. Jessie Daniel Ames, a co-founder of the biracial Association of Southern Women for the Prevention of Lynching, said, in 1936:

> White men have said over and over—and we believed it because it was repeated so often—that not only was there no such thing as a chaste Negro woman—but that a Negro woman could not be assaulted, that it was never against her will.

These attitudes continue to haunt our culture today, dividing White women from Black, distinguishing "good" girls from "bad." In an article about the Clarence Thomas–Anita Hill hearings, African American legal scholar Kimberle Crenshaw describes how sexualized images of race continue to make women into either madonnas or whores. White women are assumed to be good and pure until proven otherwise, but Black women, simply because they are Black, are assumed to be bad and whorelike. Even for an African American woman like Hill, who was a law professor at a prestigious university and a Baptist Sunday school teacher, the onus is on her to prove herself virtuous. Because of this difference in the presumed sexual natures of African American women and White women, White and Black women, Crenshaw maintains, experience differently the oppressive power of the madonna-whore dichotomy.

While White men have done much to perpetuate stereotypes about the sexuality of White women and Black women, African American men also make claims that divide White women from Black. What Black woman hasn't been told by a Black man that White women are more sexually liberated, more open to trying different sexual positions, more willing to give oral sex, and less demanding of a commitment while doing so? In stirring up a hornet's nest of interracial sexual jealousy, Black men gain the advantage. Dividing women sexually helps to keep Black women uninvolved in White feminists' campaigns to empower women and bring an end to sexual harassment, rape, and incest—much of which is intraracial. Of course, African American women have their own reasons for distrusting White women politically. But by maintaining sexual tension and jealousy between the women of the two races, African American men discourage African American women from speaking up about sexual abuse and mistreatment by African American men.

Ultimately, these damaging myths serve the interests of those with greater relative power, whether Whites in relation to Blacks or men in relation to women. Ironically, even myths about African American men's greater sexual prowess and larger penis size say less about Black men than about ensuring the separation of Black men and White women; such myths are designed to frighten White women and discourage them from pursuing African American men. It is hard to imagine men of either race claiming that "their" women are better in bed than women of the other race; such claims would serve the men no purpose. In alleging that women of the other race are sexually superior, however, men of both races are able to justify their cross-race pursuits while, at the same time, undermining the self-esteem and social stature of women of their own race.

Finally, race-based myths have the effect of silencing women so that they never talk to each about sex. This conspiracy of silence adds to an atmosphere of racial disharmony and distrust. Some people, in fact, speculate that sexual insecurity is the real basis for the continuing racial tension in this country.

How different are the sexual attitudes and practices of White women and Black women in reality? Research shows that, in fact, there are many more areas of similarity than of difference. In 1985, psychologist Philip Belcastro surveyed a racially mixed sample of a thousand unmarried undergraduates at a large Midwestern university. He found that Black and White women had roughly equal rates of premarital intercourse, intercourse with a stranger, abortion, intercourse frequency, number of intercourse partners, use of diaphragms, and percentages of pregnancies. The few areas of difference Belcastro observed suggest that White college women are more sexually active and varied in their activities than Black college women. On average, White women had more intercourse partners for six months or longer, and were more likely to perform fellatio and masturbate a partner to orgasm than were Black women. Belcastro's study has been criticized, however, because he did not control for socioeconomic differences in the women he surveyed. By using only college students, who tend to be more affluent than their counterparts in general, he limited his findings in terms of what they say about the population at large.

Another major study, conducted by Gail Wyatt, an African American psychology professor in the Department of Psychiatric and Biobehavioral Sciences at UCLA, balanced White and Black women in the study by income level and education. Wyatt also used what is generally considered a more reliable research method, conducting personal interviews with the participants. For three years, she and her team interviewed 126 African American women and 122 White women in the Los Angeles area. Her findings, published in 1989, indicate a great deal of similarity in the sexual practices and attitudes of the women. And like Belcastro, she observed some differences. Before the age of eighteen, 69 percent of White women, compared with only 31 percent of Black women, report having had four to seven one-night stands. Between the ages of eighteen and thirty-six, White women continued to have more sexual partners. Seventy-four percent had thirteen or more sexual partners, while only 26 percent of African American women reported having this many. Wyatt also found race differences in women who had oral sex or who masturbated. Among White women, 93 percent reported that they had experienced cunnilingus, and the same percent said that they had also performed fellatio. But among Black women, only 55 percent said that they had experienced cunnilingus, and 65 percent said that they had fellated. Finally, the White women in the study reported that they masturbated more frequently than Black women did.

Both Wyatt's research and Belcastro's further support the findings of a sex survey recently published by the Battelle Human Affairs Research Center, in Seattle, refuting the notion that African American women are more promiscuous than White women. In fact, White women have more sexual partners during their lifetime and are more varied in their sexual activities. As African American sociologist Robert Staples summed up, "The most popular myth is that Black sexuality has always been . . . unrestrained and unrestricted, but in reality Blacks are very conservative."

The belief that African American females are more sexually active than White females stems largely from the media's emphasis on African Americans who are poor. What is often thought to be a race difference in this country is, in reality, a class difference. Nowhere is this more true than in the presumed rates of early sexual activity of White and Black teenage girls.

According to Wyatt, White and Black girls of the same socioeconomic background have their first sexual experiences at roughly the same age, around sixteen. But when class is not factored in, national studies indicate that African American teenage girls, proportionately more of whom are poor, experience intercourse, on the average, two years ahead of White teenage girls, proportionately more of whom are affluent. Thus, between the ages of fifteen through nineteen, African American teenage girls, overall, have a rate of sexual intercourse twice that of White teenage girls. Even this gap is rapidly closing, however. A recent study by the Centers for Disease Control reveals that the sexual activity of Black teenagers has now leveled off, while the rate for White teenage girls continues to climb. By the age of nineteen, roughly 80 percent of the women in both groups have had sexual intercourse.

There are several factors associated with class that encourage early sexual involvement. Poor children do less well in school, and poor academic performance in itself is a predictor of early sexual activity. There is also a connection between obesity and sexual maturity, as we noted earlier. All other things being equal, obese children, proportionately more of whom are Black, mature faster than children of normal weight. And early sexual maturity is associated with early sexual experimentation. Those who are more developed are granted more freedom by their parents and are allowed to associate more with older friends than those who are less physically mature. Both of these factors heighten the chances of early sexual involvement. There is even some evidence that certain events in a child's life can actually trigger early sexual development and experimentation. According to sociobiologist and psychologist Jay Belsky, of Pennsylvania State University, when a father is chronically absent or sexually abusive, a biologically based survival mechanism kicks in, increasing hormone production and early sexual maturity, thereby helping daughters more quickly to escape the distressing situation.

Sexually active Black teenage girls are not necessarily having more "fun" than their sexually active White counterparts, however. A two-year longitudinal study by Edward Smith and J. Richard Udry, published in 1985, examined patterns of teenagers' sexual behavior and revealed some interesting race differences. The researchers found that White girls tend to move much more slowly from necking to clothed petting to unclothed petting and finally to intercourse than do African American girls, whose only activity before intercourse is oftentimes necking. Because women, in general, are aroused more slowly than men, the more rapidly a male moves to intercourse, the less likely his partner will experience orgasm. Sexologists further observe that prolonged petting leads to greater sexual satisfaction in women. In fact, what is commonly referred to as "foreplay" by both men and women is actually "the play" for women, many of whom report that they experienced more orgasms when they were only petting, before intercourse began.

During this prolonged petting stage, White women also learn more varied sexual activities. That is, as White girls seek to delay losing their virginity, and "do everything else but," they gain the skills to masturbate a partner to orgasm, to give and receive oral sex, as well as to discover what should be done to them to satisfy their own sexual desires.

In a 1994 *Essence* article entitled "Am I the Last Virgin?" the twenty-four-year-old African American Tara Roberts discusses her rushed sexual experiences with Black men, bemoaning the near absence of gentle touching and prolonged foreplay. Roberts describes the one time she came closest to having intercourse with a "Zimbabwean brother":

> We rushed back to his place and with little foreplay, he whipped it out and went straight for the gusto. I tried to slow him down. "Hey," I said softly, "I'm here." I searched for his soul in those beautiful eyes and confirmed for both of us that I wasn't going anywhere. I tried touching and exploring him, hoping he would understand that we had

all night under that magical Zimbabwean sky. But soon, without touching my body at all, he was ready again.

Roberts goes on, "My dream lover has to know that sex is more than just a pounding on the pelvis or an act that ends with the release of his semen."

White psychologist Michelle Fine finds that neither Black nor White teenage girls are allowed to experience their sexual nature in the same way that boys are. Investigating the missing "discourse of desire" in adolescent girls' sex education, from classes to informal talks with their girlfriends, she found that sex for teenage girls is most often framed in terms of victimization and fear, especially the fear of being raped. Not that this isn't a realistic concern for teenage girls. Statistics issued in 1994 by the Justice Department reveal that half of all rapes in this country happen to young women under the age of eighteen.

Teenage girls additionally fear unwanted pregnancy, sexually transmitted diseases, and losing their reputation. While these fears equally affect all teenage girls, African American girls are most adversely affected by the loss of reputation. Because White girls are assumed to be "good" until proven otherwise, they can often get away with sexual activity with their boyfriends as long as both parties keep quiet. But African American teenage girls, because they are presumed to be "bad" to begin with, must work hard to avoid the appearance of sexual impropriety. Perhaps this is why the 1987 Stanford studies of adolescent sexual behavior found that, across the socio-economic spectrum, there are some Black parents who deliberately delay letting their daughters date. This double standard in dating behavior creates resentment on the part of some African American teenage girls, as reflected in the following comments of Derelle, a seventeen-year-old African American high school senior from St. Louis:

I attend a Catholic high school, and just knowing that my parents are spending their money to send me here, instead of the public school, means I have to be extra careful about what I do. I don't date because everyone knows where that will lead, and I don't want a baby. But it really makes me mad to see all these "good White Catholic girls" getting pregnant, and having all these abortions like there's no tomorrow. Nothing will ever stop them from going to college.

It is obviously unfair to compare the realities of lower-class Black girls with those of middle-class White girls. But to ignore completely how perceptions of race and class interact in the sexual arena would be misleading. Many White girls believe, for example, that Black girls pepper their speech with sexually explicit language, and in general use "dirty" words in an aggressive way, more than White girls do. Poor Black girls also come across as more openly willing to discuss their sexual experiences with one another, even experiences that are negative, such as a painful first intercourse. Former Black Panther Elaine Brown, in her autobiography, *A Taste of Power,* talks about this kind of sexual frankness while growing up in the projects in Philadelphia. In one scene, Brown tells of listening to a girlfriend who confessed that her "cherry had been broken." The girl bluntly described the less-than-tender first sexual experience: "He took off my skirt and then he took off his pants . . . Then he got on top of me and pushed it in. Girl, I cried. I screamed my head off. Then all this blood came out me." To Elaine, who was thirteen at the time, the experience sounded dreadful, and she vowed never to endure it.

A White woman named Nana, now in her thirties, similarly recalls a Black girl in high school describing how she came to be pregnant. Nana was particularly shocked by the girl's bluntness.

I was thirteen years old and had just started high school, when this Black male counselor invited ten students to go on this retreat with him. One of the students was a Black girl who was sixteen and visibly pregnant. The counselor asked her—inappropriately, I might add— "How'd you get pregnant?" In this real matter-of-fact tone, this girl replied, "I was sitting in the front room and my boyfriend—he was in the bedroom—says, 'Hey girl, give me some pussy,' so I did."

Penelope, a White teenager from New York, was similarly surprised by a casual reference about sex made by her Black girlfriend Toni. Toni, who grew up in a lower-class neighborhood, was talking about her thirteen-year-old sister, whom she described as "fast." Penelope's face must have registered her surprise, because Toni quickly added, "You know, in the Black community, a distinction is made between being 'fast' and being 'a slut.' Being fast means only that you have sex with your boyfriend, and there's nothing wrong with that. Being a slut means that you will sleep with anyone, anytime, and that is definitely bad." Penelope privately concluded that even if that were true in the White community, White girls wouldn't talk about sex in such a casual way. In fact, she was somewhat intimidated by hearing about a thirteen-year-old girl who was sexually active.

While such stories are hardly scientific in revealing race differences in early sexual experiences, they do suggest that economically disadvantaged Black girls, if not more likely to be sexually experienced at an earlier age, are certainly more willing to talk about their good and bad sexual experiences. White teenage girls, on the other hand, even those from tough, working-class neighborhoods, tend to be more close-mouthed when it comes to their sexual activities. Of course, nothing informs others faster about one's sexual activities than a pregnancy.

Pregnancy outside marriage has always been viewed as a condition of shame. This is particularly true in the White community. Before the sixties, sexually active teenage girls who got pregnant were shuttled off to relatives, where their babies could be born in secrecy and then given up for adoption. In contrast, unwed Black girls who got pregnant often kept their babies, with other family members pitching in to help raise the child.

Rickie Solinger, author of the 1992 book *Wake Up Little Susie: Single Pregnancy and Race Before Roe v. Wade,* notes, however, a major race bias in societal reactions to pregnancies outside marriage. While White girls are individually shamed, unwed Black teenage girls are collectively shamed, "blamed for the population explosion, for escalating welfare costs, for the existence of unwanted babies, and for the tenacious grip of poverty on blacks in America." To this day, conservative White male politicians paint "black single pregnancy as an affront to white taxpayers and as a display of wanton, racial disobedience."

Despite this negative social pressure, Black teenagers faced with unwanted pregnancies are still more likely to keep their babies than are White teenagers in the same predicament. But a recent six-year-long national study by the Alan Guttmacher Institute concludes that "the higher a teenager's socioeconomic status, the more likely she is to terminate a pregnancy by abortion, regardless of race." As University of California sociologist Jewell Taylor Gibbs sees it, "It isn't the middle-class [Blacks] who are having these babies." Once again, the intersection between race and class tends to obscure the truth.

Black teenage girls are roughly half as likely as White girls to use contraception regularly. Unfortunately, myths about Black women's wanton sexuality actually has the effect of discouraging, rather than encouraging, responsible Black teenage girls from using birth control. An African American teenager named Rochelle, interviewed by education psychologist Deborah Tolman, commented, "When you get birth control pills, people automatically think you're having sex every night, and that's not true." Tolman acknowledges this dilemma, which she feels is particularly acute for Black girls. "Being thought of as sexually insatiable or out of control may be a fear intensified for African American girls, who are creating a sexual identity in a dominant cultural context that stereotypes Black women as alternately asexual and hypersexual." The dilemma for Rochelle is that if she uses birth control, she risks being labeled "bad," but if she doesn't use birth control, she risks an unwanted pregnancy.

Race differences in the use of contraceptives predictably translate into varying rates of unwanted pregnancies and the need to abort. According to 1990 Alan Guttmacher Institute statistics, Black women are roughly twice as likely to have abortions than White women (5.4 per hundred for Black women and 2.2 per hundred for White women). Nonetheless, Blacks have a disproportionate share of adolescent births; while making up only 15 percent of the adolescent population, they represent 29 percent of the adolescents who give birth. But because of White women's greater numbers in the population, their nonmarital births still exceed those of Black women. In 1991, for example, there were 707,500 children born to unmarried White women, accounting for 22 percent of all White women's births, compared to 463,800 children born to unmarried Black mothers, for 68 percent of Black women's births. (These figures are for babies born to all unwed mothers, not just those who are under twenty.) Yet if Black teenage girls who gave birth married their boyfriends as often as White teenage girls do, the out-of-wedlock ratio for Black teenagers would drop to what it is now for White teenagers. Despite these figures, the media continue to emphasize pregnancy rates among the poor, especially Black teenage girls, because they are viewed as the mothers draining welfare rolls and receiving AFDC (Aid to Families With Dependent Children).

According to Marian Wright Edelman, founder and president of the Children's Defense Fund, Black teenage girls' higher rates of nonmarital pregnancy have to do more with varying responses to unwanted pregnancy than with differences in sexual activity. Single motherhood is more acceptable in the African American community; it also causes fewer setbacks in achievement for Black teenage girls compared to White teenage girls. A

Black teenager named Catherine, with a two-year-old child named Tiffany, explains, "If I didn't get pregnant I would have continued on a downward path, going nowhere. They say teenage pregnancy is bad for you, but it was good for me. I know I can't mess around now; I got to worry about what's good for Tiffany and for me." Catherine appears to be right. Research by psychologists Diane Scott-Jones and Sherry Turner indicates that as long as multiple teen pregnancies are avoided, there are only modest differences in educational attainment and income between Black teenage girls who become pregnant and those who delay pregnancy. At most, delaying pregnancy relates to a gain of less than two years of education and $1500 in yearly income. Findings from the National Longitudinal Survey of Youth also confirm that compared to White adolescent mothers, Black adolescent mothers have higher high school completion rates and suffer fewer economic consequences. Jean Rhodes, a community psychologist, notes: "When a White teenage girl gets pregnant, her pregnancy breaks more of a norm within the White community and as a result, this behavior tends to cluster around other expressions of deviance, including heavy drinking and drug taking."

African American girls growing up in the poorest, most crime-ridden neighborhoods find that having a baby gives them status and someone to love. These girls have the least knowledge of how contraception works. Some believe such folklore as "You can't get pregnant standing up," or "If you eat greens, you won't get pregnant." Many distrust the White establishment so much that they think contraception is a strategy to limit the number of Black babies born in this country, and react strongly when told to postpone having babies. White women health care educators and practitioners, who don't understand what it means to grow up in gang-infested neighborhoods, where random acts of violence are common occurrences, are completely ineffectual when working with impoverished Black teenage girls. At the very least, White nurses, social workers, and teachers working in the inner city should be aware of the enormous pressures that some Black teenage boys put on Black teenage girls to have their babies *now*. As one sixteen-year-old African American male gang member put it, "If she ain't gonna drop that load, and I mean real quick-like, then we can't deal. Hell, I'm a Black man and don't know how much longer I'm gonna be here. I got to have me some namesakes." The girlfriend this Black teenager was referring to was only thirteen years old. In contrast, many White teenage boys, seeking to avoid the responsibilities of fatherhood and child care payments,

are inclined to put pressure on a pregnant girlfriend to abort. Poorly understood cultural difference in attitudes toward teen pregnancy and unwed
motherhood can cause tensions to run high among Black and White female
activists working together to improve young women's lives.

Interracial Dating and Marriage

Interracial sexual relationships are quite possibly the biggest source of tension among women of the two races. Were there no history of racism in
America, such relationships would barely arouse curiosity. Were there no
unequal treatment of women in society, men and women would cross the
color line with equal freedom and enthusiasm. Such is not the case.

For nearly three hundred years, Blacks and Whites in this country were
legally prohibited from marrying each other. The policy was initiated by the
White political establishment, concerned lest their blood be mixed with that
of people seen as inferior. Remarkably, laws prohibiting interracial marriage
were not banned until 1967, when the U.S. Supreme Court, in *Loving* v.
Virginia, finally struck down as unconstitutional all antimiscegenation stat-
utes. By that time, a host of other barriers to integration were beginning to
fall, making it more likely that Whites and Blacks would meet and fall in
love at school and in the workplace. In fact, the sweeping sociological
changes set in motion by the Civil Rights Movement are reflected in the
following rates of interracial marriage. In 1970, only 1.5 of every thousand
marriages was racially mixed; by 1990, the figure had almost tripled, to four
out of every thousand, with the majority being White-Black.

Of course, many interracial sexual relationships do not result in marriage.
The sixties also witnessed a sexual revolution, and sex outside marriage
became more common. Men and women, Whites and Blacks, were ready
and willing to experiment sexually. During the ensuing decades, several
patterns in interracial sexual relations began to emerge. Middle-class Blacks,
who often grow up in predominantly White neighborhoods, attend predominantly White colleges and universities, and work in integrated environments, are more likely to date interracially than are Blacks from lower-class
backgrounds. In addition, many more Black men and White women date
than Black women and White men. According to African American scholar
Robert Staples, during the "free love" era of the late sixties and early seven-

ties, as many as 90 percent of the Black males on some college campuses had at least one interracial dating experience. A high percentage of White women, too, said that they had dated a Black man.

For a variety of reasons, Black women seem to be far less interested in crossing the color line. Only about 30 percent report having dated a man of another racial background. This difference is reflected, as well, in statistics on interracial marriage. As of the early 1990s, 71 percent, or 156,000 of all Black-White interracial marriages, involved African American men marrying White women, and only 29 percent, or 75,000, involved African American women marrying White men.

In recent years, Black-White dating and mating has been the subject of numerous articles and books, but none has specifically focused on how the issues affect the relationships of White and Black women. Because of the disproportionate number of Black men marrying and dating White women, one effect has been to drive Black and White women apart. Not surprisingly, African American women have become angry at White women for "stealing" Black men, already in short supply.

Statistics show that in the general population there are about seven Black men to every ten Black women. Among Whites, there are ten men to every nine women. While certainly not every woman, Black or White, is looking for a man, the more Black men who turn to White women, the fewer are available for interested Black women. These differences are reflected in recent Census Bureau findings indicating that by the age of thirty, three fourths of all White women are married, but by the same age, fewer than half that number of Black women are. And by the age of forty, the statistics are more grim. As few as one in ten White women has never been married, but nearly one in four Black women who reaches the age of forty has never been married. The situation is even worse for college-educated, successful African American women, perhaps because there are fewer suitable Black men for them to marry. But what infuriates Black women the most is that the more successful an African American man is, the more likely he is to marry a woman who is light-skinned, either Black or White. This pattern was first identified by anthropologist Melville Herskovits during the sixties, and documented again in the eighties by sociologists Elizabeth Mullins and Paul Sites. These researchers found that eminent Black men were far more likely to have light-skinned partners than were eminent Black women. For the average African American woman, though, the pattern of successful

African American men marrying light and especially White is confirmed by simple observation. Everywhere they look, they see Black male celebrities, from composer and record producer Quincy Jones, to Supreme Court Justice Clarence Thomas, playwright August Wilson, and actors Sidney Poitier and James Earl Jones, married to White women. Even more disturbing is the perceived trend of celebrity Black men, most notably O. J. Simpson, divorcing a first wife who is Black and replacing her with one who is White once fame and wealth are achieved. Instead of being angry at Black men for doing this, it is more expedient for African American women to blame White women. So deep, in fact, is the rage at White women for marrying successful African American men that, on hearing that O. J. Simpson had battered and possibly brutally murdered his beautiful White wife, Nicole, more than a few African American women were heard to mutter, under their breath, that it served her right, and him, too, for messing around with her.

Anger over this issue goes back at least as far as the Civil Rights Movement, when White women and Black men, working together to register Blacks to vote, first realized and acted upon their sexual attraction to each other. The distrust continues. Among White and Black women working together for common political causes, fears about interracial dating can destroy sisterly relations. Carolyn Rodgers, an African American, captured the uneasy feelings in her 1976 poem "I Have Been Hungry," an excerpt of which appears as one of this chapter's epigraphs.

White women who date or marry Black men, on the other hand, are often taken aback and confused by the fury of Black women over this issue. Among those surprised by the rage of African American women is Gail Mathabane, co-author of *Love in Black and White*. Gail expected her marriage to a Black man to irritate White bigots, but she never dreamed that it would anger Black women. "I was made to feel that I had committed some sort of unspoken crime against the black community, particularly black women." Gail Mathabane clearly was more baffled than upset by the reactions of African American women to her interracial marriage. But some White women respond with hostility: "Yes, Black women are angry, and no, I'm not going to obsess over it. If they didn't give their Black men so much shit all the time, maybe their men wouldn't seek out White women."

Most White women, however, are simply disappointed and hurt by Black women's anger, as in the case of Lynn, an attractive, tall collegiate volleyball player with blond hair and green eyes. When Lynn started dating an African American star basketball player on campus, the Black female athletes began ignoring her. Commenting on the subject of interracial dating, Lynn said, "If I were them, I would be happy about it. I would think, there goes someone who is not prejudiced, someone who accepts us for who we are." White women who date or marry Black men often see themselves as positive race ambassadors, helping to bridge the racial divide. African American women, however, do not, in part because the reverse situation does not equally apply. White women who claim, "I don't have a problem with Black women dating White men, so why should they have a problem with White women dating Black men?" tend to infuriate African American women. They simply don't believe that the issues are interchangeable when there is no shortage of White men, and when the reasons for Black men choosing a White woman or even a light-skinned Black woman are so rooted in color prejudice.

Interracial dating can be something of a mine field; sympathic White women aren't sure how to react. They do not know what such relationships may mean to Black women in personal or political terms. An attractive middle-aged White woman, who for several years has been dating an African American man named Stanley, reflected on the complexities of this issue:

> I understand their anger; I really do. But I love Stanley. I didn't plan to fall in love with him. It just happened. And now that it has, am I supposed to give him up just because Black women I don't even know don't like it? That just doesn't make sense to me. And he's happy, too. What about him?

Deborah, a White woman of Jewish faith, after moving in with a Black man whom she met during the Civil Rights Movement, found herself paralyzed by her own feelings of guilt. She was unable, for example, to establish any positive relationship with her boyfriend's Black female friends. She even confessed to letting these women verbally abuse her, something that, as a feminist, she did not tolerate from anyone else. Finally, her boyfriend snapped at Deborah, "Why don't you stand up to them? They're losing respect for you, and frankly, so am I. I thought you were stronger than that." But Deborah could think of nothing to say in her defense. Her relationship ultimately fell apart, in large part, Deborah now thinks, because of her private sense of guilt and betrayal of her African American "sisters."

Ironically, White women who claim they would never date a Black man can still insult Black women. Although most African American women don't want White women to date interracially, in theory they would at least like White women to find African American men attractive. A White woman named Deana discovered this when she mentioned to her African American girlfriend Temple, "I don't care if Whites or Blacks date or marry each other; I just wouldn't do it. I would never date a Black guy." Temple shot back, "Are you telling me that you are superior to other people? Are you telling me that it is okay for others to do something, but that you are somehow above it?" The implication was that Deana's reaction was racist. Yet Black women feel free to express their distaste for dating White men. A White college student named Susan recalls asking a Black girlfriend whether she would ever consider marriage to a White man. The friend replied, "Never. White men smell funny and don't look good at all to me. They're all ugly."

On the whole, White women don't seem to feel threatened by the possibility that some White men find Black women more physically attractive. After all, it is White women in our society, not Black women, who set the culture's ideals of feminine beauty and attractiveness. When a White man pursues an African American woman, most White women just think his taste in women is quirky. But when a Black man pursues a White woman, it confirms a deep fear in some Black women that they are not pretty enough by society's standards.

A 1992 article in the *New York Times* by African American novelist Bebe Moore Campbell describes just how fast these raw feelings of insecurity can surface among even the most successful and competent of African American women. Campbell told of the time that she and several of her African American girlfriends were eating lunch at a "trendy Beverly Hills restaurant." Suddenly, a good-looking, well-known Black actor walked in, trailing behind him a White woman. As if on cue, Campbell and her friends threw down their forks and moaned and cursed under their breath. Only later did Campbell reflect on why they had reacted so strongly:

For many African-American women, the thought of black men, particularly those who are successful, dating or marrying white women is

like being passed over at the prom by the boy we consider our steady
date, causing us pain, rage and an overwhelming sense of betrayal and
personal rejection . . . For sisters, the message that we don't measure
up is the nightmare side of integration.

Social psychological research on the roles of physical attractiveness and
race in interracial relationships confirms African American women's worse
fears. Interracial love doesn't just happen randomly; it is the result of careful, if unconscious, consideration of what the other person has to offer, an
exchange in the interpersonal marketplace. This is exactly what White social
psychologist Bernard Murstein and his colleagues hypothesized in a 1989
study—that the Black members of courting interracial couples would be
relatively more attractive than the White members. That is, in a White-
dominated, racially unequal culture, the lower status of being Black would
have to be offset by relatively greater physical attractiveness. To test this
hypothesis, the physical attractiveness of each member of twenty married
interracial couples was judged by a panel of four, made up of two men and
two women, two of whom were White and two of whom were Black. Their
findings were mixed. The Black men were rated as significantly more attractive than their White female partners, but the Black women were rated
neither higher nor lower in attractiveness than their White male partners.

Another study, by African American clinical graduate student Camille
Baughn, yielded similar results in 1993. Male and female research participants were asked to view eight pictures of people of the opposite sex of
varying race and physical attractiveness. The subjects were asked to indicate
how attractive they thought each person was, and how willing they would
be to date each one. African Americans and Whites of both sexes generally
expressed higher dating preferences for members of their own race and for
those of greater physical attractiveness. In general, men expressed higher
interest in cross-race dating than women, and African Americans rated
Whites as more physically attractive than Whites rated African Americans.
However, Baughn also observed that African American men rated White
women as more desirable to date than African American women rated
White men. Baughn concluded that African American men and women
embrace the notion that "Black is Beautiful" differently.

In a society where race has played such a pivotal role, White women are
still too often viewed as the ultimate prize for successful African American

men. White women, even those who aren't seen as particularly attractive, can still lighten the line for African American men in a way that no African American woman can, no matter how beautiful she is.

Not all Black and White women condemn interracial dating, though, and some women of different races are brought together by it. A White school administrator named Nancy B., for example, one day asked an African American female colleague whether she would mind keeping a lookout for her boyfriend. "He's bringing by some greens for me." Her colleague, putting two and two together, guessed that anyone bringing by "greens" must be African American. She asked Nancy, "Is your boyfriend, by any chance, Black?" When Nancy replied, "Yes," the Black woman said, "Well, guess what? My boyfriend is White!" The two of them celebrated by doing a little jig together. They also began confiding in each other things that before they had kept to themselves. Anecdotal evidence like this suggests that, compared with Black women who claim they would never go out with a White man, African American women who date interracially tend to be more accepting of White women who similarly cross the color line. In addition to understanding the nature of cross-race attractions, such African American women are less personally threatened by the shortage of available Black men.

For both groups of women who date and marry interracially, female relatives of the male partner are another potential source of cross-race connection. Sonya, an African American who is currently engaged to a White Italian named Johnny, gets along very well with her fiancé's mother. "Not long after meeting her, I told my future mother-in-law that I respected the non-gendered way in which she had raised her son. From then on, there was never any question that we would get along fine. After all, we were both feminists." White women, too, report stories of love and acceptance with the women in the family of their African American boyfriend or husband.

More often, though, White and Black women report difficult relations with the relatives of their cross-race lover or spouse. An African American female college student named Jamillah, who was dating a White man, became aware that his mother and sisters were sabotaging the relationship by not relaying her phone messages to him. As a result, their plans were constantly being derailed. When her boyfriend broke up with her, Jamillah was convinced that his relatives were largely responsible. Many African American family members, especially mothers, are similarly inclined to respond poorly to a White girlfriend brought home by a son or brother. In fact, some

African American men are expressly told never to do this. The Black writer
Darrell Dawsey explains why he would never date interracially:

> Some of the distance I kept from White women resulted from my up-
> bringing . . . my mother did not approve of interracial romance. Not
> unlike other African American women, she had suffered the pain of
> being marginalized by a racist, sexist mainstream that fraudently pro-
> motes white women as the benchmark of womanhood . . . The rule
> quietly in place around Ma's house was . . . "If she can't use your
> comb, don't bring her home."

When attitudes like this prevail, a White woman, no matter how politically aware or racially sensitive she may be, will find it difficult, if not
impossible, to establish good relations with the female relatives of her African American boyfriend or husband. Needless to say, such tensions only add
to the stress of making interracial relationships work.

Despite such resistance from family members and friends, interracial dating and mating continue to grow in popularity. And as they increase, there
is a growing backlash. In March 1994, a White principal named Hulond
Humphries, of Wedowee, Alabama, allegedly told a mixed-race female student that she was a "mistake" (for having been born of a White-Black
union), and also attempted to ban interracial dating at the upcoming school
prom. Although Humphries was suspended for his racist actions, he was not
immediately fired. The prom went on without the ban, but sometime later
the school was destroyed by a fire of suspicious origins.

As members of both races struggle with the significance of interracial
sexual relationships, women's relations with one another suffer. African
American poet and essayist Audre Lorde believes, however, that the hostility
so many Black women feel toward White women for dating Black men is
misdirected and ultimately destructive:

> It can never result in true progress on the issue because it does not ques-
> tion the vertical lines of power or authority, nor the sexist assumptions
> which dictate the terms of that competition. And the racism of white
> women might be better addressed where it is less complicated by their
> own sexual oppression. In this situation it is not the non-Black woman
> who calls the tune, but rather the Black man who turns away from him-

self in his sisters or who, through a fear borrowed from white men, reads her strength not as a resource but as a challenge.

Interracial Lesbian Relationships

The rate of interracial sexual involvement among lesbians is even greater than it is among heterosexuals, although exact figures are hard to come by. Perhaps because lesbians have already challenged one of society's fundamental taboos, they are more open to challenging others. For whatever reason, the interracial relationships formed by White and Black lesbians are often emotionally charged.

Like their heterosexual counterparts, lesbian women who cross race lines for love and sex must contend with societal racism and sexual inequality. In addition, lesbians must also deal with antigay sentiment—what is termed homophobia or, more recently, heterosexism. These sources of discrimination uniquely challenge White and African American lesbians romantically involved with each other.

Having been raised in a pervasively heterosexual society, most lesbians, regardless of race, must first overcome their own homophobia—the internalized fear and self-hatred leading them to wonder whether something is wrong with them for being attracted to members of their own sex. African American lesbians, in particular those who go out with White women, must additionally ask themselves whether their interracial dating reflects an expression of their own internalized racism or self-hatred, something that perhaps renders them incapable of loving another woman who is Black. Having grown up in a color-conscious, racially biased culture, Black lesbians are not immune from the usual prejudice that lighter is somehow better, a step up. Such anxieties, in fact, are poignantly captured in the following excerpt from "does it matter if she's white?" by Dajenya, a lesbian biracial African American–Jewish poet:

> does it matter if she's white?
> does it matter
> if sistahs and brothahs
> look at me askance
> not only cause she's a she
> but cause she's white?

does it matter
if dykes of color even think there's something
wrong with me
some auntie Tom
in my soul
some self hate
that must exist
if I would choose
a white woman?

does it matter
if I try to justify
defend
if I point out that
my mother's white
so you see
it's only natural
any relationship I enter into
is necessarily
interracial

As Dajenya's poem suggests, in addition to their own questioning of their sexual and color preferences, they must contend with the accusations of other "dykes of color." Many African American lesbians are quick to assign ulterior motives to others in their community who love White women. "Black lesbians who date White women are suffering from self-hate," says one Black lesbian named Rhonda. "They think some White woman is going to lift them up." African American scholar Brenda Verner similarly claims, "Like Black men who have become obsessed with white women, many black lesbian feminists are caught in the net of 'jungle fever.' "

Such strident criticism of interracial dating from both lesbian and heterosexual members of the Black community can make it doubly hard on African American lesbians who do enter into relationships with White women. Mary Morten, former president of the Chicago chapter of NOW, described what happened to her one evening:

I was at a party with my White girlfriend, and this Black woman started hitting on me. When my White lover saw what was going on, she came over and sat next to me, kind of making it clear that the two of us were together. Well, this other woman, who was being so nice and friendly, all of sudden turned vindictive. Then, after finding out that I was president of NOW, she very snootily commented, "Oh, that's why you've got a White girlfriend."

Such attitudes also undermine the feelings of White lesbians who date Black women. One White lesbian began to wonder whether her Black partner was going with her only to gain status. Other White lesbians who date interracially worry that they are a liability for their Black girlfriends, who are put in the position of having to defend their choice of a White lover to other Black lesbians. And still other White lesbians, including Shawna, are disturbed by what they see as "Black liberal guilt" in regard to their interracial dating.

My Black girlfriend once dropped my hand when a group of radical Black lesbians walked in the room. It really made me mad, and I think her attitude about me being White was something that ultimately led to us breaking up. It is very hard on Black lesbians to have other Black lesbians accuse them of being politically incorrect, or betraying Black sisterhood.

Certainly not all African American lesbians believe that having a White lover implies a lack of self-esteem or absence of racial pride. African American lesbian scholar Cheryl Clarke is among those who defend interracial relationships. In her article "Lesbianism: An Act of Resistance," Clarke writes:

It cannot be presumed that black lesbians involved in love, work, and social relationships with white lesbians do so out of self-hate and denial of our racial-cultural heritage, identities, and oppression. Why should a woman's commitment to the struggle be questioned or accepted on the basis of her lover's or comrades' skin color? White lesbians engaged likewise with black lesbians or any lesbians of color cannot be assumed to be acting out of some perverse, guilt-ridden racialist desire.

Clarke's argument that White lesbians who date interracially cannot be presumed to be acting out of "guilt-ridden racialist desire" relates to another common accusation: that they are only "ethnic chasers." Ethnic chasers, according to White lesbian psychologists D. Merilee Clunis and C. Dorsey Green, in their book *Lesbian Couples: Creating Healthy Relationships for the '90s,* are White women who pursue Black women because they feel guilty about being White. They seek "color by proximity" to prove just how liberal they really are.

The fear that White liberal guilt, or some other misguided attraction based solely on color, is what's really driving a White woman's pursuit can leave some African American lesbians wondering whether they are just an "exotic fantasy." Marilyn, a Black lesbian Chicago-based filmmaker, after being actively pursued by a White woman, decided not to date the woman because of her constant references to Marilyn as an "African Goddess."

Another issue that women in interracial lesbian relationships must contend with is how their different skin color grants them different privileges in society. Kim Hall addresses this point in an essay entitled "Learning to Touch Honestly: A White Lesbian's Struggle With Racism":

> Because I am white, I have benefited and continue to benefit from white skin privilege, even though being a lesbian has denied other privileges. Being a lesbian does not change the fact that my physical being in the world is safer than that of a lesbian of color. My white skin remains.

While it may be true that White lesbian women are more sensitive than heterosexual White women to what it means to be part of an oppressed minority, lesbians can still hide their "stigma" whenever they choose. That is, unlike race and color, sexual preference cannot be discerned from appearance alone. As Patty K., a Black lesbian from USC, puts it, "When we walk through any door, no one really knows whether we are gay or not. But one thing they know for sure is that we are Black." bell hooks makes a similar point: "Often homophobic attacks on gay people occur in situations when knowledge of sexual preference is indicated or established—outside of gay bars, for example. Blacks can't hide their color."

To cope with the often heavy baggage of self-doubt, guilt, and resentment that can accompany interracial lesbian relationships, lesbian couples frequently turn to support groups. Cynthia W., a White lesbian, and her Black lover, after moving from Chicago to New York in the early eighties, decided to start one of their own. Once a month, women in the group took turns holding potluck dinners and discussing in depth the issues facing them. The women found it especially helpful to reserve part of the evening for those of each racial group to talk separately to each other.

Of the many issues that came up at the meetings was the fact that when the interracial couple was at home alone, their racial differences were rarely an issue, but when the two went out together, race was nearly always a problem. In restaurants, White waiters would often approach the White woman first and, at the end of the meal, give her the check. Dance clubs also appealed to either a mostly White or mostly Black clientele, and when a racially mixed couple went out, one of them commonly felt out of place. Housing, too, was a problem. Cynthia recalled the time when she looked for an apartment to share with her lover. After finding what she thought was the perfect place, she brought her Black lover to show it to her, and discovered that the landlord had had a sudden change of mind about the apartment's availability. For White women not used to such blatant racism, it can be an eye-opening and a devastating experience. While it also hurts Black women, most have developed emotional armor over the years that helps to protect them from the constant harsh realities of racism.

Because Black lesbians, in particular, face discrimination on so many different fronts—from Whites for being Black, from men for being female, and from other Blacks for being lesbian—many have sought and found relief in exclusive African American lesbian support groups, such as the Black Lesbian Support (BLSG) in Washington, Chicago's African American Womyn's Alliance, Cleveland's Sistahparty, and L.A.'s Lesbians of Color (LOC). Some White lesbians take offense at Black lesbians segregating into their own groups. A thirty-year-old White lesbian named Jennifer Ann H. said, "As lesbians we must all stick together. We can't afford to show any hint of division. Groups shouldn't be created that exclude any other lesbian." But Lisa P., a Black lesbian from the University of Chicago, disagreed. When asked whether she felt that Black lesbians organizing among themselves would breed contempt for White lesbians, or whether clubs for "gay wimmin of color only" would be detrimental to lesbian alliances, Lisa responded:

It is important that White lesbians understand that although we share a lot of the same struggles, Black lesbians have a unique set of

battles that we must confront as well. We may have being lesbian in
common, but our biggest and most obvious difference still remains
—our color. And, yes, racism is alive and well in the gay community.

For Lisa, as for many Black lesbians, issues of race will always come
ahead of those having to do with being gay. Venus Medina, a project officer
at the CDC in Atlanta, says that "most Black lesbians identify as Black
women first and lesbians second." Yet the notion that race supersedes sexual
orientation remains a difficult one for many White lesbians to accept.

In comparison to White lesbians, African American lesbians may have a
special need to come together for support, given the greater hatred against
them in their community. An African American author, Ann Allen Shockley, discusses just how strong this homophobia is in her 1974 novel *Loving
Her,* dealing with an interracial lesbian affair. The Black heroine, Renay,
who falls in love with a White woman, considers whether she should "come
out" to her best straight Black friend Fran. Deciding against it, Renay
reflects:

> Black women were the most vehement about women loving each
> other. This kind of love was worse to them than the acts of adultery
> or incest, for it was homophile. It was worse than being inflicted
> with an incurable disease. Black women could be sympathetic about
> illegitimacy, raising the children of others, having affairs with mar-
> ried men—but not toward Lesbianism, which many blamed on
> white women.

Black lesbian scholar Barbara Smith, in *Home Girls: A Black Feminist Anthology,* analyzes why many in the African American community remain
strongly opposed to homosexuality:

> Heterosexual privilege is usually the only privilege that Black women
> have. None of us have racial or sexual privilege, almost none of us
> have class privilege, maintaining "straightness" is our last resort.

In other words, to give up the one privilege that African American women
enjoy seems to others an act of suicide—or, worse yet, an act of genocide.

This attitude is certainly reflected in the following comments of Bernita, a forty-year-old Black mother of four:

> If the Black community supports gay life, then what is to happen to the Black family, which is already in danger? And Black lesbians? I just can't accept this. We are the mothers of this earth. Without us there will be no more Black children. No MLKs [Martin Luther King] would ever be born again, no Sojourner Truths, no great Black men and women. The Black family is the backbone of our community, and we all have a responsibility to preserve it.

Even the respected Black psychiatrist Frances Cress Welsing voices such concern when she states, "If we endorse homosexuality, then we have endorsed the death of our people." Ironically, despite the fear of some Black heterosexuals that lesbianism is just "another trick the Man pulled out of his genocide trickbag," Black lesbians are actually far more likely to have children than White lesbians.

Regardless of whether antigay sentiment is stronger among Blacks or Whites—and some lesbians believe there is no difference in the rates of homophobia—negative attitudes toward lesbianism are stressful. And the stress is especially great for women involved in interracial relationships, if only because they stand out more than lesbian couples of the same race. Smith has written about this issue, as well: "Whenever I had a lover of a different race, I felt that it was like having a sign or billboard over my head that said—'These are dykes. Right here.' " In the book *Lesbian Psychologies*, a White Jewish middle-class lesbian named Sarah commented:

> What I was very aware of, at the beginning of our relationship, was how visible I felt with her. And I was aware of the whole ideal of being with a black woman. When we would walk down the street, I felt that it was like wearing placards that said "lesbian." And that was very unsettling.

Obviously, it is to lesbians' advantage to avoid standing out in public or otherwise calling attention to themselves. Research on hate crimes indicates that racism, sexism, and homophobia cluster together, especially among religiously conservative men, who are among the most homophobic. To such people, the sight of a White and Black woman together, in love and having fun, fans the flames of intolerance. More than any other relationship, an interracial lesbian relationship challenges the "traditional" structure of society.

In addition to the hostile reactions of strangers, a lesbian woman who dates interracially may have to fend off the hostilities of her partner's family. Amy, a White lesbian, talks about what happened the one time her Black lover, Nancy, took Amy home to meet the parents:

> It was clear that Nancy's parents did not like me, but it was hard to tell what bothered them more—that their daughter was gay—I was the first woman that she had brought home and came out with to her parents—or that she was with someone White. All I know is that being in her parents' home was one of the most uncomfortable experiences of my life.

An African American lesbian named JoAnn W. confesses that it was difficult enough for her mother to accept that her daughter was lesbian, but when JoAnn introduced her White lover, her mother demanded to know, "Why couldn't you at least bring home a Black woman?" It can be equally hard on African American lesbians visiting the homes of their White girlfriends, although the issues may be slightly different. Black women, for example, resent it when White girlfriends act as though their parents are so liberal that race doesn't matter, when they know that it always does.

That two women of varying racial backgrounds can passionately love each other should offer hope to other women trying to come together, for whatever purpose. Ann Allen Shockley writes of the promise as well as the mystery of interracial love in *Loving Her*. In one scene, Renay, who is light-skinned, reflects on her growing attractions for her White lover, Terry:

> Tracing the whiteness of Terry's skin with her finger, Renay thought, *It is amazing how I can lie here and see and feel this skin and not think of the awful things others of her color have done to us. And yet, my skin is light—tinged with the sun. Someone, somewhere in the past, must have done and thought and felt like this with another—or hated in a different and helpless way.*

Interracial relationships require honest communication and a lot of hard work if they are to succeed. Regardless of whether the couple is heterosexual or homosexual, each member must make a determined effort to understand the other's cultural uniqueness. This means, among other things, granting a partner the freedom to express his or her differences. Compared with White Americans, who are often raised with a sense of "rugged individualism," African Americans tend to have a more communal sense of identity, to see themselves as part of a larger group. Blacks also tend to be more bicultural —that is, more adept at operating within both the White culture and the Black culture. Members of the dominant culture frequently know only how to interact comfortably with others of their own race. Thus, at social gatherings, a White lover in a group of African Americans is more likely to feel self-conscious and out of place than would an African American lover in a group of Whites. These differences need to be understood by White and Black women alike if they are to get along.

Sexual Violence and Exploitation

The intersection of sex and violence is another major source of tension between women of European and African descent, even if that intersection is usually controlled by men. With rare exceptions, women do not assault, batter, molest, or stalk one another. Lesbian rape, for example, accounts for less than 1 percent of all rapes. But relations between African American and White women are still affected by sexual violence and exploitation, if only because of the women's different responses to them. In general, White women view rape, harassment, and battering solely in terms of gender. Most African American women, however, view sexual abuse first in terms of race and only second in terms of gender. This fundamental difference in perspective and interpretation of sexual abuse strains women's political alliances.

For African American women, rape historically, as noted earlier, is linked with slavery; White slave owners forced themselves sexually on Black women, who had no legal recourse to stop their abuse. (Nor did they have protection against rape by slave men.) Only White women could bring charges of rape. With regard to interracial rape, this meant that only those cases involving White women and Black men were heard, even though there were far many more incidents of White men raping Black women.

The history of rape also conjures up incidents involving White women's false accusations against Black men, accusations that have led to the lynchings of innocent fathers, sons, and brothers. That some White women made such accusations remains difficult for African Americans of both sexes to accept. Although White women as a group were politically powerless to stop either the rape or lynching of slaves, that so few tried is cause for continuing distrust by Black women of their White "sisters."

In conjunction with this bitter history, there are contemporary reasons, as well, that African American women view rape more in terms of race than of gender. The most disturbing has to do with racial inequality in law enforcement and the criminal justice system. To this day, police officers are less likely to believe, or treat respectfully, Black women who claim to have been raped. African American women have found their version of events often dismissed by police. A twenty-nine-year-old Black hairdresser named Mary Kay explains why she didn't bother to report when she was raped. "Saying something won't make a difference. They would only say that I asked for it anyway. I'm a Black woman, you know. And it was a Black man who took advantage of me." A Black manicurist known as K.K. called the police after her ex-boyfriend assaulted her. "He held me down and tried to smash his penis in my face. When I called the police and they saw I was Black and found that I'd once dated my attacker, who was also Black, they treated me as if I'd wanted it. It's just not worth it for me. Knowing what I know, I probably just shouldn't have called the police anyway. All they do is think Black women are sluts and Black men only have sex on their minds." Of course, many White women's reports of acquaintance rape are treated similarly by police officers, but White women don't have their race as an additional factor working against them.

Research indicates that when rape cases do make it to court, the accused is more likely to walk when the victim is Black than when she is White. African American legal scholar Kimberle Crenshaw cites a case revealing all too well how this can happen. After hearing evidence that a Black teenager was raped, one White juror argued for acquittal on the grounds that a girl of her age from "that kind of neighborhood" probably wasn't a virgin, anyway. In those rare circumstances when a rape conviction is obtained, the average prison sentence for a man raping a Black woman is two years, compared with the ten years he is likely to get for raping a White woman. Justice is even more skewed in the case of interracial rape. No White male in this country has ever been given the death penalty for raping a Black woman, yet many Black men, innocent and guilty, have been sentenced to death for raping White women.

Despite reports in the media, most rapes are not interracial. According to the U.S. Department of Justice, among those cases involving a single offender, about seven out of every ten White victims were raped by a White offender, and about eight out of every ten Black victims were raped by a Black offender. But it is interracial rape that makes the big headlines and stirs public reaction.

Nowhere was this more evident than in the highly publicized case of the Central Park jogger, a White woman who was beaten and gang-raped by a group of Black teenagers out "wilding." During that same week, there was another gang rape involving a young Black woman from Brooklyn. A New York prosecutor described her attack as "one of the most brutal in recent years." She was raped, sodomized, and thrown fifty feet off the top of a four-story building. Witnesses testified that the victim "screamed as she plunged down the air shaft." Both her ankles and legs were shattered, as well as her pelvis, and she suffered extensive internal injuries. But few in America know about this woman's fate. Not only was she Black, but so were her assailants.

An African American woman who is raped by a member of her own race thus faces a dilemma. If she brings charges against the Black man, especially one as well known as Mike Tyson, she is harshly criticized by others in the community for bringing down a Black man. She also plays a role, however unwittingly, in perpetuating the stereotype that Black men are sexually dangerous. Thus, a Black woman who is raped by a man of her own race must always consider whether it is better to keep quiet about the attack, thereby saving the reputation of Black men who are innocent, or to speak out and thereby possibly save other women from the same fate. A White woman is not placed in this quandary. When she accuses a White man of rape, whether her charges are believed or not, they do not become a collective indictment of White men. Because of their different experiences in this regard, White women usually discount the importance of race in the politics of rape. They find it difficult to understand Black women's reluctance to report instances of rape. To White women, if a man rapes, no matter what his color, he should be caught and punished.

These differences in reactions to rape can fiercely divide women, even those working together to reduce sexual violence in their communities. In 1993, an interracial rape case involving a Black man assaulting a woman of Asian descent was reported on the campus of a well-known Midwestern university. The women's studies faculty members gathered to discuss how the school should respond. The White female faculty members were angry that the university was not doing enough to make the campus safe for its female students, staff, and faculty. But the African American faculty were angry over the university's posting throughout the campus a police sketch of the accused. One African American woman present at the meeting argued that the pictures were not helping to solve the crime, but were promoting the stereotype that all Black men were criminally dangerous. In reaction to her position, a White woman responded, "So, are we, as women, to put our lives at risk just to protect the reputation of Black men? No way! This guy needs to be caught and caught now, and if that means blanketing the campus with his picture, then that's what has to be done." The meeting broke up with nothing resolved but with new tension between the White and Black faculty members that took months to dissipate. Nearly a year later, the White woman who had spoken up at the meeting learned that the issue for the Black faculty member was not so much that the pictures of a Black man were being posted, but that the quality of the pictures was extremely poor. They were so unclear that the man looked indistinguishable from any other Black man. Even a relatively minor miscommunication like this, though, can have a major divisive effect on women's cross-race relationships.

Crime statistics show that African American women are more likely to be raped than White women. One reason has to do with the impoverished neighborhoods that proportionately more Black women than White women are forced to live in, and the generally higher levels of violence that accompany conditions of poverty. Statistics indicate that low-income African American women are the most likely to be raped. This sexual violence against Black women is, in the words of Audre Lorde, "a disease striking the heart of Black nationhood, and silence will not make it disappear."

Increasingly, however, African American feminists are encouraging others in their community to speak up about their abuse. *Ms.* editor Marcia Gillespie is among those who hope that African American women will hold their men "accountable for [their] everyday acts of incest, battery, rape, domestic violence and sexual harassment." She also maintains that those African American women who do speak up about sexual violence at the hands of Black men must stop being turned into "pariahs," as happened to Desiree Washington, the young Black woman who brought the charges of sexual assault against Tyson.

As Gillespie's remarks make clear, rape is by no means the only issue of sexual violence that needs to be addressed by the African American community. Incest, battering, domestic violence, and harassment also terrorize women. Again, it is mostly White feminists who have brought much of the needed attention to these areas. But in articulating concerns about sexual violence, White feminists have missed an opportunity to bridge the cultural gap between themselves and Black women; they have not always been sensitive to how the issues may affect those who are African American. For example, when White women first raised sexual harassment as a problem in the workplace, they focused nearly exclusively on its occurrence in white-collar jobs—the kind of jobs that middle-class White women were starting to occupy. They virtually ignored the long history of sexual abuse and harassment of those in domestic service—the kind of work that was traditionally performed by mostly African American women.

The same inequality of attention hinders discussion of domestic violence. White feminists generally see the issue in terms of an imbalance of power between men and women, while African American women see domestic violence growing out of racial oppression. This difference is evident in the trial of O. J. Simpson. The majority of White women claim to be color blind in their reactions to the case. Nicole was a wife apparently battered by a man who held the purse strings. In stark contrast, African American women see race as central to the trial, believing that whether O. J. Simpson is innocent or guilty, the media blitz that followed his arrest would not have been nearly as great had he been White or been married to a woman of his own race.

That women of European and African descent have such different takes shows how important it is that White and Black women recognize and acknowledge their different perceptions and reactions to events like this. Each group has something to gain from listening to the other.

Prostitution and pornography are two other areas involving women's sexual images and exploitation that are magnified by race. White feminists took the lead in arguing for better protection of women in the sex industry and documenting the harmful effects of pornography, but African American feminists, including Alice Walker and bell hooks, have also been active in pointing out the ways in which issues of race and sex collide.

That racial inequality exists in the sex industries can hardly be disputed. One indication is the racial makeup of the women who are prostitutes. Becoming a prostitute is not a career that a young woman aspires to, nor is it something that just happens to anyone. Nearly every prostitute has had a prior history of sexual abuse. When this history is combined with little formal education or professional job training—conditions that exist more frequently among African American women than White women, the result is a disproportionate number of Black women walking the streets. According to statistics compiled by the Women's Action Coalition, 40 percent of all street prostitutes are women of color.

Arrests and conviction rates are even more biased by race. An estimated 50 percent of prostitutes rounded up by the police are Black, and an estimated 85 percent of all prostitutes sentenced to jail are women of color. Race differences in arrest records also mean that when African American prostitutes later try to get out of the business, they are plagued more heavily by their past than are their White counterparts.

White prostitutes are less likely to work the streets, where most arrests for soliciting occur. Compared with Black prostitutes, White prostitutes do more escort servicing, which pays better and is considered relatively prestigious. Yet even when White prostitutes and Black prostitutes do work side by side on the street, White prostitutes make more money. One reason is that when a White john picks up a prostitute—and most johns are White—he calls less attention to himself when he walks away with a woman who is White. As a result, White prostitutes are more frequent flyers. As one Black prostitute angrily put it, "White whores get paid way more than Black whores and we turn better tricks." When a prostitute named Blanca worked the streets, some of the Black prostitutes resented her simply for being White. To get them to like her, Blanca had to find ways to lessen the racial tension. "After I showed the Black women that I was not going to 'georgia' [steal] their man, they would relax with me, and perhaps we could even become friends. But for some Black women, there was always that mistrust for me just because my skin was white."

The pornography industry is another area where racial inequality explosively combines with sexual inequality to exploit and debase women. Psychologists Gloria Cowan and Robin Campbell, analyzing pornographic videos in a 1994 study, concluded that blatant racism exists in the sex industry. Cowan and Campbell set out to explore whether there were race differences in the kinds of sexual acts that Whites and Blacks were asked to perform. Four coders analyzed twenty interracial videos. They discovered that Black women were subordinated more and subjected to greater physical and nonphysical aggression than White women. One video in particular, *Let Me Tell 'Ya 'Bout Black Chicks,* shocked Cowan and Campbell. It portrayed an African American woman willfully having sex with two White men in KKK hoods, who enter her bedroom window after observing her masturbating to gospel music. Such racist images perpetuate the myths handed down from the time of slavery. As Alice Walker put it, in writing about pornography in her 1984 book *You Can't Keep a Good Woman Down,* "Where white women are depicted as human bodies if not beings, black women are depicted as shit."

As White and Black women increase their efforts to bring an end to sexual violence, perhaps they will find that issues of race and culture will lead them to fight more of their battles together. For example, White and Black female activists worked together to denounce the practice of female genital mutilation in parts of Africa. White women can offer their support on the issue, but they risk coming across as racist if they try on their own to stop it. Ultimately, this is a topic that must involve women of African descent, as well. Ironically, even Alice Walker, who has done so much to raise awareness of female genital mutilation, has been criticized by some African leaders for interfering in the traditions of those on another continent. But instead of discouraging women from speaking out and presenting their views as a united front, such criticisms should only remind Black and White women that their different reactions and perspectives help to counter criticism along the lines of race or politics.

There are many such arenas in which White and Black women can work —and fight—together. Only by doing so can they hope to bring an end to attitudes and beliefs that severely limit women's sexual expression and freedom.

Chapter Five

Making Friends:

Relationships on the Campus, in the Workplace, and Beyond

I used to envy the "colorblindness" which some liberal, enlightened, white people were supposed to possess . . . But I no longer believe that "colorblindness"—if it even exists—is the opposite of racism; I think it is, in this world, a form of naivete and mere stupidity. It implies that I would look at a black woman and see her as white, thus engaging in white solipsism to the utter erasure of her particular reality.

—*Adrienne Rich, "Disloyal to Civilization,"*
Lies, Secrets, and Silences, *1979*

White women are beginning to examine their relationships to Black women, yet often I hear them wanting only to deal with little colored children across the roads of childhood, the beloved nursemaid, the occasional second-grade classmate—those tender memories of what was once mysterious and intriguing or neutral.

—*Audre Lorde, "The Uses of Anger:*
Women Responding to Racism,"
Sister Outsider, *1984*

For African American and White women who never interacted as children, attending college and sharing dormitory rooms may provide a crash course in getting to know women of the other race. For women who didn't go to college or who attended schools where students were predominantly of the same racial background, the workplace may be the site of their first cross-race female relations. For still other women, sustained interracial relations may not develop until they meet as neighbors or as members of a political, religious, or social organization. But wherever it is that White and Black women first come into regular contact, some will be able to form lasting friendships, while others will run into conflict, hampered in their ability to get along by swirling undercurrents of racial inequality and societal segregation.

Higher Education, Past and Present

During the nineteenth century, the majority of institutions of higher learning were carefully segregated, not only by race, but also by sex. With the exception of a small number of students attending coeducational land grant universities in the West, and progressive, private liberal arts colleges such as Oberlin, in Ohio, most White male students received their higher education at one institution, and the women and Blacks fortunate enough even to go to college got their education at another. For working- and middle-class White women, there were private and state colleges, where most were trained to become teachers, nurses, or secretaries. Wealthier White women attended expensive private women's schools, such as Vassar, Bryn Mawr, and Smith, where many received training in the arts in preparation for their future roles as wives to successful men. Middle-class Black women attended historically Black private and public colleges and universities, the most prestigious of which was Spelman College, in Atlanta.

As the twentieth century unfolded, educational opportunities for women of both races expanded dramatically. With the country's engagement in two major world wars, and many of its young men serving in the armed forces, many all-male institutions were forced to admit women in order to survive financially. Other prestigious private universities, like Harvard and Yale, and even some of the more exclusive state schools, like the University of Virginia, which never suffered from shortages of qualified male applicants, were finally forced by new legislation, Supreme Court rulings, and the changing mores in the sixties and seventies to admit women. The most important bill passed by Congress at that time was the 1972 Equal Education Act, which made it illegal for any institution of higher learning that received federal funding to discriminate on the basis of sex. Today, nearly all public and private colleges and universities in this country are coeducational.

It was after World War II that previously all-White colleges and universities began to desegregate by race. The initial push to do so came from the landmark 1954 Supreme Court decision of *Brown* v. *Board of Education,* which overturned Jim Crow laws and racial segregation in education. The Court held that compulsory segregation in public education denied Black children equal protection under the law, and all schools were directed to desegregate immediately. Subsequent Court decisions further instructed all public educational facilities, state colleges and universities as well as private institutions that received federal funding, to comply with this mandate. The Civil Rights Movement, too, did much to change attitudes about race. By the late nineteen-fifties and early sixties, many private and state-run all-White colleges and universities, even without the Court rulings, were beginning aggressively to recruit qualified African American students and faculty.

The actual process of desegregation was painfully slow, however, so it was not until the early seventies that significant numbers of college students were first faced with the prospect of sharing living space with someone of a different race. Before then, at those predominantly White colleges and universities that had already begun to desegregate, African American students were typically placed in dorm rooms by themselves. During the sixties, college housing officials surveyed all incoming White students on their racial attitudes so that only the most progressive among them would be assigned rooms with Black students. Ironically, at the same time, in the wake of the more militant Black Power movement, a growing number of Black college students, both male and female, began demanding separate housing on predominantly White college campuses.

Today, it is illegal to make dormitory or room assignments by race, and all incoming freshmen and transfer students are informed on housing application materials that the school does not discriminate on the basis of race, sex, religious affiliation, and, in most places, sexual orientation. To avoid even the suspicion that race is a factor in room placement, questions about racial identification are carefully omitted on survey forms, while matters like smoking, drinking, and study habits are assessed in great detail. Although some housing applications may still include such vague questions as "What do you want in a roommate?" as a way to tap potential racial prejudices, in general the concern has shifted away from White students who might be uncomfortable in having to live with someone who is Black, and toward African American students who would suffer from being forced to live with someone who is racist. Also, some colleges and universities continue to offer separate living quarters for African American students who desire them, in the guise of "special interest housing." That is, those students, including White students, who wish to live with others interested in, for example, African American studies, can check an appropriate box. In general, though, most schools simply take the position that an important part of a student's total educational experience is learning to get along with persons from different backgrounds, and therefore most room assignments are made randomly. While this makes for an interesting mix of students suddenly thrown together for the first time, it also creates the potential for intense racial conflict.

To help diffuse racial tensions before they begin, first-year students at all colleges today are required to attend lectures on multiculturalism and respect for human diversity. Brought together in huge auditoriums, or divided into small focus groups, White and Black students from rural to urban America are encouraged to get along. With some, the message seems to take, but others greet the lectures with skepticism. In theory, colleges and universities are supposed to be models of tolerance, but lately they have become spawning grounds for racial tensions. White students see varying admission standards for White and Black students, and cry "reverse discrimination," and, increasingly, African American students, tired of defending often lower test scores on what they see as culturally biased admission tests, step up demands to segregate from White-dominated campus culture. Such volatile issues are usually omitted from multicultural orientation lectures, however, where the emphasis is placed on togetherness rather than on the issues that divide Black and White students.

Ironically, another topic typically left out of human diversity talks is gender—specifically, how gender and race interact. The unspoken assumption on campuses seems to be that men and women respond in the same way to racial conflict. While in some cases this assumption may hold true, in many others it does not. Research suggests that men and women often have different interpersonal communication styles, especially during same-sex interactions. In general, men tend to be more direct with each other, to the point of making what may seem to be rude or even hostile comments regarding issues of race. But at least, through such communication, they have a chance to clear the air. Women, however, seem to avoid as long as possible mentioning that there is "an elephant in the room." That is, most will make the polite effort of pretending everyone is racially the same and that the interactions between racially mixed groups of women are perfectly fine. But unspoken racial differences have a way of festering, sometimes erupting into major conflict with seemingly little provocation.

Men, through sports and other competitive activities, such as playing pool and computer games, have an outlet for releasing pent-up racial tensions. During a pickup game of basketball, for example, a White man may yell at a Black roommate, who has just missed an important shot, "You shoot like a White boy." Such a comment serves not only to acknowledge their racial differences but also to defuse them. The African American roommate may, in turn, save face by responding with something like, "Yeah, well, at least I can dunk, White boy." While certainly not all men successfully work out their racial differences in this way, the strategy seems to work quite well for those who do.

In comparison, women have fewer activities together in which to release racial tensions. Many women still narrowly judge both themselves and others according to how pretty and popular they are. College years, especially, are a time of intense courtship for many. Even a woman who excels in the classroom, or is a star athlete, may not, unless she is also physically attractive, garner much admiration from other women, whatever her race. The one place where women expect to address their looks in privacy is in the sanctity of their own dorm room, the very place where they are suddenly thrown together with women from different cultural backgrounds. Here they are forced to witness for the first time each other's intimate daily grooming rituals. Most women look at dorm life as a chance to relax and enjoy life outside the stress of the classroom. But in a racially mixed environment, differences in grooming habits can create unwelcome tension. As Ladonna M. Sanders, a former residence hall director on a racially mixed urban campus, says of the reactions of some African American female students, "After dealing with issues of race all day, the last thing you want to hear when you come back to your dorm room—your new home—is 'Why do you do this and that to your hair?' When I'm home, I want to be on vacation from race."

As we saw in the chapter on beauty, a continuing area of misunderstand-

ing among African American and European American women has to do
with the textural differences in their hair. Hair is, by and large, a uniquely
feminine preoccupation. Along with skin color, hair texture is one of the
more obvious physical manifestations of race. But unlike skin color, hair can
be altered by special grooming techniques—heat and chemicals—to conform with our culture's generally White standards of beauty.

According to Sanders, questions and complaints about hair are among the
earliest raised by women sharing dormitory space. African American
women are frequently barraged with questions about their grooming, as if
the way they groom their hair is not the norm. Tensions over grooming
habits are further compounded by the fact that many African American
women first begin to confront and grapple with their minority status during
their college years, when they actively reject European standards of beauty.
The following comment by an African American woman student named
Tara reflects the resentment that can develop:

White girls are always tripping on Black hair. I used to have to tell my
White roommate to butt out. She was so fascinated by my hair and always wondering how I could go two weeks without washing it. I remember one time hearing her on the phone telling her mom how
Black people can go two whole weeks without washing their hair. I
wasn't on the phone telling my mom how when White people wash
their hair it smells like a wet dog.

African American women are particularly sensitive about, and offended
by, White women's complaints about their use of the hot comb. During the
first few weeks of college an African American student named LaRay assumed that she and her White roommate were getting along well. But
unknown to LaRay, her White roommate despised the smell of "burned
hair" from LaRay's daily use of the hot comb. One night things reached a
boiling point when LaRay innocently plugged in her electric hot comb, only
to find herself the target of a sudden, malicious verbal assault. Another
Black student, Brigette, who attends a small suburban university in the
Midwest, had a similar run-in with her White roommate, who asked, "Why
do you have to burn your hair every two weeks?" Later she griped that
Brigette's hot comb was making the suite smell like an "incinerator." "She
would make me so mad," recalled Brigette. "I can't help that she grew up in

'Honkeyville' Iowa and her mamma never took her around Black folks. We had more arguments about my hair."

Both White and Black college women benefit from being educated about cultural differences, and sensitized to the concerns and values of each other. Of course, not every question can be answered in a public forum, and there will be times when racial issues will need to be privately discussed. Sanders feels that roommates should open discussion of racial issues by first getting permission to ask some things that might "move the other beyond her usual comfort zone." And if the time is not good for a sensitive discussion of race, roommates must learn to indicate that, and to respect each other's wishes to wait.

Many African American women hold a part of themselves in abeyance when sharing a room with a White woman, fearful of the day their roommate may say or do something racist. One African American woman, for example, invited her brother, who was a doctor and of whom she was quite proud, up to her dorm room to show him around. Her White roommate saw the brother's beeper, and after he left she asked, "Is he a drug dealer?" —which understandably infuriated the African American student.

Of course not all White women are so naïve or insensitive. But ironically it is often those White women trying their hardest to be friendly who inadvertently cause the greatest friction. After all, how do you tell someone who is well-meaning that she is acting out of ignorance? It was exactly this dilemma that faced Mokita, an African American college student, when she found herself the only Black woman assigned to live in a town house dormitory suite with seven White women during their year of college. It took about four months for Mokita and her roommates to move beyond the stage of "let's avoid talking about race." Then they went through an awkward phase during which some of the women made inevitable blunders in their efforts to connect with Mokita. One woman began greeting Mokita with "Hey, homegirl, what's up?" Another confided to Mokita that she had been told by friends that "she had a body like a Black girl." As time went on, the White woman began to repeat the comment in a giggling way as justification for borrowing Mokita's clothes. A third woman brought Mokita a newspaper article on male rap artists, which at first Mokita appreciated, until her suitemate pointed to the picture accompanying the article and asked, "Why do Black men wear their hair like that?" To lump all Black men into one sweeping category infuriated Mokita. "Not *all* Black men do wear their hair that way," she replied. Yet Mokita realized that her White roommates were trying to understand her and Black culture, and she learned to forgive their sometimes rude or woefully naïve questions and comments. Unfortunately, African American women are more often the victims of such racial ignorance than their White roommates are. Since they grow up in a society that is predominantly White, they are more familiar with White culture, fashions, and mores than White women are of Black culture.

Another source of tension between the women is the very fact that proportionately more White women than Black women grow up assuming that they will attend college. Money is less often an obstacle to White female students; the financial means to pursue higher education through savings, loans, and other sources are more frequently found for middle-class White women. And if such women decide not to attend college, there is a greater expectation that they will either get married to men who can support them financially, or that they will be able to find paying jobs that don't require a college degree. But the chance for many African American women to go to college is still considered special, not something to be taken for granted. This difference in opportunity and attitude toward college makes some African American women angry. In response to a general question about women and issues of race, feminist scholar Barbara Smith commented:

> An example I can think of and which drives me crazy is the arrogance that some white women display about "choosing" not to finish school, you know, "downward mobility." But what they think is that they don't have to worry about being asked, "Do you have a degree," and then being completely cut out of whole range of jobs and opportunity if they don't. Race is a concept of having to be twice as qualified, twice as good to go half as fast.

In *Talking Back: Thinking Feminist, Thinking Black,* bell hooks notes other differences in attitudes between White and Black women on the college campus. For hooks, White women are more used to ignoring or brushing aside the academic humiliations that some professors seem to inflict on students. African American women, who have had to resist and challenge all their lives those who would deny their academic potential, are more apt to take such humiliations personally. For example, a White woman may casually warn a Black woman that even though a certain male professor claims his class is too hard for women, she should just ignore him and take the course anyhow. To the White woman, the professor seems sexist and unfair. But to the Black woman, the professor seems to be directly attacking her competence because she is female *and* Black. As hooks puts it, "Those of us who were coming from underprivileged class backgrounds, who were black, often were able to attend college only because we had consistently defied those who attempted to make us believe we were smart but not 'smart enough.'"

Unfortunately, some students arrive on college campuses less academically prepared than others, and this is more often true of students who have attended underfunded public, inner-city high schools. Also, some of the best and brightest Black high school graduates today are choosing to attend historically Black colleges and universities. As a result, fewer qualified Black students are left in the recruitment pool to meet minority goals at many predominantly White colleges and universities, with the result that such schools sometimes accept Black students whose grade-point averages and standardized test scores are lower than those of White students. This difference in qualifications is one factor responsible for the disparity in graduation rates. Recent figures show that 66 percent of White students graduate within five years, but only 27 percent of Black students do. This difference also means that, in order to "catch up" to the other students, some African American women have to devote more time to studying than their White female counterparts do, another factor that can breed racial hostility.

It was this kind of tension that dissolved the potential for friendship between Elaine, a White New York Italian American woman who attended the University of North Carolina in the mid-eighties, and Wendy, her first-year roommate, a Black woman who was the best musician from her eastern North Carolina high school. Wendy had come to Chapel Hill to play in the university band. Both women were proud to be attending one of the South's best universities. Initially the two got along well; at one point Wendy told Elaine, "Oh, you're Italian. I don't even think of Italians as White people. They're more like us!" Elaine realized the comment was a genuine attempt to bridge the cultural gap between them. But as the school year progressed and differences in their academic abilities became apparent, the relationship began to deteriorate. Elaine thrived at Chapel Hill, winning a competitive scholarship to study abroad, while Wendy found her classes intimidating, and started to stay away from them. She decided against trying out for the marching band because the other musicians seemed so much better than she was. More and more, Wendy just sat in their room, watching soap operas. Elaine found herself bouncing back and forth between trying to figure out what she could do to help Wendy and being angry at her for giving up. Wendy went from academic probation to eventual dismissal, and the two never spoke again.

Nowhere is the tension greater between Black and White college women than when it comes to the age-old college tradition of "partying." While the media sometimes leave the impression that Blacks drink more alcohol and do more drugs than Whites, research confirms that the opposite is true, especially for women. Many African American college women come to resent White women for getting away with socializing activities that are stereotypically—and negatively—associated with them. An accountant named Lynda, an African American who graduated from college in the eighties, remembered one White coed who lived across the dormitory hall from her.

> GiGi was her name and gin was her game. This White girl drank so much, or "partied," as she would call it, that I'm surprised she made it to her junior year. Nearly every night she had a flurry of activity going on in her apartment. Music, booze, and men, many of them Black. All night you could hear music going. Eventually she had to drop out, but even then I recall thinking how unfair it was that the Black girls were always seen as acting irresponsibly, and how much trouble they would have gotten in had it been any of us acting like that.

Mokita, whom we introduced earlier, was similarly taken aback by the amount of drinking and partying that her seven White suitemates did. "Even on week nights, these women always seemed up for a party."

College sports, too, can be a source of conflict between Black and White women. In general, a woman's sense of identity is less centered on her athletic abilities than a man's is. However, for those women who do play varsity sports, an athletic identity is very important, and certain racial assumptions, like the one that Black women are stronger or faster than White women, can cause conflict. According to a White student named Lyn, who plays both volleyball and basketball, some Black female athletes have a hard time accepting athletically gifted White women. "The Black women don't think we are as tough as they are, and that's just ridiculous." Lyn found that the Black women who are on athletic scholarships look down on White women who are not, making such comments as, "You White girls are here only because your Daddy supports you." Yet in team sports, Lyn says, when a team wins, racial tensions all but fade away. Indeed, at the annually televised NCAA women's basketball tournament, White and Black members of the winning teams often hug and cry on each other's shoulders.

How well Black and White athletes get along depends to a degree on which sport they are playing. Sports like basketball, and track are more "Black identified," and even at predominantly White colleges it is not uncommon to find more Black women than White women participating in them. These are also the very sports in which Black women are seen as having innate superiority, sometimes to the annoyance of White teammates. But in more "White identified" sports, like tennis, gymnastics, golf, and swimming, in which more White women than Black women usually participate, race is not seen as a factor in the White women's dominance, and perhaps for that reason there appear to be fewer overt racial tensions. Tina S., the only African American woman on her school's tennis team, could recall only one racial incident in the four years during which she played. And that incident took place after their team lost in a tournament against an all-Black school. All day long the matches were heated, and at one point the Black male coach of the other school even referred to one of Tina's teammates as a "bitch." Later, in the van on the way home, his comment triggered a fight between Tina and one of her teammates, who claimed, "Blacks just use more profanity than Whites." The sweeping generalization angered Tina, and when she challenged her teammate, the White woman defensively replied, "I'm not racist and I'm tired of being told that I am."

Such conflicts are not uncommon. Inside and outside athletics, some White women complain that it is impossible to be friendly with Black women on campus because they are so ready to call Whites racist. Others claim that it is the Black women, not the White women, who want to keep their distance. And it is true that African American women do sometimes face peer pressure from other African Americans—especially from men—to avoid befriending White women.

Despite such pressures, a surprising number of White and Black women do become friends during their college years. Mokita, even with the ups and downs of having seven White women suitemates, now says of the experience, "I loved it. It wasn't all roses, peaches, and cream. There were times when we were angry at each other, but in the end it was a sisterlike thing. None of us would trade it, and for the most part, we did get along well." Another African American college student commented, "Such relationships definitely help to break down racial stereotypes. When you get older, it is harder to do that." Many White women who miss out on developing cross-race friendships during their college years may come to regret it. One such student is Page A., who graduated from Virginia Tech in 1994.

> During the summer before my freshmen year, I worried myself sick about who my college roommate was going to be, convinced that she was not White because her name sounded suspiciously Black. Well, "Shona" turned out to be White, but we still didn't get along, and by the end of the first semester, I had to request another roommate. It's funny—some of my high school friends with the same prejudices as me were assigned Black roommates, and they ended up getting along really well, even staying together all four years. I bet they'll even keep in touch in the future. Now, I'm really sorry that I never got to know even one Black woman the entire time I was in school. I finally realized that skin color is less important than sharing values and fundamental attitudes about the important things in life.

And cross-race college relationships can be lasting friendships. African American writer Audrey Edwards has been "tracking birthdays" with her White college girlfriend Jo for twenty-five years. The two first met at the University of Washington during the sixties, and were quick to realize that they had a lot in common. In an article entitled "Sisters Under the Skin" for the *New York Times Magazine,* Audrey described their friendship:

> Race, in some ways, has mattered the least in our friendship. And then, of course, in other ways, it has mattered most. Being black on big white college campuses in the mid-60's was not without cachet, even as it isolated those of us in the first wave of integration. I always knew Jo thought it was "cool" to have black friends. In those days it was. But what I would continue to love about Jo is that she never stopped thinking it was cool to have black friends.

More than just a meeting place for students, the campus is also a place where women of different races come together as students and professors, as administrators and colleagues, within the same departments as well as across larger academic fields. Cross-race work relationships that develop at universities are shaped by different forces from those of society at large, perhaps because the academy is the only institution where the seeking of truth and knowledge is valued over the making of money. Within the rarefied atmosphere of academia, the uncomfortable and unmentionable truths often are spoken in the name of academic freedom, and unacceptably racist or intolerant remarks are censored in the name of political correctness. And somewhere in the middle of those competing high ideals, African American and European American women try to "work it out."

Two departments where emotions tend to run particularly strong are women's studies and African American studies, both of which grew out of the political activism of the sixties and early seventies. These two interdisciplinary areas have breathed new life into many campuses in the form of innovative course offerings and scholarship. Yet they are also easy targets for criticism. African American women enrolled in women's studies classes often feel that the course material is too Eurocentric, while White women taking African American studies classes sometimes feel that they are blatantly ignored in class, or are graded more harshly, simply because they are not Black.

Despite such complaints, White women and Black women brought together in the two departments may come to appreciate for the first time each other's cultural strengths and differences. In recent years, women's studies programs, in particular, have done much to meet the goals of multiculturalism in the curriculum and racial diversity among the faculty. One African American student in her thirties, Lynn R., discussed the fondness she developed for her White women's studies instructor:

> My first semester back in school, I fell in love with this White woman who taught me psychology of women. I ended up taking every other course she offered, and even switched my major to women's studies largely because of her influence. So many things started to come together for me in her classes. I began to realize how much of what I had been taught to believe was true by members of my own community was not necessarily so, and in some cases, also not good for me as a woman. Even now, whenever I see this fortysomething White woman walking across campus, I give her a big bear hug, which I think both pleases and embarrasses her.

There are also those White female students who become intensely attached to their African American female professors. Even here, however, experiences differ. Some young White women, who see their own lives as too privileged, turn to older African American women for their authenticity of experience, thereby romanticizing the instructors. Other White female college students confess to feeling nervous around their Black female professors, afraid of saying something that might smack of political incorrectness. A White woman named Sandi commented:

> I learned so much from this African American woman who taught a course on race and families. She helped me better than anyone else to really understand the subtleties of racism. But I always felt so tongue-tied in her presence. I never got over the feeling that she was going to pounce on me—you know, just waiting for me to say something ignorant about Blacks—I mean African Americans—so that she could correct me.

Another former student stated:

> I once had this really radical Black woman for a teacher, and she was always making examples of the White women in class about how racist we all were. For example, once I made the mistake of referring to this White girlfriend of mine "as a real American beauty with girl-next-door-kind of looks." Well, the words were barely out of my mouth when my teacher accused me of being racist because that kind of description always precludes women who are Black. Maybe so, but it's just an expression. I don't think that I deserved to be chewed out in the front of the whole class for saying something like that.

Some White faculty members, too, admit to having an unsettled feeling in their stomachs whenever they interact with powerful African American women on campus, especially administrators. In one instance, a White female associate professor, at a midsize university on the West Coast, served as the acting dean of her college before an African American woman was brought in to replace her. At first the White professor was thrilled that a woman of color was hired as the dean. But gradually her feelings began to change. "I came to realize that our new dean was using the fact that she was female and Black to control and intimidate the other, mostly White, faculty members," she said. She elaborated on her growing discontent:

I can't tell you how many times this Black woman works into the conversation her own personal history of growing up poor, and all the racial obstacles she had to overcome to get where she is today. Now, I don't doubt for a moment that everything she says is true; it's just that she then uses all that stuff as some sort of license to do only what she wants to, without input from others. Anyone who dares to challenge her gets interrupted and basically shot down, and that's just not the way things are done at our school. While I do still appreciate what this feisty woman has done to shake up the White male establishment, she is unfortunately such a tyrant that I seriously doubt that her contract will be renewed.

The traditional White male hierarchy is noticeably intact at most universities today, making it especially difficult for African American women faculty and administrators to assert themselves. With both race and gender working to their disadvantage, African American women often feel they cannot rely on a low-key approach and at the same time command respect. For example, a tenured White male professor can readily grant permission to students wanting to turn in term papers late without incurring any loss of respect, but an African American female faculty member, especially a young, untenured one, may not feel free to do the same. She may fear that if she relaxes her standards for even a moment, her authority in the classroom will be challenged. The same holds true for many African American female administrators; sometimes they feel they have to bellow just to be heard. The resulting difference in interpersonal style can strain relations, especially for African American and European American women functioning at different levels in the university hierarchy.

Within the politically charged atmosphere of the university today, relations between White and Black women at all levels can suffer. One example is in course material. Because for so long the history and experiences of Blacks were all but ignored in research and course material, some African American women on college campuses have become territorial regarding which areas of study "belong" to them. White woman professors who dare to venture into those areas designated as "Black" can expect resistance. In her book *Segregated Sisterhood,* White feminist Nancie Caraway is critical of the way in which some Afrocentric female scholars dismiss their White female colleagues, even to the point of rendering "invisible a White woman who comes to a public lecture on a major campus to hear a Black professor speak about 'African Goddess Myths.'" Caraway claims that it is grossly unfair when more radical African American women professors characterize White women as "cultureless, parasitic on the literature, customs, food, and music of Third World people."

Co-author Midge Wilson of this book ran up against the cultural private property issue when she first began work on *The Color Complex*. One day, an African American female colleague pulled Midge aside and told her in no uncertain terms to get off the book, because "the topic of intraracial skin color discrimination belonged to African Americans." The words stung, not only because Midge had long been conducting scholarly research on colorism and was well versed in the field, but also because she was but one of the three authors, along with Kathy Russell and Ronald Hall, both of whom are Black.

Of course the majority of African American women on campus do not hold such territorial views about research, but the strident attitudes of a few can wreak havoc on a faculty. An African American female director for Northwestern University's Center on African American Studies recently discovered this when she made the "mistake" of inviting a White female professor from another university to speak. Although the White professor was doing research in an area of interest to many Blacks, the other African American faculty and students, on learning that the intended speaker was a White woman, balked, leaving the director in the embarrassing and awkward position of having to withdraw the invitation.

This political gerrymandering of courses and research topics may leave White female professors with the feeling that they can do no right. They are lambasted by Black faculty and students on campus for not doing enough research and not including enough course material on African American women, but when they do, they are criticized because they themselves are not Black. As Audre Lorde has observed, no one would dare question the appropriateness of a female professor teaching Molière when she is neither male nor French. Why, then, are women criticized when they teach courses and do research not derived from their own personal experiences?

Yet across the country there are also thousands of White and Black women who are warm and supportive colleagues. African American women are often heartened to discover that when it comes time for tenure and promotion, it is often White female colleagues who are among their staunchest supporters. As bell hooks herself once observed, "Racism and sexism do not always shape all experiences" on the college campus today.

The Workplace

Outside the university, tensions between African American and European American women are often shaped by different concerns. As in the university, though, only fairly recently have large numbers of White women and Black women worked side by side. Except for a brief time during World War II, when women of all races and classes joined together to support the war effort, most White women who worked either did so in large segregated work settings, whether offices and factories, or helped their husbands run small family-owned businesses, such as restaurants and farms. Before the 1970s, though, most middle-class White women did not expect to work their entire lives. Their ambitions were to marry and raise children, ultimately withdrawing from the paid workforce. In contrast, most Black women did expect to have to earn a living, even after marriage. They were not likely to be cushioned by the financial success of a husband. As far back as 1920, for example, 45 percent of single White women worked, compared with 58.8 percent of single Black women; a mere 6.5 percent of married European American women worked, while 32.5 percent of married African American did. To some extent, this trend continues, even at a time when most women want and expect paid employment. According to 1988 U.S. Bureau of the Census statistics, 55.3 percent of married White women are in the paid labor force, compared with 65.8 percent of married Black women.

Historically, poor White women, especially those who were married, felt stigmatized by having to work. The only group left between them and the absolute bottom social stratum were Black women. Thus, perhaps to preserve what little status they had, many refused to work beside Black women or to perform the same chores they did. This meant that when Black women went looking for employment, frequently the only jobs left for them were domestic service and the most unpleasant and numbing of factory jobs, jobs that working-class White women refused to take. While Black women stripped the tobacco from plants in hot and poorly ventilated rooms, White women packaged it elsewhere; while Black women pulled the candy out of hot ovens, White women wrapped it when cooled; while Black women greased and lifted the heavy pans in bakeries, White women made the batter and decorated the cakes; and while Black women washed soiled linens in damp basements, White women folded and counted the sheets upstairs. As

African American author Zora Neale Hurston wrote, in her 1937 novel, *Their Eyes Were Watching God,* "De nigger women is de mule un de world."

Even Black women who were well educated and able to enter the two primary professional occupations generally open to all college-trained women, nursing and teaching, rarely worked side by side with Whites. Until recently, most hospitals and schools were racially segregated, which also made it easier for management to pay White and Black teachers and nurses different salaries. For example, in the 1920s, Darlene Clark Hines reveals in her 1989 book, *Black Women in White,* the Commonwealth of Virginia paid its White nurses $125 per month at public hospitals, and paid its similarly trained Black nurses only $100.

Passage of Title VII of the 1964 Civil Rights Act, prohibiting discrimination in hiring, firing, promotion, and benefits "on the basis of race, color, religion, national origin, or sex," as well as both the women's and the civil rights movements, did much to open up employment opportunities for women. Now, at least in theory, all women, regardless of color, have legal access to some of the better-paying and more prestigious jobs previously unavailable to them. Sadly, however, more than thirty years after passage of this important legislation, widespread occupational sex segregation persists. An estimated 77 percent of women employed today still work as teachers, nurses, social workers, hairdressers, salesclerks, secretaries, receptionists, or in the food industry as waitresses, handlers, processors, and cafeteria workers. Because these jobs are held mostly by women and so often low-paying, they have been labeled "pink collar." More than anything else, it is this skewed distribution of women in the workforce that explains why women still earn only seventy cents to each dollar that men earn.

For African American women, the employment picture is even grimmer. According to 1989 U.S. Bureau of Labor statistics, White women earn an average of $318 a week compared with Black women's $238. While women of both races have experienced occupational gains in recent decades, for many Black women the shift has been only from low-status domestic or factory work to minimum-wage clerical work, while for many White women the shift has been from clerical work to more administrative and middle management positions. This persistent race difference in women's employment is reflected in a saying within the African American community: "Careers are what White women have; jobs are what Black women do."

As a result, Black women have not been as enthusiastic as White women in crediting the women's movement for recent career advancements. In fact, among those stuck in the lowest paying and most dead-end positions, real liberation would mean the economic freedom to quit working altogether and stay home to raise their children. There is a perception among many Black women that feminists' demands to be treated like a minority in the workplace have hurt the Black community. Plum positions that were once designated for African Americans, including many in the corporate sector, are now being filled by women who are White. To some Black women, it seems as though White women are eager to advance their own careers at the expense of women who are Black.

The truth is that Black women and White women are both deserving of greater occupational gains, and the career opportunities of one group should not be gained through the losses of the other. This "either or" stance serves to divide and conquer women, and ultimately deny them the right to work together and attain their full potential. But in a country where every major institution, financial, military, religious, educational, or political, is topheavy with men, particularly White men, it is difficult for women not to feel that they are competing against each other for advancement.

Corporate America is among the worse offenders in terms of promoting women into top positions. The wealthier the company, the less likely it is to have a woman in top management. A recent Korn/Ferry International survey found that among Fortune 1000 companies, less than 5 percent of the top executives and board members are female. Even in the nineties, the majority of women of either race who enter white-collar careers traditionally held by men will advance no further than middle management. Most will encounter the "glass ceiling"—the invisible and impenetrable barrier through which the successes of others can be viewed but not realized.

It is on this uneven playing field that many of today's best and brightest White and Black women meet and compete. Given their limited opportunities for promotion, it is no surprise that they conflict with one another. One clear example of the potential for conflict can be seen in the experiences of an African American lawyer named Sandrya and a White lawyer named Rebecca. As the only women hired one year at a midsize L.A. law firm, the two at first became friends, setting their sights on making partnership within the standard six-year review period. Whenever one was feeling low about her prospects, the other was always there to offer just the right words of encouragement. But as the time for review grew near, Rebecca and Sandrya found their words of support coming less easily. Each had come to worry that only one of them would make it, and each feared it would not be she. Sandrya was convinced that the firm was racist and would hold some perceived shortcoming against her as justification for letting her go; Rebecca was certain that the firm wanted to become more racially diverse and, given two women of roughly equal qualifications, would decide to keep the Black woman. Fortunately, both Sandrya and Rebecca were granted partnership. It was only then that they were able to resume their friendship.

Bebe Moore Campbell explored the tension between race and sex in the corporate sphere as part of the plot of her 1994 best-selling novel, *Brothers and Sisters*. Two women in middle management at two different departments in an L.A. bank, a White named Mallory and an African American named Esther, initially come together when a White male regional branch manager ogles and calls them both "honey." Esther teaches the more timid Mallory how to use her anger to confront men who dare to treat her in such demeaning fashion. Things get considerably more complicated, however, when a new Black male senior vice president sexually harasses Mallory. Esther, who develops an attraction for the new man, finds herself torn between wanting to protect someone of her race and wanting to support her friend Mallory.

Through the characters of Esther and Mallory, Campbell tackles a number of racial issues affecting women in the corporate workplace. Esther, who has an M.B.A., challenges Mallory, who does not, to think about the fact that African American women have to be twice as qualified to go half as far as White women. At one point, she tells her friend, "Mallory, there are white women with high school degrees who make more money than I do." In fact, statistics compiled by the Women's Action Coalition show that the average salary of a Black female college graduate in a full-time position is even less than that of a White male high school dropout.

African American scholar Letha A. Lee unearthed evidence of similar racial tension in her interviews with professional African American women. Several of the women complained that their higher education provided less job mobility and fewer salary raises than it did for White women. Others expressed distrust of White women's career ambitions, claiming that when rare positions in upper management do open up, White women always seemed to grab them first. As one Black woman put it, "There is no such thing as 'togetherness' with white women. The agendas they set and the jungle behavior they exhibit is strictly for their advantage." Another woman compared White women's management style with that of White men's:

When white women are placed in top-level management positions, they imitate white men. They make an all-out effort to expel the myth that women feel and men think. In top management, white women have no role models except men, so they become "unfeeling."

In fact, some White female managers think it necessary to be especially hard-nosed to offset male notions that they are too sensitive, weak, and passive to be effective leaders. Black women, long seen through racial stereotypes as stronger, tougher, and more assertive, would seem, at first glance, to have an advantage in the business world, where such attributes are valued. But such is not the case. African American women in corporate America are often penalized for being too aggressive, a view reflected by yet another African American woman interviewed by Lee.

Once we had a black woman in top management, but she was labeled "rigid," "aggressive," "strong." While employed here, this woman eliminated favoritism, equalized the staff, rewrote job descriptions, cast out the "old boy" network, and raised the caliber of the organization. If a woman is black, strong, and assertive, she is a threat to both white men and white women. This woman did not last long. She was fired, and white women assisted in the process.

In a 1993 paper entitled "Quadruple Jeopardy: Black, Female, Professional, and in Charge," African American psychologists Janet R. Brice-Baker and Beverly Greene claim that African American professionals in management positions continue to be hampered by stereotypes. If they act tough and assertive, they risk being labeled a Sapphire, the cantankerous character of "Amos 'n' Andy"; if they are nice and nurturing, they invoke images of Mammy. If they are not mammy-like, others act disappointed; if they are attractive, they become Jezebel and are blamed for inciting sexual harassment. Brice-Baker and Greene further claim that White women still balk at being supervised by women who are Black; they stated, "White women are more used to relating to Black women as members of the housekeeping staff, or as secretaries, than they are as bosses."

One of the most frustrating issues for many African American women in the corporate workplace remains White women's misconception that Black women have an advantage in their "two for one" status. Rebecca, the White lawyer mentioned above, held exactly this belief when she thought she wouldn't be granted partnership because Sandrya was both Black and female. Yet according to the results of a recent study, conducted by Audrey Murrell of the University of Pittsburgh School of Business, Black women, far from having an advantage in a "double minority" status, are less likely to get ahead than either Black men or White women. African American women trying to make it in White corporate America face not only the glass ceiling, but in many cases a "glass wall" in getting hired. Despite the popular belief that affirmative action policies give unfair advantages to Blacks in general, as of 1991 only 7.2 percent of Black women (and Black men) were executives, administrators, or managers in corporate America. This figure compares to 12 percent of White women in such jobs, and 14.7 percent of White men.

The reality remains that few women of either race experience great success in traditionally male White-collar jobs, and those who do are viewed as exceptional. Oddly, even being thought of as exceptional can be a source of conflict between European and African American women. While many White women in high power occupations take secret pleasure in being told that they are different from (that is, better than) most other women, Black women, as a group, despise being told that they are different from (better than) most other Blacks. One apparent reason for this difference is that Whites, in general, are raised with more sense of individuality; as a result, being told that they are better than others reinforces their feeling of personal achievement. African Americans, however, are generally raised with more of a collective identity, one reflecting their larger community; as a result, being told that they are better than other Blacks is insulting to other Blacks. Ellis Cose, an African American journalist and author, touched on the anger that this generates in many middle-class Blacks in corporate America today in *The Rage of a Privileged Class,* published in 1993. Cose described an incident in which an African American female scientist, who had been working for a year and a half at the National Research Council, mentioned to a White colleague who was also a friend that it was a shame there were so few other Blacks on staff. The White woman agreed wholeheartedly, adding, "Yes, it's too bad that there aren't more blacks like you." While the statement was meant as a compliment, to the African American scientist her White colleague really seemed to be saying that Blacks as a group lacked the intellect that she was lucky enough to possess. Unfortunately, in a country with a long history of racial inequality, what is viewed as complimentary by one group may be laden with racist implications for the other.

African American women also question why the onus always seems to always be on them to educate not only White men but also White women about racism. They feel it is exhausting and even risky always to be the bearer of such bad news in the workplace, and no professional Black woman wants to develop a reputation for being "overly sensitive" about issues of race. Bebe Moore Campbell touches on this issue in *Brothers and Sisters* when Mallory expresses her surprise on learning that Esther is so angry about racism. "But why do you sound so bitter? . . . Look at you. You've done so well." In response, Esther attempts to explain to Mallory why she remains angry and why affirmative action is still necessary:

> You think America is a meritocracy? You've had affirmative action for white folks ever since this country got started. Every time a black person couldn't get the job because he was black, that was affirmative actions for white people . . . So hell, yeah, I want some affirmative action for black people. I want some jobs reserved for me. I want some prime real estate reserved for me. I want spots in the best schools set aside for me. I want the Justice Department to bend the law my way.

To survive in traditional White male work climates, African American women must learn to pick and choose their battles. For example, when a White female supervisor told Raquel, an African American medical sales representative, that her dialect was better than that of other Blacks, Raquel informed her boss that dialect does not necessarily relate to intelligence, and to assume that it does unfairly dismisses those Blacks who don't necessarily speak like her. But Raquel has thus far kept to herself the seething resentment she feels over the way her boss solicits her opinion about new job applicants only when they are Black, and never when they are White.

Yet White women in the corporate ranks say that it is exhausting for them to be constantly on guard in front of Black female colleagues for fear of being called a racist. A White woman named Karen, who is a manager at a major computer firm, began hearing complaints from customers about the communication skills of an African American woman colleague named Alice. Karen decided to try to help Alice by discussing what she had heard so that Alice wouldn't get fired. After their talk, however, Alice went to someone higher up in the company, claiming that Karen was racist because she didn't like the way Black people spoke. Another White woman, Maureen, an editor at a video production house, similarly found herself being accused of racism by one of her Black female co-workers after taking a White male client on a tour of the company's facilities. When Maureen opened the door to an editing room, she discovered a Black female colleague eating lunch there. This was common practice; many employees took lunch and coffee breaks in unused editing rooms. When the client expressed concern about disturbing someone, Maureen casually commented, "Oh, it's okay. She's just having lunch." What Maureen didn't know, however, was that the remark triggered deep feelings about the assumed invisibility of Black domestic workers. The next thing Maureen knew, she was being told to develop more racial sensitivity—ironically, by a White female supervisor.

While there is no question that some White women in the corporate workplace are, consciously or unconsciously, prejudiced, there are also Black female employees who hide behind allegations of racism to insulate themselves from criticism. In social psychology, this behavioral strategy is referred to as self-protective, and its use is not limited to African Americans. Research shows that members of stigmatized groups, whether they are Black, Latino, gay, or persons with physical disabilities and facial disfigurements, often learn to hold on to a sense of self-esteem by continually attributing life's setbacks to the prejudices of others. In fact, not to adopt such a strategy could be devastating for such individuals. However, overreliance on the self-protective strategy is not healthy, either. In one study demonstrating its effect, Black students received negative criticism from a White evaluator about a paper they had written. The criticism lowered self-esteem only when the students were led to believe that the evaluator did not know their race. In other words, when the students thought that the White evaluator knew they were Black, they attributed the criticism to prejudice, and not to their own inadequacies as writers. Unfortunately, in relying on self-protective strategies, stigmatized individuals may miss opportunities to learn what it is that they are failing to do correctly, and what it is that they could do to improve themselves.

These are but some of the problems faced by women of different races in corporate America. Actually, many White and Black women in blue-collar jobs face similar concerns. Both are often distinct minorities in the workplace, and remain clustered in the least prestigious and lowest-paying positions of their chosen field. And whether they work in a factory or pour cement at a construction site, they know that only a limited number of women will be able to rise above the low-paying jobs.

Even women who own their own businesses can run into conflict with other businesswomen over the issue of race, especially in the awarding of government contracts to minority- and women-owned firms. While most Whites believe that African Americans unfairly benefit from programs that set aside certain percentages of government business to minority-owned firms, statistics show in fact that it is White women who have benefited the most from these programs. For example, in 1994 the Illinois Minority and Female Business Enterprise Program awarded $140 million to White businesswomen and only $21.6 million to Black businesswomen. Of course, there are many more White women than Black women in the population, and thus the argument can be made that disproportionately more Black women than White women are getting these state funds. Yet few African American women see it that way. Many believe that White women are unfairly claiming minority status and "stealing" business away from discriminated-against racial groups.

For the majority of women who work with other women in pink-collar jobs, issues of race are often somewhat different. Unlike entrepreneurs, or women engaged in white- or blue-collar employment, pink-collar women are often supervised by other women. And, predictably, more White women than Black women become supervisors, occupying proportionately more of the better paying and higher status pink-collar positions.

The color gap persists in large part because proportionately more Black women continue to enter the workplace with less education and fewer skills than White women. It is primarily this difference in educational background that creates the often two-tiered pink-collar work environment for White and Black women. For example, approximately 9 percent of clerical workers are African American, yet they represent a full 25 percent of file clerks, the lowest paying and most routine of secretarial work; only 7 percent of all registered nurses are African American, but Black women represent a full 31 percent of hospital aides, the most custodial and least prestigious of all nursing responsibilities. In such environments, race problems are bound to develop.

Many White women report difficulties in supervising Black women. Ann L., a White nurse practitioner, is director of a nursing home in Chicago, where she finds herself constantly struggling with this issue. Some of the Black women Ann L. oversees are nurses' aides who are attempting to get off welfare for the first time in their lives. Although Ann L. is supportive of these women in their efforts to improve their lot in life, she feels compromised by their frequent requests that she lie when called by the public aid office. The Black women typically want Ann L. to say that they are working fewer hours than they actually are, because if they work too many hours they will lose their family coverage. Ann L. finds herself vacillating between sympathy with the women's financial plight and anger at their not working harder to get off government aid altogether.

> These women need jobs, but they are being told, in effect, "What you do is not worth being paid a decent wage." So I give them slack, but on the other hand, isn't it racist not to hold other people to the same standards that you hold yourself? Sometimes I think I'm not as good a supervisor as I could be because of my own fear of being racist. And, of course, I suffer from that incurable disease of needing to be loved all the time. I just try to keep some justice in the situation, but it's always a struggle.

Another White nurse, Anne Z., discussed her mixture of sympathy and embarrassment in regard to an African American woman she supervised at a large, predominantly White hospital in Minneapolis. Like Anne Z. herself, her colleague had a master's degree in nursing, but still made many spelling and grammatical errors when writing up patient reports; for example, writing chicken pox as "chicken pops." Anne Z. knew enough about this woman's poverty-stricken, dysfunctional family background to respect the drive and effort it had taken her to get where she was, but she also believed that the nurse's poor language skills were hurting the professional image of other nurses, especially among the doctors. Yet the one time Anne Z. tried to correct something that her colleague had written, she was rebuked. In the end, she had to decide to let gross spelling mistakes slide, and to focus instead on the good her colleague did in her interactions with the hospital's Black patients.

Unfortunately for African American women trying to get ahead in pink-collar employment, strong language skills are often a prerequisite. Unlike most blue-collar work, where the skills and labor required are more manual and craft oriented, jobs as teachers, librarians, nurses, secretaries, word processors, receptionists, and bank tellers require the ability to write and speak well. Many African American women have these skills, yet proportionately more Black women than White women grow up in homes where learning to speak and write the King's English is not encouraged, and is sometimes even ridiculed. Regardless of the cultural value of nonstandard Black English, or ethnic differences in dialect, phrasing, intonation, and enunciation, the reality in the workplace is that employees are often judged by how well they communicate in standard English.

For some African American women, the pressure to use standard English in the workplace and Black English at home has led them, in effect, to speak two different languages. Some predominantly Black high schools and community colleges offer classes specifically designed to help African Americans improve their oral communication skills. As Darlene, a Black computer technician, explains, "When I talk to my boss or my customers, I sound like a White girl, but when I talk to my friends or someone who pisses me off, I talk Black. Basically, I'm bilingual."

In addition to having differences in language in the workplace, Black women and White women also employ different terms of emotional expression at work. According to the book *Black and White Styles in Conflict,* by White author Thomas Kochman, Blacks tend to engage in louder and more intense language when trying to resolve differences, while Whites are more solicitous and collegial. Kochman maintains that the "Black mode" of negotiating conflict is "high-keyed: animated, interpersonal, and confrontational," while the "White mode" is "relatively low-keyed: dispassionate, impersonal, and nonchallenging." Thus, in arguments, Blacks are more likely to engage both their mind and body in ways that are emotionally and even spiritually invigorating, while Whites tend to value self-restraint and calm discourse as the means to demonstrate their rationality. This difference in communication style can make some White women in the workplace fear the intensity of Black women, and can make some Black women think of White women as timid and less committed to something that is supposed to be of great importance to them. Kochman's book has been heavily criticized for its class bias, however; he drew comparisons in his study between the communication styles of Blacks who were from the inner city, and were more frequently lower-class, and Whites who were more middle class.

To minimize this bias, African American communications scholar Stella Ting-Toomey surveyed the styles of Whites and Blacks from similar socioeconomic backgrounds. She found that middle-class White and Black men did not significantly differ in their patterns of speech, but that White and Black women did. Her research suggests that middle-class White women use "more compromising strategies to dispel disagreements," and middle-class Black women are "slightly more verbose and emotionally expressive."

Cultural differences in communication skill and style are especially likely to cause conflict among women employed in public and private schools, perhaps because it is these women's responsibility to teach others to speak properly and to conduct themselves appropriately. Again, it is not very long that White and Black women have taught together in the same schools. Before the nineteen sixties, most public schools were racially segregated, as were the majority of universities and workplaces. That situation has been rectified legally, but it is hardly the case today that all public schools show perfect racial balance. Most of them continue to reflect the racial makeup of their surrounding communities, and since most neighborhoods in this country are still racially segregated, most schools are predominantly one race or another. Although some schools are predominantly Hispanic or Asian, for the most part White teachers and Black teachers end up working at schools that are either mostly White or mostly Black.

Race relations among the White and Black female faculty and staff at any one school often depend on the larger racial makeup of the school. At many mainly White suburban schools, African American women feel discriminated against when it comes time for promotion, and resentful of the way White women treat them. Sharon A., for example, who has been working since the late eighties as a circulation librarian at a racially mixed but predominantly White high school on Chicago's North Shore, complains that the White librarians always ask her to reprimand a noisy Black student. Sharon notes, "Some of those White women have been there for fifteen to twenty years. They should know what to do better than I." Sharon also resents that the other librarians always ask her whether she knows the Black students' names, as if she should just because she is Black. "I know the names of as many White students as Black students, but the White librarians only learn the names of White students. Is that fair?"

White women who work in inner-city, predominantly Black schools run into a different set of problems. One such woman, Nancy B., who until recently was an administrator at a predominantly Black inner-city elementary school, had this to say about her experience:

> It seemed to me that the White and Black teachers would always start
> off the school year getting along fine, but then after the parents came
> around on Parents' Day, racial tensions would start to flare. The Black

parents do not believe that a White teacher knows enough about the Black community to help "their babies." To allay such fears, the Black teachers would put their arms around the Black mothers and say things like, "Don't you worry, I'll take good care of your baby." Unfortunately, that too often translated into them not teaching a child anything, just providing them with nurturing. This was frustrating to the White teachers who wanted to push the Black children more academically.

Another White teacher, Trish, who taught fourth grade at the Sojourner Truth Elementary School near Chicago's infamous Cabrini Green public housing project, was shocked by what she termed "the total lack of nurturing within Black culture." Trish said that she was constantly ridiculed for her attempts to reason with misbehaving children, rather than slapping them. According to Trish, the African American teachers would tell her, "The only thing these kids understand is a good whack." She was taken aback by the way the Black teachers seemed to threaten the children with violence, saying things like, "If you don't stay in line, I'm gonna knock your teeth down your throat." To Trish, the use of such threats only perpetuated the violence she observed among the Black children. She couldn't help comparing her own childhood educational experiences at a predominantly White school, where none of the kids seemed to fight, to her experiences at the school where she currently taught, in which the students were constantly fighting.

Other White women who teach at mainly Black, poor, inner-city schools say that they have received clear and hostile messages from Black teachers that they are not wanted. Such was the case with a White teacher named Karen P., who joined the Teach for America Program after college graduation. At first Karen was excited to be placed at a school near South Central L.A., where she thought she could make a difference. Instead, she encountered enormous resistance and even hostility from the Black teachers working there.

They were ready to interpret everything that I did in the most negative light. They constantly questioned my motives for being there, believing that I surely had wanted a teaching position in a White school but had been placed there instead. They didn't understand or want to believe that I wanted to help, and they totally mocked my idealism.

Karen felt ostracized throughout the school year, and no more so than during Black History Month. She remembered one incident in which she was supposed to lead her class in singing the inspiring song "We Shall Overcome." Karen didn't know all the words, but when she admitted this before the other Black teachers, one of them, disgusted with her, yelled, "Don't even get me started."

For their part, African American women teaching in predominantly Black inner-city schools do get angry at White teachers who act as though they deserve a medal for being there. African American women feel as though they must pay dues every day in this country just for being Black. That may be why they are generally not receptive to suggestions made by White teachers to do things differently. The very notion that an inexperienced White teacher knows better than members of the Black community what is best for Black students is insulting.

Those White and Black women who teach at the same schools only seldom become close. Jackie R., a White woman teaching high school science at a racially mixed school in Hampton, Virginia, said, "The White and Black teachers are cordial enough when we pass in the hallways, but at lunch we never sit together, and after school we never do anything together socially. It's as though we live in two different worlds." Her comment was echoed by nearly every White and Black teacher interviewed for this book. The one exception was an African American woman named Frieda, who once taught at a racially mixed school in Chicago's Hyde Park, one of those rare successfully integrated neighborhoods. In that school, according to Frieda, "the White and Black teachers got along extremely well, and we often did things together after work."

Ironically, in other predominantly Black employment environments, White women report more positive workplace experiences and peer relationships. Being the only White person in an otherwise all-Black work environment used to be practically unheard of, but the incidence is on the rise, a fact reflected in the new phrase "the only marshmallow in the hot chocolate," to balance the longer standing and more common experience of a Black's being "the only chip in the cookie." A recent article in *Ebony* entitled "Reverse Integration" discusses the "marshmallow" experiences of several White women, including Louise Lindbolm, who was hired to be the media director at the National Urban Coalition. Lindbolm said, "There's a sense of community—a sense that everyone is pulling together for something—that seems to be more prevalent in a Black workplace than a White workplace." She also discovered an unexpected benefit in her minority status. "If I do something silly, I'm automatically excused for it. My colleagues just shake their heads and say, 'What does she know? She's White.'" A second White woman featured in the *Ebony* article, Carole Borgreen, is an administrative coordinator of special projects at Howard University. Being hired in a Black-dominated workplace made Borgreen better appreciate what it means to live in a world in which you must constantly disprove racial stereotypes. Thinking back on when she was first hired, she noted:

> I didn't know what to expect. And as I was going over the possibilities in my mind, imagining the hostility I might face, I developed a real sensitivity for what it must be like to have to deal with that question all the time.

A White woman named Robin P., interviewed for *Divided Sisters,* was once the only White woman in *Ebony*'s fashion show; she now works in London as the only White marketing representative for the Johnson Company's Fashion Fair cosmetic line. "I've never tried to relate to my colleagues in racial terms," says Robin. "People are people. There is always competition in the workplace, and maybe more questions are asked when race differences are present. But at the end of the day, it all comes down to competence in the job. Overall, my work experience has been positive."

The issue of race is more frequently stressed when the only White woman present is also the one in charge, as was the case with Shirley, a White registered nurse hired to supervise an all-Black staff on the psychiatric ward of a Michigan state hospital. It is difficult enough for anyone to walk into a new work situation and manage those who have been there longer, but it is especially hard when the situation re-creates the standard hierarchy of race in the larger society. Shirley described her experience this way:

> I tend to have a blunt interpersonal style of management, and I don't care if you are White or Black; if you're not doing your job right, you're going to hear from me about it. But because I was White and

they were all Black, some of the nurses mistook my no-nonsense way of speaking to them as racist. Believe me, that made for a long and difficult adjustment. Now that things are settling down, my main complaint is that no one I've met at work can give me a good recommendation for where I can get my hair done in this town!

Too often, perhaps, this chapter has drawn relations between Black women and White women in the workplace as negative. For that reason alone, it is an incomplete portrait. There are many positive relationships that develop among White and Black women colleagues. In fact, the workplace remains the one place where adults are most likely to make new friends, and this holds true for African American and White women. Even at the strife-ridden bank portrayed in Bebe Moore Campbell's novel *Brothers and Sisters,* by the end, Mallory and Esther triumph over their differences, and their friendship survives. In the real world, women on both sides of the racial line are discovering their similarities. A White secretary named Lucy said, "In our office, we recently hired this Black woman who is a real joy to work with. She's totally competent and comes to work every day in a great mood. Her easy laugh and quick wit have improved the mood of everyone else working here, most especially me. We're starting to have lunch together and I would be really sad if she left."

Many African American women, too, display a willingness to befriend White women at work. A television production assistant named Keisha sees her situation this way:

I think I must send out some sort of signal to White women that I am available to be their friend because they just flock to me. I grew up with a lot of Whites, so maybe they can tell I am very comfortable with them. For whatever reason, it has been my experience that if you just give White women half a chance, most do want to be nice to you.

An African American woman who works at a huge accounting firm observed that "from the onset, the White women I met at work went out of their way to be accommodating. I was glad that they did, especially since the only person in the office who wasn't nice to me was another Black woman. It was like I had dethroned her queen bee status, or something like that.

Whatever, it really made me mad." Finally, other African American women, like Raquel, the medical sales representative mentioned earlier, admit to one advantage in being "the only chip in the cookie":

> Racism is a funny thing. I mean it can even help you in a weird sort of way. White women try so hard not to come across as racist that I'm often treated better because of it. They won't be mean to me because they don't want to be accused of being racist. I think I even sell more for that reason. And White women also seem to feel better about themselves in being nice to me. Then they can then say to themselves, "I knew I wasn't racist," and that's fine with me.

Sometimes, of course, when White women at work try to get too friendly too fast, it can make African American women uncomfortable. In *The Black Women's Health Book,* African American therapist and author Julia Boyd touches on this issue, drawing on an incident from her own life. Boyd was doing volunteer work at a women's center when another therapist, a White woman named Beth, confided that Julia was her best friend. Julia did not feel the same way about her. "How do you tell a white woman that it's still politically dangerous to have white folks for best friends, even if it is the 1990s?" Thus, while Boyd realized that Beth was trying hard to bridge the gap between them, she was still trying to gauge her emotional reactions to Beth's overture. "What she doesn't understand is that it may take me longer to come over the water, because bridges have a way of not being stable when the winds blow too strong."

Friendships

For those White and Black women who do first meet in the workplace, a big step in developing a true friendship is getting together after work. Unfortunately, many of women's cross-race friendships that thrive during lunch breaks and daytime shopping trips don't extend after hours. Because so many neighborhoods are in fact racially segregated, to come together at night and on weekends means White women have to travel into a predominantly Black setting to visit, or, more typically, Black women have to travel into a predominantly White setting to visit. Either way, one is a fish out of water and the other may be conscious of violating the norms in her community by inviting someone of another race to her home.

When White women visit Black girlfriends, several concerns can arise. African American women claim that if they bring a White girlfriend, especially a pretty blond one, to an all-Black private party or club, the Black men fall all over themselves trying to impress her, and the other Black women end up getting mad. The issue of perceived safety is also a factor. A thirtysomething African American woman sighed and explained, "Whenever my White girlfriend comes over to my place, she makes me walk her down the street. She claims that I protect her from street harassment and worse. Whether that's true or not I do not know, but it's a strain to have to be someone's escort all the time." And then there is plain old racial hatred. A White artist named Jill recalls the extreme discomfort she felt when a Black girlfriend, with whom she was traveling, took her to the home of another Black friend, in the projects in Baltimore:

> I am sure that I was the only White woman for blocks around, and it was clear my girlfriend's friend's family did not like me being there. At first, they just did their best to ignore me, like playing pinochle and not inviting me into the game. That was fine; I sat in the corner and did some sketching. But then, this older Black woman came into the room and I guess I turned into some sort of lightning rod for every hostile pent-up feeling she ever had toward Whites. She started taunting me, at one point even demanding that I dance for her so that the others could all laugh at me.

And when African American women visit the homes of White girlfriends, there are other issues to contend with. While a Black woman in a White neighborhood doesn't arouse the same degree of paranoia that a Black man might, there is still the embarrassing possibility that a White neighbor may question her motives for being there, or mistake her for somebody's housekeeper. A White girlfriend may also fret about inviting a Black friend to a party at which she will likely be the only Black person. In an effort to make her party more racially integrated, a White woman may even compound the problem by inviting other African Americans whom she doesn't know very well. However well meaning that strategy may be, it is usually obvious and can backfire. Cheryl, who worked at a large, predominantly White advertising agency in Chicago, remembers a party thrown by another White woman in their office. The only African American woman employed at the agency was also invited. As Cheryl described it:

> It was a summer evening and the party spilled out onto the back porch, attracting the attention of a Black man in the alley below. He was probably homeless, saw people drinking and started coming upstairs. Well, the White hostess, plagued by a terminal case of White liberal guilt and not wanting to make a scene in front of her Black colleague, actually invited the guy in to have a beer. But the Black woman who witnessed this became furious, as if this White woman was somehow equating her status with that of this down-and-out Black man's simply because they shared the same race. Long after he was finally asked to leave, racial tension remained in the room.

There are other stumbling blocks, as well, that cross-race friendships must overcome before they can thrive. White women's behavior with a Black girlfriend too often seems to fall into one of two extreme categories: either they try to relate to her solely terms of her race, or they try to deny completely race as a factor between them. Crystal, a Black woman from Ohio, claims that her White friend Ann is always telling her that she, Ann, knows a lot about Black music and culture. Whenever Ann sees a Black actress or model in a magazine or on TV, she makes a big deal of stating how beautiful that actress or model is. Not surprisingly, Crystal gets annoyed by such obsequious behavior. LaTisha, a Black woman from L.A. who works in television, has had similar experiences. "My friendships with White women have always been a bit trying. They always seem to want to prove to me that they understand Black culture."

Too many White women act as if they expect their Black girlfriends to be experts on every topic relating to race. While some African American women enjoy serving as consciousness-raising vehicles for White women, most Black women do not relish the role. They especially don't like being asked a lot of questions about how to handle so-called Black-identified social problems. Lois, a Black woman in her late thirties who works at the Mars candy factory, remembers an incident that nearly destroyed her budding friendship with a White woman whom she had met at work:

I'll never forget the first time I called this White woman and said to her on the phone, "Hey, what's going on Nigger?" That was my way of saying we were friends, but it threw her off. She got used to that, though, and we were getting along real fine until the time she called me up in a big panic to ask what she should do about her teenage daughter who had gotten pregnant. I definitely got the feeling that just because I was Black, she thought that I was supposed to be some kind of expert on unwed pregnancy. So I asked her, real angry like, "Well, why should I know?"

In an article for *Ms.* magazine entitled "Friendship in Black & White," Bebe Moore Campbell describes a similar incident between a Black woman named Betty Ann and a White one named Peggy. The two journalists first met during the mid-seventies at the Associated Press office. Asked to reflect on the early days of their relationship, Betty Ann said, "When I got to AP, I was very inexperienced. There were very few other black women there. I really appreciated Peggy's concern, her sisterliness." Eventually, the two women began talking on the phone in the evening and getting together socially. But one night Peggy made the mistake of calling Betty Ann in the middle of the night to ask her how to handle some Black neighbors who were fighting and being loud. Betty Ann's response was chilly. "She gave me a very clear message," recalled Peggy. "Don't expect me to help you solve your problems with your rowdy black neighbors, because I wouldn't know what to do with those folks either." While Betty Ann denies that there was anything Peggy has done to really test their friendship, she nonetheless admitted that there was probably a part of her racial identity that she didn't reveal to Peggy. Still, Betty Ann says, "I think black women and white women should be friends. It helps to have bridges. It's a start if women can get along; they can make men get along." And Peggy added, "I think our friendship transcends race, though we're never unaware of it."

While African American women do not appreciate being related to only in terms of their race, neither do they like being "whitefaced" and having their racial identity ignored. It is no compliment for a Black woman to have a White friend tell her, "I don't even think of you as Black." When Deana, a White woman, said something along these lines to her new Black girlfriend, Temple, Temple cautiously asked Deana what she meant. Deana replied, "Your blackness doesn't faze me. I see you as my best friend, as a person with no color." Temple became angry. "A major part of who I am is that I'm a Black woman. For you not to see me as Black really hurts."

White girlfriends similarly make the mistake at times of denying the existence of societal racism. A twentysomething middle-class Black woman named Carla experienced this sort of thing when she recently ran into a former White childhood friend, Tyler. As Carla explains it:

> I hadn't seen Tyler in about two years, and as we were catching up on what we had been doing lately, we discovered that we had both made a stab at modeling. She talked of her successes in Europe—she was tall, beautiful and blond—and I spoke of my failures because of racism in the modeling industry. "Oh, I can't see how that could be. You are so gorgeous," she kept saying. I kept reiterating that my beauty had nothing to do with it—some advertisers just don't want to use Black women. Still, Tyler couldn't seem to understand. I swear White women like her think that just because they aren't racist, then no other White person is, either.

Of course, White women, too, have their grievances. A surprising number are bothered by Black girlfriends' tendency to be late, and for failing to return phone calls promptly. Many of the White women we interviewed also reported that African American women don't seem to think it as necessary to apologize for these lapses as a White girlfriend might. Although it is risky to make generalizations of any sort about either race, it is interesting to note that the African American psychologist James M. Jones has posited a model of cultural differences that may help to explain such behavior. Jones uses the acronym TRIOS to identify the themes of *t*ime perception, *r*hythm, *i*mprovisation, *o*ral tradition, and *s*pirituality to differentiate Black culture from White. With respect to time, he feels those of European descent have, for various reasons, a more linear and rigid relationship with the clock than those of African descent, who, he claims, have a more spatial and casual relationship with the fourth dimension. This difference in relating to time is reflected in the popular African American expression "being on CPT, or Colored People's Time," as a handy excuse for tardiness in the Black community. Confessed one White woman named Heather, "I've simply gotten in the habit of telling my Black girlfriend that something starts about an hour earlier than it actually does so we have some chance of being on time.

Even then, I still get so mad at her for being so incredibly slow. To me, it's like our friendship doesn't mean that much to her, if she can't try even a little to accommodate my needs to be on time."

On the whole, Black women seem more circumspect regarding the value of an interracial friendship than White women, reflecting perhaps the habits of those more powerful and less powerful in the world at large. For example, women living in a male-dominated world, must study the behavior and habits of men, so that their coming to know any one man well will yield fewer revelations about men in general. In the same vein, African American women feel as though they know plenty about White women from having to pay more attention to them in a White-dominated society—certainly more attention than most White women have paid to Black women. In other words, White women stand to gain more from relationships with Blacks than African American women do from friendships with Whites.

This difference in the perceived value of cross-race relationships sheds light on why African Americans become so irked by the cliché "Some of my best friends are Black." Whites tend to use the statement as a way to defend themselves and to verify that they are not prejudiced. Karla, an African American woman who owns a bicoastal entertainment production company, recalls the night her White girlfriend Annette announced in Karla's presence, at a dinner party with all of Annette's White friends present, that she was proud to have a friend who was Black. To Karla, what Annette really seemed to be announcing was that she was an "expert on Black love, Black sensibilities, the plight of the Black race, and now all her White friends can look up to her for being such a rebel." African Americans resent that some Whites think having a friend who is Black is "cool." As African American Tina put it, "White people don't say it's cool having White friends, or that some of their best friends are White. It's as if Black people are abnormal and to have one as a friend is something that needs to be announced."

Sociologists Mary Jackman and Marie Crane, using an interview sample of nearly two thousand adults, 70 percent of whom were White, studied whether interpersonal contacts with Blacks actually changed a White person's racial attitudes. The survey asked questions about the racial makeup of the respondents' friends and acquaintances, along with questions assessing racial prejudice, such as beliefs about personality trait differences between Blacks and Whites. Jackman and Crane found that only 9.4 percent of Whites could even name one "good friend" who was Black, although 21.4

percent said that they had at least one Black "acquaintance." The authors' primary discovery, though, was that for Whites, having a Black friend did little to change their racial prejudices. That is, the good Black friend was simply subtyped as "exceptional," and traditional racial prejudices remained intact. However, when the Whites respondents who claimed to have Black friends were divided into three groups—those whose Black friend had relatively lower socioeconomic status, those whose Black friend had similar socioeconomic status, and those whose Black friend had relatively higher socioeconomic status—the picture changed. When a Black friend is of equal or higher socioeconomic status, overall racial attitudes of Whites do begin to move in a more favorable direction. Jackman and Crane's research seems to imply that if significant progress in women's race relations is to be achieved, White women must begin to deal with Black women as equals—and not as beloved nursemaids or domestic servants.

In a paper on women's interracial friendships, presented by African American psychologist Althea Smith and White psychologist Stephanie Nickerson at a recent meeting of the Association of Women in Psychology, the authors asked, "How pervasive is racism in interracial friendships today?" Their short answer was "very." For Smith and Nickerson, though, the solution was not in trying to teach women to be nonracist—in today's culture, that seemed to them impossible. Instead, they advocated that cross-race friends admit to each other their racial stereotypes. In that way, the air can at least be cleared. For example, many African American women believe that White women are "exploitative, condescending, incompetent, silly, or untrustworthy," while many White women believe, at some level, that Blacks as a group are intellectually inferior to Whites. Nickerson and Smith concluded that for women's cross-race relations to be lasting, both partners must have "good intentions about race relations and a commitment to improving race relations in society."

While we've covered a lot of issues pertaining to interracial friendships in this chapter, we have unfortunately barely scratched the surface. There are simply too many variables to consider them all, too many circumstances under which European American and African American women can run into conflict or come together. As America changes, so too does the nature of both men's and women's cross-race relationships. Yet, historically, little attention has been paid to the many ways in which interracial relations differ by gender. Over shared cups of coffee in the workplace, while doing laundry, or making baby-sitting arrangements, women often connect in ways that are at once intimate and mundane. As the less empowered members of society, and therefore those with more to gain and less to lose, the women, rather than the more politically entrenched men, may well be the ones to find the keys to future racial harmony.

Chapter Six

Social Activism:

Shared Agendas and Uneasy Alliances

Black feminism is not white feminism in blackface.

—*Audre Lorde*
Sister Outsider, *1984*

It is a lie to say that feminism is White, middle class, and Western. As long as there has been a patriarchy, there have been women resisting it.

—*Robin Morgan, keynote address,*
Association of Women in Psychology
Conference, March 1993

"It was the women's vote that won it, kind of a wild, exciting outpouring," declared Sue Purrington of Chicago NOW on March 18, 1992, the day after the Illinois senatorial primary election. All over the state White women like Purrington were taking much of the credit for the surprise victory by the Cook County deeds recorder, Carol Moseley Braun over the incumbent, Alan Dixon. Braun's campaign had been sparked by Dixon's pro–Clarence Thomas vote, and Dixon's defeat came at the hands of a coalition of African Americans and liberal Whites. Exit polls also indicated that a significant number of White Republican women, in the white-collar counties outside Chicago and downstate Illinois, jumped parties to help put the first female candidate on the ballot for the November general election.

Among those celebrating the primary results was Molly, a thirtysomething White female and a member of Chicago's so-called Lake Front liberal community. On hearing that Braun had won, Molly was ecstatic, filled with hope that White and Black women could finally come together for a specific political purpose—in this case, the defeat of Senator Dixon. Molly called her African American girlfriend Tandra to share the excitement. From the opening moments of their conversation, Molly realized that Tandra was just as happy about Braun as she was, but for a completely different reason. To Tandra, Braun's election was all about an African American winning. Finally, Molly blurted out, "Don't you feel good that a woman won tonight? Wouldn't a Black woman celebrate a liberal White female candidate defeating a conservative African American male candidate?" "Probably not," came Tandra's reply. "Listen, Molly, it's hard to imagine African American women feeling good about anything a White woman has done, but I'm glad you're happy that a sister won tonight." When Molly hung up the phone, her enthusiasm for Braun had considerably dampened. After all, if Black women would never feel good about White women winning a similar election, why should she care so much about Braun? It just didn't seem fair.

The different reactions of Molly and Tandra to Carol Moseley Braun's successful bid for the Democratic candidacy are not surprising, in light of the separate histories of African and European women in this country. As we saw earlier, Black women became suspicious of White women's political motives during the nineteenth century, when, first, they were banned from White women's social reform meetings, and, later, their vote was nearly sacrificed by White female suffragists. These suspicions were rekindled in

....
188

the sixties, when White women appeared to coat-tail on the issues of Black
civil rights, causing that movement, in the eyes of many, to suddenly lose its
momentum. It is this recent historical legacy that we now examine to explain why African American women like Tandra maintain a cautious stance
in their political relations with White women today.

The Civil Rights Movement

While African American men and women have been fighting for their basic
liberties since the day they arrived in this country, the modern Civil Rights
Movement is said to have begun on December 1, 1955. On that day in
Montgomery, Alabama, Rosa Parks refused to give up her seat on a bus for
a White male passenger who had just boarded. Parks was hardly the first
Black person to resist conforming to the Jim Crow laws of the South, but
her arrest gave the local NAACP the perfect test case to bring charges of
race discrimination against the Montgomery bus system.

Another Black woman important early on in the Civil Rights Movement
was Ella Baker. In 1957, at the age of fifty-two, she helped to found the
Southern Christian Leadership Conference (SCLC), becoming its first full-
time executive secretary. Following the court ruling that struck down segregation in public transportation, the momentum of activism associated with
the year-long bus boycott in Montgomery was about to come to an abrupt
halt. Baker believed that a new group, other than the NAACP, was needed
to keep things going in the South. She had in mind an organization that
would specifically recruit church leaders and train them in the use of nonviolent protest as a means to win Southern Blacks their basic civil rights.
Baker worked hard to make it happen. Thus, while Martin Luther King,
Jr., was recognized as the official head of the SCLC, by all accounts it was
"Miss Baker," as she was respectfully called, who helped get the SCLC up
and running.

College campuses, too, became the site of much political activity during
the late fifties and early sixties. Inspired by Rosa Parks, four male students
from North Carolina's all-Black Agricultural and Technical State University, in Greensboro, challenged Jim Crow restaurant laws by walking into a
Woolworth store on February 1, 1960, to order Coca-Cola at the all-White
lunch counter. Although they were immediately arrested, their actions
launched the student sit-in movement. Within a week, similar sit-ins took

place in fifteen other Southern cities in five different states, and within eighteen months an estimated seventy thousand people had participated in them, and some thirty-six hundred arrests had been made.

Again, it was Ella Baker who first grasped the true significance of what was taking place. Within a few months of the Greensboro sit-in, Baker encouraged the students to organize, and persuaded the SCLC to contribute $800 for them to hold a conference. In April 1960, more than three hundred male and female students, Black and White, from fifty-six different colleges across the South and nineteen colleges in the North, convened at Shaw University to form the Student Nonviolent Coordinating Committee (SNCC). Beyond organizing even more sit-ins, SNCC joined the SCLC in the campaign to register Southern Blacks to vote.

Young Black women were active in SNCC from the beginning. Diane Nash helped to organize the Freedom Rides that brought thousands of student volunteers on buses to rural areas of the South, and Ruby Doris Smith went on to become SNCC's executive secretary in its Atlanta office. Scattered throughout the South, young White women also became actively involved in the burgeoning student movement.

White women in the Civil Rights Movement experienced a revelation about the potential strength and toughness of women. Besides being exposed to such powerful Black women as Miss Baker and Rosa Parks, White women also became aware of the courage of the often uneducated, completely impoverished Black women living in the most remote areas of the rural South. When SNCC entered a new region, White women were surprised to learn that it was the women, not the men, who were contacted first. This was because there was usually at least one Black woman—referred to as the "mama"—who was willing to catch hell for her beliefs. She, more than anyone else, could cajole the others in her community into taking whatever risks were necessary to register to vote. For White women, groomed in a tradition of passivity and sweetness, the mamas, as well as the other Black female SNCC staff members, made quite an impression. As the White student activist Dorothy Dawson Burlage recalled, "For the first time I had role models I could really respect."

Throughout the early sixties, a virtual flood of White and Black student volunteers headed south to participate in the voter registration drives there. They boarded buses that traveled from campus to campus during the early summer to take them to the rural areas where they were needed most. In fact, so many students from Northern campuses went south during the summer of 1964 that it came to be known as Freedom Summer. Before 1964, SNCC policy prohibited White women from being on the front lines of voter registration drives, because their presence in rural areas was known to spark racial violence. However, in the summer of 1964, that policy was changed. Black SNCC staff leaders realized that the sight of White women helping Southern Blacks made good press. Ultimately, it helped to draw much needed national media attention. While the plan worked, it also caused a rift between White and Black women working in SNCC offices. It bothered Black female staff members, especially those who had risked their lives and been thrown in jail for their beliefs, to see the national media suddenly focus on White female volunteers who were there for the summer.

Sending White women into the field that Freedom Summer produced another unintended effect that further eroded relations between the White and Black women in SNCC. A significant number of the White women volunteers, especially those from the North, found themselves attracted to the sexually explicit manner of some of the Black men with whom they were working. To those volunteers, having sex with a Black man seemed a good way to demonstrate their lack of racial prejudice. The Black male students, too, responded favorably to the presence of friendly White women. Having sex with White women was yet another way to defy the White man's authority.

The breakdown of taboos against White women sleeping with Black men drove a wedge between veteran Black and White female SNCC staff members. Understandably, many of the Black women became enraged at the sight of Black men falling for young White female volunteers. Their rage, however, got directed not at the Black men involved, but at the White women willing to sleep with them. Ultimately, all White women working in SNCC offices became suspect. As feminist historian Sara Evans noted in *Personal Politics,* "The rising anger of black women would soon become a powerful force within SNCC, creating a barrier that shared womanhood could not transcend."

The 1964 Freedom Summer was also a violent summer, and by its end, SNCC was left in a near state of disarray. Thousands of volunteers had been mobilized, hundreds had been arrested, a few had been killed, and permanent staff members were overworked and short-tempered. SNCC had grown bigger than anyone had dreamed it would, and the time had come to assess the group's direction and focus. One issue that needed to be addressed was whether SNCC was going to embrace other issues of injustice, or continue devoting itself to the single goal of Black liberation. A conference to consider these and other matters was scheduled for autumn of 1964 in Waveland, Mississippi. Among those invited to attend were veteran White staff members Mary King and Casey Hayden.

King and Hayden had devoted several years to the cause of fighting racial injustice. Recent experiences within SNCC, however, had led them also to begin defining themselves politically as women. The two decided to prepare a paper on the position of women in SNCC for distribution at the Waveland conference; because of the paper's controversial topic, King and Hayden kept their names off it. They cited numerous examples of sexual discrimination, detailing how assumptions of male superiority were limiting women's leadership opportunities in SNCC, drawing an analogy between the treatment of Blacks by Whites and the treatment of women by men:

> The average white person finds it difficult to understand why the Negro resents being called "boy," or being thought of as "musical" or "athletic," because the average white person doesn't realize that he assumes he is superior. And naturally he doesn't understand the problem of paternalism. So too the average SNCC worker finds it difficult to discuss the woman problem because of the assumption of male superiority. Assumptions of male superiority are as widespread and deep-rooted and every [bit as] . . . crippling to the woman as the assumptions of white supremacy are to the Negro.

The paper was not well received. Just about everyone figured out who had penned it, and King and Hayden found themselves criticized and ridiculed. Even the Black women scoffed at most of the points made in the paper, noting that the ill treatment of Rosa Parks and thousands of other Black women in this country had nothing to do with their sex and everything to do with their race. They held that it was only White women whose leadership opportunities were being curtailed in SNCC—that Black women were not treated in sexist fashion. The most infamous reaction to the paper, however, came from a Black man, Stokely Carmichael, who quipped, "The position of women in SNCC is prone!" (Although this comment tends to anger women who hear it today, according to King, who was present at the time it was made, Carmichael meant to be funny, and even she laughed.)

A year later, in November 1965, King and Hayden wrote another paper on women that came to be called the Manifesto. In it, they further developed their ideas about the treatment of women in society, describing the existence of a caste system that kept women subordinate to men. Forty copies of the document were sent all over the country to women involved in political groups. This time, King and Hayden received a tremendously positive response from the mostly White women who read their paper. From their Black women friends, they heard very little.

By the mid-sixties, a rising spirit of Black nationalism and even separatism was transforming the once peaceful Civil Rights Movement into something far more radical and dangerous. Black Power was in, and the feminine values of passive, nonviolent forms of protest were being replaced by a more masculine style of demonstration that included knotted fists, angry verbal threats, and even physical violence. The few remaining White women in SNCC fled, some of them joining other radical White groups, such as the Students for a Democratic Society (SDS).

Even though many Black women were relieved to see White women abandon SNCC, they too were affected by the more macho style in the organization. Angela Davis claimed that when she was helping to organize a rally in San Diego in 1967, she was constantly told that, as a woman, her role was to inspire the men, not to lead them. A year later, in Los Angeles, Davis again found herself reprimanded for trying to take over SNCC. The women were always stuck with the most boring organizational work, she said, and instead of getting credit for what they had done, they were told by the men to keep quiet:

> Some of the brothers came around only for staff meetings (sometimes), and whenever we women were involved in something important, they began to talk about "women taking over the organization," calling it a matriarchal coup d'état. All the myths about Black women surfaced. [We] were too domineering; we were trying to control everything, including the men—which meant by extension that we wanted to rob them of their manhood. By playing such a leading role in the organization, some of them insisted, we were aiding and abetting the enemy, who wanted to see Black men weak and unable to hold their own.

Kathleen Cleaver, wife of Black Panther leader Eldridge Cleaver, recalls that she practically had to "genuflect" before speaking. As Black men asserted their power, Black women were expected to give up theirs. One pamphlet issued by the Black Nationalists during the early seventies described men and women's responsibilities as follows:

> We understand that it is and has been traditional that the man is the head of the house. He is the leader of the house/nation because his knowledge of the world is broader, his awareness is greater, his understanding is fuller and his application of this information is wiser . . . Women cannot do the same things as men—they are made by nature to function differently.

It is ironic that while men in the Black Power movement were working hard to dispel notions of genetic inferiority based on color and race, they were still emphasizing principles of biological determinism when it came to matters of sex.

At a Black Power Conference in 1967, an official statement was issued, opposing the use of any contraception, on the grounds that it was akin to genocide for Black women to control their fertility. Although Black Panther Regina Jennings recalls that some of the women in the organization resisted the edict, eventually they were overruled by the party's central committee, which made them feel that they were bringing "bourgeois" beliefs into the vanguard army. For the sake of Panther unity, the sisters yielded their position. Some politically minded Black women, alarmed by this turn of events, began to speak up about what they saw happening. In 1972, writer Barbara Sizemore observed that it looked as though Black women were to "become chattel once again, with good and loving masters, to be sure, but chattel nevertheless."

Radical White men were no more progressive in their attitudes toward women. In 1968, when a group of radical White students from the SDS took over the administrative building at Columbia University, the women found themselves stuck with all the cooking responsibilities. When they rebelled, Mark Rudd, the most prominent student leader in the Columbia takeover, arrogantly told his girlfriend that she should go to "chicklib" classes while he was busy doing more important things. The following year, as a White SDS woman was speaking at a protest on the day of Richard Nixon's inauguration, a White SDS male cried out, "Take her off the stage and fuck her!" Incidents like these radicalized many White women, turning them into instant feminists.

The Women's Movement

As the decade of the seventies turned, the women's movement gained momentum. Beside the distribution of King and Hayden's Manifesto, several events had taken place to spur the movement on. The first was the passage of the 1964 Civil Rights Act. When the bill was first being debated in Congress, Representative Howard Smith of Virginia, who opposed it, proposed that Title VII, which governs issues of employment discrimination, be amended by adding sex as a protected category along with race, color, religious preference. He believed the inclusion of sex as a protected category in the workplace would effectively kill the bill. His plan backfired. Representative Martha Griffith of Michigan, who intended for more legitimate reasons to add sex to Title VII, was able to marshal enough support from other politicians, some of whom were outraged at Smith's sexist tactics, to get the bill passed with the sex provision intact. But Howard Edelsberg, who was appointed founding director of the Equal Employment Opportunity Commission (EEOC), which was to be the enforcement arm of Title VII, made it clear from the outset that he opposed the sex provision. He intended to ignore all complaints of sex discrimination complaints brought before the new agency.

In large part, it was Edelsberg's arrogant attitude that led to the development of another organization that boosted this country's second wave of feminism—the founding in 1966 of the National Organization for Women (NOW). As originally conceived, NOW was to be a sort of NAACP for women, ensuring that women's civil rights, most specifically Title VII protections in the workplace, would be safeguarded. NOW's founding president was Betty Friedan.

Betty Friedan was already important to the burgeoning women's movement because of the enormous success of her 1963 book, *The Feminine Mystique,* which put forth the radical thesis that the unfulfilling role of housewife lowered women's self-esteem, even driving some a bit crazy—as Friedan termed it, the "sickness without a name." To fix the problem, she demanded women's full and equal participation in the workplace. Friedan, who herself was White and upper middle class, wrote the book from her own perspective, and no doubt intended to speak to other women similarly situated. However, *The Feminine Mystique* made such sweeping generalizations about women that it ended up alienating and angering those who did not fit her particular profile. Her statement "I never knew a woman, when I was growing up, who used her mind, played her own part in the world, and loved, and had children," struck a raw nerve among poor, working-class Black mothers who had been doing nothing but those things all their lives. To them, the idea that a housewife was oppressed was laughable. In fact, many Black women were fighting for the exact opposite of what Friedan called for. They longed for a time when their economically oppressed husbands could make enough money for them to stay at home with their children. Yet, as Michele Wallace notes in her book *Black Macho and the Myth of the Superwoman,* in wanting to be racially liberated as Blacks, and yet taken care of like Victorian models of womanhood, Black women's desires were inherently contradictory.

While *The Feminine Mystique* failed to resonate with Black women, it spoke volumes to hundreds of thousands of White women. Armed with Friedan's book and dog-eared copies of King and Hayden's Manifesto, middle-class White women all over the country formed and joined consciousness-raising (CR) groups throughout the seventies. As they talked, many of them emerged from their silence, isolation, and paralysis to share with others for the first time the private pain of their illegal abortions, the batterings they had received at the hands of boyfriends and husbands, and their thwarted career ambitions. One by one, White women came to the realization that the "personal is political," and that yes, they too were victims of systematic discrimination. They also started saying such things as "women are the niggers of the world" and "woman as slave" to help explain their oppression to others. In so doing, White women assumed that they were establishing a link with Black women and their historical experiences. They could not have been more wrong. The "woman as slave" analogy in particular enraged Black women.

CR groups struck many Black women as frivolous and, at some level, insulting. The very idea that you could have reached adulthood without knowing that you were oppressed did not ring true with the experiences of Black women. No matter what your socioeconomic status—or sex, for that matter—you had some history of discrimination and oppression. Because so many Black women were still dealing with issues of "survival," rather than higher issues of "fulfillment," they came to ridicule middle-class White women's enthusiasm for CR groups. But what Black women didn't realize is that White women needed CR groups because White culture fosters a

greater spirit of antagonism and competition among its women than does
Black culture. In addition, many Black women already had in place a social
mechanism that fostered the kind of sisterhood White women were now
finding for themselves. That mechanism was the beauty parlor.

While White sisterhood may have been celebrated in the play and film
Steel Magnolias, trips to the beauty parlor for most White women are primarily functional. Most of their time is spent in isolation under noisy hair
dryers: the point for many is to get in and out as fast as possible. In contrast,
when African American women go to the beauty parlor—and this was
especially true when so many more were "hot combing"—there is a lot of
time to share problems with others. In an article for *Z Magazine,* bell hooks
described the beauty parlor experience this way:

> The beauty parlor was a space for consciousness raising, a space where
> black women shared life stories—hardship, trials, gossip; a place where
> one could be comforted and one's spirit renewed. It was for some
> women a place of rest where one did not need to meet the demand of
> children or men.

African American poet Willie M. Coleman also reflects on the consciousness
raising that took place during "hot combing" in her poem "Among the
Things That Use to Be":

> *Use to be*
>
> *Ya could learn*
> *a whole lot of stuff*
> *sitting in them*
> *beauty shop chairs*
>
> *Use to be*
>
> *Ya could meet*
> *a whole lot of other women*
> *sitting there*
> *   along with hair frying*
> *   spit flying*
> *   and babies crying*

Use to be

you could learn
a whole lot about
how to catch up
*   with yourself*
and some other folks
*   in your household.*
Lots more got taken care of
*   than hair.*
Cause in our mutual obvious dislike
*   for nappiness*
we came together
*   under the hot comb*
to share
*   and share*
*   and share*

But now we walk
*   heads high*
naps full of pride
with not a backward glance
at some of the beauty in
*   that which*

use to be

Cause with a natural
there is no natural place
for us to congregate
to mull over
our mutual discontent

Beauty shops
could have been
a hell-of-a-place
*   to ferment*
*   a . . . . . . revolution.*

Actually, during the seventies some Black feminists did try to establish CR groups with their friends, but most such groups failed to thrive. In the end, the sentiment developed among many that "White women feel, Black women do."

But White women "did." In 1968, they organized a protest against the all-White Miss America pageant. Signs that greeted passersby were scrawled with "Welcome to the Miss American Cattle Auction" and "Miss America Is Alive and Angry—in Harlem," referring to the fact that no Black women had as yet participated in the national contest. Inspired by the draft-card burning by Vietnam protestors, the female demonstrators designated a "Freedom Trashcan" into which they tossed copies of *Playboy* and *Vogue,* along with girdles, false eyelashes, and possibly bras, for burning. (Although there is some dispute about whether or not any bras were actually among the items thrown into the Freedom Trashcan, this is where the derogatory term "bra burners," used to describe feminists, originated.) Some of the protestors bought tickets for the pageant; during the crowning ceremonies, they unfurled a huge banner that unmistakably read WOMEN'S LIBERATION for millions of TV viewers at home. They were immediately arrested, and the Black civil rights lawyer Flo Kennedy was called to help bail them out.

Flo Kennedy was among only a handful of Black women who were members of NOW. While NOW's leadership viewed itself as extremely sympathetic to issues of race, and welcomed any and all Black women as members, the organization could not seem to shake its image of being comprised of spoiled middle-class White women. Most Black women were turned off by it. It was even rumored that Betty Friedan had a Black maid present at one of the meetings in her New York apartment. Some Black women also resented that the rise of the women's movement coincided with the decline of the Civil Rights Movement, and they blamed feminists for stealing their thunder. Finally, some Black women rejected NOW because whenever they made derogatory comments about White women and their "silly" liberation movement, many Black men applauded them.

As the seventies opened, NOW began experiencing its own growing pains. Younger, more radical White women, some of whom were openly lesbian, were joining, and most of them believed Friedan to be hopelessly bourgeoise. Meanwhile, mainstream White women feared that lesbians were trying to take over the organization, and that a "I'm more radical than thou" mentality was developing in its ranks. Recalling her early experiences in the women's movement, feminist author Susan Brownmiller commented, "It was very difficult to survive. People used to say that the only person who can get up and say something and not be shouted down was a black lesbian single mother on welfare." Only four years after the founding of NOW, Betty Friedan stepped down as president. In March 1970, she was replaced by Aileen Hernandez, who identified as Black.

Relinquishing the presidency of NOW did not mean that Friedan was ready to give up control of the women's movement. Not long after she stepped down, she announced to the media, without telling anyone else beforehand, that a march for women's equality was going to be held in New York City to commemorate the fiftieth anniversary of women's suffrage. Her announcement threw NOW members into a panic, as such events require huge amounts of time and energy to plan, and if they fail, the movement as a whole suffers. However, somehow things all came together, and on the evening of August 26, 1970, an estimated twenty to fifty thousand women, Black and White, took over Fifty-seventh Street to walk in the biggest march for women's equality this country had ever witnessed. Participants included Gloria Steinem, who went on to found *Ms.* magazine in 1972, Representative Bella Abzug from New York, Beulah Sanders of the National Welfare Rights Organization, Flo Kennedy, and Representative Shirley Chisholm, who claimed to have suffered more discrimination as a woman than she ever did as a Black. It looked as though a coalition of White and Black women had finally joined forces to support feminism.

Behind the scenes, however, racial tensions flared. A Black feminist group known as the Third World Women's Alliance (TWWA) wished to carry a sign reading "Hands Off Angela Davis." Earlier that year, Davis had been dropped from her teaching post at the University of California and, more recently, had been charged with first-degree murder, first-degree kidnaping, and conspiracy to commit both. Some guns that had been used to kidnap a judge, several jurors, and the district attorney during a trial for a Black prisoner had been registered in her name, and even though she was not present at the scene of the crime, Davis was "wanted" by the FBI. Members of TWWA were greatly concerned about Davis, especially in light of the recent violence directed at Black Panther members by government officials. Their political sympathy for Davis was not shared by the White women organizers of the anniversary march, though. As Frances Beal of the TWWA recalled, "One of the leaders of NOW ran up to us and said angrily, 'Angela Davis has nothing to do with the women's liberation.' "

Beal shot back at her, "It has nothing to do with the kind of liberation you're talking about, but it has everything to do with the kind of liberation we're talking about."

There were other signs of racial divisiveness. The following year, award-winning author Toni Morrison wrote a piece for the *New York Times Magazine* in which she was highly critical of the "White women's" movement. Morrison stated, "The faces of those white women hovering behind that black girl at the Little Rock school in 1957 does not soon leave the retina of the mind . . . It is a source of amusement even now to black women to listen to feminists talk of liberation while somebody's nice black grand-mother shoulders the daily responsibility of childrearing and floor mopping."

At the same time, there were signs of support for feminism among a growing number of women in the Black community. In 1971, the National Women's Political Caucus was formed to help get women elected and appointed to political office, and many women of color, including those who were conservative, found this group far more appealing than NOW. The following year, approximately thirty Black women from the New York area formed their own group, the National Black Feminist Organization (NBFO), to "address the specific needs of the Black female who is forced to live in a society that is both racist and sexist." NBFO founding member Eleanor Holmes Norton confessed, "It took us some time to realize that we had nothing to fear from feminism." Within a year, NBFO's membership grew to over two thousand members in ten chapters. By 1974, however, the NBFO was in decline.

Activist Black women found themselves torn between loyalty to their own community and a growing desire to struggle for women's rights. Most ended up fighting a two-front war for equality. Audre Lorde neatly summed up their conflicting sentiments in a 1973 poem entitled "Who Said It Was Simple":

WHO SAID
IT WAS SIMPLE

There are so many roots to the tree of anger
that sometimes the branches shatter
before they fall

Sitting in Nedicks
the women rally before they march
discussing the problematic girls
they hire to make them free
An almost white counterman passes
a waiting brother to serve them first
and the ladies neither notice nor reject
the slighter pleasures of their slavery.
But I who am bound by my mirror
as well as my bed
see causes in color
as well as sex

and sit here wondering
which me will survive
all these liberations

Despite Black women's reluctance to join NOW, and their less visible involvement in the women's movement in general, surveys indicated that, as a group, Black women were actually supporting feminist issues more than White women were. In 1972, a Louis Harris–Virginia Slims poll revealed that 62 percent of Black women endorsed efforts to change women's status in society, while only 42 percent of White women did. The survey also found that 67 percent of Black women were sympathetic to women's liberation groups, compared with only 35 percent of White women. By the end of the decade, in 1980, another study yielded similar results, finding that Black women embraced the precepts of the women's movement as much, if not more, than White women. Taken together, these two studies showed that it was simply not true that Black women were uninterested in women's liberation. Instead, what Black women opposed was the label *feminist,* which they equated with man-hating lesbians, and the perceived, and in some cases actual, racial prejudice of the White women running feminist organizations.

In 1979, former NOW president Hernandez concluded, in a minority task force report, that NOW had been silent for too long on issues of racial inequity. Her hopes for change faded, however, after the 1979 annual election of officers at NOW's national convention. Although a Black candidate named Sharon Parker was running for secretary for the second year in a row, an all-White panel of officers was elected. For Hernandez, this was the final straw. In a fit of anger, she accused NOW of being "too White and middle class," and called for the resignation of all its non-White members.

The fallout from this racial rift may have cost NOW, and the women's movement in general, passage of the Equal Rights Amendment. Instead of going after the support of Black and working-class women, who had the most to gain from ERA, NOW mostly sought the support of women who were White and middle class. When ERA did not receive the necessary number of state endorsements, some say the momentum of the women's movement died along with it.

Women's Studies and Feminist Scholarship

Feminist issues were kept alive in the conservative eighties on the college campus. CR groups evolved into women's studies, the first of which was a course offered in 1970 at SUNY–Buffalo, called "Women in Contemporary Society." The women's studies movement spread so fast that, by 1976, a student at San Francisco State University could earn a B.A. in the subject. Today over six hundred universities offer courses in women's studies. With the emergence of women's studies as a discipline, there came a virtual explosion of books and articles on feminist theory and gender analysis.

A White middle-class bias inevitably dominated much early women's studies scholarship, with the result that Black women once again felt excluded. One theory in particular angered Black feminists—the assertion that patriarchy, not racism, was the root of all oppression. As long as White feminist scholars believed that resisting patriarchy was a more legitimate goal than resisting racial oppression, the voices of women of color would not be heard, and they would not be attracted to women's studies.

Unfortunately, the voices of Black female scholars were often not heard at all. Throughout the seventies, their unique perspective fell between the cracks of African American studies classes, where much of the material focused on men's issues, and women's studies courses, where much of the material was devoted to White middle-class women's issues. This situation changed somewhat in 1982, with the publication of Gloria T. Hull, Patricia Bell Scott, and Barbara Smith's book *All the Women Are White, All the Blacks Are Men, but Some of Us Are Brave,* the first Black women's studies book. But the gap was hardly filled. The reputation of women's studies faculty being insensitive to issues of race persisted. In fact, on the national level, accusations of racism at the National Women's Studies Association (NWSA), the discipline's only professional organization, founded in 1976, were so bad that the group nearly dissolved in the late eighties. (NWSA has since regrouped, and appears to be better on track, with a more multicultural orientation.)

During the eighties, bell hooks emerged as the Black community's premier feminist scholar. In her debut 1981 book, *Ain't I a Woman,* hooks admonished White women for failing to consider race and class privilege in their original analysis of women's conditions. hooks was also critical of Black women who responded to racism in the women's movement by forming their own feminist groups. According to her, such a move would only endorse and perpetuate the very racism that Black feminists were trying to erase.

In hooks's second book, *Feminist Theory: From Margin to Center,* she claimed that White women's demands for equality had a hidden racist agenda: it was really equality with White men, not Black men, that White women wanted. Were Black women, then, supposed to desire equality only with Black men? hooks also took to task White feminists for claiming to wish that more women of color would join the women's movement, and saying it was not the fault of Whites that more Black women had not done so. According to hooks, White women were acting like the hosts of a movement they did not own.

Another influential African American feminist scholar to gain recognition during the eighties was Audre Lorde, who admonished White feminists for their tendency to homogenize all women's experiences, thereby erasing the particularities of Black women's lives. In her 1984 book, *Sister Outsider,* Lorde wrote:

> By and large within the women's movement today, white women focus upon their oppression as women and ignore differences of race, sexual preference, class, and age. There is a pretense to a homogeneity of experience covered by the word *sisterhood* that does not in fact exist.

For their part, White feminists failed to realize that it was not enough to declare that they were not racist; it was necessary to identify the advantages of being White in a primarily White society. In 1988, White feminist scholar Peggy McIntosh first spoke of the invisible package of benefits that one receives simply by being White in a society that is racially unequal. Among the nearly fifty advantages she noted were (1) I can go shopping alone most the time, fairly well assured that I will not be followed or harassed by store detectives, (2) I can easily find academic courses and institutions that give attention only to people of my race, (3) I am never asked to speak for all the people of my racial group, and (4) if I declare there is a racial issue at hand, or there isn't a racial issue at hand, my race will lend me more credibility for either position than a person of color will have.

Despite recent attempts in the women's movement and women's studies curricula to become racially inclusive and multiculturally diverse, relatively few Black women publicly identify as feminists. A continuing reason appears to be the word itself. In her 1983 book, *In Search of Our Mother's Gardens,* Alice Walker proposed that African American women might be more comfortable identifying themselves as womanists. Walker defined a womanist as one who is committed to the survival and wholeness of entire people, male *and* female. By keeping men in the definition, she hoped that Black women would not reject the term as readily as they had *feminist.* Reactions to the new term have varied. While some women in the African American community, including Spelman College president Johnnetta Cole, embrace the word *womanism,* others, including bell hooks, reject it. For hooks, *womanist* lacks the tradition of radical politics that *feminist* has.

In reality, most women of both races do not label themselves either *feminist* or *womanist.* This does not mean, however, that women in general have not benefited from the many changes brought about by the women's movement. In fact, health care is probably the single area where feminist activism has most directly affected the average woman's life.

Health Care

Beginning in the seventies, feminists challenged the predominantly male medical profession, particularly gynecologists, obstetricians, and psychiatrists, for their insensitive and sometimes abusive treatment of female patients. Feminist health care activists helped women realize that they had to be more in charge of their own bodies and health. As a result, some women today, especially those living in urban areas, go to health care centers run exclusively by and for women.

The concerns of Black women and White women surrounding issues of health can vary, though, and White female activists have not always been sensitive to those differences. One difference is in the childbirth experience. In recent years, middle-class White women have sought to demedicalize and naturalize giving birth. A growing number are turning to midwives to assist in their deliveries, and most are now choosing to breast feed, instead of formula feed, their newborns. Ironically, in the early twentieth century both of these practices, midwifery and breast feeding, were associated almost exclusively with poor Black women in this country.

Until as recently as the sixties, Black women in rural areas across the South were routinely denied access to good medical facilities, and were forced to rely on midwives to assist them. For them, health care dramatically improved when they were finally allowed to have their babies in hospitals. Most of them also had no choice but to breast feed; baby formula was too expensive. In both rural and urban areas, health care got better when government-sponsored health care programs, such as Women, Infants, and Children (WIC), made it possible for them to feed their babies with formula.

White women and Black women continue to hold vastly different attitudes toward breast feeding. White gynecological nurse practitioner Anne Zachman observed these differences after she moved from working with primarily poor Black women at an inner-city health clinic, in north Philadelphia, to a women's health care center serving predominantly professional White women, on Chicago's North Side. Zachman confessed that in Philadelphia she eventually gave up trying to convince Black women that it was better for them and their babies if they breast fed. It seemed to her that these women viewed breast feeding as inconvenient, vaguely primitive, and somewhat nasty and shameful. In contrast, the majority of White professionals that Zachman saw in Chicago believed that they should breast feed their newborns, and if they were wavering, Zachman said, "I could usually convince them to do it." While Zachman thinks that these attitudes toward breast feeding may reflect class as much as race differences between the two populations of women, she maintains that even among middle-class Black women there is a tendency to avoid the "stigma" of breast feeding, because the practice has so long been associated with Black women who were too poor to do otherwise. In fact, data from the 1988 National Maternal and Infant Health Survey indicate that only 27 percent of African American women breast feed their newborns, while 61 percent of White women do, and that these differences hold across socioeconomic status.

The most visible and controversial change in women's health care brought on by feminists has been the legalization of abortion. Before 1970, when New York and Hawaii became the first states to legalize abortion, well-to-do women with unwanted pregnancies flew to England or one of the Caribbean islands, where the procedure was legal, to take care of the "problem." For poor women, this was not an option. In fact, statistics revealed that before abortion was made legal in New York city, 80 percent of the deaths caused by botched abortion attempts involved women who were either Black or Puerto Rican. Clearly the health of proportionately more Black women than White women stood to benefit by the legalization of abortion in this country. Why, then, have so few Black women been active in the abortion rights campaign?

To most prochoice middle-class White women, the abortion issue is about a constitutional right to privacy having to do with personal control over their bodies. The perception of abortion among many African American women has been affected by this country's shameful history of sterilization abuse. At the turn of the century, White social scientists and politicians claimed that Blacks, immigrants, and poor people were reproducing at a much faster rate than well-to-do Whites. To stop the perceived genocide of the human race (that is, of intelligent White people), many encouraged birth control as a "duty" for poor people not to reproduce so much. Only later did birth control take on the meaning of a "right" of women who wished to control their fertility.

The best-known crusader in the birth control movement was White social activist Margaret Sanger. While often hailed as a courageous feminist leader, she too was influenced by the ideology of her day. Sanger once stated that the chief goal with respect to birth control was "more children from the fit, less from the unfit."

The government gradually came to accept that one way to stop undesirable women from having children was to surgically remove their womb. The eugenics movement, as it was called, spread so fast that, by 1932, twenty-six states had passed compulsory sterilization laws, and the government provided federal assistance to states to help pay for the services. As recently as the sixties, mentally retarded women, or any women deemed unfit for motherhood, were at risk of the mutilating surgery. Predictably, statistics revealed that proportionately fewer White women than Black women were forced to undergo the procedure.

In 1973, while White feminists were celebrating the *Roe* v. *Wade* Supreme

Court decision, many Black women did not view the legalization of abortion as anything to feel good about. Even Black feminists who recognized the important health benefits for their community resulting from legalizing abortion ended up angry and frustrated at White feminists who repeatedly glossed over the matter of sterilization abuse in their public discussions of women's reproductive rights. Angela Davis believes that had White women been more sensitive to concerns about this abuse, more African American women would have joined in the fight to prevent the erosion of women's reproductive rights in the years that followed. And it's particularly unfortunate that this didn't happen, as poor Black women were hardest hit by the movement's setbacks.

In 1977, Congress passed the Hyde Amendment, prohibiting the use of any federal funds to pay for abortions. This meant that women on welfare, proportionately more of whom were Black, had to come up with their own money to pay for the procedure. Even today when such women arrive at hospitals and clinics for abortions, they may find themselves being persuaded into getting sterilized at the same time. While the federal government continues to find it morally unacceptable to pay for abortions for poor women, it is quite willing to foot the bill for poor women to undergo sterilization.

In addition to the Hyde Amendment, there have been other setbacks in women's abortion rights that seem to contain a hidden agenda. The predominantly White antichoice groups, such as Operation Rescue, seldom mount their protests at places that help poor Black women to terminate their pregnancies. As Davis sees it, "While women of color are urged at every turn to become permanently infertile, white women enjoying prosperous economic conditions are urged, by the same forces, to reproduce themselves." Whatever the reasons, statistics compiled in 1990 by the Alan Guttmacher Institute indicate that in this country, Black women are more than twice as likely to have abortions as White women (5.4 per hundred Black women compared with 2.2 per hundred White women).

Of course, African American women as a group remain as much divided on the abortion issue as White women. On the prochoice side there have been such visible African American women as Faye Wattleton, who for years served as the national director of Planned Parenthood, and Byllye Avery, founder and director of the National Black Women's Health Project (NBWHP). But unlike prochoice White women, who focus primarily on the safety and legality of the abortion procedure, prochoice African American women view unwanted pregnancies as symptomatic of larger economic and social problems in the Black community. At NBWHP clinics, Black teenage girls with unwanted pregnancies can receive, if necessary, individualized instruction to help earn a GED and job-training skills to help them become self-sufficient.

Although more African American women today have become involved in the abortion rights movement, only about 5 percent of the estimated 300,000 marchers who attended the April 1989 Abortion Rights Rally in Washington were women of color. The majority of prochoice activists continue to be middle-class White women.

Prolife African American women also see the reasons for opposing abortion somewhat differently from prolife White women. Irene Esteves, national director of the Professional Women's Network, contends that White women are grossly insensitive to the tradition of extended family support within the African American community, which ensures that all babies will be taken care of. Black Americans for Life spokesperson Akua Furlow believes that "Black women do not realize that the people forcing abortion on our people as a panacea to our social problems have a long history of beliefs in eugenics. They have a long history of racism." Nonetheless, a recent survey by the National Council of Negro Women reveals that 73 percent of minority women believe the decision to abort is one that women must make for themselves; only 11 percent believe that birth control and abortion are strategies by Whites to reduce the Black population.

Another area in which the women's movement resulted in change for the average woman is mental health care, particularly outpatient services. Traditionally, most psychotherapists were White men, and most of their patients were White women. African American women did not generally embrace the concept of having a paid professional sort out their emotional problems for them.

During the seventies and eighties, there was a huge influx of women into the field of mental health care. Many female clients began to prefer working with a female therapist. But White female psychotherapists who work with African American women are frequently disappointed to find that they cannot gain their clients' trust. African American women are often taught that it is a sign of weakness to put your "business on the street," especially when that street is outside the Black community. In contrast, White culture tends to encourage its women in disclosing information about themselves as a socially acceptable way to establish trust with new people, especially other women. This difference in communication can create tension and misunderstanding between White female therapists and Black female clients. And many African American female psychotherapists report that they must work harder with White female clients than with their Black clients to establish themselves as competent and credible.

Nonetheless, Black women are far less likely to consider and commit suicide as a "way out" than White women, even though disproportionately far more African American women endure poverty and violence. According to the U.S. Bureau of Census, White women are more than twice as likely to commit suicide than Black women. African American poet Kate Rushin captures the attitudes of Black women toward suicide in the following poem:

> IN ANSWER TO THE QUESTION:
>   HAVE YOU EVER CONSIDERED SUICIDE?

> Suicide?!?!
> Gurl, is you crazy?
> I'm scared I'm not gonna live long enough
> As it is

> I'm scared to death of high places
> Fast cars
> Rare diseases
> Muggers
> Drugs
> Electricity
> And folks who work roots

> Now what would I look like
> Jumpin offa something
> I got everything to do
> And I ain't got time for that

> Let me tell you
> If you ever hear me
> Talkin about killin my frail self
> Come and get me

Sit with me until that spell passes
And if they ever
Find me layin up somewhere
Don't let them tell you it was suicide
Cause it wasn't

I'm scared of high places
Fast moving trucks
Electricity
Drugs
Folks who work roots
And home-canned string beans

Now with all I got
To worry about
What would I look like
Killin myself

Despite a history of generally negative attitudes toward psychotherapy on the part of many African American women, there is some indication that such views are starting to change. A growing number now realize the benefits of talking honestly and openly about their anxieties. Violence, and the threat of violence, are taking their toll. According to one estimate, six out of every ten Black women in this country suffer from some type of major physical disorder related to their emotional well-being. As African American psychotherapist Julia Boyd succinctly puts it, "Our silence isn't golden; it's deadly."

Black women are also joining White women in exploring how low self-esteem affects them politically. In her 1992 book, *Revolution From Within: A Book of Self-Esteem,* Gloria Steinem revealed for the first time her private struggles in learning to accept herself. She turned around the popular feminist slogan of the seventies, "The personal is political," to say, "The political is personal." Boyd appears to have reached a similar conclusion in her 1993 book, *In the Company of My Sisters: Black Women and Self-Esteem.* She warns Black women that before they can get ahead, they must learn to love themselves, and she details how to do just that.

The Church

Traditionally, of course, Black women suffering from emotional stress and low self-esteem turned to the church for comfort. In recent years, even this staid institution has undergone political change.

During the sixties, some Black male theologians began identifying the ways in which Christianity was used to perpetuate racial inequality. They questioned why Black people were encouraged to worship the image of a White-looking God, pointing out that Jesus probably did not have blond hair and blue eyes, but was likely a dark-skinned man of some African descent. But when feminist theologians began raising analogous questions in relation to why God was male, and how the Bible was used to undermine women, they received little support. Black theologians and ministers may have been ready and willing to reject Paul's biblical command to slaves to be obedient to their masters as a valid justification of slavery, but they did not appear to question Paul's comments about women. Indeed, Black ministers, according to the Episcopal priest and lawyer Pauli Murray, seemed to fashion their own liberation theology after "super-male chauvinistic traditions."

Black women were slow to embrace feminist theology for many of the same reasons they failed to support other feminist notions: issues of race and racism were overlooked or ignored. A prime example of this tendency, and the distrust that resulted, can be seen in the work of Mary Daly, the most widely known of the radical feminist liberation theologians. She attacked the presence of male-dominated language and symbolism in the Bible in her classic 1973 book, *Beyond God the Father,* arguing that the problem could not be fixed by simply adding feminine pronouns to all references to God. Daly called for *God* to become a verb—"the Verb of verbs." She argued that only through such radical and dynamic transformation of the word *God* could women in the larger society break free of its masculine influence.

In her 1978 *Gyn/Ecology: The Metaethics of Radical Feminism,* Daly further developed her ideas. Unfortunately, she returned to the tenet that racism was only a manifestation of patriarchy, the larger problem in society. Black feminist scholars were frustrated by the audacity of a White woman, who has herself never experienced the destructive effects of racism, deciding which problem was more central. Clearly, Daly meant to be racially inclusive. She specifically made a point of inviting Black women to participate with White women in returning to a goddess spirituality, to become a part of what she termed the Sisterhood/Be-Friending process. Yet the goddess images Daly included were all White, Western, and European. Audre Lorde responded in an "open letter" to Daly, stating, "What you excluded from *Gyn/Ecology* dismissed my heritage and the heritage of all other non-european women, and denied the real connections that exist between all of us."

African American women may have rejected some elements of White feminist criticisms of religion, but they have had their own complaints about the church. African American theologian Theresa Hoover has been quite outspoken about the fact that Black women give the most to the church and get the least back. As she puts it, without Black women's "stick-to-itiveness," most Black churches would have failed to keep their doors open or their preachers fed.

However, most African American women defend their high level of involvement in the church, claiming that Christianity has given them a heightened sense of community and connectedness that many White women lack. They also see Black women successfully moving into church leadership roles, pointing, as an example, to Barbara Harris, an African American who in 1988 became the first woman ever to be elected an Episcopal bishop. African American female pastors are starting to organize, too; they gathered for the first time in November 1993 to analyze their particular issues. One of the topics discussed at this history-making conference was the difference between Black and White women in the church. Audrey Bronson, who is pastor of Sanctuary Church, believes that Black women are more likely than White women to establish their own churches, because "White women will stay and fight the system, while Black women feel they don't have to take it."

Politics

The influences of the women's movement continue to be felt politically. In most states, women can now bring charges of sexual assault against abusive husbands and have ex-lovers arrested for stalking, and in some states lesbians can now legally adopt and get custody of their own children from a previous marriage. Every year, more women are elected to public office; they presumably better represent the needs of women, children, and the poor.

The women's movement has also made the workplace a friendlier place for women. Title VII of the 1964 Civil Rights Acts was expanded and amended to protect women from being fired, or held back from promotions, because they were pregnant or refused to conform to sex-role stereotyping. It was also Title VII that served as the legal basis for women's right to work free of hostile and intimidating sexual harassment.

Unfortunately, there is an enormous gap between the ideals of the law and the realities of millions of working women in this country. Nowhere was this gap more apparent than in the 1991 accusations that Professor Anita Hill brought against Judge Clarence Thomas. During Thomas's confirmation hearings for appointment to the Supreme Court, Hill claimed that Thomas harassed her while she was working at the EEOC, the agency charged with hearing such cases. While much has been said and written about the Hill-Thomas spectacle, there is no question that these hearings revealed how differently White and Black women are apt to respond to issues where race and sex intersect.

Feminist White women rallied to Hill's defense, viewing the situation in terms that were strictly gender-based, while many African American women, even those who believed Hill, were convinced otherwise. Many believed that the charges saw the light of day only because Thomas and Hill were both African American. bell hooks, who has written extensively on the topic, maintains that had Hill been White, the establishment would have demanded respect for her privacy and blocked the spectacle from ever happening. African American economist and columnist Julianne Malveaux also believes that a major reason for many White women's enthusiastic support of Anita Hill was that she was "well-educated, soft-spoken, dignified, and aloof." Malveaux questions whether this level of support would have been extended to a poor working-class Black woman not as refined as Hill.

The Thomas-Hill case also marked a turning point for White and Black women's political relations in this country. Even if they didn't always agree with each other, the hearings did manage to get women of both races talking again about matters that particularly concern women. Here are just some of the many changes that have taken place as a direct or indirect result of Anita Hill's testimony. In its wake (1) nearly a dozen political organizations and new groups were formed by African American women, including the Philadelphia-based Ain't I a Woman Network, and the nationally networked African American Women in Defense of Ourselves; (2) the number of women elected to the Senate has grown from two to seven, and twenty-four new female representatives joined twenty-three incumbents in the House of Representatives, raising the number of women in the House to an all-time 11 percent of the House; (3) the Supreme Court has become more liberal in its interpretation of Title VII protections for women, ruling in *Harris* v. *Forklift Systems* that women do not have to demonstrate severe psychological harm from sexual harassment but need prove only that the harassment interferes with their job performance; (4) accusations of sexual harassment at the 1991 Navy Tailhook Association Convention were taken seriously, and resulted in the dismissal of some top naval officers; (5) all branches of the military, including its academies, have been put on alert regarding the discriminatory treatment of women in the armed services. Women of both races were rudely awakened to the truth that the fight for women's rights is far from over. In response, Rebecca Walker, daughter of Alice Walker and goddaughter of Gloria Steinem, established what she calls the Third Wave, a new political group for younger women of different races, classes, and ethnicities to carry on the fight for women's political rights.

Meanwhile, the women's movement continues to become more multicultural. At the 1990 national conference, NOW delegates, inspired perhaps by Alice Walker's novel *Possessing the Secret of Joy,* unanimously passed a resolution pledging support and money to the Inter-African Committee working to bring an end to female genital mutilation in Africa and the Middle East. NOW has also played an active role in the distribution of *Warrior Marks,* a film documentary on the subject. More African American women are moving into positions of leadership within NOW at both the local and national levels. In Chicago in 1988, on the twenty-fifth anniversary of the founding of NOW, Mary Morten became the first African American elected president of a major NOW chapter. And in 1993, Marcia Ann Gillespie was appointed the first African American editor in chief of *Ms.* magazine. As former editor of *Essence,* Gillespie has brought much-needed attention to issues concerning women of color.

At the same time, charges of racism continue be leveled periodically at NOW and other feminist organizations. Most recently, Efia Nwangaza, a Black South Carolina lawyer who ran unsuccessfully for the presidency of NOW, angrily claimed that White feminists still disregard their own role in the oppression of people of color. Some African American feminists also maintain that NOW was too slow in its defense of African American Lani Guinier when it became clear that her nomination for assistant U.S. attorney general was in trouble. They feel that had Guinier been White, NOW would have more vigorously and publicly supported her. On the other hand, few African American women came to the defense of White female candidates Zoe Baird and Kimba Wood when their nominations for attorney general faltered.

Despite such brushfires, the political relationship between White and Black women has much improved since the beginning of the modern women's movement in the 1960s. African American women activists are beginning to accept that it is not necessary for them to agree with White female activists to appreciate the new terrain they helped open up for all women. White feminists are finally starting to listen when African American feminists state that women's rights are not always going to be their top priority.

African American women will continue to play a pivotal role in politics, in part because they have the best chance of drawing the necessary support from both the African American and the liberal White communities. In fact, according to statistics compiled by the Women's Action Coalition, African American women are the fastest-growing group in American electoral politics today. In Congress, their numbers have increased from four to ten, and their voices, though small, can be heard in two major caucuses: the forty-eight-member Congressional Caucus for Women's Issues and the forty-member Congressional Black Caucus. Because African American women stand at the crossroads of issues concerned with race and gender, in many ways they may be able to suggest new solutions to problems in society. It is African American women's turn, as well, to make a difference.

Within months of being put in office, Senator Carol Moseley Braun demonstrated her potential to transform "politics as usual." In a move that angered many conservatives, but cheered liberal White and Black women alike, Braun effectively blocked the renewal application of a design patent for the insignia of the United Daughters of the Confederacy—which featured the flag of the Confederacy. She was the first person in the history of the Senate singlehandedly to turn around a vote on something that had previously been approved. While certainly the issue is symbolic, Braun's victory stands as a promise of far greater things to come for activist women everywhere.

Chapter Seven

Relations on the Home Front

So, people in the South loved the blacks as individuals, but not as a group. And people in the North loved them as a group, but would have no part of them as individuals. I would imagine that the blacks in the South felt the same way—that they feared whites as a group but loved them as individuals. I think this is true still, that there are many blacks who have good relations with individual whites but don't with a group.

> —*Elinor Birney, White domestic employer,*
> *from Susan Tucker's*
> Telling Memories Among Southern Women:
> Domestic Workers and Their Employers in the
> Segregated South, *1988*

In private, we were often like sisters, laughing and chatting and enjoying one another's company . . . But whenever other people were around, the barrier of color went up automatically. Without acknowledging that we were doing so, we became more distant to one another. She became the rich, white lady author, and I became quiet, reserved, and slipped into her shadow, the perfect maid.

> —*Idella Parker,* Idella:
> Marjorie Rawlings' Perfect Maid, *1992*

Among women's interracial relationships, perhaps none is more deeply personal yet emotionally enigmatic than that between a Black domestic and her White employer. Born of inequality, with historical links to slavery, this cross-race relationship has survived well into the twentieth century. Although the number of Black domestics working for White women has declined dramatically in recent decades, there nonetheless remain many women, especially older women living in the South, whose primary connection to a woman of another race is of this kind. Some White women point with pride to the positive relations they have with their Black housekeepers as evidence of their lack of racial prejudice. The attitudes held by Black domestic servants are often more varied and complex. Many are understandably resentful that they have been forced into domestic service because of the lack of job opportunities for Blacks, and feel bitter toward the White families for whom they work or worked. But other Black domestic servants develop warm and lasting relations with their White female employers, and especially the White children, whom they may have once nurtured as their own.

Black Domestics and White Employers

For Black women, the tradition of working in the homes of White women goes back hundreds of years. Initially, Emancipation did little to change the quality of life of most Southern Black women. Those who had been house slaves before the Civil War carried on in that capacity, only now as employees with meager financial compensation. Most of those who previously had slaved in the fields abandoned such work for more appropriately feminine chores in the home, but rarely was the home their own. While a small number of Negro women—mostly those who had lived free before Emancipation—did have husbands who made enough to allow them to stay home, most of the Black women in the South were desperately poor. To manage, they turned to the only work they could get: cleaning White women's homes and taking care of White women's children, often at the expense of their own. In the process, the racial-caste system of the South was left solidly intact.

In the North, the situation was slightly different, if only because fewer Black women lived there. Since the formation of the colonies, there had

....

always been some free Negro women who worked in the homes of Whites. Yet there were never enough to meet the demand, so Northern Black women shared this lowly occupation with immigrant White women, especially those of Irish descent. In fact, 1850 census figures show that a full 70 percent of domestics in the Boston area were born in Ireland. In general, White servants were considered less reliable, because as soon they got married, most quit working. Black women, married or not, were usually too poor to afford that luxury, and most remained chained to menial household labor all their lives.

Still, to many newly freed slaves, the North seemed the Promised Land in comparison with the South. From the late nineteenth century to the Great Depression of the 1930s, a steady stream of Black women migrated northward in hope of a better way of life. Most were disappointed. At the turn of the century, as the country became increasingly industrialized, working-class White women were able to abandon domestic chores for better paying factory and office work, but when Black women applied for positions as clerks, stenographers, typists, and bookkeepers, they were usually turned away. Instead, Black women were forced to fill the gap in domestic service left behind by White women. As a result, in both the North and South, Black women cleaned the homes of Whites. Reflecting the changing demographics, in 1890, Black women constituted only 28.8 percent of all domestics in the country, but by 1920, they made up close to 46 percent. Regional differences remained significant: in 1920, only 18 percent of female domestics in the North were Black; in the South, Black female domestics made up a full 82 percent.

The status of White women who had Black domestic servants varied from one part of the country to the next. Because there were relatively fewer Black women in the North, it was considered far more prestigious for a Northern White family to have a Black housekeeper, especially one who was a live-in, than it was in the South. Below the Mason-Dixon Line, even many working-class White women were able to afford someone else to clean their homes. In fact, as recently as the 1950s, the South was referred to as a "White housewives' utopia" because of the abundance of inexpensive Black domestic servants.

As late as 1940, 60 percent—over two million—of all employed Black women in this country identified themselves as domestic servants. Even twenty years later, as many as a third of Black women continued to list domestic service as their primary occupation. It was not until after passage

of the 1964 Civil Rights Act that employment opportunities for Black
women finally opened up. And once they did, Black women left domestic
work in droves. By 1970, only 18 percent of employed Black women categorized themselves as "private household workers" in the official census—the
first time in history that the category did not head the list of occupations of
African American women.

In 1992, only 876,000 persons, nearly all of them women, remained in
private household work. In that same year, among the total number of
domestic servants, the percentage who identified themselves as Latino (19.6
percent) for the first time surpassed those who identified themselves as Black
(18.6 percent). Today, a domestic worker is more likely to be an immigrant
from Central or South America or one of the Caribbean islands. But given
the history and sheer number of Black women who have worked or continue to work in the homes of Whites, it is not surprising that Black author
Alice Childress, in her 1956 book, *Like One of the Family,* declared, "It's a
rare thing for anybody to find a colored family in this land that can't trace a
domestic worker somewhere in their history."

Until recently, the personal relationships between Black domestics and
White female employers were never considered worthy of serious study.
The world of women working in the home was less visible, and was considered less important, than the often more public lives of men. However, since
the emergence of feminist scholarship in the late seventies, research has
expanded to include the realities of working women's lives. The day-to-day
interactions between Black domestics and their White employers have been
the subject of two recent books. The first, *Between Women: Domestics and
Their Employers,* published in 1985, was based on the doctoral research of
African American sociologist Judith Rollins, who worked as a domestic
servant, between September 1981 to mid-May 1982, for ten different White
women in the Boston area. She supplemented her personal experiences with
interviews of twenty White female employers of domestics and twenty Black
housekeepers. Her research brings to light how very differently domestic
work is viewed from the perspective of the Black employee and the White
employer.

The second book, *Telling Memories Among Southern Women: Domestic
Workers and their Employers in the Segregated South,* published in 1988, was
written by a White researcher named Susan Tucker. Tucker, with the help
of an African American assistant, Mary Yelling, interviewed over forty
Black women and White women about domestic service in the South today.

A Southerner herself, Tucker was primarily interested in the insights of other Southern women on the rapidly changing roles of women there.

Taken together, these two books reveal that regional differences still exist regarding the nature and longevity of domestic servitude. In the North, where racial attitudes are considered generally more liberal, White women and Black women traditionally had more opportunity to meet and interact in places other than a White woman's home. Also, most African American women who turned to domestic service did not expect to stay in that occupation very long. But in the South, with its history of Jim Crow laws, many workplaces, schools, and neighborhoods were strictly segregated, and domestic employment was often the only point of connection between Black and White women. Although in recent decades the South has become more integrated, even today it is possible to find Black women who have worked for the same White family for thirty years or more. In some cases, multigenerational connections can be traced back a hundred years between the two families, White employers and Black domestics. The greater longevity of domestic employment in the South also leads more Southern Whites to invoke the phrase "like one of the family" when describing a particularly loyal and much beloved Black servant.

Not surprisingly, few Black domestics, in either the South or North, respond favorably to this quaint expression. As paid employees, and frequent victims of prejudice both within and outside White households, Black women are far more attuned to the many ways in which they are *not* treated as "one of the family." For example, family members, unlike their domestic servants, eat in the dining room, not in the kitchen. And even though Black domestics often recognize that they are very much loved by their White female employers, privately they do not consider themselves "family members." That is the White employer's fantasy, not theirs.

Susan Tucker reported that nearly every White female employer she interviewed singled out her own Black domestic servant as exceptional. As Tucker noted, if White women truly believe that their servants are somehow exceptional, what must they think of most Blacks in general? Apparently, not much. Nonetheless, in the South many White women do sincerely believe that their Black domestic servants are special women, deserving high-quality care and the best medical treatment. Stories abound of those Black maids too old or infirm to work anymore being financially supported by their White employers. If a former maid is in need of surgery that she cannot afford, it is often the White family that covers the expenses. This

attitude of personal responsibility is as yet another defining difference be-
tween many White employers in the North compared with those in the
South, a difference reflected in the chapter epigraph by Elinor Birney, a
White woman interviewed by Tucker.

Regardless of where in the country the women live, there are many more
similarities than differences in the domestic work relationship—similarities
that arise because the protagonists are women. The domestic-employer relationship is qualitatively different from any other. Work interactions in the
home are less formal than in an office. The division of responsibilities is less
clearly defined. Compared with men, at work in a more structured environment, White housewives may find it difficult to know exactly where their
role as the homemaker ends and the job of the hired servant begins. This
issue is compounded by the fact that housework is largely devalued. No
matter how good a job a domestic servant may do, her work is rarely
praised or viewed as worthy of special recognition.

This widespread devaluing of housework, along with the blurred boundaries of the job, affects how domestic employers handle their managerial
responsibilities. While some White women are content to supervise another
woman, others find it difficult to exercise their authority—a task made even
harder if the servant is perceived of as equal in status to themselves. Perhaps
this explains why historically most White women preferred housecleaners
who were Black rather than White. With racial differences, there was less
confusion about who had the power and status in the relationship—and
who did not. These complex, interrelated issues of race, as well as class, are
evident in the following story told by a forty-six-year-old White female
advertising executive named Mike about her mother:

> I grew up during the fifties and sixties outside Detroit. My father was
> a doctor, and my mother, as a doctor's wife, of course, always had a
> maid. Actually, we had several different housekeepers while I was
> growing up, and they were all Black, except this White one who was
> from Eastern Europe and hardly spoke a word of English. She was
> also the wife of a new doctor in residency at the hospital where my
> father worked. My mother could hardly handle the guilt—a White
> maid who was another doctor's wife! Instead of having this woman
> work, my mother spent all day teaching her how to speak proper En-
> glish. My sisters and I hated it because it meant we got stuck with all
> the housework that the maid wasn't doing. Looking back on it,

though, I guess, from my mom's perspective, it was more like "There but for the grace of God go I." It must have been extremely uncomfortable for her.

Ironically, some White women today, suffering from White liberal guilt, are more comfortable hiring a White domestic servant than one who is Black. It is easier for them to pretend that the obvious status differences between the employer and the domestic help are less great. Alice, a White college professor, recently described her feelings about hiring an older Black domestic servant:

> I used to have a White Polish college student who cleaned my house, but then she graduated and quit. My friend Toy recommended her housekeeper, a Black woman in her sixties named Jasmine. Even though Toy assured me that Jasmine was excellent, I hesitated for the longest time calling. I was paralyzed with guilt—guilt about hiring an older Black woman, and guilt about not hiring her. When I finally broke down and offered Jasmine the job, I ended up doubling her salary from what I had been paying the college student, just to assuage my own guilty feelings about hiring an older Black woman to clean up after me.

The home environment is also unique in fostering a type of intimacy between women not commonly found in other work situations. Caring for another woman's children and helping her to plan and successfully carry off a huge dinner party require a good relationship. From the perspective of both parties, the success of many domestic arrangements is measured in personal terms alone. During an interview conducted by Judith Rollins, a White female employer named Karen Edwards described what she looks for in a housekeeper: "I want reliability, honesty, niceness. The quality of the work is probably the least important thing." In the same study, a Black domestic named Elizabeth Roy commented:

> The worst thing that can happen in domestic work is a poor understanding with your employer. A bad relationship makes the work that much harder. That's it; a bad relationship. Then you've really got a hard job. You dread it.

When asked why she likes doing domestic work, Zelda Greene, a Southern Black domestic, told Susan Tucker, "I tell you, it's not so much the work—it's the people you're working for. That's what makes the difference."

Beneath this veneer of sociability, however, lie irrefutable status differences that undermine the development of a real friendship. White and Black women both know this, albeit in slightly different ways. As the employee, a Black woman is well aware that at any time she can be summarily dismissed, both emotionally and occupationally, by her White female employer, regardless of how nicely she acts. As the employer, the White woman, foolishly, may overestimate the extent to which her Black domestic really cares about her. Judith Rollins discovered from her own experiences as a domestic servant that "part of being a domestic was acting like the person the employer wanted her domestic to be." If at times that means acting like a best friend, then that is what a Black domestic will do. And if at other times, that means acting subservient, then that is what she will do.

In addition to being "invisible" at times, the domestic servant is required to listen sympathetically to an employer's problems, even when those problems seem trivial. A housekeeper is never free to say to her employer, "I'm sorry. I don't feel like listening to you right now," or, worse, "You think that's bad; let me tell you about my situation." Between women of equal status, the latter type of exchange would be common; reciprocal disclosures and shared emotions are what signal trust in a developing friendship. A White employer's intimate disclosures to her Black housekeeper are ultimately meaningless because they entail no risk. The social worlds of domestic employers and their servants are too far apart for even the most embarrassing and shameful confidences to have any consequences for the White woman. Nonetheless, Black domestic servants are expected to listen attentively to the problems of their White employers for the sake of the relationship between them.

Servants are required to be deferential in other ways, as well. These may include using only the back door, addressing employers as "ma'am" but being addressed back more intimately, wearing a "maid's" uniform, and acting grateful when given unwanted gifts.

Not long ago, a Black woman entering the front door of a White family's home would have caused the neighbors to talk. Restricting servants to back entrances was a hypocritical gesture, however, done for appearances' sake only. As Ruby Lee Daniels, a former domestic interviewed by the White author Nicholas Lehmann for his 1991 book *The Promised Land: The Great Black Migration and How It Changed America,* angrily noted, "This white woman thinks I'm good enough to nurse her baby and to make the meals that her family eats. Why am I not good enough to go in her house by the front door?"

Asymmetry in the use of names also bothers domestic servants. Addressing their employers as Miss, Mrs., or Ms. while being called by their first names, especially by the children, is insulting. Even the Southern practice of placing "miz" before the first name of an older domestic servant is not a true gesture of respect; her last name is still not being used and, in many cases, is not even known by most White family members.

Requiring a domestic to wear a uniform similarly serves to demarcate her status from that of her White employer. For that reason, many domestic servants today refuse to wear uniforms.

In yet another show of deference, Black domestics are expected to act grateful for gifts given to them by their White employers, even for items that are clearly unwanted or obviously useless. Like most employees, Black domestics would rather have a bonus or a raise than be burdened by such offerings. In recent years, many have begun to inform White employers that they don't "tote"—take food or other material goods home. Others, however, such as Ellen Samuel, continue quietly to accept the often useless "gifts." "I didn't want most of that junk. But you have to take it. It's part of the job; makes them feel like they're being so kind to you. And you have to appear grateful. That makes them feel good."

David Katzman, in his 1978 book, *Seven Days a Week,* termed gift-giving an expression of maternalism, the way a nurturing but controlling mother might take care of her young. The White employer seems to feel that, without her help, the Black domestic servant would be hopelessly lost. As one smug White female employer commented, regarding the benefits Black domestic servants receive when working in White households, "They live with people of higher refinement and education than themselves and feel that influence . . . They are given a chance to learn order, system and economy, patience and forbearance, and thus are better fitted to be themselves thrifty housekeepers." Not surprisingly, domestic servants hold such employers in contempt. As a Black housekeeper, Joan Fox, commented, "I wouldn't want to be in her place . . . I would never want to live like that, sitting around, talking foolishness, and doing nothing."

Nonetheless, Tucker concluded, from her research in the South, that gift-giving by some wealthy White female employers is in many cases a sincere attempt to express care, and even love, for a long-term domestic servant.

Black domestics give to their employers something far more precious than anything material—leisure time, an intangible benefit seldom granted to Black domestics, who are often expected to hold everything together for everyone else. Poet and scholar Adrienne Rich feels that the presence of Black domestic servants in the homes of White women allows them to regress emotionally. These same White women, however, sometimes turn around and infantilize Blacks, calling them "irresponsible, lazy, intellectually inferior, and childlike."

The cumulative effect of such indignities is that, without warning, the Black domestic may quit. When this happens, the White employer is often stunned. In interview after interview, White women who had had this happen to them said, "But I treated her so well. I thought that we were friends. She was 'like one of the family.' If she was unhappy, why didn't she tell me what was wrong? I can't believe that she would walk out on me at a time when she knows how much I need her." Yet such women never seemed to notice the emotional mask that their housekeepers were forced to wear, or the times that their employees had to censor their true thoughts to maintain the appearance of getting along so well.

Often a last straw for a Black domestic is being accused of stealing. Every family loses things from time to time, but when there is a housecleaner around to blame for the loss, it becomes all too easy to do just that. Not all Black domestics are honest, nor are all White employers suspicious, but thoughts about stealing—whether or not it happens—do seem to permeate nearly every domestic arrangement. It is a painful and difficult subject. For some White women, it becomes impossible to ask a Black housecleaner where a lost item is for fear of sounding accusatory. To Black women who have tried very hard to prove themselves honest and hard-working, being suspected of theft is devastating and enraging. In reaction, long-suppressed anger over other indignities may finally erupt, sometimes in dramatic fashion. According to Black activist lawyer Flo Kennedy, her mother, Zella, "said it all" when she was falsely accused of theft, as Marcia Cohen relates in her book *The Sisterhood:*

Zella was at work in the home of a woman who was "quite preoccupied with dirt." One day Zella's employer approached her with a list of complaints—not unheard of, certainly, but this time, added to her normal harangue, was the accusation of theft. To be accused of stealing was beyond Zella's endurance. In a tantrum of rage, the young domestic removed every article of her clothing, down to her sanitary napkin. Then, her anger still unspent, the outraged Zella pulled off that last soiled item and shook it in her employer's shocked face.

Despite the rage, guilt, distrust, and active disdain that may accumulate between many Black domestics and their White employers, real and lasting affection can also be found. In the South particularly, many older Black housekeepers are secure in the knowledge that they are very much beloved by the White family for whom they work—or once worked. And many older White women, as well as their grown daughters, are confident that the love that they bestow upon a long-term Black female domestic is freely returned. Again, this affectionate bond between women of disparate race and class is nurtured in large part by the environment in which it takes place. It is hard to remain emotionally neutral in the face of such intensely positive and negative life events as childbirth, love, marriage, family violence, divorce, and death.

Black Domestics and Children

Black domestic servants and the White children they are asked to watch often develop strong attachments. African American women's studies scholar Bonnie Thornton Dills investigated the psychological strategies used by Black domestic workers in caring for another woman's children. The exchange of money for maternal love is a strange, if not impossible one to evaluate. How does one shell out X amount of affection to a helpless child in return for X amount of money without becoming emotionally involved? As Dills notes:

> Because most young children readily return love that is freely given and are open and accepting of people without regard to status factors that have meaning for their parents, the workers probably felt that they were treated with greater equality and more genuine acceptance by the children of the household.

Some Black domestic servants even have to contend with White children mistakenly believing them to be their real mother. Such maternal confusion produces a curious mixture of pride and pain in Black women domestics, as Mattie Washington said of her experience:

There's long time she [the child] use to thought I was her mamma. She would ask me why is my skin white and your brown, you my mamma? I tell her I'm not your mammy and I see the hurt coming in her eye. You know like she didn't want me to say that. I said there's your mamma in there, I'm just your nurse. She said no, you my mamma.

Such maternal confusion is usually resolved by the time the child is three. But as they develop a sense of gender identity, girls in particular begin to form a more fundamental connection with this other woman in their life. Perhaps that explains why White daughters far more than sons are likely to develop meaningful lifelong relationships with their Black housekeepers.

Black child care workers express a range of attitudes toward their White charges. Some Black women don't like the White children they watch over, yet others develop strong feelings of maternal love for them. However, they soon learn it is best to keep positive feelings in check, since the relationship between them is always tenuous. At any time, it can be severed by the White mother-employer. Some White mothers become jealous when their daughters start confiding more in the Black housekeeper than in them. And unlike the White employer's ultimately meaningless disclosures, the secrets told to a Black domestic servant by a White daughter display real trust. After all, if the Black domestic were so inclined, she could confide to the child's mother whatever her daughter has said. But what is perhaps most infuriating to White mothers is that most Black domestics do not.

White girls who grew up with a Black servant in the home similarly report a range of feelings for the woman. Most report having been greatly affected by the experience. Some feel that having another woman around made it easier for them to separate emotionally from their mother. Others admit that they patterned their self-image on both their biological mothers and the Black women who helped raise them. A few feel that the love they received from their Black servant seemed more genuine than the love they got from their own mother. After all, one's real mother was obliged to love them, but the Black domestic servant seemed to love them for no reason at all.

A White physician, Tara, who grew up in South Carolina, reveals just how emotionally interdependent the White daughter–Black domestic relationship can be:

> I'm in therapy right now and recently realized that I have spent more time talking about my early relationship with my Black maid, Sally, than with my own mother. Sally was the one I went to whenever I did anything bad, and she never ever judged me or told Mama, which was great. To this day—even though I'm forty-three—Sally still calls me her "baby."

Virginia, a thirtysomething White flight attendant who grew up in Louisiana and now lives up North, remains passionately devoted to her former Black caregiver. To this day, Virginia keeps a framed black-and-white photograph of herself and the uniformed "Miz Lil" on her dresser. Recently, she was teased by a close friend about the picture of her "mammy." Virginia was angered. "But I love Miz Lil. She helped raise me and is like a second mother. Why, Miz Lil would be more upset than my own mom if ever I forgot to send a card on Mother's Day."

And a White woman of Jewish faith named Lynn, who grew up on Chicago's North Shore, credits her Black domestic servant with educating her early on about matters of race. One day, when she was seven or eight, she was innocently dancing around the house singing a little ditty that she had heard at school: "Eenie meenie minie mo. Catch a nigger by the toe." Cora, the family housekeeper, came storming out of the kitchen and shook Lynn by the shoulder, saying, "Don't you ever say that word again!" Lynn was frightened; she had never seen Cora angry, and she didn't know which of the many words she had used was offensive. But once she figured it out, with the help of her mother, she was forever impressed by the power words have to hurt people.

Too often, however, the time and energy that many Black domestics devote to helping to raise White children are in inverse proportion to the time and energy that they have to spend on their own children. A Black domestic servant's absence from home deeply affects her own daughters especially. Resentment at being abandoned by their mothers can leave a deep wound in Black children. Years later, when the daughter is grown with children of her own, the wound may reopen when she sees her mother finally giving the grandchildren all the love and attention earlier denied to her. It's an issue that April Sinclair addressed in her touching coming-of-age novel, *Coffee Will Make You Black,* published in 1994. Set in the sixties, this story centers on a young Black girl named Stevie. In one scene, she listens as her mother, Evelyn, and her maternal grandmother fight about how the latter is spoiling Stevie. Evelyn reminds her mother how differently she treated her own children when they were all young:

> You raised us to be tough. I remember having to get myself dressed, help little Sheila and the boys get ready, fix breakfast, make Daddy's biscuits. Sometimes we went out wearing mismatched clothes, hair half combed, looking like ragamuffins, 'cause you'd left before day to go take care of some white family.

Toni Morrison, in *The Bluest Eye,* also explores the disruption in a Black family stemming from the mother's having to care for children who are White. In one particularly poignant scene, eleven-year-old Pecola, who is Black, and her two Black girlfriends, Claudia and Frieda, visit the White household where Pecola's mother, Pauline Breedlove, cleans and cares for a little White girl. While she is there, Pecola accidentally knocks a blueberry pie onto the floor. Mrs. Breedlove is so mad at Pecola for having caused the mess that she is almost speechless, yet still she manages to find time to comfort the young White girl upset by the spill:

> "Crazy fool . . . my floor, mess . . . look what you . . . work . . . get on out . . . now that . . . crazy . . . my floor, my floor . . . my floor." Her words were hotter and darker than the smoking berries, and we backed away in dread.
>
> The little girl in pink started to cry. Mrs. Breedlove turned to her. "Hush, baby, hush. Come here. Oh, Lord, look at your dress. Don't cry no more. Polly will change it." She went to the sink and turned tap water on a fresh towel. Over her shoulder she spit out words to us like rotten pieces of apple. "Pick up that wash and get on out of here, so I can get this mess cleaned up."

Tragically, Pecola comes to believe that if her eyes were blue, like this White girl's, everyone, including her mother, would love her more.

The daughters of White employers and the daughters of Black domestics do sometimes become friends, at least when both girls are young. Throughout the South, Black domestics still bring their young daughters to work with them to play with the White daughters of their employers. And White mothers, albeit not as often as they used to, still drop their daughters off at the maid's home for baby sitting or simply to play. That a White mother would leave her child at a Black family's home may strike some Whites, particularly Northerners, as incredible, but it does happen. Tara, the White South Carolinian mentioned earlier, vividly recalls visiting Sally's home as a child and playing with her children. April Sinclair mentions the innocent practice, as well as regional differences in race attitudes that contribute to its existence, in *Coffee Will Make You Black*. When Stevie asks her grandmother if she ever had a White girlfriend, the older woman tells Stevie about Kathy Jo, the White daughter of her mother's domestic employer:

> Once my mother was working for a family and I spent a lot of time over there. I grew up with Kathy Jo. We even took baths together. That was common in the South. We couldn't sit together on the street-car, but we could share the same bathwater. Figure that out . . . Kathy Jo's mother thought nothing of throwing her in the bed between me and my sister if she wanted my mother to keep Kathy Jo on a Saturday night. White folk in the South don't mind getting close to you as long as it's clear who works for who. White folk in the North don't care how big your house is, so long as you're not their neighbor.

The "friendship" abruptly ended when Stevie's grandmother failed to get an invitation from Kathy Jo to her tenth birthday party. As Black and White girls get older, status differences strain the relationship, ultimately breaking it apart.

Having been exposed to White middle-class childrearing practices, some Black women raise their own children differently. A Black domestic named Willa Murray claimed that the White family for which she worked taught her the "value of talking with the children, reasoning with them, explaining things and hearing their thoughts and opinions on various matters . . . Telling your children that you trust them places greater emphasis on self-direction than giving them orders to follow. Even if it means kids talk back, it can be good."

However, most Black domestics are critical of the way White mothers coddle their children. Aren't kids more likely to misbehave, they wonder, when they know that the only punishment they will receive is a "good talking-to"? Black mothers are more likely to use physical force and issue sharp verbal warnings to discipline their own offspring. For one thing, a good spanking takes less time than a lecture about why something is wrong, and time is the one thing that working Black mothers have precious little of. Such observed differences in the mothering styles of White and Black women may be reflective of class-based differences; economically disadvantaged women, regardless of race, tend to rely more on physical than verbal means of controlling their children. But it is interesting to note that even in fiction, most Black writers portray Black mothers as stern figures. As African American feminist scholar Gloria Wade-Gayles observes, "Mothers in Black women's fiction are strong and devoted . . . but . . . they are rarely affectionate."

Fortunately, Black daughters often have in their lives another woman—perhaps an aunt, a grandmother, or just a neighbor—who spoils them with unconditional love and emotional support. As discussed by Patricia Hill Collins in the article "The Meaning of Motherhood in Black Culture and Black Mother-Daughter Relationships," such women in the Black community are referred to as "othermothers." They assist bloodmothers in mothering responsibilities and play an especially important role in mentoring Black girls.

Othermothers are unique to the Black community, and may reflect the sentiment of the ancient African proverb "It takes a village to raise a child." Rarely do White mothers turn to other family members or friends to help raise their children. Instead, when a White woman needs assistance, she hires outside help, oftentimes a Black woman. Ironically, a Black housekeeper may thus serve for White girls the same function that an othermother serves for Black girls—that of a loving confidante and go-between with the biological mother.

Mothers and Biracial Daughters

A very different kind of cross-race relationship exists between the mother and daughter in a biracial marriage. Statistics derived from the 1990 census indicated that approximately four out of every thousand married couples, or

211,000 marriages in the United States that year, were racially mixed, Black and White. Just twenty years earlier, only 1.5 of every thousand marriages were mixed this way. The number of biracial offspring has similarly risen, from an estimated 8700 births in 1968 to nearly 45,000 in 1989. These figures are probably inaccurate, though, as many Black-White biracial babies born to unwed mothers are classified as monoracial. There is no dispute, however, that the number of biracial children born in this country will continue to grow. How do biracial children fare when raised by a White mother rather than a Black one?

Psychologists have begun to explore whether biracial children are more or less well-adjusted than monoracial children. In 1992, Raymond Vagas compared girls who were biracial, Black, and White, and concluded that biracial status is unrelated to overall social functioning. In another study, published in 1993, psychologists Nishimura and Priest looked at various strategies used by mothers in raising biracial children. The researchers discovered that mothers try to raise their biracial children by (1) denying that race is important, (2) promoting one parent's racial identity over the other's, or (3) acknowledging the child's biracial heritage.

Depending on other factors, either the second or third strategy can be successful. The first, however—denying that race is important—is nearly always disastrous, especially when the mother is White, which is likely to be the case, since 70 percent of all biracial marriages in the United States are between White women and Black men. Fortunately, most of these mothers do discuss the issue of racial identity with their children.

Yet even in the healthiest biracial family, subtle and not-so-subtle psychological challenges may arise, according to Candy Mills, the African American founding editor and publisher of *Interrace* and *Biracial Child*. Mills should know. In addition to editing two magazines that address issues of race, she is happily married to a White man and the mother of two biracial children, a boy and a girl. Mills has noticed an important but often overlooked factor in studies of biraciality, and that is the child's physical appearance. Although the appearance of offspring of any White-Black union is a complete genetic toss-up, White and Black mothers are affected differently by a child's racially mixed looks. For many Black women, especially those suffering from a color complex, certain social advantages may be seen in having a child, especially a daughter, with light skin and "good" hair. Such an attitude may be reinforced by Black relatives who exclaim what excellent coloring, facial features, and hair the child has. Relatives on the White side of the family hardly ever make such comments. Black mothers also expect that their biracial children will look essentially Black. There is already so much White—and Native American—blood pumping through the veins of the Black community that even in public, the presence of a dark-skinned mother with a light-skinned child typically does not provoke much speculation. Most strangers simply assume that this Black woman married, or perhaps "dated," a Black man much lighter than herself.

The White mother of a biracial child, however, contends with vastly different issues, since the child's biracial status is more "marked" for others to see. Even in public, strangers will usually be able to tell, by looking at a child's skin color, facial features, or hair texture, that he or she has some Black blood. In addition, because of this country's widespread acceptance of the one-drop rule—in which an ounce of Black blood renders full Black identity—as well its lack of a legal concept of biraciality, racially mixed children are usually designated as Black. A White mother, then, may experience more anxiety than a Black mother about how her biracial child will be identified.

Candy Mills believes that when biracial daughters are very young, they think of themselves as Black or White depending on the race of the mother. But as they enter the critical developmental phase during which individuation takes place, questions about their racial identity come to the fore. Conflict is especially likely to develop when the mother and daughter do not look alike; that is, when the mother is Black but her daughter looks White, or when the mother is White but her daughter looks Black. Such a situation can even trigger an identity crisis of sorts in the mother. This is what Mills confessed happened to her.

My daughter Gabriela is very light-skinned, and in public, perfect strangers used to come up to us to ask, "Is she your daughter?" Some people even assumed that I was Gabriela's nanny, which was really beginning to upset me. When Gabriela was around four, I started putting her in the sun, hoping that if her skin turned darker, we wouldn't get so many of these type comments. It worked, but then I began covering up Gabriela so that she wouldn't get too dark—the old color complex thing. Finally, I realized what I was doing, and was able to stop. Good thing, too, because Gabriela was starting to pick up that something funny was going on.

Mills added that when Gabriela turned eight, she asked her mother, "What race should I choose?" Candy replied, "You can only be what you are. You are biracial." But Gabriela persisted: "No, if I *had* to choose, what race should I be?" Candy this time told her, "Choose what is easier for you, what makes your life easier. Each individual must lead his or her own life."

The process of establishing racial identity when the mother is White may be particularly challenging for a biracial daughter. According to psychologist Nancy Chodorow, in her 1978 book *The Reproduction of Mothering,* gender differences, traceable to early childhood experiences with the mother, support such a contention. Between the ages of three and five, boys realize that they are different from their mothers, and form much of their masculine identity around these differences. The result is that boys are primed to grow up with a strong sense of self; but because they suffered a break with their first love, the mother, they may be less strong in their ability to connect fully with others. During this same developmental phase, girls are repeatedly told that they are the same as their mother and, in fact, one day will grow up to be just like her. Since she is never challenged to make that psychological break with her primary caregiver, the girl may retain the ability to connect with others, but her sense of self may become weak. In psychological terms: she lacks good ego boundaries between herself and others. What happens, then, to biracial daughters, who are simultaneously told that they are like their mothers but also that they are not?

For many biracial daughters, there are clear psychological advantages. Some have both well-established ego boundaries and a strong sense of connectedness with others. Perhaps this helps explain why so many biracial women are extraordinarily successful. The list of such women includes celebrities like film and television actresses Jasmine Guy, Jennifer Beals, Halle Berry, pop singers Mariah Carey and Paula Abdul, television news reporter Sue Simmons, and *Village Voice* columnist and author Lisa Jones. Each of these women was raised by a mother who is White, and, in some cases, without the benefit of a Black father around. Halle Berry recalls with pride how her White mother handled the issue of her racial identity:

My mother cleared it up for me when I was very young. She said when you look in the mirror you're going to see a Black woman. You're going to be discriminated against as a Black woman, so ultimately, in this society, that's who you will be. And that's made my life very easy. I think if you're an interracial child and you're strong enough to live "I'm neither Black nor White but in the middle," then more power [to you]. But I needed to make a choice and feel a part of a culture. I feel a lot of pride in being a Black woman.

Lisa Jones, who also identifies herself as Black, once asked her mother why she decided to raise her children to be Black, not biracial. Her mother's response was "I was not about to delude you guys into thinking you could be anything different in this country. And, frankly, I didn't think that being anything other than black would be any more desirable." And Mariah Carey, who actually identifies herself as multiracial, also gives credit for her lack of racial confusion and her success in life to the White woman who bore and raised her:

I am very much aware of my Black heritage, but I'm also aware of the other elements of who I am. And I think sometimes it bothers people that I don't say "I'm Black" and that's it. But it's not true. I have a mother who is 100 percent Irish who raised me from birth and who is my best friend. So if I were to say that I'm Black only, that would be negating everything she is. So when people ask, I say I'm Black, Venezuelan, and Irish, because that's who I am.

Regardless of whether a racially mixed daughter decides to identify herself as Black, biracial, or multiracial, she clearly need not be impaired by the experience of having a White mother. That is not to say that all biracial daughters are healthy or remain untouched by the emotional challenge of coming to terms with their mixed racial identity. In "Mama's White," an essay in her book *Bulletproof Diva: Tales of Race, Sex and Hair,* Lisa Jones discusses the discomfort the issue can cause:

Are you still staring: Let me guess. My white mother presents a different set of enigmas to you based on your own racial classification. Those of you who are black might find "evidence" of my white parent reason to question my racial allegiance. For those of you who are white, evidence of my white lineage might move you to voice deep-seated feelings of racial superiority. You might wonder why I would choose to identify as "fully" black when I have the "saving grace" of a white parent. I have no time for this sort of provinciality either. I realize both sets of responses display an ignorance of our shared cultural and racial history as Americans.

White mothers may also suffer psychologically from having to give up their daughters to another racial identity, a phenomenon known as the White Mother Martyr Syndrome.

Some biracial daughters clearly do not have good relations with their mothers. Conflicts and serious adjustment problems are especially likely when a White mother tries to hide the daughter's biracial status from family members, or regrets to the point of denial her relationship with a Black man. Black mothers, too, may be unhappy about having a daughter who is half-White. Some try to force a daughter who would like to acknowledge her biraciality to fully identify herself as Black; others even try to withhold the knowledge that the absent father is White. While it is generally easier for Black mothers to deny the Whiteness of their biracial daughters than it is for White mothers to deny the Blackness of their biracial daughters, in both cases it largely depends on how the child looks. When a girl's physical features are at odds with how she wants to identify herself, she is most vulnerable to low self-esteem and psychological confusion.

Ultimately, the success or failure of the relationship between a mother and her biracial daughter depends on the two individuals. Some mothers and biracial daughters are better equipped than others to handle the stress this situation can produce.

Transracial Mothering

Another way a White woman may mother a Black girl is to adopt her. The National Association of Black Social Workers (NABSW) believes, however, that this is a bad idea. Since 1972, as pointed out earlier, this organization has officially opposed the adoption of Black children, even biracial ones, by White parents. Largely because of the NABSW's position, many states during the seventies passed laws restricting adoptions across racial lines, and the number of transracial adoptions in this country was cut in half. In 1975, an estimated 2 percent of all adoptions were of White parents with Black children, but by 1987, this figure had dropped to only 1 percent.

Because of the widespread ban on transracial adoptions in this country, and a shortage of available White babies for adoption, thousands of White

Americans have been forced to go elsewhere to adopt—in some cases to countries where no such restrictions are in effect. Many White Americans would adopt babies here if it were possible. The National Committee for Adoption reported in 1984 that of the approximately two million couples waiting to adopt, about 68,000 would willingly adopt transracially. Meanwhile, American-born Black and biracial children languish in foster care.

The primary reason for NABSW's objection to transracial adoption is that White mothers are presumed incapable of instilling in Black children a positive sense of racial identity. Yet the findings of several recent longitudinal studies indicate that only about a fifth of transracially adopted children suffer any significant psychological problems. The self-esteem level of the majority of transracial adoptees, especially girls, is no different from that of other children.

The comments of both mothers and daughters involved in transracial adoptions would seem to support the positive nature of the experience. Jessica Zang, a fourteen-year-old Chicago Black teenager who was adopted when she was five days old, was asked whether having a White mother had ever caused her problems. She replied, "I get that strange kind of look a lot, you know, is that really your Mom? But I always answer very confidently, 'This is my Mom.'" Jessica's mother, Ellen, added, "I cannot consider that this is the wrong thing. How can I when I look at her? She has enriched my life so much."

Certainly not all members of the Black community endorse the NABSW's strong opposition to transracial adoptions. Many Black leaders are now revisiting this issue in light of growing concerns about the sheer number of Black children in foster care. In 1994, Senator Carol Moseley Braun introduced a bill in Congress that would make it illegal for federally funded adoption agencies to deny or delay placing a child solely on the basis of race. Many states also are starting to modify their policies. In Illinois, for example, the adoption code was recently amended to limit the time the state can spend trying to match children racially with adoptive parents. The new code recognizes that, all else being equal, it is probably in the child's best interest to grow up in a family of the same race, but if a same-race family is not found after three months, then a couple of another race may proceed with adoption.

Some family court judges are also starting to hand down more liberal decisions in transracial adoption cases. In one such case, in Washington, D.C., the color line as well as the sexual-orientation line was crossed. In

February 1994, a male judge granted custody of a Black child to a White lesbian couple who had been serving as the child's foster parents. The judge based his decision on the previously unstable child's excellent progress while under the care of these two White women.

Despite the movement in recent years to challenge antitransracial laws, and some recent favorable court decisions in the area, the number of transracial adoptions remains small. For every case in which White foster parents finally get custody of a Black child, there are many more in which White parents are denied. Sadly, it is the innocent Black foster children who suffer the most—suddenly removed from the only home they may have ever known for reasons having more to do with politics than with their welfare.

New Birth Technologies

The development of new birth technologies has added another layer of complexity to transracial mothering. Now, a woman of one race can actually carry in her womb and give birth to a child of another race. The process is called surrogate motherhood, and takes several different forms. In the first and most common form, a woman, known as the surrogate, is hired, for anywhere from $10,000 to $20,000, by a couple with viable sperm but no eggs. At ovulation, the surrogate is artificially inseminated with the man's sperm, and, assuming conception takes place, carries to term this fetus, which is genetically half hers. At birth, the baby is turned over to the waiting infertile couple.

In the second, more complicated case, the woman and the man have viable eggs and sperm, but the woman's womb does not properly function. The couple can still genetically reproduce, however, if the infertile woman's eggs are surgically removed and fertilized outside the womb in a petri dish. Such a procedure is known as *in vitro* fertilization (IVF). The fertilized egg, or zygote, is placed in the womb of the surrogate, who carries the baby to term. In this case, only the surrogate's womb is needed, and she makes no genetic contribution to the baby.

In the third case, the womb of an infertile woman is fine, but her eggs are not. In this instance a surrogate donor has her eggs surgically removed from her body and fertilized via IVF with the sperm of the infertile woman's partner. The zygote is placed in the womb of the "infertile" woman, and she then carries the fetus to term. Most recently, postmenopausal women in their fifties and even sixties have used this procedure to give birth.

While still relatively rare, there have been nearly four thousand surrogate births in this country since the 1970s. The procedure is considered a godsend for otherwise infertile couples, but enormous legal and ethical complications can develop if the surrogate mother changes her mind and wants to keep the baby at birth. The most widely known case of this sort involved a White woman, Mary Beth Whitehead, and a White couple, Betsy and William Stern. After giving birth to a baby girl from her own egg and the sperm of William Stern, Whitehead realized that she did not want to give up her baby. The Sterns sued to get custody of the child, who, they believed, contractually belonged to them. In a controversial decision, the judge ruled joint custody on the basis of genetic contribution. The little girl would jointly belong to Mary Beth Whitehead and William Stern.

In another, less publicized, case involving the second IVF procedure, a Black surrogate mother, Annie Johnson, changed her mind and sued for custody of the White baby that she carried to term. (Johnson was actually of mixed African American, Irish, and Native American ancestry, and the couple who hired her was interracial; Mark Calvert was White and his wife, Crispina, was a Filipina.) In this case, the judge ruled that Johnson was a genetic stranger to the child that she bore, so she had no right even to joint custody.

These cases and court decisions have disturbing implications. There is growing concern among Black female activists about the class and race abuses that may spring from this new birth technology. Will well-to-do White women begin hiring poorer women of color to carry their babies for them? In an article for *Essence*, Lelia McDowell-Head notes the historical bond between poor women like Mary Beth Whitehead and slave women from centuries past whose wombs were considered the property of White masters:

> How long will it be before "renting" a womb becomes the fashion for the affluent, for the career woman who doesn't want to take nine months out to "ruin" her figure? The rented wombs will undoubtedly be those of poor women, who in moments of financial desperation may enter into agreements they later regret. How many abusive boyfriends will coerce girlfriends into making a "quick" 10 or 20 thousand dollars, or whatever the going price of a uterus is?

There are other concerns with regard to race. A White woman sued a sperm bank for negligence and medical malpractice because it apparently mixed up her White husband's sperm with that of a Black man, and the baby looked Black. While the White woman's lawyer maintained that his client "loves her three-year-old daughter very much," the child is unfortunately the repeated target of "racial teasing and embarrassment." The White mother decided to sue for monetary damages, because her biracial child faces prejudice. Black legal scholar Patricia Williams, in her book *The Alchemy of Race and Rights,* ironically reflects on the significance of this woman's suit:

I ponder this case about the nightmare of giving birth to a black child who is tormented so that her mother gets to claim damages for emotional distress. I think about whether my mother shouldn't bring such a suit, both of us having endured at least the pain of my maturation in the racism of the Boston public school system. Do black mothers get to sue for such an outcome, or is it just white mothers?

Yet Williams also sees cause for hope in White women nurturing Black children:

The image of a white woman suckling a black child; the image of black child sucking for its life from the bosom of a white woman. The utter interdependence of such an image; the merging it implies; the giving up of boundary; the encompassing of other within self; the unbounded generosity and interconnectedness of such an image. Such a picture says there is not difference; it places the hope of continuous generation, of immortality of the white self in a little black face.

Whether through new birth technologies, transracial adoptions, or biracial unions, Black and White mothers and daughters have achieved what no one else in society has been capable of—radical acts of racial integration. Beyond the power posturing of the workplace, the political struggles of social activists, or the petty concerns about differences in beauty and sexual desirability, Black and White women in the home—the one sphere traditionally defined as theirs—have managed in some cases to transcend the divisiveness of racial intolerance.

There remains something unsettling about the various cross-race relationships discussed in this chapter. While there is nothing inherently wrong with one woman doing the child care or housekeeping chores of another— after all, there will always be women in need of domestic assistance, just as there will always be women willing to give it—it is the one-sided racial nature of the relationship that smacks of prejudice. Why is it a Black woman working in a White woman's home, and rarely the opposite? And why is it that more White women want to adopt Black children than Black women adopting White children? The answer is found in the economics of racial inequality that govern the public sphere. As long as the distribution of wealth and educational benefits in the larger society remains unchanged, the many positive instances of White and Black women finding common ground in the home will remain isolated incidents. Until White and Black women work with equal frequency inside each other's homes, and learn to love with equal fervor each other's children, domestic color barriers will not truly be broken.

Chapter Eight

Pop Culture and the Media

When I get big, I'm gonna have blond hair, blue eyes, and I'm gonna be white. I told my mother I don't wanna be black no more.

—Whoopi Goldberg,
in her stage show and video
Whoopi Goldberg Live, *1985*

When I was a little girl, I wished I was black. If being black is synonymous with having soul, then, yes, I feel that I am.

—Madonna,
in Vibe *magazine article, 1992*

I n the fall of 1994, the NBC weekly drama "Sweet Justice" made its debut. Set in New Orleans, the show featured the Academy Award–winner Cicely Tyson and the Emmy-winner Melissa Gilbert as two liberal lawyers working together at the same firm. At first glance, "Sweet Justice" seemed to represent a gigantic step forward in the popular media's portrayals of White and Black women. Never before had a major network showcased in a prime time slot the relationship between two women of different races compatibly engaged in such nontraditional work.

On closer inspection, however, "Sweet Justice" appears to have recycled some familiar, though updated, racial stereotypes of women. As the pampered daughter of a wealthy White Southern patriarch, Gilbert's Kate Delacroy comes across as naïvely idealistic and also a little hysterical when things don't go her way. Carrie Grace Battle is the older but wiser African American woman for whom Kate Delacroy works; as her name implies, the character played by Tyson is "battle"-scarred from her participation in the South's Civil Rights Movement and yet full of moral "grace." She is the contemporary strong Black woman, possessing not so much physical strength as uncompromising ethical principles. If there is any doubt about how stereotypical these two female characters are, imagine their roles reversed, with the younger, more emotional woman being Black, and the older, more worldly woman being White. It simply wouldn't fly.

And therein lies the problem. The media, in all their forms, ultimately mirror and maintain popular notions of women and African Americans. This is particularly true when it comes to a commercially sponsored television show like "Sweet Justice." Regardless of media form, the result is usually the same, because in mainstream culture Whites create and control the images of those who are not part of the mainstream, Blacks. The media constitute a powerful tool for influencing culture, and for that reason they also hold for Black women and White woman the greatest hope for social change. In the right hands, the media have the power to transform cross-race relations in America. This chapter takes a historical and contemporary look at the way relations between Black women and White women have been portrayed in fiction, films, and television, as well as in advertising, modeling, and music.

Early Portrayals

The earliest representations of relations between White women and Black women can be found in nineteenth-century American novels. Stories of romance and adventure were a wonderful source of entertainment throughout the 1800s; they were especially popular with White women, an estimated 90 percent of whom were literate. But romances were also read by those Black women fortunate enough to have received an education, and women of both races wrote novels during the nineteenth century.

The best-known American writer of the period was probably Harriet Beecher Stowe, author of *Uncle Tom's Cabin* (1851). A White Northern abolitionist, Stowe wished to tell a tale that would raise an alarm about the brutalities of slavery and help bring it to an end. The book's success must have exceeded Stowe's dreams. *Uncle Tom's Cabin* became an instant best seller, and to this day holds a prominent place in American culture.

Although *Uncle Tom's Cabin* is usually remembered for its stark antislavery sentiment, it was also instrumental in creating the myth of warm relations between White plantation mistresses and Black female house slaves. Again, this was an important message to convey: if women of such disparate circumstances could be friends, surely there was hope for others to share in a common humanity. Mrs. Shelby, the plantation mistress in *Uncle Tom's Cabin,* was never cruel and was always sympathetic toward her house slave, Aunt Chloe. And Aunt Chloe was never spiteful and always forgiving of her White mistress. Chloe was, in fact, a mammy, as the African American cultural critic Patricia A. Turner notes in *Ceramic Uncles and Celluloid Mammies: Black Images and Their Influence on Culture* (1994):

> Dark-skinned, loyal to her master and mistress, an able cook and housekeeper, plump, asexual, good-humored, Aunt Chloe was one of the first of a long line of fictional black women whose characters comforted and assuaged.

Portraying Black female house slaves as happy and content to wait on the White household served other purposes as well. White female authors and readers alike could successfully avoid thinking about their own ethical responsibilities to the Black slaves. Clearly slavery was the fault of White husbands, never that of the wives. In the pens of White authors, the Black female house slave was also stripped of any sexual allure. Since the mammy was always described as dark-skinned, overweight, and unattractive, her presence in the home of a White woman could more easily be tolerated. No White husband would be sexually interested in such a woman. Of course, in reality, sexual relations between female house slaves and White masters were a common and painful experience for the slaves, some of whom were brutally raped. The illicit relations were also humiliating for White wives because of their inability to stop them. In novels, at least, it helped not to dwell on such unpleasantries. No wonder White women much preferred to read about loyal mammies than to hear the sober truth about what really went on in the lives of enslaved Black women. Stowe's novel helped White women readers feel good about opposing slavery, and her book, and the books of other White women writers who followed similar formulas sold well.

Although it was a time of widespread educational disadvantages, the nineteenth century also managed to produce the first Black women novelists. Among them was Harriet Wilson, whose 1859 largely autobiographical book *Our Nig* is now considered by literary scholars to be the first novel ever written by a Black woman in this country. Nearly lost to obscurity, *Our Nig* was discovered and reissued in 1983. Not surprisingly, when Black women like Wilson assumed creative control, relations between White and Black women were painted rather differently. *Our Nig* centers on the story of a mulatto indentured servant named Frado—presumably Wilson herself—living in the North, and her difficulties with a cruel White female mistress, Mrs. Bellmont, who had an even meaner daughter, Mary. Although not every White female in *Our Nig* is portrayed as cold and unfeeling, enough of them were that the book did not make for pleasant reading by White women. In fact, this may be one of the reasons the book failed to find commercial success when it was first published. Wilson made it clear that she was writing for a Black reading audience, not a White one, but at that time there were not enough literate Blacks in the country to support such a literary endeavor.

The paucity of Black readers was a problem that continued to plague other early African American female novelists. If a Black woman author hoped to make a living by writing books, she had to make her story appeal to White female readers as well. One early African American novelist who managed to do just that was Frances Ellen Watkins Harper. Her novel *Iola*

Leroy (generally thought to have been published in 1888, although some scholars date its publication as early as 1863) featured a fair-skinned mulatto heroine named Iola, who meets and falls in love with an aristocratic White doctor. When the doctor discovers Iola's true ancestry, he decides that he loves her anyway, and proposes that the two of them run away together. But in a surprise move that comforted both Black women and White women readers, Iola turns down the good doctor's offer. Concerned about the fate of future mulatto children, she remains true to her race. The book sold well.

Racially mixed women like Iola were common in the novels of many White women, too, but in their hands such heroines were nearly always killed off by book's end. Along with the stock mammy character, there emerged another image of Black women in early American literature—the beautiful but tragic mulatto. Like the mammy figure, the tragic mulatto seemed to meet a strong though somewhat different psychological need in White women, particularly those of the South. It was comforting for them to read about the tragic consequences awaiting the offspring born of sexual relations with their men. For those White women outside the South, stories about the fate awaiting any racially mixed woman, especially one who dared to pass and to pursue White men, may have helped soothe growing anxieties about race mixing in this country. In fact, well beyond the era of Reconstruction, novels about tragic mulattoes continued to sell well.

In the 1920s and early thirties, there was a virtual explosion of books, art, plays, and music written and performed by Blacks, the period is called the Harlem Renaissance. As exciting as this creative era was for African American artists, musicians, performers, and authors, most of them still had to make their work appeal to largely White producers, publishers and gallery owners. Black women writers such as Nella Larsen, who wrote *Quicksand* (1928) and *Passing* (1929), and Jessie Redmon Fauset, who wrote *There Is Confusion* (1924) and *Plum Bun* (1928), were most successful when they followed the formula, penning stories of beautiful mulatto heroines tragically struggling with their racial identity. But unlike their White counterparts, Harlem Renaissance authors included in their works White women characters who were often cruel or indifferent to the problems of Black women.

Toward the end of the period, a few women writers, like the poet Gwendolyn Brooks and the novelist Zora Neale Hurston, began writing specifically for Black audiences and worried less about whether White audiences would approve or understand. Although Hurston's novel *Their Eyes Were Watching God* (1937) has now claimed its rightful place in American literature, at the time that it was first published, it did not sell well. The story is of a racially mixed heroine, Janie, who, instead of meeting an unhappy end, triumphs. That simple but crucial departure from formula has since led scholars to credit *Their Eyes Were Watching God* as the first feminist African American novel. But because White women hardly figured in the story at all, it was not a book that Whites recommended to their friends. To make ends meet, Hurston was forced to survive on secretarial wages, unemployment benefits, welfare checks, substitute teaching, and domestic work.

The most popular female novelists of the thirties continued to be White women who stuck to familiar genres. Among them was Fannie Hurst, for whom, ironically, Hurston once worked as a secretary. Hurst wrote one of the all-time classic tragic mulatto stories, *Imitation of Life* (1933). Drawing on racial stereotypes, Hurst portrayed a dark-skinned Black woman named Delilah who is warm and subservient in her relations with her White employer, Bea. Although she is not a slave, Delilah still functions very much like a mammy. She remains loyally devoted to Bea even after the White woman makes a financial success from marketing, of all things, Delilah's famous pancake recipe. Both women have daughters, but it is only the light-skinned Black daughter, Peola, who is tragically fated. In her attempts to pass as White, Peola pretends, in scene after scene, to deny that Delilah is her mother. And in the end, before Peola realizes the error of her ways, Delilah dies, leaving a guilt-ridden daughter behind. So popular was this tale that only a year after it was published, *Imitation of Life* was made into a movie.

The new industry of film became yet another powerful medium through which the stereotypes of Blacks and White women were perpetuated. Nowhere was this more evident than in the film *Gone With the Wind*, based on the 1936 novel by Margaret Mitchell. The movie was released in 1939 by MGM, and went on to win a record ten Academy Awards. *GWTW* remains to this day one of the all-time top grossing films in history.

Although many of the relationships in *GWTW* left indelible marks in the minds of viewers, one of the most enduring was that between the White plantation mistress Scarlett O'Hara and her house slave, Mammy. Who can forget the scene before the Wilkes's big picnic in which Mammy (portrayed by large, dark-skinned Hattie McDaniel, who won the Best Supporting Actress Oscar) fusses over the dress to be worn by the spoiled but ever resourceful Miz Scarlett, (portrayed by the delicately beautiful Vivien Leigh, whose performance netted her the Best Actress award)? Like Aunt Chloe in

Uncle Tom's Cabin, Mammy is completely devoted to Scarlett, highly maternal, and devoid of any sexual allure. In *GWTW,* Mammy emerges as the conscience of the story. It is she who "tsk, tsk, tsk's" over Scarlett's constant scheming ways, and it is Mammy whose approval the charming White Rhett Butler seeks.

Another big-budget film about the antebellum South released during the thirties was Warner Brothers' *Jezebel* (1938), which featured a feisty yet self-centered Southern White woman named Julie, played by Bette Davis. She, too, has a devoted house slave, Zette, played by Black actress Theresa Harris. The plot centers on Julie's refusal to conform to the Old South's restrictive codes of femininity, especially the genteel ways of her banker fiancé, Pres. The pivotal scene takes place at the Olympus Ball, an event at which all unmarried women were expected to wear white. To embarrass and shock Pres, Julie decides to wear a red dress—an act of defiance that ultimately leads Pres to leave her. By the film's end, Julie is labeled a Jezebel, the Biblical by-word for a wicked female.

According to the film scholar Richard Dyer, *Jezebel* is notable for the way in which it used color to symbolize Julie and Zette. Whiteness was associated with order, rationality, and conformity to social convention; blackness conveyed disorder, irrationality, and looseness. The Black characters in *Jezebel* were also more natural, emotional, sensual, and spiritual than any of the White characters. This dichotomy was further reflected in Julie's insistence on wearing the red dress to the ball, seen merely as dark in this black-and-white film. While White family members and associates found the dress vulgar, Zette was attracted to its bold and flashy color. And when Julie finally realized the error of her ways, the dress was passed to Zette, who presumably had a much better time wearing it.

In the years before the activist sixties, there was one other big-budget movie that bears mentioning, a remake of *Imitation of Life.* Released in 1959, on the eve of the Civil Rights Movement, *Imitation of Life* starred Lana Turner as the White woman, Sandra Dee as the White daughter, Juanita Moore as the Black maid, and White actress Susan Kohner as the light-skinned Black daughter. For the remake, the story line and character names were all updated. Instead of marketing a pancake recipe (too much like Aunt Jemima), the White woman, now called Lora, abandons her domestic ways to become a glamorous Broadway star. This leaves the Black woman, Annie, less a business partner than an ever-constant, smiling domestic servant. Annie also functions as the surrogate mother for the White daughter, abandoned by her overly ambitious, career-minded White mother. The light-skinned daughter, now called Sarah Jane, still tries to deny her racial heritage; and in keeping with the stereotype of the sexually aggressive woman of mixed race, it is she, not the White daughter, who is recklessly promiscuous. At one point, Sarah Jane runs away to become a stripper in a seedy nightclub. The ending remains intact. Once again the Black mother dies before her ungrateful daughter can properly apologize for her actions. There is even an elaborately staged funeral scene, complete with soaring strains of Mahalia Jackson, during which Sarah Jane hysterically flings herself on Annie's coffin, begging for forgiveness.

Although in many ways the plot of *Imitation of Life* seems laughable today, in the context of the fifties it was a fairly liberal film. Not only did the story line center completely on women, rather than men, but it also portrayed a real friendship that crossed racial lines. In scene after scene, a genuine intimacy between Lora and Annie was evident. Of course, Annie was still Lora's devoted servant, and in that regard the film ultimately placated White audiences as much as it challenged them. Thus, while the tears of White women helped to make this Universal release one of the studio's highest grossing films, Black audience members may have been more inclined to laugh in disbelief at the absurdity of Annie's being so blindly devoted to a White employer.

The fifties witnessed the rise of yet another image-making medium, and that, of course, was television. In 1951, only 12 percent of American homes had a television set. By 1963, that number had risen to close to 90 percent. In the beginning, Black people barely existed at all on TV, except for a few superstars like singers Nat King Cole and Diahann Carroll. A few more were featured in all-Black comedies, like "Amos 'n' Andy," where no opportunities for cross-race relations existed. This popular but highly racist show is memorable for creating yet another stereotype of the Black woman, the loud-mouthed, strong-willed, emasculating Sapphire.

One show in the early fifties did feature in its title role a Black woman: "Beulah." Portrayed by the plump, dark-skinned actress Louise Beavers, Beulah was, naturally, a maid. The message the show presented was clear: every White family should be lucky enough to have a maid like Beulah. She was always there to assist the White mother with her children, and never seemed to have concerns about her own Black family, even on holidays. For years, the medium of television clearly did no better than film in advancing the image of Black women.

White women, too, were at first narrowly portrayed on television, primarily as happy homemakers, whose main concern in life was taking care of husband and children. During the fifties, this limited image of middle-class White women was seen in shows such as "Father Knows Best," "Leave It to Beaver," and "The Adventures of Ozzie and Harriet."

In the decades that followed, all forms of the media were forced to react to the growing demands of the civil rights and, later, the women's movement, to improve their representations of African Americans and women. Publishing was among the first outlets to respond to the activist winds of change.

Literature

For African Americans, the outpouring of literature and arts following the Civil Rights Movement became another Black Renaissance. At last, the missing discourse of Black voices in American fiction was being heard, and this time there was a large, literate, and hungry Black reading audience ready to support it.

One early book by a Black author to come out of that era set the tone for a new portrayal of women's cross-race relations; it was Margaret Walker's *Jubilee* (1966), a Civil War epic, for which the author won the Houghton Mifflin Literary Fellowship. Based in part on the true story of Walker's great-grandmother, *Jubilee* takes place in the South, where all its major characters experience the sweeping effects of the Civil War. The book is often called the Black *Gone With the Wind,* because the events are told not through the eyes of a White heroine, but through those of a Black house slave named Vyry (Walker's grandmother). Another difference is that in *Jubilee* many Black female slaves suffer horribly. It was Walker's best seller that finally presented a less idealized depiction of female house slaves at the hands of White mistresses in the South. But at the book's ending, Walker has Vyry forgive the vicious cruelty of the older, now dying, White Southern woman. With that simple gesture, *Jubilee* ultimately celebrates the humanist spirit while suggesting a future in which relations between White women and Black women might be better.

It is interesting to note just how many Black women authors of the sixties and seventies portrayed their Black female characters in service to White women. Given the degree to which domestic work was so long the principal form of employment for Black women in this country, perhaps this is not surprising. Yet, as Black literary scholar Trudier Harris makes clear in the title of her 1982 book, *From Mammies to Militants: Domestics in Black American Literature,* Black maids in the hands of Black authors were no shrinking violets. Their White female employers were nearly always portrayed as grossly insensitive, incapable of befriending a Black woman, or even of treating her with any degree of fairness or kindness. For African American novelists, it was pay-back time.

This anti-White woman sentiment is evident in many of the novels written by Toni Morrison, the most critically acclaimed African American female writer to come out of this era. *The Bluest Eye* (1970), set in Ohio before the Civil Rights Movement, follows a poor, uneducated Black woman named Pauline, who works as a maid for a White woman, portrayed in an extremely negative light. In *Song of Solomon* (1977) Morrison returns to roughly the same time and place, although the White employer, Michael-Mary Graham, is a poet and thus slightly more sensitive. The main female protagonist, a Black woman named Corinthians Dead, is college-educated and middle class; it is societal racism that forces her to work as a domestic. But while the circumstances and personalities may be somewhat more sympathetic, Morrison still makes clear that no real human connection can be made between these two women of different races.

In *Tar Baby* (1981) Morrison first offers a glimmer of hope for the development of an interracial friendship, in this case between a White woman named Margaret and her Black domestic servant, Ondine. Their interactions are helped by the fact that Margaret grew up dirt poor and has at least some understanding of being disadvantaged. It is only because she marries well that she is now able to afford a domestic servant. Although much that happens in this story serves to drive Margaret and Ondine apart, in the final chapter Morrison offers the possibility that the two women may form a friendship.

"Ondine? Let's be wonderful old ladies. You and me."

"Huh," said Ondine, but she smiled a little.

"We're both childless now, Ondine. And we're both stuck here. We should be friends. It's not too late."

Ondine looked out of the window and did not answer.

"Is it too late, Ondine?"

"Almost," she said. "Almost."

Racial tension between Black and White women is similarly explored in the work of Alice Walker. Although most of Walker's books, notably *The Color Purple* (1982) and *The Temple of My Familiar* (1989), focus primarily on Black characters in predominantly all-Black environments, *Meridian* (1976) suggests a new treatment of White women in Black women's literature, that of disadvantaged sisters. Set in the South during the Civil Rights Movement, *Meridian* follows the activist commitments of a Northern White Jewish woman, Lynne Rabinowitz, and the book's title character, a Southern Black woman named Meridian Hill. Complicating their cross-race relations is a Black man named Truman, who marries Lynne but in times of need seeks out Meridian. Despite this, Meridian comes to respect and even to like Lynne.

Among the other African American women authors associated with this period are poet laureate Maya Angelou, author of the autobiographical *I Know Why the Caged Bird Sings* (1969), playwright Ntozake Shange, who wrote *For Colored Girls Who Considered Suicide/When the Rainbow Was Enuf* (1975), and Gloria Naylor, whose novel *The Women of Brewster Place* (1982) won the National Book Award. While none of these works dealt primarily with women's cross-race relations, all were embraced by progressive White women.

A new generation of White women authors also emerged in the sixties and seventies, writing about themes of new-found independence and sexual liberation for women. Such authors included Marge Piercy *(Small Changes,* 1972; *Women on the Edge of Time,* 1976), Marilyn French *(The Women's Room,* 1977), Erica Jong *(Fear of Flying,* 1974), Lisa Alther *(Kinflicks,* 1976), and Rita Mae Brown *(Rubyfruit Jungle,* 1977; and *Six of One,* 1978). Unfortunately, Black women in these stories were either ignored or relegated to maids' roles, though they were maids who were paragons of virtue, strength, warmth, and wisdom. That portrayal was especially common in the books of Southern White women, such as Alther and Brown.

By the eighties, a small trickle of White women writers, most of them Southern-born, attempted to move beyond the stereotypes of Black women and White women. Among this group is Ellen Douglas, whose *Can't Quit You, Baby* (1988) examines not only the barriers separating Black women servants from their White female employers, but also their many unacknowledged bonds. Douglas is unusual in that she dares to have her Black female character steal something from the White family for which she works as an expression of Black rage. In the end, the Black woman and the

White woman finally talk and come to some understanding of why they acted as they did toward each other.

Another White Southern author to move her characters beyond the stereotypes is Gail Godwin. In her novel *A Mother and Two Daughters* (1982) she reverses the power relations between a White woman and a Black woman as a means of raising issues about race and gender. A subplot centers on Lydia, one of the two White daughters referred to in the book's title, who is a divorcée with two young sons. She returns to college in her late twenties, and there she encounters a Black woman professor named Dr. Renée Peverell-Watson, who teaches a course on the history of female consciousness. It is Renée who serves as the means of raising Lydia's consciousness about women in society. The two women initially become friends because they are the same age and both are single parents. But in the book's final chapter, which takes place years later, at the wedding of their two children, clearly the friendship has become strained. Having quit her teaching position following a local incident of racial terrorism, Renée is too busy studying to become a civil rights lawyer to make it to her own daughter's wedding, and Lydia has gone on to become the host of a popular Martha Stewart–like television show.

In more recent years, a few African American women writers have dared to explore women's interracial relationships in nonstereotypical ways. At the forefront of this group is Bebe Moore Campbell, whose best-selling novel *Brothers and Sisters* (1994) delves deeply into both the rewards and discomforts of a female friendship that crosses racial boundaries. Increasingly, children's book authors are also exploring themes of cultural diversity and girls' interracial friendships.

Film

Hollywood, too, began responding to the Civil Rights Movement, and in several ways. One was to begin making big-budget films about Black families, from *Sounder* (1972), starring Cicely Tyson, to *The Color Purple* (1985), starring Whoopi Goldberg and Oprah Winfrey. The seventies also saw the rise of so-called blaxploitation films, such as *Shaft* (1971) and *Superfly* (1972), which featured Black men in heroic but ultimately stereotypical roles. Today, this genre has surfaced again in the form of "gangsta" films, like *New*

Jack City (1991), starring Wesley Snipes. When women of either race appear in these films, they have been relegated to being either ornamental girl-friends or the targets of rape and physical abuse.

For the first time, Hollywood also began making such films as *A Patch of Blue* (1966) and *Guess Who's Coming to Dinner* (1967), which touched on themes of interracial attraction. More recently, there has been Spike Lee's *Jungle Fever* (1991), starring Wesley Snipes and Annabella Sciorra, *Made in America* (1993), starring Whoopi Goldberg and Ted Danson, and *The Body-guard* (1992), starring Whitney Houston and Kevin Costner.

The buddy film was another genre that focused to an extent on interracial relations, although most of them featured men only. In the sixties, there were films such as *Robin and the Seven Hoods* (1964), starring Rat Pack members Frank Sinatra, Dean Martin, and Sammy Davis, Jr.; in the seven-ties, *Silver Streak* (1976), starring Richard Pryor and Gene Wilder. In the eighties *48 Hours* (1983), starring Eddie Murphy and Nick Nolte, became a big hit, and recently, *White Men Can't Jump* (1992), with Wesley Snipes and Woody Harrelson, did well at the box office. Clearly the interracial male buddy genre has been a formulaic success and, as a marketing strategy, has the added advantage of appealing to audiences of both races.

Women, however, have had no such vehicle for exploring cross-race rela-tions on the big screen. In fact, films about women, and especially their relationships with each other, have not been particularly popular in Holly-wood's eyes. Black male directors, many of whom emerged on the scene during the late eighties and nineties, have rarely bothered to focus on the lives of Black women. The one exception is Spike Lee, in the film *She's Gotta Have It* (1986), about a Black woman named Nola Darling, who must have her sexual freedom, although in one scene she pays for it with rape. Lee has been criticized for his portrayals by some African American women, including author and columnist Julianne Malveaux, who, in an article enti-tled "Spike's Spite," wrote:

> While Lee treats black women peripherally, he treats Angie (Annabella Sciorra), the white woman who has an affair with Flipper (Wesley Snipes), in a careless, offhand manner . . . We never know how she feels about the affair, herself, her life. Like Nola Darling, she has to pay for her sexuality [and] like Nola, Angie Tucci is a reactor, not an actor. These passive women are painted in activist garments, as women

who are liberated and courageous. But Lee's view of women is that we
play it as it comes, exercising little choice.

The few films in recent years that have addressed women's interracial
relationships are nearly always set in some earlier historical era. In that
way, Black women can once again be acceptably cast in service to White
women. Thus, we have such films as *Cross Creek* (1983), starring Mary
Steenburgen as author Marjorie Kinnan Rawlings, and Alfre Woodard as
her domestic servant, Idella Parker, and *The Long Walk Home* (1991), starring Whoopi Goldberg and Sissy Spacek. *The Long Walk Home* takes place
in the fifties during the Montgomery bus strike. Spacek plays a middle-
class White woman who is torn between her allegiance to a racist White
husband and her growing respect for their maid (Whoopi Goldberg), who
must now walk miles to work rather than take the bus. In the end, Spacek
sides with truth and justice, joining Goldberg at a civil rights rally. Once
again it is the Black woman who functions as the moral center of the story.
   The career of Whoopi Goldberg is interesting to look at not only because she is one of the highest paid actresses in Hollywood today, but also
because of the frequency with which she has been cast as a maid. In addition to *The Long Walk Home,* Goldberg has been a domestic servant in
Clara's Heart (1988) and *Corrina, Corrina* (1994), both of which were also set
in earlier eras. When not playing a maid, Goldberg is invariably the one in
the film who brings color, life, and spiritual awakening to the White female characters. In *Sister Act* (1992), she plays a Las Vegas lounge singer
who opens the convent doors, letting in life and laughter to a group of
cloistered White nuns; in *Ghost* (1990), for which Goldberg won the Best
Supporting Actress award, she is a fortune teller named Oda Mae Brown
who can make contact with the recently deceased boyfriend of a young
White professional woman, Molly (played by Demi Moore). Goldberg's
Oscar was the first won by a Black woman since Hattie McDaniel's Oscar
for *Gone With the Wind*. Of the character played by Goldberg in *Ghost,*
African American film scholar Donald Bogle writes that it is, "decades old
—the matronly black woman who deals with spirits and whose eyes pop
open wide at the appropriate moments . . . The role is a nurturer for a
white couple, and Goldberg has this feistiness that mammies in the past
often had."
   Among Black actresses in film today, Goldberg is hardly alone in being
asked to play the role of a maid to a White woman. In *Fried Green Tomatoes*

(1991), set in an earlier era, Cicely Tyson plays a cook in a restaurant owned by two White lesbians. *Driving Miss Daisy* (1989), again set in an earlier era, casts Theresa Merritt as a domestic servant working for White actress Jessica Tandy; and *Passion Fish* (1992) stars Alfre Woodard as a live-in nurse's aide assisting a recently disabled and self-pitying White soap opera star.

At least in *Passion Fish,* made by independent White male director John Sayles, Woodard's character is fully fleshed out with some flaws of her own, instead of being dully perfect. Ultimately, this is a story of triumph in which two women help each other to enjoy life again. *Passion Fish* is one of the few films in recent history, placed in a contemporary setting, that has at its center the developing relationship between a White woman and a Black woman. In general, Hollywood has failed miserably to advance the images of White women and Black women and their relations to each other.

Television

Television has done little better in this regard. Following the activism of the sixties, the networks were forced to re-evaluate and alter stereotypical images of both Blacks and women. Not surprisingly, it was the men, not the women, who were given first crack at exploring cross-race relations. The male buddy show "I Spy," starring Bill Cosby and Robert Culp as two detectives, ran from 1965 through 1968.

"Julia" (1968–1971), a sitcom starring the beautiful Black actress and singer Diahann Carroll as a single mother who is a nurse, was the first show built around a Black woman who wasn't a domestic servant. But Julia's acquaintances all seemed to be White. Her boss was White, and her best friend was a White woman named Marie, who lived next door in the same high-rise apartment complex. In being cast as a perky nurse with no racial opinions of her own, Julia came across as little more than a domestic servant. As Diahann Carroll herself said of the show in 1968, "At the moment we're presenting the white Negro. And he has very little Negro-ness."

Following "Julia," television producers began creating more shows about Blacks who lived and worked among other Blacks, from "Sanford and Son" (1972–1978), to "Good Times" (1974–1979), to "What's Happening?" (1976–1979). But in so doing, they eliminated from the picture Whites, especially White women. Issues of race were sometimes raised, but never directly dealt with in relation to White characters. Meanwhile, the majority of other sitcoms and dramas continued to have all-White casts. With the notable exception of "All in the Family" (1971–1978), which had a Black family move next door to the Bunker household, Whites and Blacks on the small screen seemed to live in parallel universes throughout the sixties and seventies.

During the politically conservative and financially booming eighties, a few shows did deal with race. The first was "The Cosby Show" (1984–1992), which finally brought dignity and style to a Black family on television. Unfortunately, White women rarely entered the Cosby world. However, a spinoff from that show, "A Different World" (1987–1992), in which Cosby daughter Lisa Bonet leaves home to attend a prestigious Black college in the South, did. Her roommate was a White woman (played by Oscar winner Marisa Tomei), apparently the only White woman in attendance at the school. In some of the show's early episodes, women's cross-race relations were discussed. But gradually plots began to center on the romantic tension between Whitney (Jasmine Guy) and Dwayne (Kadeem Hardison), and by the second season, the White woman student had transferred out.

Another long-running, top-rated show of the eighties notable for its treatment of race was the nighttime soap opera *Dynasty* (1981–1989). It too attempted to integrate its cast, at least for one season, when Diahann Carroll showed up as a fabulously wealthy singer named Dominique Deveraux, who claimed to be the half-sister of patriarch Blake Carrington (John Forsythe). Although such a plot twist could have lent itself to a searing discussion of race and racism in America, with the many White women in Carrington's life feeling conflicted or threatened by Deveraux's sudden presence, no such discussion ever took place. The tension surrounding Deveraux's claim to some of Carrington's great fortune was never linked to her being Black and everyone else in the family being White. Once again, the talented Diahann Carroll was forced to portray another white-faced Black woman.

In the nineties, various weekly drama shows, such as "L.A. Law," "Picket Fences," and "NYPD Blue," have attempted to frame more realistically, in contemporary settings, issues of race and racism in America. Unfortunately, most of the plots have centered on men. With the exception of "Sweet Justice," women's cross-race relations in a contemporary setting have taken a back seat. The only two shows that do touch on women's race relations, "I'll Fly Away" and "The Homefront," are once again set in earlier times, with Black women back in the homes of White women.

More time has been devoted to exploring women and their race issues on daytime television. One obvious reason is that women make up the bulk of daytime viewing audiences, and African Americans, in particular, constitute nearly 38 percent of it. As a result, the producers of soap operas have been forced to find ways to attract and satisfy these otherwise often ignored market segments.

As of 1992, there were fourteen Black women working on eight of the eleven daytime soaps. In some soaps, the characters these actresses play are nonstereotypical and highly visible regular members of the casts. Most African American daytime actresses complain, though, that ultimately they function as either the love interests for White men or as the token friends of White women in the show.

African American actresses have fared better in some of the big-budget made-for-TV movies, most notably *Queen* (1993), the story of Alex Haley's paternal grandmother, starring Halle Berry and Jasmine Guy, and *The Women of Brewster Place* (1989), the adaptation of Gloria Naylor's book about eight Black women living on the same dead-end street. Without the backing of the executive producer, Oprah Winfrey, however, *The Women of Brewster Place,* which starred Winfrey along with Cicely Tyson and Robin Givens, would likely never have seen the light of day.

In recent years, a few cable and network movie productions have featured White and Black women together, but the formula is nearly always the same—a weak-willed, mixed-up White woman is saved by a morally stronger Black woman. The fact remains that few shows on television have addressed women's cross-race relations in nonstereotypical ways.

Advertising

Advertising is another powerful influence shaping images of Black and White women in America. Here, too, stereotypes rule. Aunt Jemima, for example, is one of the most enduring advertising images of a Black woman, and despite her weight loss and handkerchief removal in recent years, she remains a mammy. While Black men and White men in commercials and print ads work, play sports, and drink beer together, women still seem mostly to pitch cleaning, food, and beauty products in racially segregated worlds.

According to research conducted by psychologist Carolyn West, Black women are sexualized more often than White women, even in the same advertising campaign. White women in the Virginia Slims cigarette ads, for example, are typically placed in a historical setting, such as early twentieth century, where they are dressed in assertive, masculine attire and shown working hard for women's suffrage. Across the bottom of such ads reads the slogan "You've come a long way, baby," which manages both to promote a woman's independence and to deny her adult status. In contrast, the Virginia Slims ads featuring African American women convey themes of covert sexuality. In one such ad, a Black woman is dressed in tight-fitting clothing; across her chest is an iridescent strip with the slogan "Change is ok, big bills are better." Although the ad could be interpreted to depict a woman's right to be financially ambitious, because of how the woman in the ad is dressed and where the ad copy is placed, another interpretation is that she is essentially a tramp or a prostitute.

In 1992, *Advertising Age* surveyed a racially mixed sample of 470 marketing and media executives on race and racism in the advertising industry and found that more than half agreed that advertising has played a role in the country's current racial problems. Roughly the same number admitted that there were no Blacks working in their departments, other than in clerical or other low-level positions. If more African Americans held creative and executive positions in the advertising industry, perhaps they would have a louder voice for change. As one African American respondent in the survey noted, "All we ever see is a bunch of us dancing to a good beat and smiling. That's not how we are. Ads just perpetuate stereotypes."

There is a need for advertising to be more sensitive to the subtle interplay of the racial and sexual stereotyping of women, in particular. In 1993, Foote, Cone, and Belding, in San Francisco (FC&B–SF), began airing a series of five thirty-second commercial television spots, with such titles as "Woman with a Purpose" and "Woman Getting It Off Her Chest," for their Levi's for Women campaign. Designed to sell Levi's to women, all but one of the spots featured abstract animated White female figures in blue-colored jeans expressing their independence and assertiveness. The fifth in the series, entitled "Woman Not Feeling Blue," was specifically aimed at promoting the Levi's line of multicolored jeans for women, and it was the only spot to feature an animated Black female figure dancing to the sounds of house music. Halfway into the commercial, a female voiceover, with an obviously Black accent, teasingly intoned, "Girl, pick yourself a color." Taken together, the commercials were an immediate success. "Woman With a Purpose" was awarded a Clio, the advertising world's equivalent of an Oscar, and the media watchdog consumer group Women in Communication (WIC) awarded FC&B–SF its annual Leading Change Award for its positive portrayals of women. But in an unprecedented move, WIC also gave the negative Needing Change Award to the one spot entitled "Woman Not Feeling Blue." Why is it, WIC asked, that the only woman shown dancing in the overall campaign was the only Black female figure?

White copywriter Mimi Cook, who was among those at FC&B–SF to work on the Levi's account, admitted, "Instead of depicting a general feeling, which is what all the spots were supposed to do, the 'Woman Not Feeling Blue' one ended up saying 'This is what a Black woman is all about.' I now realize that once you skew toward someone who is Black, Hispanic, or Asian, you necessarily make a bigger political statement than if you use a White character." Not all African American women who saw the "Woman Not Feeling Blue" commercial found it objectionable. In fact, it seemed to Cook that most women, regardless of race, thought the spot made a positive statement that applied to all women.

Modeling

Just as actresses of both races have had to weigh concerns at being cast in stereotypical roles against their desire to make a living, so too have models. A 1991 report entitled *Invisible People,* issued by New York's Department of Consumer Affairs, documented the extent to which African Americans are underutilized in advertising. The percentage of Black models appearing in over eleven thousand ads in twenty-seven different national magazines was tabulated and compared against the percentage of Black readers for the magazines. While 11 percent of the magazines' readers were Black, only 3 percent of the models in the magazine ads were Black. And when African American women models were featured in ads, they usually appeared as little more than token figures in the background of a group of White models. Apparently, some businesses fear having their products become associated through advertising images with Blacks, with the possible consequence of alienating their larger market of White consumers.

A more subtle form of racism in advertising shows in the choice of which African American female models appear in the ads. The Department of Consumer Affairs report found that most of the Blacks were light-skinned.

Dark-skinned African American women with natural hair styles were the most "invisible" of all the women in print magazine ads.

Only in the world of fashion, where the point seems to be to create trends that run counter to the mainstream, can beautiful dark-skinned women, such as Naomi Campbell and Iman, find great success. Here skin color is treated more as an accessory than as a racial feature. As the high-fashion designer Givenchy says, regarding his preference for dark-skinned African American fashion models, "Their bodies are perfect for my clothes . . . the colors I use look more beautiful on darker skin." Every year the houses of LaCroix, Chanel, Versace, and Saint Laurent book dark-skinned women of African descent to display their haute couture in the runway shows of Paris, Milan, and New York.

The appearance of a few highly paid African American supermodels ultimately does little to alter the perception that it is still White women whose images are most valued in our culture. One indication of this can be found in the sales figures of beauty magazines. Some magazines suffer a clear loss of revenue when a Black woman is featured on the cover. Another indication of how marginalized Black models continue to be is found in *Vogue*'s 1992 book *On the Edge: Images from 100 Years of Vogue*. Conspicuously absent was African American supermodel Beverly Johnson. In 1974, she became the first Black woman to appear on the magazine's cover, but somehow the editors of this historical look-back into the world of fashion modeling deemed her not important enough to be included. In a letter to *Vogue*'s owner, S. I. Newhouse, Johnson angrily addressed the racism behind this glaring omission:

> I was proud to be the Jackie Robinson of the fashion world. To ignore that moment in history is to discredit all African American contributions in fashion as a people. I waited a year to write because I was shocked and traumatized by the incident.

While clearly an incident like this is brought about by the individuals in power rather than the models themselves, it nonetheless creates tension between the Black women and White women who work in the modeling industry.

In an effort to raise awareness of just how prejudiced the world of modeling can be, a consortium of powerful Black fashion models, including Naomi Campbell, Tyra Banks, Veronica Webb, Beverly Peele, and Iman, decided to organize into the Black Girls Coalition (BGC). In November of 1992, they held a press conference attended by more than a hundred journalists. Devoid of their high-fashion personas, these sought-after models asked some serious questions about African American women still getting so much less modeling work than their White counterparts. Campbell asked why the industry seemed able to single out only one Black model at a time to be its latest supermodel. "You can have ten or twenty White supermodels, and no one is saying, 'You're the new one; you'll bump out So-and-So.'" And Iman spoke of how racist it was to tell her that she looked like a "White woman dipped in chocolate," and, worse, how the comment was delivered as though it were a compliment. Other models told of constantly being asked to wear wigs, weaves, and falls to emulate the flowing hair of White women. While some people have criticized the BGC as spoiled, rich Black women asking for more at a time when more "girls" with "ethnic" looks are finding work as models, the founders of the BGC remain adamant in their determination to bring an end to prejudice in the modeling industry.

Beauty Pageants

Beauty pageants are yet another place where White women and Black women compete around their perceived attractiveness. The mother of all beauty contests remains the Miss America Pageant. It began in 1921 in the resort town of Atlantic City as a gimmick to boost sagging business sales over Labor Day, the summer's last holiday weekend. Each state in the union was asked to send its most attractive young White woman to parade in a bathing suit up and down the boardwalk in the hope that she might be crowned "the most beautiful woman in America." The event was a huge success. It was later brought inside, and contestants were judged on the basis of talent and poise, in addition to their appearance in a bathing suit. And the winners also were awarded huge college scholarships. But Black women were barred from competing. In response, the Black community formed its own contest, the Black Miss America pageant.

It was not until 1970 that the first Black woman, Cheryl Browne of Iowa, appeared on stage in the national Miss America contest. A Black woman did not win the pageant, however, until 1984, when Vanessa Williams was hailed the "most beautiful woman in America." Her crown sparked controversy in the Black community. While many were proud that one of their own had finally won, others were angered. With her green eyes, light skin, and sandy, long hair, she seemed to resemble a White woman rather than a Black woman. That controversy was soon overshadowed by another when *Penthouse* published a series of nude pictures of Williams. In response, pageant officials took Vanessa Williams's crown away from her. Another Black woman, Suzette Charles, who was the runner-up that year, stepped in to finish out, uneventfully, the remaining two months of Williams's term. The African American community now rallied behind Williams, perhaps realizing that no matter how "White" her features, she was still vulnerable to attack by the White mainstream media. Williams has since gone to become not only a respected actress, but also a Grammy Award–winning singer.

Nonetheless, it wasn't until 1990 that pageant officials were ready to take a chance on another Black winner: African American Debbye Turner won the Miss America crown that year. The following year, another African American woman, Marjorie Judith Vincent, was crowned. Vincent's victory was considered a real breakthrough by some, because, despite the requisite shoulder-length hair, she has skin that is somewhat dark and facial features that are more Black in their characteristics than White. And then in 1994, yet another African American contestant, Kimberly Aiken, became Miss America.

Performing Arts

Beauty pageants aren't the only stage from which Black women, until recently, have been excluded. It wasn't until 1987 that the Radio City Music Hall Rockettes hired their first Black dancer, and she was only an alternate. Before that time, the director of the Rockettes, a White woman named Violet Holmes, defended the all-White mirror line on the grounds that its symmetry and precision would be ruined by the presence of "one or two black girls." African American cultural critic and legal scholar Patricia Williams wrote a scathing criticism of Holmes's rationalization in *The Alchemy of Race and Rights:*

> Mere symmetry, of course, could be achieved by hiring all black dancers. It could be achieved by hiring light-skinned black dancers, in the tradition of the Cotton Club's grand heyday of condescension. It could be achieved by hiring an even number of black dancers and then plac-

ing them like little black anchors at either end or like hubcaps at the
center, or by speckling them throughout the lineup at even intervals,
for a nice checkerboard, melting-pot effect. It could be achieved by letting all the white dancers brown themselves in the sun a bit, to match
the black dancers—something they were forbidden to do for many
years because the owner of the Rockettes didn't want them to look
"like colored girls."

From two to four, usually light-skinned, African American women now
routinely appear in the kicking line, and audiences have coped just fine with
the "disruption" of the show's harmony. Such a color-blind solution to the
problem is no doubt abetted by the larger trend in theater productions of
nontraditional casting. African American actresses and actors are now appearing in leads and secondary parts in what were once all-White productions by such playwrights as Shakespeare and Tennessee Williams.

For African American actresses, the benefits of nontraditional casting
have been genuine. Not only are more of them finding work, but many are
earning rave reviews for injecting new life into old lines. While one effect of
nontraditional casting has been to allow more Black actors to play what
were once White-only roles, the reverse—White actresses and actors playing
Black roles—has not been successfully realized. In fact, the few attempts
have created a firestorm of controversy.

African American director Phyllis Griffin, of DePaul University's acclaimed Theatre School, encountered some resistance when she decided to
cast White women in Ntozake Shange's play *For Colored Girls Who Have
Considered Suicide/When the Rainbow Is Enuf* (1975). Her decision to do so
did not come easily, and in the *Playbill* notes she went to great lengths to
give her reasons. Her primary one was that DePaul's Theatre School never
seemed to have enough African American women students to take the
different parts. As a result, year after year the play kept getting shelved.
Finally, Griffin, who is the only African American faculty member on staff,
decided it was better to cast Shange's play nontraditionally than not produce
it at all. Thus it was that, in December of 1993, *For Colored Girls Who Have
Considered Suicide/When the Rainbow Is Enuf* opened with four White
women and three African American women playing the seven lead roles
originally written for an all-Black female cast.

Griffin describes the experience of putting on this play as "surreal." More
than a year after it closed, she confesses to having "intense dreams about the

incomplete communication associated with that show." The African American actresses were mixed in their feelings about the production, while the White actresses were intimidated by being asked to portray African American women. If they overacted, they risked grossly stereotyping Black women, but if they underacted, they were accused of not using their bodies fully or taking their parts seriously. During a critique of the show, Griffin found one of the White actresses backstage crying after she was told by one of the African American actresses that White women playing Black women simply didn't "cut it."

This splitting of female roles into noninterchangeable parts is particularly evident among singers. Sixties rock legend Janis Joplin, for example, was constantly described as singing more like a Black woman than a White woman. Joplin herself once remarked that she had two distinct singing styles, her White choir voice and her Black gospel voice, inspired by the likes of Bessie Smith, Mavis Staples, and Big Maybelle. Regardless of a woman's race, if she sings or moves soulfully and provocatively, she is said to be "Black," but if she sings or moves classically, or even in a pop style, she is said to be "White." Yet because of the cliché that Blacks have better rhythm than Whites, it is viewed as more insulting to a Black woman to be told that she moves and sings like a White woman than it is for a White woman to be told that she moves and sings like a Black woman. In fact, for many White women rock and blues singers, from Joplin to Bonnie Raitt and Rickie Lee Jones, the latter comment is considered a huge compliment.

Actress-singer-comedian Sandra Bernhard confronted the issue—that White women feel they must steal from Black women to have soul in their performance—in her stage show, *Without You I'm Nothing,* which was also released as an independent film in 1990. In the show, Bernhard appears before a largely disdainful Black audience at a Black nightclub. In one absurd scene, an older White woman, identified only as Bernhard's manager, tries to argue the following point about Sandra:

And let's be frank—she doesn't have any influences, she doesn't need any. And if you want my opinion, they've all stolen from her. Donna Summer, Tina Turner, Whoopi Goldberg, Nina Simone. And I have even seen traces of Sandra in Diana Ross.

Bernhard follows with a searing parody of Diana Ross. But the punchline —and point—is subsequently made not by Bernhard, but by the beautiful

Black model Cynthia Bailey, who mysteriously pops in and out of several scenes. In the film's final moments, which take place in the now empty nightclub, Bailey glares at Bernhard. She then pulls out of her purse a tube of bright red lipstick and writes on a white tablecloth, "Fuck Sandra Bernhard." In effect, the Bailey character is saying, "You may *think* you're black, but I'm the one who has paid the dues." Freelance writer James Ledbetter, in an article about White wannabes in the music industry for *Vibe* magazine's premier issue, had this to say about Bernhard:

> It is a rare white performer who is capable of pointing out the irony, and often the absurdity, in the ways in which white people appropriate blackness. In doing this, Bernhard goes even further: she is willing to play the idiotic white person—functioning, in essence, as the butt of her own jokes. So who better than Sandra Bernhard to break down this whole white-people-who-think-they're-black thing for us?

The music industry itself has played a part in stereotyping and dividing White and Black female performers. As in film and television, there has been a curious absence of cross-race pairings among female musicians and singers. From Benny Goodman's integrated swing band of the forties, to Paul Simon's world beat sound of the nineties, there is a rich history of White men and Black men performing music together. But White women and Black women musicians rarely record or perform on stage together.

While this is partly due to women's smaller presence and influence in the music industry at large, it also has to do with the way in which White women and Black women are sexualized and marketed for primarily male viewing audiences. To become successful in the music industry, especially as a singer, a woman, no matter how much raw talent she may possess, has an enormous advantage if she has a sexy body and a pretty face. Ultimately, whether she is an actress, model, beauty pageant winner, or singer, a woman on stage becomes a sexual object for male viewers. And it is here that the issue of race comes in. White women on stage sing to, and become the sexual objects primarily of, White men; when Black women sing, they are performing for, and being gazed at by, men of both races. Even Madonna, who has pushed the sex envelope more than any other White woman singer, has never appeared before a predominantly Black audience. Somehow, the image of a White woman sexually stirring an assembly of Black men remains vaguely taboo in our culture. Yet sexy Black women singers like Tina Turner are given free range to whip into a virtual frenzy an auditorium full of White men. Turner, for example, has appeared on stage and "privately danced" alongside a strutting Mick Jagger for a live worldwide concert broadcast before mostly White fans. But it is nearly impossible to conjure up the opposite image, that of a beautiful and scantily clad White woman sexily cavorting beside a Black male singer before a predominantly African American audience. The reason goes back to the role Black women have played as the objects of White men's sexual fantasies, as well as our history of White women long having been off limits to Black men. This lingering tension around race and women's sexuality ultimately explains why White women and Black women so rarely perform together. Occasionally, a woman of another race may be inserted as a background singer, but almost never do women of the two races actually sing together as equals. It would simply be too uncomfortable for most audiences. Perhaps that is why the one big hit that Black and White woman artists did do together, "Sisters Are Doin' It for Themselves" (1985), by soul legend Aretha Franklin and White rock star Annie Lennox, was more of an anthem intended for female audiences than a sexy duet designed to seduce and entice men.

The emphasis on marketing women's sexual appeal in music became more pronounced during the eighties, with the emergence of music videos. Although a few women, such as African American songwriter and guitarist Tracy Chapman and White rocker Chrissie Hynde of the Pretenders, have successfully managed to escape being portrayed as sex kittens, many others have not. Sex sells, and the mostly male music producers know this. Some singers, like Madonna, have deliberately played up their sexuality, while others, like Annie Lennox, have begun to experiment with feminine images. Still others, like Whitney Houston, are so talented and strikingly attractive that they simply play it straight and sing to the camera. But, with notable exceptions like Houston, there has been a disturbing trend among both African American and White female singers to sell themselves sexually.

Violence against women in contemporary music is another issue that frequently divides Black and White women. Misogyny in lyrics is hardly new. Popular performers and groups from James Brown to the Beatles have written lyrics at one time or another that objectified and demeaned women. What is new is the extreme level of violence against women in the music of certain gangsta rappers. Most White women—and much of White society— are strongly opposed to lyrics that condone the rape of a woman, yet some

Black women justify misogynist lyrics in rap music on the grounds that they are legitimate expressions of urban Black culture. But is it free speech that these women are protecting? Many African American women have simply been conditioned to defend whatever Black men do, even if their actions are potentially harmful to Black women. They fear that if they challenge Black men on such behavior, they will be ridiculed and ostracized for associating themselves with the politics of White feminists.

Indeed, this is what happened to African American Jamie Foster Brown, who publishes the women's hip-hop magazine *Sister 2 Sister*. She once sat in a meeting with a group of Black male recording executives listening to an about-to-be-released rap CD. One of the songs contained some sexually offensive lyrics, and Brown expressed her opposition to them. An executive responded, "Ah, why do you want to keep a Black man from making an honest dollar?" Another chimed in, saying that Brown was letting "White feminists influence her judgment." Brown angrily retorted, "I don't need a White woman to tell me that these lyrics are offensive."

One prominent African American woman who has joined in the fight against misogynist rap music is C. Delores Tucker, chair of the National Political Congress of Black Women (NPCBW). Under her leadership, the NPCBW unanimously passed a resolution in 1993 condemning any song containing "words, lyrics, and images that degrade and denigrate African American women with obscenities and vulgarities of the violent nature." Some prominent Black male leaders, including nationally syndicated newspaper columnist William Raspberry, are also calling for an end to this madness. In a 1993 column, Raspberry asked why it was that when "Ross Perot addresses a black audience as 'you people,' we go ballistic. Rappers call our women 'bitches' and 'ho's,' and we develop lockjaw." A growing number of all-Black music radio stations, including KACE-FM in Los Angeles, have decided that they will no longer play music advocating violence or disrespect for women. Nonetheless, music executives and the rappers themselves have continued, unabated, to reap profit from such lyrics. Unfortunately, an unintended side effect of radio stations refusing to play music advocating violence against women is brisk business for gangsta rap CDs. Ultimately, African American women will have to join their White sisters in bringing an end to such misogyny.

As we've seen across the various media outlets, White women and Black women have been grossly stereotyped, maligned, and, worse, ignored altogether. Women's cross-race relations are without representation in most media outlets. In large part, this is because women, and particularly Black women, throughout history have lacked creative and marketing control over their portrayals. And the more expensive and influential the medium is, the less likely their chances to change the situation. Even when an African American female film director such as Euzhan Palcy is given the opportunity to make a major Hollywood film, she must exercise great restraint when choosing a project if she hopes to remain a player. Millions of dollars are required to produce and market major CD releases, music videos, television series, and films, and the companies and individual backers tend to be conservative. In fact, Palcy's understanding of the politics involved is reflected in her explanation for choosing to direct *A Dry White Season* (1989), a film about the effects of apartheid in South Africa not on a Black woman or a Black man, but on a White man (acted by Donald Sutherland).

I knew as a black filmmaker I now needed to do something about apartheid. I also know that no one wants to put any money into a film about black people. Black in Hollywood isn't commercial . . . I hate the idea that every time you talk about something like Vietnam, you have to have a white hero. But I want to scream to people who say this; they should write more, and they should join me and fight against those who have the money and the power to produce a movie.

While Palcy's call to "fight against those who have the money and power" was targeted specifically at filmmaking, it can also be understood as a call to arms to women of all races to seize control of how they are depicted. The portrayal of Black women and White women in literature, television, advertising, modeling, beauty pageants, music videos, and rap lyrics has begun to change, but given the politics of money and power, White women and Black women would present a stronger, more united front if they joined forces to abolish their stereotypes. Both Black and White women must look at the interests and issues they have in common rather than focusing only on those which drive them apart. Only when Black women and White women change the way they interact with each other can they hope to challenge the limited and predictable portrayals of that interaction in the media.

Epilogue: Sisters Beneath the Skin

It is easy to identify how others with more power discriminate against you. What is harder to realize is how you, by virtue of your membership in some privileged group in society, may discriminate against others. Only when we finally work to bring an end to even those types of discrimination that don't personally affect us, will we truly be sisters beneath the skin.

—*Midge Wilson, 1995*

SISTERS

Sisters in Joy, Sisters in Sorrow,
Sisters Today, Yesterday, and Tomorrow.
Strong, Determined,
Spirited and Unshaken.
Through our differences we find commonality,
Through our weaknesses we find greatness.
Black Women, White Women
Reach deep within.
As we build our sacred trust
We are Sisters Beneath the Skin.

—*Kathy Russell, 1995*

As any marriage counselor, labor mediator, or peace negotiator will tell you, in order to begin the work of repairing relations between two parties in conflict, it is first necessary to catalogue the reasons for their strife. That has been the intent of this book—to describe the various tensions that continue to exist between Black women and White women. The issues are real and are not subject to quick fixes. Spouting platitudes such as "sisterhood is global" and issuing desperate pleas to "just get along" do little to change Black and White women's realities. Real work must be done if progress is to be made in cross-race relations, and the process should begin with naming the problem, as we've attempted to do here. Beyond that, what steps must be taken to bridge the gap between Black and White women in this country?

Beginning in elementary school, more material about the history of women's cross-race relations must be presented. Although great strides have been made in recent years to change and improve school curricula, nonetheless the history of women and the history of Blacks are still treated as parallels, with little understanding of where they converge. The result is that few girls graduate from high school knowing anything about the issues of racism, gender, and equality that have affected Black women and White women from the antebellum South through the discriminatory practices of the abolitionist and suffragist movements of the late nineteenth and early twentieth centuries. Fewer yet know about the interracial tensions that erupted during this country's second wave of feminism, and how those tensions linger to this day, affecting women of different races as they work on political initiatives.

How can we rectify this? First, concerned parents can become involved in their local school boards and demand that the interplay of Black women and White women's lives be better covered in school. After all, "those who do not learn from 'herstory' are doomed to repeat it."

Parents can also try to encourage their daughters' interracial same-sex friendships. Since playing with dolls continues to be a popular activity for young girls of both races, one thing that parents can do is buy dolls of other races in addition to those of their own. Dolls can help get girls to open up about their feelings of guilt, confusion, and resentment, and serve as a springboard to discussions about race and racism. Most important, parents can examine their own attitudes and casual pronouncements about race, as racial prejudice often begins in the home.

....

Parents can also teach their daughters to become more critical consumers of the media. As long as the images of girls and women in children's books, on television, and in films and in magazines focus on racial and gender stereotypes, the attitudes and perspectives of the past will be perpetuated. Children should be encouraged to question why the female characters in stories and shows are more vain or less heroic than their male counterparts, and why Black female characters, in particular, are either missing or given lesser billing.

Finally, parents can actively seek out material that tries to overcome the usual gender and racial stereotypes. There is a growing collection of children's books that do just this. Among books for four- to eight-year-old readers that specifically address girls' interracial relationships are *Black Like Kyra and White Like Me* (1992) by Judith Vigna, *Amazing Grace* by Mary Hoffman, and *The Story of Ruby Bridges* (1993) by Dr. Robert Coles. And for older girls, there is Jacqueline Woodson's *I Hadn't Meant to Tell You This* (1994), about two girls' cautiously developing interracial friendship.

Because African American girls grow up learning the customs and culture of an America that is still predominantly White, Whites need to make a greater effort to learn about the culture of African Americans. For example, most Black girls who have never had a White girlfriend still know about White beauty habits, but few White girls who have not had a Black girlfriend know anything about why she might perm, dreadlock, and hot comb her hair.

The college dormitory is a place where White women and Black women are often thrown together for the first time, and as we've seen, ignorance of each other's culture can lead to fear and alienation. It is also a place where constructive measures can be taken to improve women's cross-race relations. During orientation-week activities, a gender-segregated session should be scheduled so that Black and White women can be encouraged by trained group leaders to openly and honestly discuss everything from beauty practices to interracial sexual attraction and jealousy. These sessions can be ongoing, designed to promote more cross-race friendships among women in college.

For those women who do not attend college, other outlets, from reading groups to community seminars, are available to educate each other. Sharing activist commitments can be another source of connection and empowerment among women of the two races.

In the past, many White female activists made the mistake of equating their own issues of feminism with those of Black women, to the disdain and fury of Black feminists. Mindful of this history, today's White feminists are often paralyzed with indecision about how to work together.

Such concern was evident at a Chicago Women's Action Coalition (WAC) meeting in the spring of 1994. Although the meeting was open to all women, and scheduled in a part of the city that was accessible to women of different racial and ethnic groups, only about thirty White women were present. Sincere in their efforts to make the world a better place for women, these concerned White women discussed and planned various action projects. One issue up for discussion that night was what could be done to help raise awareness about the rape of Bosnian women in the former Yugoslavia. One of the White women mentioned that there were Black women being raped by rival Black male gang leaders right here in Chicago, for reasons not unlike those of the Serbian men. Discussion quickly segued into what could be done to help. Clearly, a group of White women marching into a Black neighborhood carrying signs that read "Stop the rape of Black women" would be met with outrage rather than appreciation. In the end, they could think of nothing to do that would be positively received, so they returned to their original discussion and mission to help White women who were thousands of mile away.

What *can* women do to help other women who are disadvantaged, whatever their race? How can White women, in particular, assist without appearing patronizing when those they seek to help are Black? To begin, White women, no matter how well intentioned, must realize that one-time interventions do not work and may leave them open to accusations of grandstanding by African Americans in need of real aid. White women who truly want to make a difference must be willing to develop long-term relationships with local community groups and organizations that are already in touch with the cultural needs of those they are meant to serve.

This was but one of the many lessons learned by a White artist and activist named Carmella Saraceno when she tried to help poor inner-city women living in two racially mixed neighborhoods, one in New York and the other in Chicago. While living in Manhattan, Carmella tried to build a multi-use cultural space for the Black residents of a neighborhood in the South Bronx. Although she did not realize it at first, there were political, economic, and social forces at work against the proposal. These forces were not insurmountable, but because Carmella did not actually live in the affected neighborhood, she was unable to move the project forward, and it failed. Learning from her mistake, when Carmella moved to Chicago, she and her husband bought housing in a racially mixed gang-populated neighborhood on the West Side. Because she was then a resident of the neighborhood that she wanted to improve, Carmella was able gradually to earn the trust of her neighbors, many of whom now regularly come to her for assistance in dealing with White-run agencies. Carmella also has been instrumental in helping her mostly Black and Hispanic neighbors organize a community policing program to eradicate gang activity and stop drug selling on nearby corners. And, finally, she founded an organization called Artists and Children Create Together (ACCT) to help divert young children from joining gangs by getting them involved in community-based art projects.

While few of us can make the kind of sacrifices that Carmella has, there is no doubt something that every woman can do to help her sisters. It may entail speaking up about racism in the workplace or helping to elect more African American women into positions of power and influence. It may involve assisting a co-worker who is struggling with her communication skills. Both Black and White women must come to view helping those who are less privileged as a positive thing, and if necessary to ignore criticism from other members of their community for doing so.

As we mentioned in the opening pages of this book, the slogan "sisters beneath the skin" was criticized by many as a simplistic color-blind notion of race relations that had failed women in the past. Yet we cautiously and optimistically return to this notion, while acknowledging the important differences of skin color among women, both as a reality and a symbol of cultural difference. Despite our embattled history, White women and Black women are connected by the fact that they are women. We have the ability —and the need—to move beyond the notion of sisters who are divided to become sisters who are united.

Black women and White women can no longer afford to waste time bickering among themselves. Now, more than ever, we must come together to fight racial inequality, preserve the ideals of affirmative action, and give children of all backgrounds the necessary educational and financial tools to prosper and grow. Some political leaders envision a return to a mythical time when every family was a happy two-parent unit, and Mom stayed home to take care of the children. Such representations are disrespectful of the many single mothers and working women of this country who must pitch in financially to help their families survive. Too many politicians today are determined to undermine the fragile support systems that allow single, financially disadvantaged mothers to take care of their children at home. Rather, we need to work together for adequate day care facilities and after-school programs to assist women of all economic backgrounds to better care for their children. To prevent the erosion of the rights and address the particular concerns of women by those in government, we must change the face of Congress so that it more closely resembles the overall gender and racial makeup of the citizens of this country. But for that to happen, women of all races must pitch in as the sisters they are, as the sisters they need to be.

There is reason to hope that women's cross-race relations are on the path to improvement. The media themselves are sources of renewed optimism. As this book goes to press, the first interracial on-the-road female buddy film, *Boys on the Side* (1995), starring Whoopi Goldberg, Mary-Louise Parker, and Drew Barrymore, is doing well at the box office. The movie tells the story of a loving cross-race friendship among three women, and for once, the African American female lead is not in service to any of the White women. And a growing number of commercials and television programs portray White and Black women in a more even and positive light. In recent years, the multicultural educational movement has done much to educate scholars, politicians, teachers, and ordinary people alike to the issues of race and equality.

Clearly, there is a revolution going on in this country regarding race and gender. Relations between the races and the sexes have undeniably changed in the past two decades, and there is no going back. It is our belief that these forces for understanding and change will prevail, and women, in all their diversity, will lead the way together into the twenty-first century.

Notes

Chapter 1
History
The Divisions Begin

p. 11 Mary Boykin Chesnut quote, in C. Vann Woodward (ed.), *Mary Chesnut's Civil War* (New Haven, CT, 1981), pp. 59, 729.

p. 11 Harriet Jacobs quote, in Harriet Jacobs, *Incidents in the Life of a Slave Girl* (Coral Gables, FL: Mnemosyne Publishing Co., 1969), p. 119.

p. 12 Mission of shipping "maydens," in Suzanne Lesbsock, "No Obey," in Nancy A. Hewitt, *Women, Families, and Communities: Readings in American History,* vol. 1; *To 1877* (Glenview, IL: Foresman–Little, Brown Higher Education, 1990), p. 12.

p. 12 First Africans in Jamestown, in Lerone Bennett, Jr., *Before the Mayflower: A History of Black America* (Chicago: Johnson Publishing Co., 1982), pp. 34–35.

p. 13 Discussion of first female English immigrants, in Suzanne Lesbsock, "No Obey," Hewitt, op. cit., pp. 12–14; and Bennett, op. cit., p. 35.

p. 13 Census data on first Negroes in America, in Bennett, op. cit., p. 36.

p. 13 Law about pregnant indentured servants, in Suzanne Lesbsock, "No Obey," Hewitt, op. cit., p. 14.

p. 14 Opportunities for upward mobility, Suzanne Lesbsock, "No Obey," Hewitt, op. cit., pp. 15–16.

p. 14 Changing laws about slavery and the status of mulatto children, in Joel Williamson, *New People: Miscegenation and Mulattoes in the United States* (New York: Free Press, 1980), p. 8, and Bennett, op. cit., p. 45.

p. 15 Ratio of Africans to White bound laborers arriving in the colonies, in Suzanne Lesbsock, "No Obey," in Hewitt, op. cit., p. 19.

p. 15 Why slavery came to be abolished in the North, in Jean R. Roderlund, "Black Women in Colonial Pennsylvania," in Jean E. Friedman, William G. Shade, Mary Jane Capozzoli, *Our American Sisters: Women in American Life and Thought* (Lexington, MA: D. C. Heath & Co., 1987), pp. 55–69.

p. 16 Phillis Wheatley, in Bennett, op. cit., pp. 71–72.

p. 16 Percent of female slaves working as fieldworkers, in Jacqueline Jones, *Labor of Love, Labor of Sorrow: Black Women, Work, and the Family from Slavery to the Present* (New York: Basic Books, Inc., 1985), p. 14.

p. 16 Anne Firor Scott quote, in Anne Firor Scott, "Women's Perspective on the Patriarchy in the 1850s," in Friedman, Shade, Capozzoli, op. cit., p. 156.

p. 16 Expected roles of slave women and White mistresses, in Deborah Gray White, *Arn't I a Woman: Female Slaves in the Plantation South* (New York: W. W. Norton & Co., 1985), p. 17.

p. 17 Mistresses working hard and related quotes by Harriet Martineau and slave Polly Colbert, ibid., pp. 51–52.

p. 17 Mistress about Christmas, in Anne Firor Scott, *The Southern Lady: From Pedestal to Politics 1830–1930* (Chicago: University of Chicago Press, 1970), p. 30.

p. 17 Mary Chestnut's beliefs about slavery, in Elizabeth Fox-Genovese, *Within the Plantation Household: Black and White Women of the Old South* (Chapel Hill: NC: University of North Carolina Press, 1988), pp. 47–48.

p. 17 White men being invested in White women's beliefs about the good of slavery, in White, op. cit., p. 58.

p. 17 George Fitzhugh's views of slavery and its effects on women, in White, op. cit., p. 45; Fox-Genovese, op. cit., p. 199.

p. 18 Thomas Dew's beliefs about slavery, in Fox-Genovese, op. cit., pp. 197–198.

p. 18 William Drayton quote, in White, op. cit., p. 44.

p. 18 White women not being convinced that slave women as prostitutes was advantageous, in Ann Firor Scott, *The Southern Lady: From Pedestal to Politics 1830–1930* (Chicago: University of Chicago Press, 1970), p. 53.

p. 18 White women sharing beliefs that slave women were promiscuous, in White, op. cit., pp. 38–40.

p. 18 Rape of slave women, in Gerda Lerner (ed.), *Black Women in White America: A Documentary History,* (New York: Vintage Books, 1972), p. 158;

in Joel Williamson, *New People: Miscegenation and Mulattoes in the United States* (New York: Free Press, 1980), p. 42.

p. 18 Some slave women as concubines, in Stanley Feldstein, *Once a Slave: The Slave's View of Slavery* (New York: William Morrow & Co., 1970), pp. 133–134.

p. 18 Mistresses been treated badly by their husbands, in White, op. cit., p. 40.

p. 19 Mary Chesnut quote, in Woodward, op. cit., p. 29.

p. 19 Mistress beating thirteen-year-old girl, in Feldstein, op. cit., p. 132.

p. 19 Mulatto hypothesis and discussion of skin color beliefs and slaves, in Kathy Russell, Midge Wilson, and Ronald Hall, *The Color Complex* (New York: Harcourt Brace Jovanovich, 1992), pp. 126–127.

p. 19 Quote by son regarding his mother's relationship with a house slave, in Anne Firor Scott, *The Southern Lady: From Pedestal to Politics 1830–1930* (Chicago: University of Chicago Press, 1970), p. 48.

p. 19 Clothes and slaves being dressed better than farmers' wives, in Fox-Genovese, op. cit., pp. 216–219.

p. 20 Story about Sarah Gayle, ibid., p. 22–26.

p. 20 Slave's cynical comment about mistress crying, ibid., p. 131.

p. 20 Failure to give slaves housecleaning instructions, in Feldstein, op. cit., p. 130.

p. 20 Fight between mistress and slave woman, in Dorothy Sterling *We Are Your Sisters: Black Women in the Nineteenth Century* (New York: W. W. Norton, 1984), p. 57.

p. 20 Owners valuing birth of slave children, in Herbert Gutman, *The Black Family in Slavery and Freedom, 1750–1925* (New York: Pantheon Books, 1976), pp. 75–76.

p. 21 Slave marriages based on real affection, in Sterling, op. cit., p. 37.

p. 21 Mary Chesnut quote, in White, op. cit., p. 97.

p. 21 Slaves not being so sexually liberated, in bell hooks, *Ain't I a Woman: Black Women and Feminism* (Boston, MA: South End Press, 1981), p. 54.

p. 21 Gender role conventions from Africa, in Fox-Genovese, op. cit., p. 290.

pp. 21–22 Medical complications associated with childbirth, in White, op. cit., p. 83.

p. 22 Slave women valuing motherhood more than marriage, in Fox-Genovese, op. cit., p. 64.

p. 22 Slave women's views about pregnancy, in White, op. cit., pp. 83–88.

p. 22 Role of Black Mammy, ibid., pp. 56–60.

pp. 22–23 White mistresses watching over slave children, ibid., pp. 53–54.

p. 23 Quote by mistress who hated watching over slaves, in Anne Firor Scott, *The Southern Lady: From Pedestal to Politics 1830–1930* (Chicago: University of Chicago Press, 1970), p. 47.

p. 24 Women's social movements and the Colored Female Religious and Moral Society, in Anne Firor Scott, *Natural Allies: Women's Association in American History* (Urbana: University of Illinois Press, 1991), pp. 13–14.

p. 24 Black women forming first antislavery group, ibid., pp. 45–46; and in Sterling, op. cit., p. xiii.

p. 24 Quaker women integrating antislavery groups, in Anne Firor Scott, *Natural Allies: Women's Association in American History* (Urbana: University of Illinois Press, 1991), p. 51.

pp. 24–25 Black women attending first national antislavery conventions, and greater acceptance of lighter-skinned women, Rosalyn Terborg-Penn, "Discrimination against Afro-American women in the woman's movement, 1830–1920," in Sharon Harley and Rosalyn Terborg-Penn (eds.), *The Afro-American Woman: Struggle and Images* (Port Washington, NY: National University Publications Kennikat Press, 1978), p. 19.

p. 25 Black women holding few illusions about marriage, in Sterling, op. cit., pp. 89–92.

p. 25 Grimké sisters, in *Compton's Encyclopedia,* Online Edition, Downloaded from *America Online,* Aug. 12, 1993.

p. 26 How women's movement came into being, in Anne Firor Scott, *Natural Allies: Women's Association in American History* (Urbana: University of Illinois Press, 1991), pp. 53–54.

p. 26 Mott and Stanton radicalized by London, in Mary Becker, Cynthia Bowman, and Morrison Torrey, *Cases and Materials in Feminist Jurisprudence: Taking Women Seriously* (Minneapolis: West, 1993), pp. 1–2.

p. 26 Seneca Falls convention, ibid., p. 2.

p. 27 Douglass, in Rosalyn M. Terborg-Penn, *Afro-Americans in the Struggle for Woman Suffrage,* a dissertation submitted to the faculty of the Graduate School of Howard University (Ann Arbor, MI: University Microfilms International, 1983), p. 29.

p. 27 Black women's demands to be heard, in Sterling, op. cit., p. 410.

p. 27 Truth beginning her participation in the women's movement, ibid., p. 411.

p. 27 Sojourner Truth in Akron, Ohio, in Rosalyn Terborg-Penn, "Discrimination against Afro-American women in the woman's movement, 1830–1920," in Harley and Terborg-Penn, op. cit., p. 20.

p. 27 Quote by Truth, in Sojurner Truth, "Ar'n't I a Woman," speech in White, op. cit., pp. 13–14.

p. 28 Women running plantations during Civil War, in White, op. cit., p. 106.

p. 28 Changes in women's role after Civil War, ibid.

p. 28 Members of Freedmen's Bureau encouraging traditional sex roles, in Sterling, op. cit., p. xi.

p. 28 Biblical injunction, in Jacqueline Jones, *Labor of Love, Labor of Sorrow: Black women, Work, and the Family from Slavery to the Present* (New York: Basic Books, Inc., 1985), p. 67.

p. 28 Black women perceiving freedom as opportunity to devote to family, ibid., p. 78.

pp. 28–29 Black husbands taking pride in buying wives fancy clothes, ibid., p. 69.

p. 29 Black women being harassed by White men," in hooks, op. cit., p. 55.

p. 29 Fourteenth and Fifteenth amendments, in Anne Firor Scott and Andrew MacKay Scott, *One Half the People: The Fight for Woman Suffrage* (Urbana: University of Illinois Press, 1982), pp. 15–16; in Mary Becker, Cynthia Bowman, and Morrison Torrey, *Cases and Materials in Feminist Jurisprudence: Taking Women Seriously* (Minneapolis: West, 1993), p. 10; Bennett, op. cit., p. 260.

pp. 29–30 Douglass, in Rosalyn Terborg-Penn, "Discrimination against Afro-American women in the women's movement, 1830–1920," in Sharon Harley and Rosalyn Terborg-Penn (eds.), *The Afro-American Woman: Struggle and Images* (Port Washington, NY: National University Publications Kennikat Press, 1978), p. 20.

p. 30 Quote by Anthony, in Eleanor Flexner, *Century of Struggle: The Women's Rights Movement in the United States* (Cambridge, MA: Belknap Press, 1975), p. 147.

p. 30 Quote by Truth, in Sterling, op. cit., pp. 411–412.

p. 30 Educated White women outraged about illiterate Blacks getting the vote ahead of them, in Anne Firor Scott, *Natural Allies: Women's Association in American History* (Urbana: University of Illinois Press, 1991), p. 135.

p. 30 Split in suffrage movement," ibid., pp. 135–136; in Becker, Bowman, and Torrey, op. cit., p. 10.

pp. 30–31 Majority of women not suffragists, in Carolyn Johnston, *Sexual*

Power: Feminism and the Family in America (Tuscaloosa: University of Alabama Press, 1992), p. 102.

p. 31 WCTU, in Rosalyn Terborg-Penn, "Discrimination against Afro-American women in the woman's movement, 1830–1920," in Harley and Terborg-Penn, op. cit., pp. 21–24.

p. 31 Amelia Bloomer, Frances Harper, and Josephine St. Pierre Ruffin, ibid., pp. 22–23.

pp. 31–32 Black and White Southern joining forces to prevent lynching, in Carolyn Johnston, *Sexual Power: Feminism and the Family in America* (Tuscaloosa: University of Alabama Press, 1992), p. 109.

p. 32 Jessie Daniel Ames, in Paula Giddings, *When and Where I Enter: The Impact of Black Women on Race and Sex America* (New York: William Morrow & Co., Inc., 1984), pp. 207–208.

p. 32 Anna Julia Cooper, in Johnston, op. cit., p. 107.

p. 32 Black men opposing suffrage, in Rosalyn M. Terborg-Penn, *Afro-Americans in the Struggle for Woman Suffrage,* dissertation submitted to the faculty of the Graduate School of Howard University (Ann Arbor, MI: University Microfilms International, 1983), p. 268.

p. 32 Quote by Mary Church Terrell, ibid., p. 269.

p. 32 Wells-Barnett, in Rosalyn Terborg-Penn, "Discrimination against Afro-American women in the woman's movement, 1830–1920," in Harley and Terborg-Penn, op. cit., p. 24.

p. 33 Sylvamie Williams's comment to Anthony, Rosalyn Terborg-Penn, "Discrimination against Afro-American women in the woman's movement, 1830–1920," in Harley and Terborg-Penn, op. cit., p. 24.

p. 33 Reference to Alice Paul, in "Discontented Black Feminists: Predule and Postscript to the Passage of the Nineteenth Amendment," Lois Scharf and Joan M. Jensen (eds.), *Decades Of Discontent: The Women's Movement, 1920–1940,* (Westport, CT: Greenwood Press, 1983), p. 264.

p. 33 Southern states that failed to ratify the suffrage amendment, in Johnston, op. cit., p. 105.

p. 34 "Historian believing the suffrage amendment would have passed soon anyhow," in Anne Firor Scott and Andrew MacKay Scott, *One Half the People: The Fight for Woman Suffrage* (Urbana: University of Illinois Press, 1982), p. 46.

p. 34 Disillusionment with enfranchisement, ibid., pp. 47–48.

p. 34 Flappers, in Mary Becker, Cynthia Bowman, and Morrison Torrey,

Cases and Materials in Feminist Jurisprudence: Taking Women Seriously (Minneapolis: West, 1993), p. 16.

p. 34 LWV and NWP, in Anne Firor Scott and Andrew MacKay Scott, *One Half the People: The Fight for Woman Suffrage* (Urbana, IL: University of Illinois Press, 1982), p. 49.

p. 34 NWP as racist and classist, in hooks, op. cit., pp. 171–172.

p. 34 Council for Interracial Cooperation, in Paula Giddings, *When and Where I Enter: The Impact of Black Women on Race and Sex America* (New York: William Morrow & Co., Inc., 1984), p. 171.

p. 34 YWCA, in Jacquelyn Dowd Hall, "A Common Bond of Womanhood? Building an Interracial Community in the Jim Crow South," in Nancy A. Hewitt, *Women, Families, and Communities: Reading in American History,* vol. 2, *From 1865,* (Glenview, ILL: Foresman/Little, Brown Higher Education, 1990), p. 107.

p. 34 Black women joining their own groups and forming coalitions with Black men, in Giddings, op. cit., pp. 93, 166.

p. 34 Nannie Burroughs, ibid., p. 210.

pp. 34–35 Disenfranchisement of Southern Blacks, in "Discontented Black Feminists: Predule and Postscript to the Passage of the Nineteenth Amendment," in Lois Scharf and Joan M. Jensen (eds.), *Decades of Discontent: The Women's Movement, 1920–1940* (Westport, CT: Greenwood Press, 1983), p. 266.

p. 35 Women's movement between 1920s and 1940s, ibid., p. 268.

p. 35 Renewed activism in late fifties and early sixties, Giddings, op. cit., pp. 261–324.

Chapter 2
Childhood
From Schoolgirls to Homegirls

p. 37 "Nikki-Rosa," in Nikki Giovanni, *Black Feeling Black Talk Black Judgement* (Detroit, MI: Broadside Press, 1973), cited in Toni Cade (ed.), *The Black Woman: An Anthology* (New York: A Mentor Book, 1970), p. 15.

p. 37 Lynda Barry, *The Good Times Are Killing Me* (Seattle, WA: The Real Comet Press, 1988), p. 29.

p. 38 Personal interview with Justine, Aug. 20, 1993.

p. 38 Personal interview with Jane, Dec. 2, 1993.

p. 39 Acquisition of racial identity, in M. A. Spencer, G. K. Brookins, and W. R. Allen, *Beginnings: The Social and Affective Development of Black Children* (Hillside, NJ: Lawrence Erlbaum Associates, 1985).

p. 39 Acquisition of gender identity, in Rhoda Unger and Mary Crawford, *Women and Gender: A Feminist Perspective* (New York: McGraw-Hill, Inc., 1992), p. 28.

p. 39 Girls being racially aware before boys, in Judith Porter, *Black Child, White Child: The Development of Racial Attitudes* (Cambridge, MA: Harvard University Press, 1971), p. 25.

p. 39 Racial awareness development stages, in Marguerite Alejandro-Wright, "The Child's Conception of Racial Classification: A Socio-Cognitive Developmental Model." Spencer, op. cit.

p. 39 Concrete thinkers, in Jean Piaget, *The Child's Conception of the World* (Totowa, NJ: Littlefield, Adams & Co., 1969).

p. 40 Quote by Christine Kerwin from telephone interview, Sept. 14, 1993.

p. 40 "Subliminal awareness" stage, in Marguerite Alejandro-Wright, "The Child's Conception of Racial Classification: A Socio-Cognitive Developmental Model." Spencer, op. cit.

p. 40 Children's lack of constancy, in Jean Piaget, op. cit.

p. 40 Personal interview with Brooke L., Jan. 12, 1995.

p. 40 Clarks' research, in J. A. Baldwin, "Theory and Research Concerning the Notion of Black Self-Hatred: A Review and Reinterpretation," *Journal of Black Psychology,* vol. 5 (1979), pp. 51–77.

p. 40 Doll choices, in Albert Roberts, Kathleen Mosely, and Maureen Chamberlain, "Age Differences in Racial Self-identity of Young Black Girls, *Psychological Reports,* vol. 37 (1975), pp. 1263–1266.

p. 41 Variation of Clarks' research in Darlene Powell-Hopson and Derek S. Hopson, "Implications of Doll Color Preferences Among Black Preschool Children and White Preschool Children, *The Journal of Black Psychology,* vol. 14 (1988), pp. 57–63.

p. 41 Children and race-related terms, in Olivera Perkins and Karen R. Long, "Kids and Color: Prejudice Begins at Home," *Cleveland Plain Dealer,* national sect. p. 1A, Oct. 29, 1993.

p. 41 Telephone interview with Alana, April 20, 1993.

p. 42 Nonphysical cues in racial classification, in Marguerite Alejandro-Wright, "The Child's Conception of Racial Classification: A Socio-Cognitive Developmental Model," in Spencer, op. cit.

p. 42 White children and awareness of race, in Porter, op. cit., p. 25; in

Judith Levine, "White Like Me: When Privilege Is Written on Your Skin," *Ms.* March–April 1994, pp. 22–24.

p. 42 Gender identity and differences in play, in Bernice Lott, *Women's Lives: Themes and Variations in Gender Learning,* 2nd ed. (Pacific Grove, CA: Brooks-Cole Publishing, 1994), pp. 33–67.

p. 43 Reference to Mattel's first Black doll, in telephone interview with Lisa McKendall, Corporate Relations Representative, Mattel Industries, Jan. 3, 1995.

p. 43 Excerpt on Claudia's Aryan-looking doll, in Toni Morrison, *The Bluest Eye* (New York: Pocket Books, 1970), p. 22.

p. 44 Dolls choices and behavior, in Joseph Hraba and Geoffrey Grant, "Black Is Beautiful: A reexamination of racial preference and identification," *Journal of Personality and Social Psychology,* vol. 16 (1970), pp. 398–402.

p. 44 Margaret Spencer's research, in Frances Aboud, *Children and Prejudice* (New York: Basil Blackwell, Inc., 1988), p. 90.

p. 44 Quote by Sara about daughter Jennifer in telephone interview, Nov. 15, 1994.

p. 45 Telephone interview with a woman in her thirties, Sept. 26, 1993.

p. 45 Personal interview with Kara, Nov. 25, 1993.

p. 45 Personal interview with Nana, Nov. 22, 1993.

p. 45 Black girls and rope-jumping, in Gregory Lewis, "Those Girls Really Know the Ropes," *San Francisco Examiner,* Feb. 27, 1994, p. E10.

pp. 45–46 Quote by Mattie about double-dutch rope-jumping from personal interview, Oct. 23, 1994.

p. 45 Quote by Annie about double-dutch, June 14, 1994.

p. 46 Children separating by gender, in Barrie Thorne, *Gender Play: Girls and Boys in School* (New Brunswick, NJ, 1993), p. 33.

p. 46 Sex segregation in play, in Martin Patchen, *Black-White Contact in Schools: Its Social and Academic Effects* (West Lafayette, IN: Purdue University Press, 1982).

p. 46 Propinquity in interracial friendships, in Maureen T. Halliman and Richard A. Williams, "Interracial Friendship Choices in Secondary Schools," *American Sociological Review,* vol. 54 (1989), pp. 67–68.

p. 47 Housing segregation myths, in Gary Tobin, *Divided Neighborhood: Changing Patterns of Racial Segregation* (Newbury Park, CA: 1987), pp. 8–9.

p. 47 "Census data," ibid, pp. 95–114.

p. 47 Lynda Barry's play, in Steve Johnson, "It's Play Time: Cartoonist Lynda Barry's Quirky Creations Take a Dramatic Turn," *Chicago Tribune,* Tempo sect. (April 19, 1989), Zone C., p. 1.

p. 47 Edna and Bonna as best friends, in Lynda Barry, *The Good Times Are Killing Me* (Seattle, WA: The Real Comet Press, 1988), p. 34.

p. 48 Unstructured time and other-race friends, in David DuBois and Barton Hirsch, "School and Neighborhood Friendship Patterns of Black and Whites in Early Adolescence." *Child Development,* vol. 61 (1990), pp. 524–536.

p. 48 Personal interview with Tracey, Nov. 19, 1993.

p. 48 Quote by Lynn from personal interview, July 10, 1994.

p. 49 Quote by Jessica from excerpt in Ann M. Martin, *The Baby Sitters Club # 22,* (New York: Scholastic, Inc., 1989), p. 3.

p. 49 Young Black girl's self-esteem in predominantly White environments, in Allison Samuels, "Teaching That Black Is Beautiful: Females Suffer More in Mostly White Social Settings, *Los Angeles Times,* Sect. Orange County Life, Part N (May 10, 1990), p. 6.

p. 49 Reference to story about girl named Sheronda from Debora M., telephone interview, Oct. 1, 1993.

p. 50 Black and White children in naturally integrated schools, in E. Mavis Hetherington and Ross D. Parke, *Child Psychology: A Contemporary Viewpoint,* 4th ed (NY: McGraw-Hill, Inc., 1993), p. 518; in Edward Zigler and Matia Stevenson, *Children in a Changing World: Development and Social Issues,* 2nd ed. (Pacific Grove, CA: Brooks/Cole Publishing Co., 1993), p. 558.

p. 50 Children in schools where Black-White ratio is nearly equal, in Frances Aboud, *Children And Prejudice* (New York: Basil Blackwell, Inc., 1988), pp. 81–82.

p. 50 Personal interview with Megan and Shawn, July 24, 1993.

p. 50 Being a girl and racial minority, in Janet Kistner, Amy Metzler, Deborah Gatlin, and Susan Risi, "Classroom Racial Proportions in Children's Peer Relations: Race and Gender Effects," *Journal of Educational Psychology,* vol. 85 (1993), pp. 446–452; in "FSU study: Minority Rejection Tied to Gender, Not Race," *United Press International,* Regional News, Dist. Florida, May 20, 1993.

p. 51 Quote by Marie, in Jacqueline Woodson, *I Hadn't Meant to Tell You This* (New York: Delacorte Press, 1994), pp. 95–96.

pp. 51–52 Quote by Lydia from personal interview, July 12, 1994.

p. 52 Personal interview, Aug. 20, 1993, with White girl who said she likes light-skinned Black girls better than dark-skinned girls.

p. 52 Skin color prejudice, in Kathy Russell, Midge Wilson, and Ronald Hall, *The Color Complex: The Politics of Skin Color Among African Americans* (New York: Harcourt Brace Jovanovich, 1993).

p. 52 Girls discriminating skin tones, in Cornelia Porter, "Social Reasons for Skin Tone Preferences of Black School-Age Children," *American Journal of Orthopsychiatry* (Jan. 1991), pp. 149–154.

p. 53 Nursery school girls and physical attractiveness, in Karen Dion "Young Children's Stereotyping of Facial Attractiveness," *Developmental Psychology,* vol. 9 (1973), pp. 183–188, 1973.

p. 53 Telephone interview with Becky, April 30, 1993.

p. 53 Dark-skinned girls and social rejection, in Morrison, op. cit.; in Maya Angelou, *I Know Why the Caged Bird Sings* (New York: Bantam, 1969).

pp. 53–54 Telephone interview with Jerrilyn, Dec. 1993.

p. 54 Biracial girls as bridges, in Christine Kerwin, "Racial Identity Development in Biracial Children of Black/White Racial Heritage," dissertation submitted to the Graduate School of Education, Fordham University, 1991, p. 126.

p. 54 Biraciality, friendship, and adjustment, in Christine Kerwin, Joseph Ponterooto, Barbara Jackson, and Abigail Harris, "Racial Identity in Biracial Children: A Qualitative Investigation," *Journal of Counseling Psychology,* vol. 40 (1993), pp. 229–230; in Raymond Vagas "The Psychological and Social Functioning of Latency Age Black/White Biracial Girls from Intact Interracial Families," *Dissertation Abstracts International,* B 52/10 p. 5571, April 1992.

p. 54 Telephone interview with transracially adopted, biracial woman named Katie, Sept. 27, 1993.

p. 54 NABSW, in Russell, Wilson, and Hall, op. cit., p. 100.

p. 54 Elizabeth Bartholet, in Ruth Richman, "Unfair, Harmful?: Law Professor Questions Same-Race Adoption Policies," *Chicago Tribune,* Womannews, Sect. 6 (April 4, 1993), pp. 1, 11.

p. 54 Biracially adopted children, in Allen Wise, "The Formation of Racial Identity in Black Children Adopted By White Parents," Dissertation submitted to the Wright Institute Graduate School (Ann Arbor, MI: University Microfilms International, 1976).

p. 55 Steve Asher's research, in E. Mavis Hetherington and Ross D. Parke, *Child Psychology: A Contemporary Viewpoint,* 4th ed. (New York: McGraw-Hill, Inc., 1993), p. 519.

p. 56 Telephone interview with fifteen-year-old Black girl, Aug. 1993.

p. 56 Barry, op. cit., p. 29.

p. 56 Telephone interview with Claudia, Oct. 10, 1993.

p. 56 Attack on two girls, in Michael Parente, "3 Teens Held in Racial Attack, *Newsday,* News section (Jan. 15, 1992), p. 26.

p. 56 Black girls accused of acting White, in Olivera Perskin and Karen R. Long, "Kids and Color: Prejudice Begins at Home," *Cleveland Plain Dealer,* National sect., (Nov. 29, 1992), p. 1A.

p. 56 Race Monitors, in article by K. C. Compton, Gannett News Service, Sect. K. C. Compton (May 30, 1989), 85th Story, Level 1.

p. 57 Black girls being heavier, in "Black Girls More Prone to Heart Disease Than Whites," *Jet,* Health sect. (Feb. 8, 1993), p. 28.

p. 57 Race difference and puberty, in Marilyn Dunlop, "Girls Entering Puberty Earlier, *Toronto Star Newspaper,* Life sect., June 5, 1993, p. F2.

p. 57 Early menarche, in J. Brooks-Gunn and A. C. Petersen (eds.), *Girls at Puberty* (New York: Plenum Press, 1983), cited in Rachel T. Hare-Mustin and Jeanne Marecek (eds.), *Making a Difference: Psychology and the Construction of Gender* (New Haven: Yale University Press, 1990). p. 108.

p. 57 Quote by Meredith from personal interview, Aug. 1994.

p. 58 White girls' loss of voice, in Lyn Mikel Brown and Carol Gilligan, *Meeting at the Crossroads: Women's Psychology and Girls' Development* (Cambridge: Harvard University Press, 1992).

p. 59 Loss of voice in White middle-class girls, in Peggy Orenstein, *SchoolGirls: Young Women, Self-Esteem, and the Confidence Gap* (New York: Doubleday, 1994), p. 159.

p. 59 Children under age eighteen with single mothers, Table no. 80, "Children Under 18 Years Old by Presence of Parents: 1970 to 1992," *Statistical Abstract of the United States,* 113th ed. (Washington, DC: U.S. Department of Commerce, 1993), p. 64.

p. 59 Living in nontraditional family, in Shere Hite, "Bringing Democracy Home," *Ms.,* March–April 1995, pp. 54–61.

p. 59 Race differences in girls' self-esteem, in *Shortchanging Girls, Shortchanging America: A Call to Action* (Washington, DC: American Association of University Women, 1991), p. 27, in article about report by Janet Leibs Dworkis, "Happy the Way She Is," *Dallas Morning News,* Today sect. (Nov. 25, 1992), p. 5C; in E. L. Horwitz, "Shortchanging Girls, Shortchanging America," *Outlook,* vol. 77, 85, no. 278.

p. 59 Quote by Janie Victoria Ward in "Shortchanging Girls, Shortchanging America, *American Association of University Women,* (Washington, DC, 1991), p. 27.

p. 60 "Those loud Black girls," in Signithia Fordham, "Those Loud

Black Girls: (Black) Women, Silence, and Gender 'Passing,' in the Academy," *Anthropology and Education Quarterly,* vol. 24 (1993), pp. 3–32.

p. 60 Quote by Fordham, ibid., p. 17.

p. 61 Quote by Becca, in Orenstein, op. cit., p. 80.

p. 61 Reference to April, ibid., p. 180.

p. 61 School suspension rates in NYC, in Billy House, "School Suspensions Hit Black Hardest," Gannett News Service (March 16, 1993), 13th story, level 1.

p. 61 High school dropout rates, in "High School dropouts," *Chicago Tribune,* Nov. 24, 1991, Zone C, p. 1.

p. 61 1994 SAT scores, in "Profiles of College-Bound Seniors: Gender and Ethnic Group Breakdown," Educational Testing Service, Princeton, NJ, from phone conversation with ETS marketing representative, Jan. 13, 1995.

p. 62 Parental expectations of children's success, in Zena Smith Blau, *Black Children/White Children: Competence, Socialization, and Social Structure* (New York: The Free Press, 1981), p. 151.

p. 62 Wexler school and quotes by teachers, in Janet Ward Schofield, *Black and White in School: Trust, Tension or Tolerance?* (New York: Teachers College Press, 1989), pp. 101–102.

p. 62 Participation in multiethnic sports, in E. Mavis Heatherington and Ross D. Parke, *Child Psychology: A Contemporary Viewpoint* (New York: McGraw-Hill, Inc., 1992), p. 259.

p. 62 Wilson Sports survey, in Gerald Eskenazi, "Girls' Participation in Sports Improves," *New York Times,* sect. A, Sports Desk (June 8, 1988), p. 29, col. 1.

p. 63 Quote by Willye White, ibid.

p. 64 Gender differences in athletics versus physical appearance, in Barrie Thorne, *Gender Play: Girls and Boys in School* (New Brunswick, NJ: 1993), p. 155.

p. 64 Excerpt, Shirley Abbott, *Womenfolks: Growing Up Down South* (New York: Ticknor & Fields, 1983), p. 110.

p. 64 Homecoming court quota, in "Blacks Upset With Homecoming Court Quota," Associated Press, Domestic News (Oct. 17, 1986).

p. 65 Alternating race of homecoming queen, in Darryl Fears, "Race Take Turns at Homecoming Title Unique Policy: Tennessee Educators Say Alternating Queens Keeps the Peace at a Majority-Black School," *Atlanta Constitution,* national news (Feb. 7, 1992), sect. A, p. 3.

p. 65 Black girls not being picked as cheerleaders, in Marie Nelson,

"NAACP Cheers for Principal, Boos Coach," *Washington Times* (June 21, 1990).

pp. 65–66 Telephone interview with Patty, Nov. 25, 1993.

p. 66 Michelle Kegley punched in the face, in Kevin Johnson "Racist Threat in Dress Dispute: Teens Harassed Over 'Hip-Hop' " *USA Today*, Life sect., Dec. 14, 1993, p. 3A.

pp. 66–67 Telephone interview with Melissa, September, 1992.

p. 67 Telephone interview with Canan, August 1993.

p. 67 Telephone interview with Tara, Sept. 1993.

p. 67 Personal interview with Donna, Oct. 1994.

p. 68 Personal interview with Renée and Jennifer, Joliet, Il, in April 1993.

p. 68 Sally at Wexler School, in Janet Ward Schofield, *Black and White in School: Trust, Tension or Tolerance?* (New York: Teachers College Press, 1989), p. 89.

pp. 68–69 Quote regarding growing up White in a predominantly Black school, in Tru Love, "What I Learned as a White Girl in a Black School", *Ebony*, vol. 48, Sept. 1993, pp. 44–50.

p. 69 Personal interview with Lana, Nov. 22, 1993.

p. 69 Personal interview with Sandra T., Nov. 22, 1993.

pp. 69–70 Telephone interview with Addie, Sept. 1994.

Chapter 3
Surface Divisions
Issues of Beauty and Style

p. 71 Susan Brownmiller quote, in "Hair," *Femininity* (New York: Fawcett Columbine, 1984), p. 73.

p. 71 Lonnice Brittenum Bonner quote, in *Good Hair: For Colored Girls Who've Considered Weaves When the Chemicals Became Too Ruff* (New York: Crown Trade Paperbacks, 1991), p. 9.

pp. 72–73 Adrienne Rich quote, in "Disloyal to Civilization: Feminism, Racism, Gynephobia," Adrienne Rich, *On Lies, Secrets, and Silence* (New York: Norton, 1979), pp. 298–299.

p. 73 Light-skinned women around the world, in Russell, Wilson, and Hall, op. cit., p. 56.

p. 73 Pale skin in European women, ibid., p. 58.

p. 73 Sun tan, in Susan Brownmiller, "Skin," *Femininity* (New York: Fawcett Columbine, 1984), p. 136.

p. 74 Mulatto hypothesis and slave jobs, in Russell, Wilson, and Hall, op. cit., p. 18.

p. 74 Quadroon balls, ibid.

p. 74 Advantages of mulatto elite, ibid., pp. 24–32.

p. 74 Colorism worse on women, ibid., p. 42.

p. 75 Attempts to lighten skin color, ibid., p. 50.

p. 75 Successful men preferring lighter skin women, ibid., p. 108.

p. 76 Excerpt about skin color and ashy skin, in Toni Morrison, *The Bluest Eye* (New York: Washington Square Press, 1970), p. 71.

p. 76 Excerpt about ashiness of skin, in Julia Boyd's *In the Company of My Sisters* (New York: Dutton Publishing, 1993) p. 33.

p. 76 Telephone interview with Liza, Sept. 1993.

p. 77 Excerpt, White women and aging, in Connie May Fowler, *Sugar Cage* (New York: Washington Square Press, 1992), pp. 201–202.

p. 77 Melanin reducing aging effects, in Karen Grigsby Bates, "Looks: A Change of Face, Cosmetic Surgery Poses Special Considerations for Black Women," *Los Angeles Times,* magazine sect., May 6, 1990, p. 38.

p. 77 Quote about race and plastic surgeon, in Bates, op. cit., p. 38.

p. 77 Reference to L. Scott Caldwell from personal interview, conducted on April 23, 1993.

p. 77 Race differences in teenage girls agreeing that women get more beautiful with age, in Michele Ingrassia, "The Body of the Beholder," *Newsweek,* April 24, 1995, pp. 66–67; in Sheila Parker, Mimi Nichter, Mark Nichter, Nancy Vuckovic, Colette Sims, and Cheryl Ritenbaugh, "Body Image and Weight Concerns among African American and White Adolescent Females: Differences Which Make a Difference," *Human Organization,* vol. 54 (1995), pp. 103–114.

p. 77 Race and gray hair, in Ellen Blum Barish, "Much Ado About Do's," *Chicago Tribune,* March 14, 1993, Sunday magazine sect., pp. 20–22.

p. 78 Curly versus straight hair growing, in Lonnice Brittenum Bonner, *Good Hair: For Colored Girls Who've Considered Weaves When the Chemicals Became Too Ruff* (New York: Crown Trade Paperbacks, 1991), p. 17.

p. 78 Good and bad hair, in Russell, Wilson, and Hall, op. cit., pp. 81–93.

p. 78 Hair-straightening practices, ibid., pp. 43–47.

p. 79 Personal interview with Dorothy, March 1993.

p. 80 Reference to Caroline, in Russell, Wilson, and Hall, op. cit., p. 84.

p. 80 bell hooks quote regarding not loving hair in natural state, in bell hooks, "Straightening Our Hair" *Z Magazine,* Sept. 1988, pp. 33–37.

p. 80 Phone interview with Hillary, Jan. 1993.

p. 81 Phone interview with Theresa, in Jan. 1993.

p. 82 Phone interview with Janie, Feb. 1993.

p. 82 *School Daze,* in Russell, Wilson, and Hall, op. cit., pp. 90–91.

p. 82 Susan Brownmiller reference, in "Hair," *Femininity* (New York: Fawcett Columbine, 1984), p. 73.

p. 82 Erma Bombeck reference, in Erma Bombeck, "Long Hair Doesn't Always Mean You're Tressed for Success," *Dallas Morning News,* Today sect., Feb. 3, 1993, p. 13C.

p. 83 Gwendolyn Brooks reference, in Brooks, "White Girls Are Peculiar People," *Children Coming Home* (Chicago: David Company, 1991), p. 3.

p. 83 Personal interview with Rhonda Hansome (Passion), Sept. 20, 1993.

p. 84 Reference to Lonnice Brittenum Bonner, in Bonner, op. cit.

p. 84 White feminists and long hair, in Katherine Viner, "What Long Hair Really Says About a Woman," *The Guardian,* Features sect., July 29, 1993, p. 14.

p. 84 Phone interview with Diana, June 1993.

p. 84 Reference to women, in Zhane Deborah Gregory, "Zhane: Here to Stay—Divas-in-Training Who Won't be Dismissed," *Essence,* Jan. 1994, p. 34.

p. 85 Susan Brownmiller quote about cutting her hair, in Arlene Vigoda, "Restyling the Concept of Femininity," *USA Today,* News Sect., Mar. 12, 1990, p. 2.

p. 85 Questions about dreadlocking, in Russell, Wilson, and Hall, op. cit., p. 88.

pp. 85–86 Alice Walker quote about dreadlocking, in Alice Walker, "Oppressed Hair Puts a Ceiling on the Brain," *Living by the Word* (New York: Harcourt Brace Jovanovich, 1988), pp. 69–74.

p. 86 Cornrow braids and Bo Derek, in Russell, Wilson, and Hall, op. cit., p. 89.

p. 86 Personal interview with Siobhan, Feb. 1994.

p. 87 Reference to Cheryl Tatum, in Russell, Wilson, and Hall, op. cit., pp. 132–133; Leah Y. Latimer, "Union Assails Policies on Cornrows: Some Hotel Rules Said to Discriminate Against Blacks" *Washington Post,* Jan. 19, 1988, Metro Sect., p. B3.

p. 87 Reference to Pamela Mitchell, in Latimer, op. cit., p. B3.

p. 88 "Renee Randall and cornrowed ponytail, in Jim Paul, "Cafeteria

Refuses to Rehire Worker With Do, Despite ACLU Complaint," Associated Press, April 19, 1988, twelfth story, level 1.

p. 88 Lawsuits about hair, in Mary Becker, Cynthia Bowman, and Morrison Torrey, *Cases and Materials on Feminist Jurisprudence: Taking Women Seriously* (St. Paul, MN: West Publishing Co., 1994), pp. 784–787.

p. 88 Black women managers with braided hair, in Leon B. Wynter, "Braided Hair Collides with Office Norms," *Wall Street Journal,* May 3, 1993, sect. B., col. 1.

p. 88 Ethnic styles strike fear in managers, in Patricia McLaughlin "Is Corporate America Really Afraid of Braids?" *Star Tribune,* Oct. 27, 1993, Variety sect., p. 2E.

p. 88 bell hooks job interview, in bell hooks, "Straightening Our Hair," *Z Magazine,* Sept. 1988, pp. 33–37.

p. 89 Personal interview with Pamela, in Feb. 1994.

p. 89 Personal interview with Rae, March 1994.

p. 89 Phone interview with Lynette, Nov. 27, 1993.

p. 90 Blond woman changing with burlesque troupe, in Corynne Corbett, "Dark Victory: Brunettes Battle for Their Place in the Sun," *Elle,* March 1992, pp. 272–274.

p. 90 Stereotyping blondes, in Dennis Clayson and Micol Maughan, "Redheads and Blondes: Stereotypic Images," *Psychological Reports, 59,* pp. 811–816.

p. 90 Dumb blond jokes, in Martha Sherrill, "Those Dumb Dumb-Blonde Jokes: They're Insensitive, Baseless, Tasteless. So Who's Laughing?" *Washington Post,* Style sect., Sept. 22, 1991, p. F1.

p. 90 Blond hair softens face, in Mary Ellen Banashek, "Go Blond: Shades of Pale," *Elle,* June 1990, pp. 174, 177.

p. 90 Personal interview with Erica, on Nov. 27, 1993.

p. 91 Streaking hair blond, in Wendy Chapkis, *Beauty Secrets: Women and the Politics of Appearance* (Boston: South End Press, 1986), p. 59.

p. 91 Reference to Cheryl Riley, in Rohan B. Preston, "Black and Blond," *Chicago Tribune,* Style sect., Feb. 24, 1993, pp. 10–13.

p. 92 Long blond associated with prostitution, ibid, pp. 10–13.

p. 92 Singers wearing blond wigs, in hooks, op. cit., pp. 33–37.

p. 93 Color contact lenses and quote by Elsie Washington, in Russell, Wilson, and Hall, op. cit., p. 114.

p. 94 Costs and side effects of collagen, in Arlene Vigoda, "Sex Appeal," *USA Today,* June 15, 1993, Life sect., p. 1D.

p. 94 Phone interview with Tammi, Dec. 1992.

pp. 94–95 Personal interview with Sheila, Jan. 1993.

p. 95 African woman creating ear piercing, in Saundra Sharp, *Black Women for Beginners,* (New York: Writers and Readers Publishing, 1993), p. 45.

pp. 95–96 Personal interview with Natalie, Jan. 1994.

p. 96 Personal interview with Yvette, Feb. 1994.

p. 96 Black woman advising others not to get a tattoo, in "Day One," ABC news magazine show airing Dec. 6, 1993.

p. 97 Black women weighing more but with higher body satisfaction, in Steve B. Chandler, Doris A. Aboood, Dae Taek Lee, Mae Z. Cleveland, and Janice A. Daly, "Pathogenic Eating Attitudes and Behaviors and Body Dissatisfaction Differences Among Black and White College Students, *Eating Disorders,* vol. 2, 1994, pp. 319–328.

p. 97 Race differences in body satisfaction and rates of dieting, in Michele Ingrassia, "The Body of the Beholder," *Newsweek,* April 24, 1995, pp. 66–67.

p. 97 White women initiating more weight control, in Denise Watson, "Go Figure: Black Women More Comfortable with Curves than White Women, Study Shows" *The Virginia Pilot and Ledger Star,* April 11, 1993, p. 11.

p. 97 Race difference in cosmetic surgery, in "Trends in Hospital Procedures Performed on Black Patients and White Patients: 1980–1987," *U.S. Department of Health and Human Services,* Provider Studies Research Note 20, April 1994, p. 39.

p. 97 Black magazines not advertising weight loss products, in Roy Allen Roberts "Ethnicity, Body Image Dissatisfaction, and Eating Disorders: The Differential Impact of Norms of Attractiveness on Black and White Women (Cultural Norms)," from the University of Louisville, 1992, in *Dissertation Abstracts International-B,* vol. 53/09, March 1993, p. 4984.

p. 97 Observations by Carolyn West about body image in paper entitled, "Developing an 'Oppositional Gaze': Black Women and Distorted Beauty Images," at the 18th Annual Women in Psychology Convention, Atlanta, March 11–14, 1993.

p. 98 Saying about a bone, in Rachel Jones, Knight-Ridder *Tribune,* "Black and Beautiful: Women's Group Works at It: Detroit Exercisers Help One Another Find What It Takes," *Arizona Republic,* April 18, 1993, Special sect., p. HW5.

p. 98 Madeleine Nelson, in Watson, op. cit., p. 11.

p. 98 Reference to Yvonne Neil-Powell, ibid.

p. 98 Thirty-four-year-old Black woman at work, in Deborah J. Bowen,

Naomi Tomoyasu, and Ana Mari Cauce, "The Triple Threat: A Discussion of Gender, Class, and Race Differences in Weight," *Women and Health,* vol. 17, 1991, pp. 123–143.

p. 99 Reference to Jessie Putnam, in Watson, op. cit., p. 11.

p. 99 Reference to Jocelyn in Becky Wangsgaard Thompson, in " 'A Way Outa No Way': Eating Problems Among African-American, Latina, and White Women," *Gender and Society,* vol. 6, 1992, pp. 546–561.

p. 99 Kim Chernin and her quote, in Rosemary L. Bray, "Heavy Burden," *Essence,* Jan. 1992, p. 54.

p. 100 Centerfolds and thinner Barbie, in Mary Crawford and Rhoda Unger, *Women and Gender* (New York: McGraw Hill, 1993), p. 332.

p. 100 Suzanne Henrick and girls' preoccupation with Kate Moss, in Louise Lague, Allison Lynn, Lois Armstrong, Vicki Sheff-Cahan, Gabrielle Saveri, and Laura Sanderson Healy, "How Thin Is Thin?" *People,* Sept. 20, 1993, pp. 74–80.

p. 100 Robinne Lee story about her obsession with Kate Moss, in Robinne Lee, "The Model Thing," *Tell,* Feb. 1994, p. 62.

p. 100 *Essence* survey, in Linda Villarosa, "Dangerous Eating: The Results of Our Survey on Eating Disorders Show That Black Women Are at Risk," *Essence,* Jan. 1994, pp. 19–21, 87; Marilyn Elias, "Eating Disorders Do Affect Blacks, *USA Today,* Life sect., Oct. 25, 1993, p. D1.

p. 101 Characteristics of women with eating disorders, in Maya Browne, "Dying to Be Thin," *Essence,* June 1993, pp. 86–87, 124, 126–127, 129.

p. 101 Rates of anorexia and bulimia, in Jane E. Brody, "Healthy," *New York Times,* Sect. B., p. 9; Maya Browne, "Dying to be Thin," *Essence,* June 1993, pp. 86–87, 124, 126–127, 129.

p. 101 Rates of obesity, in Portia Hawkins-Bond, "Information Please," *Essence,* Health Sect., Sept. 1993, p. 34; Rosemary L. Bray, "Heavy Burden," *Essence,* Jan. 1992, pp. 52, 54, 90.

p. 101 Food as drug of choice, in Becky Wangsgaard Thompson, " 'A Way Outa No Way': Eating Problems Among African-American, Latina, and White Women," *Gender and Society,* vol. 6, 1992, pp. 546–561.

p. 101 Black women and rates of hypertension and diabetes, in Leslie Laurence, "Her Health: Four-center Diet Study Offers Long-overdue Weight-loss Insights for African Americans," *Atlanta Constitution,* Dec. 28, 1993, Sect. C, p. 4.

p. 101 Study on economic and social consequences of obesity, in Steven L. Gortmaker, Aviva Must, James M. Perrin, Arthur M. Sobol, and William H. Dietz, "Social and Economic Consequences of Overweight in Adolescence and Young Adulthood," *The New England Journal of Medicine,* vol. 329, Sept. 30, 1993, pp. 1008–1037.

p. 102 Race differences in leg shaving, in Susan A. Basow, "The Hairless Ideal: Women and Their Body Hair," *Psychology of Women Quarterly,* vol. 15, 1991, pp. 83–96.

p. 102 Personal interview with Linda, Feb. 1993.

p. 103 E Style catalogue, in Marisol Bello, "Ethnic Strategy: Clothing Retailers are marketing to Minorities," *St. Louis Post-Dispatch,* Style sect. Nov. 7, 1993, p. 4.

p. 103 Black women's reactions to E Style, ibid.

p. 104 Personal interview with Crystal, Dec. 1992.

p. 105 Personal interview with Sondra, May 1993.

p. 105 Black woman dressing sexy and seen as a whore, in Wendy Chapkis, *Beauty Secrets: Women and the Politics of Appearance* (Boston: South End Press, 1986), p. 59.

p. 105 Phone interview with Alice, Nov. 1993.

p. 106 Personal interview with Ellen, March 1, 1994.

p. 106 Dressing in African-inspired fashions popular, in Nina Darnton, Sonya Vain, Howard Manly, and Shawn Doherty, "An Old Look is New Again," *Newsweek,* Life/Style sect., Oct. 16, 1989, p. 78.

p. 107 Black women feeling pressure not conforming to "radical women of color," in Nancie Caraway, *Segregated Sisterhood: Racism and the Politics of American Feminism* (Knoxville, TN: University of Tennessee Press, 1991), p. 111.

p. 107 Reference to Marcia Gillespie, in Crawford and Unger, op. cit., p. 333.

p. 107 Maya Angelou story, in Les Payne, "Seeing Whoopi for What She Is" *Newsday,* July 11, 1993, Currents sect., p. 3.

pp. 107–108 Poem about accepting one's beauty, in Ekua Omosupe, "In Magazines (I Found Specimens of the Beautiful)," Gloria Anzaldúa (ed.), *Making Face, Making Soul/Haciendo Caras: Creative and Critical Perspectives by Feminists of Color* (San Francisco: Aunt Lute Foundation Books, 1990), p. 169.

p. 109 Poem about never accepting one's beauty, in Marge Piercy, "Barbie Doll," *Circles on the Water: Selected Poems of Marge Piercy* (New York: Alfred A. Knopf, 1982), p. 92.

p. 109 Rejecting masculinist aesthetic, in Patricia Hill Collins, *Black Feminist Thought: Knowledge, Consciousness, and the Politics of Empowerment* Perspective on Gender, vol. 2 (New York: Routledge, 1990), p. 88.

Chapter 4
Sexual Tensions

p. 111 Carolyn M. Rodgers, "I Have Been Hungry," in *How I Got Ovah: New and Selected Poems* (Garden City: NJ: Anchor Books, Doubleday, 1976), p. 49.

p. 111 Gail Mathabane quote, in Maureen Downey, "Interracial Marriages Irk Black Women," *Cleveland Plain Dealer,* Feb. 23, 1993, Everywoman sect., p. C4.

p. 112 Telephone interview with Jackie, Dec. 1993.

p. 112 Interracial sexual jealousy, in Glynis Carr, "The Female World of Love and Racism: Interracial Friendship in U.S. Women's Literature, 1840–1940." A dissertation submitted to Ohio State University, 1989 (Ann Arbor, MI: University Microfilms International, 1994), pp. 204–205.

p. 113 White men sexualizing African women's nudity, in Winthrop D. Jordan, *White Over Black: American Attitudes Toward the Negro, 1550–1812* (New York: W. W. Norton, 1968), p. 39.

p. 113 Black women as animals, in Patricia Hill Collins, "Pornography and Black Women's Bodies," *Making Violence Sexy* (New York: Teachers College Press, 1993), p. 97.

p. 113 Valuing natural rhythms, in Susan Taylor, "The Divine Feminine," *Essence,* July 1993, Spirit sect., p. 49.

p. 113 The Hottentot Venus, in bell hooks, *Black Looks: Race and Representation,* (South End Press: Boston, 1992) p. 62; Saundra Sharp, *Black Women: For Beginners* (New York: Writers and Reader Publishing Company, 1993), p. 75; Collins, op. cit., pp. 98–99.

p. 113 African woman's buttocks, in Elaine Brown, *A Taste of Power: A Black Woman's Story* (New York: Anchor Books, Doubleday, 1992), p. 93.

p. 114 White women not being sexually free, in Carr, op. cit., pp. 204–205.

p. 114 Jessie Daniel Ames comment, in Jacquelyn Dowd Hall, "The Mind That Burns in Each Body: Women, Rape, and Racial Violence," in Margaret L. Andersen and Patricia Collins (eds.), *Race, Class, and Gender: An Anthology* (Belmont, CA: Wadsworth Publishing, 1992), p. 400.

p. 114 Good girl, bad girl, in Kimberle Crenshaw, "Mapping the Margins: Intersectionality, Identity Politics, and Violence Against Women of Color," unpublished paper, cited in Mary Becker, Cynthia Bowman, and Morrison Torrey, *Feminist Jurisprudence: Taking Women Seriously* (St. Paul, MN: West Publishing Co., 1994), p. 194.

p. 116 Racial tensions as sexual insecurities, in John Down, "Black/White Dating," in Doris Wilkinson, *Black Male/White Female Perspectives on Interracial Marriage and Courtship* (Cambridge, MA: Schenkman Publishing, 1975), p. 162.

p. 116 Differing statistics, in P. A. Belcastro, "Sexual Behavior Differences Between Black and White Students," *Journal of Sex Research,* vol. 21, 1985, pp. 56–57, cited in Spencer A. Rathus, Jeffrey S. Nevid, and Lois Fichner-Rathus, *Human Sexuality in a World of Diversity* (Boston: Allyn and Bacon, 1993), pp. 256–257.

p. 116 Gail E. Wyatt's research, in Walter Leavy, "Sex In Black America: Reality and Myth," *Ebony,* Aug. 1993, pp. 126–130; G. E. Wyatt, S. D. Peters, and D. Guthrie, "Kinsey Revisited: Part I: Comparisons of the Sexual Socialization and Sexual Behavior of White Women Over 33 Years," *Archives of Sexual Behavior,* vol. 17 (3), pp. 201–209; G. E. Wyatt, S. D. Peters, and D. Guthrie, "Kinsey Revisited: Part I: Comparisons of the Sexual Socialization and Sexual Behavior of Black Women Over 33 Years," *Archives of Sexual Behavior,* vol. 17 (4), pp. 289–332, cited in Rathus, Nevid, and Fichner-Rathus, *Human Sexuality in a World of Diversity,* pp. 256–257.

p. 117 Robert Staples quote, in Leavy, op. cit., p. 130.

p. 117 Teenage rates of intercourse, in "Trends in Pregnancies and Pregnancy Rates, United States, 1980–1988," Monthly Vital Statistics Report, Centers for Disease Control/National Center for Health Statistics, Nov. 16, 1992; in F. Furstenberg, S. P. Morgan, K. A. Moore, and J. L. Peterson, "Race Differences in the Timing of Sexual Intercourse," *American Sociological Review,* vol. 52 (1987), pp. 511–518.

p. 117 Wyatt's research, in Rathus, Nevid, and Fichner-Rathus, op. cit., p. 256.

p. 117 Sexually active by age nineteen, in Jerry Schwartz, "Teenage Girls Having Sex Earlier, Health Agency Says," Reuters, Feb. 1, 1990, AM Cycle.

p. 117 Obese children, in Marilyn Dunlop, "Girls Entering Puberty Earlier," *Toronto Star Newspaper,* Life sect. (June 5, 1993), p. F2.

p. 117 Early development and freedom, in Jeanne Brooks-Gunn and Frank F. Furstenberg, Jr., "Adolescent Sexual Behavior," *American Psychologist,* vol. 44 (Feb. 1989), pp. 249–257.

p. 118 Early sexual development theory, in William F. Allman, "Sexual Chemistry: Science Takes a New Look at the Ancient Game of Love," *U.S. News & World Report,* July 19, 1993, pp. 557–563.

p. 118 Race differences in making out, in Edward Smith and J. Richard

Udry, "Coital and Non-coital Behaviors of White and Black Adolescents," *American Journal of Public Health*, vol. 75 (1985), pp. 1200–1203.

p. 118 Technical virgin, in J. H. Gagnon and W. Simon, "The sexual scripting of oral genital contacts," *Archives of Sexual Behavior*, vol. 16, pp. 1–25.

p. 118 Zimbabwean brother excerpt, in Tara Roberts, "Am I the Last Virgin?" *Essence*, June 1994, p. 80.

p. 119 Missing discourse of desire, in Michelle Fine, "Sexuality, Schooling, and Adolescent Females: The Missing Discourse of Desire," Lois Weis and Michelle Fine (eds.), *Beyond Silenced Voices: Class, Race, and Gender in United States Schools* (Albany: State University of New York Press, 1993), pp. 75–99.

p. 119 Justice Department figures, in *Time*, vol. 144, July 4, 1994, p. 12.

p. 119 1987 Stanford Studies, in S. M. Dornbusch, R. T. Gross, P. D. Duncan, and P. L. Ritter, "Stanford studies of adolescence using the national health examination survey," cited in R. M. Lerner and T. T. Foch (eds.), *Biological-Psychosocial Interactions in Early Adolescence* (Hillsdale, NJ: Erlbaum, 1987), pp. 189–205, cited in Rhoda Unger and Mary Crawford *Women and Gender: A Feminist Psychology* (New York: McGraw Hill, 1992), p. 295.

p. 119 Telephone interview with Derelle, March 1993.

p. 120 Painful, first intercourse, in Brown, op. cit., p. 42.

p. 120 Personal interview with Nana, Nov. 22, 1993.

p. 120 Personal interview with Penelope, May 1994.

p. 121 Societal reactions to pregnancies, in Rickie Solinger *Wake Up Little Susie: Single Pregnancy and Race Before Roe v. Wade* (New York: Routledge, 1992), pp. 24–25.

p. 121 Black teenage girls and population explosion, ibid., pp. 24–25.

p. 121 Black teenagers costing taxpayers, ibid., p. 35.

p. 121 Guttmacher Institute study, in Sandra Gregg, "Area Teen Abortion Far Above U.S. Norm; Percentages Even Higher in Affluent Predominantly White Suburbs," *Washington Post*, April 21, 1987, First sect., p. A1.

p. 121 Jewell Taylor Gibbs statement, in Joe Frolik, "White or Black, the Poor Suffer," *Cleveland Plain Dealer*, Nov. 28, 1993, National sect., p. 17A.

p. 122 Contraception at first intercourse, in "Trends in Pregnancies and Pregnancy Rates, United States, 1980–1988," Monthly Vital Statistics Report, Centers for Disease Control/National Center for Health Statistics, Nov. 16, 1992.

p. 122 Rochelle comment, in Deborah L. Tolman, "Speaking of Desire:

Adolescent Girls, Sexuality, and A Question of Empowerment," unpublished paper presented at the 101st Annual Convention of the American Psychological Association at Toronto, Canada, Aug. 1993.

p. 122 Tolman quote, ibid.

p. 122 Differing abortion rates, in Table no. 111, "Abortions—Number, Rate, and Ratio, by Race: 1975–1992," *Statistical Abstract of the United States,* 114th ed., (Washington, DC: U.S. Department of Commerce, 1994), p. 85.

p. 122 Blacks having disproportionate adolescent births, in Diane Scott-Jones and Sherry L. Turner, "The Impact of Adolescent Childbearing on Educational Attainment and Income of Black Females," *Youth and Society,* vol. 22, Sept. 1990, pp. 35–53.

p. 122 Census figures of children born to unmarried women, from Table no. 100, "Births to Unmarried Women, by Race of Child and Age of Mother: 1970 to 1991," *Statistical Abstract of the United States,* 114th ed., (Washington, DC: U.S. Department of Commerce, 1994), p. 80; in Marian Wright Edelman, "The Black Family in America," in Evelyn C. White (ed.), *The Black Women's Health Book: Speaking For Ourselves* (Seattle, WA: Seal Press, 1990), p. 133.

p. 122 Edelman point, in Evelyn C. White (ed.), *The Black Women's Health Book* (Seattle, WA: Seal Press, 1990), p. 133.

p. 123 Catherine comment, ibid., p. 83.

p. 123 Effects of teen pregnancy, in Scott-Jones and Turner, op. cit., pp. 35–53.

p. 123 National Longitudinal Survey, ibid., pp. 35–53.

p. 123 Deviance associated with White girls, in Jean Rhodes, Phylis Gingiss, and Peggy Smith, "Risk and Protective Factors for Alcohol Use Among Pregnant African American, Hispanic, and White Adolescents: The Influence of Peers, Sexual Partners, Family Members, and Mentors," *Addictive Behaviors* (in press, 1994).

p. 123 Jean Rhodes quote in telephone interview, June 16, 1994.

p. 123 Having a baby to enhance their self-esteem, in "What We Can Do About Child Pregnancies," *New York Times,* sect. A, March 13, 1991, p. 24.

p. 123 Lack of sex education, in Schwartz, op. cit.

p. 123 Suspicious of birth control, in Dorothy Gilliam, "Black Parents Flustered Talking to Teens about Sex," *Washington Post,* Nov. 26, 1979, Metro sect., p. C1.

p. 123 Having babies young, in Laurie Becklund, "I Wanted Somebody to Love," *Los Angeles Times,* March 14, 1993, View sect., p. 1.

p. 124 *Loving* v. *Virginia,* in Isabel Wilkerson, "Black-White Marriages Rise, but Couples Still Face Scorn," *New York Times,* Dec. 2, 1991, B6.

p. 124 Barriers to integration falling, in Robert Staples, *The World of Black Singles: Changing Patterns of Male-Female Relations* (Westport, CT: Greenwood Press, 1981), pp. 138–139.

p. 124 Black-White marriages from 1970 to 1990, in Jack Kroll, Vern E. Smith, and Andrew Murr, "Spiking a Fever," *Time* magazine, June 10, 1991, pp. 44–47.

p. 125 90 percent of Blacks males, in Staples, op. cit., pp. 138–139.

p. 125 White women and interracial sex, ibid., p. 143.

p. 125 Gender differences in ratio of interracial marriages, in Jack Kroll, Vern E. Smith, and Andrew Murr, "Spiking a Fever," *Time* magazine, June 10, 1991, pp. 44–47; in J. Kroll, V. Smith, and A. Murr, "A black-white affair is the catalyst for Spike Lee's panoramic view of a culture in a color bind." *Newsweek,* June 10, 1991; in Laura Randolph, "Black Women/White Men: What's Goin' On?" *Ebony,* March 1989, p. 156.

p. 125 Interracial marriage angering African American women, in Downey, op. cit., p. C4.

p. 125 Race differences in getting married, in Cynthia Hanson, "Love in the 90s Means Commitment," *Chicago Tribune,* Womanews sect., April 11, 1993, p. 1.

p. 125 Difficulty of African American women finding husband, in Susan Mitchell, "Changing Marriage Patterns Add Up to Changing Lifestyles," *Boomer Report,* March 15, 1993, Lifestyles sect., p. 7.

p. 125 Successful men marrying light-skinned women, in Melville Herskovits, *The American Negro* (Bloomington: Indiana University Press, 1968), p. 64; in Elizabeth Mullins and Paul Sites, "The Origins of Contemporary Eminent Black Americans: A Three-Generation Analysis of Social Origin," *American Sociological Review,* 1984, pp. 672–685.

p. 126 Interracial couples, in Lynn Norment, "Black Men/White Women: What's Behind the New Furor?" *Ebony,* Nov. 1994, pp. 44, 46, 48, 50.

p. 126 Interracial dating during Freedom Summer, in Paula Giddings, *When and Where I Enter* (New York: William Morrow, 1984), p. 301.

p. 126 I Have Been Hungry, in Rodgers, op. cit., p. 128.

p. 126 Gail Mathabane quote, in Downey, op. cit., p. C4.

p. 126 Telephone interview with anonymous White women about Black women dating White men, April 1993.

p. 126 Personal interview with Lynn, May 12, 1994.

p. 127 Personal interview with middle-aged White woman dating Black man named Stanley, Feb. 12, 1994.

p. 127 Personal interview with White woman named Deborah, April 1993.

p. 128 Personal interview with White woman named Deana, April 1994.

p. 128 Comment by Black friend, in Ranjeet Singh, "Interracial Relationships," unpublished paper, March 11, 1994.

pp. 128–129 Excerpt by Bebe Moore Campbell, in "Hers; Brothers and Sisters," *New York Times,* Aug. 23, 1992, sect. 6, p. 18.

p. 129 Race and physical attractiveness, in Bernard Murstein, Joseph Merighi, and Thomas E. Malloy, "Physical Attractiveness and Exchange Theory in Interracial Dating," *The Journal of Social Psychology,* vol. 129 (1989), pp. 325–334.

p. 129 Dating preferences, in Master's thesis, Camille Baughn, Psychology Department, DePaul University, Chicago, IL, 1993; in Midge Wilson, "Race, Skin Color, and Physical Attractiveness: The Politics of Interracial Dating," invited Paper, Midwestern Psychological Association, May 5, 1995.

p. 130 Personal interview with Nancy B., Dec. 15, 1993.

p. 130 Personal interview with Sonya, May 12, 1994.

p. 130 Personal interview with Jamillah, Feb. 1994.

p. 131 Darrell Dawsey quote, in Darrell Dawsey, "I Don't Date White Women, and Here's Why," Gannett News Service, Oct. 28, 1992, 150th story, Level 1.

p. 131 Prom incident, in "Race Remarks Prompt Suspension: Principal Tried to Ban Interracial Dating at Prom," *Chicago Tribune,* March 15, 1994, sect. 1, p. 12.

pp. 131–132 Fury of Black women, in Audre Lorde, *Sister Outsider: Essays and Speeches* (Trumansburg, NY: Crossing Press, 1984), pp. 47–48.

p. 132 Black lesbian pressures, in D. Merilee Clunis and G. Dorsey Green, *Lesbian Couples: Creating Healthy Relationships for the '90s* (Seattle: Seal Press, 1993), p. 138.

p. 132 Poetry excerpt, in Dajenya, "does it matter if she's white?" in Jan Hardy (ed.), *Sister/Stranger: Lesbians Loving Across the Lines* (Pittsburgh: Sidewalk Revolution Press, 1993), pp. 118–121.

p. 133 Personal interview with Rhonda, May 1993.

p. 133 Brenda Verner statement, in Brenda Verner, "African Womanism —Why Feminism Has Failed to Lure Black Women," from a 1993 packet of promotional material.

p. 133 Personal interview with Mary Morten, Nov. 16, 1991.

p. 134 White women wondering why, in Clunis and Green, op. cit., p. 140.

p. 134 Telephone interview with Shawna, Dec. 1993.

p. 134 Cheryl Clarke quote, in Cheryl Clarke, "Lesbianism, An Act of Resistance," Cherríe Moraga and Gloria Anzaldúa (eds.), *The Bridge Called My Back: Writings by Radical Women of Color* (New York: Kitchen Table: Women of Color Press, 1983), p. 135.

p. 135 "Ethnic chasers," in Clunis and Green, op. cit., p. 140.

p. 135 Telephone interview with Marilyn in June 1992.

p. 135 Kim Hall excerpt, in "Learning to Touch Honestly: A White Lesbian's Struggle With Racism," in Jeffner Allen (ed.), *Lesbian Philosophies and Cultures* (New York: SUNY Press, 1990), pp. 317–326.

p. 135 Telephone interview with Patty K., Feb. 1993.

p. 135 Quote by bell hooks in *Talk Back: Thinking Feminist, Thinking Black* (Boston: South End Press, 1989), p. 125.

p. 135 Personal interview with Cynthia W., Jan. 13, 1994.

p. 136 Black Lesbian Support Group, in "The Black Lesbian Support," *Essence,* April 1992.

p. 136 Cleveland's Sistahparty, in Nick Charles, "A Struggle for Dignity: Cleveland's Gay Community Joins an Emerging Fight for Rights," *Cleveland Plain Dealer,* Living sect., Nov. 29, 1992, p. 1G.

p. 136 Lesbians of color, in Gloria I. Joseph and Jill Lewis, *Common Differences: Conflicts in Black and White Feminist Perspectives* (Boston: South End Press, 1981), p. 36.

p. 136 Personal interview with Jennifer, June 1992.

p. 136 Telephone interview with Lisa P., May 16, 1992.

p. 137 Venus Medina statement, in Alvin Poussaint, "An Honest Look at Black Gays and Lesbians," *Ebony,* Sept. 1990, p. 131.

p. 137 Excerpt by Ann Allen Shockley from *Loving Her: A Novel* (Indianapolis: Bobbs-Merrill Co., 1974), p. 31.

p. 137 Barbara Smith regarding heterosexual privilege, in Smith and Smith, op. cit., p. 193.

p. 138 Personal interview with Bernita, in June 1993.

p. 138 Frances Cress Welsing, in Gloria I. Joseph and Jill Lewis, *Common Differences: Conflicts in Black and White Feminist Perspectives* (Boston: South End Press, 1981), p. 37.

p. 138 Homosexuality as genocide, ibid., p. 37.

p. 138 Barbara Smith on lesbianism and feminism, in Barbara Smith and Beverly Smith, "Across The Kitchen Table: A Sister-to-Sister Dialogue," in

Cherrie Moraga and Gloria Anzaldúa (eds.), *The Bridge Called My Back: Writings by Radical Women of Color* (New York: Kitchen Table: Women of Color Press, 1983), p. 125.

p. 138 Homophobia among Blacks, in Cheryl Clarke, "The Failure to Transform: Homophobia in the Black Community," in Barbara Smith (ed.), *Home Girls: A Black Feminist Anthology* (New York: Kitchen Table: Women of Color Press, 1983), p. 205.

p. 138 Comment by Barbara Smith, in Jewelle L. Gomez and Barbara Smith, "Taking the Home Out of Homophobia: Black Lesbian Health," in Evelyn C. White (ed.), *The Black Women's Health Book: Speaking for Ourselves* (Seattle: Seal Press, 1990), p. 207.

p. 138 Comment by Sarah, in Norma Garcia, Cheryl Kennedy, Sarah F. Pearlman, and Julia Perez, "The Impact of Race and Culture Differences: Challenges to Intimacy in Lesbian Relationships," in Boston Lesbian Psychologies Collective, *Lesbian Psychologies: Explorations and Challenges* (Urbana: University of Illinois Press, 1987), p. 153.

p. 139 Personal interview with Amy, Dec. 1993.

p. 139 Personal interview with JoAnn, Jan. 13, 1994.

p. 139 Excerpt from Shockley, op. cit., p. 100.

p. 140 Group versus individual identities, in Clunis and Green, op. cit., pp. 138–139.

p. 140 Black women's views on sexual assault, in Mary Becker, Cynthia Bowman, and Morrison Torrey, *Cases and Materials on Feminist Jurisprudence: Taking Women Seriously* (St. Paul, MN: West Publishing Co., 1994), p. 229.

p. 140 Rape and legal recourse, ibid., p. 121.

p. 140 Rape and lynching, in Michele Wallace, *Black Macho and the Myth of the Superwoman* (New York: Verso, 1991), pp. 119–120.

p. 141 White women and lynching, ibid., p. 230.

p. 141 Black women and criminal justice system, in Patricia Hill Collins, *Black Feminist Thought: Knowledge, Consciousness, and the Politics of Empowerment* (New York: Routledge, 1990), p. 178.

p. 141 Telephone interview with Mary Kay, May 1993.

p. 141 Telephone interview with K.K., Jan. 1994.

p. 141 Court case and Black teenage girl, in Kimberle Crenshaw, "Mapping the Margins: Intersectionality, Identity Politics, and Violence Against Women of Color," unpublished paper, p. 27, cited in Mary Becker, Cynthia Bowman, and Morrison Torrey, *Feminist Jurisprudence: Taking Women Seriously* (St. Paul, MN: West Publishing Co., 1994), p. 194.

p. 141 Race differences in prison terms, ibid., p. 194.

p. 141 White man and death penalty, in Joseph and Lewis, op. cit., p. 278.

p. 141 Rapes being interracial, in Caroline Wolf Harlow, *Female Victims of Violent Crimes,* U.S. Department of Justice, NCJ–126826, Jan. 1991.

p. 142 Media headlines, in Marcia Ann Gillespie, "In the Matter of Rape," *Ms.,* Jan. 1993, p. 60.

p. 142 Central Park "wilding" incident, in Crenshaw, op. cit., p. 194.

p. 142 Dilemma of Black women, ibid., p. 194.

p. 142 Conflict in women's studies meeting, from anonymous interview, April 1993 and Nov. 1993.

p. 143 Race differences in rape, in Joseph and Lewis, op. cit., p. 278; in Caroline Wolf Harlow, *Female Victims of Violent Crimes,* U.S. Department of Justice, NCJ–126826, Jan. 1991.

p. 143 Audre Lorde quote, in Becker, Bowman, and Torrey, op. cit., p. 535.

p. 143 Quote by Gillespie, in Marcia Gillespie, "What's Good for the Race?" *Ms.* (Jan.-Feb. 1993), p. 81, cited in Mariah Burton Nelson, *The Stronger Women Get, the More Men Love Football: Sexism and the American Culture of Sports* (New York: Harcourt Brace, 1994), p. 143.

p. 144 Black domestic workers being sexually harassed, in Collins, op. cit., p. 176.

p. 144 O. J. Simpson case, in Jill Smolowe, "Race and the O. J. Case," *Time,* vol. 144, Aug. 1, 1994, pp. 24–26.

p. 145 Percent of prostitutes, (115 Spring St, NY 10012: The Women's Action Coalition, 1993), p. 42, and in "Prostitutes Say They are AIDS Scapegoats," UPI, San Francisco, June 30, 1988.

p. 145 Quote by Blanca in Lynn Rousseau, "An Interview With A Friend," unpublished paper, March 11, 1994.

p. 145 Race differences in acts women perform in pornographic videos, in Gloria Cowan and Robin R. Campbell, "Racism and Sexism in Interracial Pornography: A Content Analysis," *Psychology of Women Quarterly,* vol. 18 (1994), pp. 323–338; in Gloria Cowan, "New Feminist Research on the Harm of Pornography," panel presentation at the Speech, Equality, and Harm: Feminist Legal Perspectives on Pornography and Hate Propaganda Conference, Chicago, March 5–7, 1993.

p. 145 *Let Me Tell 'Ya 'Bout Black Chicks,* in Cowan and Campbell, op. cit., pp. 323–338.

p. 146 Alice Walker quote, in Alice Walker, "Coming Apart," *You Can't*

Keep a Good Woman Down (New York: Harcourt Brace Jovanovich, 1981), p. 52.

Chapter 5
Making Friends
Relationships on the Campus, in the Workplace, and Beyond

p. 147 Adrienne Rich quote, in "Disloyal to Civilization: Feminism, Racism, Gynephobia," *Lies, Secrets, and Silences* (New York: W. W. Norton, 1986), p. 300.

p. 147 Audre Lorde quote, in "The Uses of Anger: Women Responding to Racism," *Sister Outsider: Essays and Speeches* (Trumansburg, NY: Crossing Press, 1984), pp. 125–126.

p. 148 Women and Blacks going to college, in Mary Frank Fox, "Women and Higher Education: Gender Differences in the Status of Students and Scholars," in Jo Freeman (ed.), *Women: A Feminist Perspective,* 4th ed. (Mountain View, CA: Mayfield Publishing Co., 1989), pp. 217–235.

p. 149 *Brown* v. *Board of Education* and Court ruling, in Norman Dorsen, "Civil Rights and Civil Liberties," *Encarda* (Microsoft Corporation, 1993).

p. 149 College housing placement policies at most colleges today, from telephone interview conducted with Ladonna Sanders, former residence hall director at DePaul University, Chicago, on July 26, 1994.

p. 150 Multiculturalism lectures during orientation week, ibid.

p. 150 Gender differences in avoiding conflict, in Deborah Tannen, *You Just Don't Understand: Women and Men in Conversation* (New York: Ballantine Books, 1990), pp. 163, 183.

p. 151 Sports central to improved race relations for boys not girls, in Richard L. Zweigenhaft and G. William Domhoff, *Blacks in the White Establishment?: A Study of Race and Class in America* (New Haven: Yale University Press, 1991), p. 50; in E. Mavis Hetherington and Ross D. Parke, *Child Psychology: A Contemporary Viewpoint,* 4th ed. (New York: McGraw-Hill, Inc., 1993), p. 518.

p. 151 Quote by Ladonna Sanders from telephone interview, July 26, 1994.

p. 152 Quote by Tara from telephone interview, Jan. 1994.

p. 152 Reference to LaRay from telephone interview, Nov. 1993.

p. 152 Quote by Brigette from telephone interview, July 1993.

p. 153 Reference to Ladonna Sanders from telephone interview, July 26, 1994.

p. 153 Black female student's brother with a beeper, ibid.

p. 153 Reference to Mokita from telephone interview, Aug. 3, 1994.

p. 154 Barbara Smith quote about "downward mobility," in Barbara Smith and Beverly Smith, "Across the Kitchen Table: A Sister-to-Sister Dialogue," in Cherrie Moraga and Gloria Anzaldúa (eds.), *This Bridge Called My Back: Writings by Radical Women of Color* (New York: Kitchen Table: Women of Color Press, 1983), p. 113.

p. 154 White women more accepting of academic humiliation, and quote about Blacks having to defy them, in bell hooks, *Talking Back: Thinking Feminist, Thinking Black* (Boston: South End Press, 1989), pp. 58–59.

p. 155 Race differences in admission standards and SAT scores, in Walter E. Williams, "Campus Racism," in Susan F. Feiner (ed.), *Race and Gender in the American Economy: Views From Across the Spectrum* (Englewood Cliffs, NJ: Prentice Hall, 1994), pp. 158–161.

p. 155 Race differences in dropout rates, in Claude M. Steele, "Race and the Schooling of Black Americans," in Feiner, op. cit., pp. 172–182.

p. 155 Story of Elaine and Wendy from telephone interview with Elaine, Dec. 1993.

p. 156 Race differences in women's drinking and drug taking, in Harry Avis, *Drugs and Life* (Madison, WI: WCB Brown and Benchmark, 1993), p. 143.

p. 156 Telephone interview with Lynda, Feb. 13, 1994.

p. 156 Personal interview with Lyn, May 12, 1994.

p. 157 Personal interview with Tina S., Dec. 7, 1993.

p. 157 Quote by Mokita from telephone interview, Aug. 3, 1994.

p. 158 Quote by African American woman advocating cross-race friendships by Raquel W., from telephone interview, June 11, 1994.

p. 158 Quote by Page A. from personal interview, July 27, 1994.

p. 158 Comment by Audrey about her White friend Jo, in Audrey Edwards, "Sisters Under the Skin," *New York Times Magazine,* Sept. 19, 1993, p. 35.

p. 159 Quote by Lynn R. from personal interview, Sept. 20, 1994.

p. 160 Quote by Sandi from telephone interview, Aug. 15, 1994.

p. 160 Additional quote by White female student from interview, July 1994.

p. 160 Anonymous quote by White female former dean, telephone interview, June 1994.

p. 161 Cultural private property and Caraway quote, in Nancie Caraway, *Segregated Sisterhood: Racism and the Politics of American Feminism* (Knoxville: University of Tennessee Press, 1991), p. 114.

p. 162 Reference to African American female director of Northwestern University, telephone interview with Carla Sperlock-Evens, Oct. 1993.

p. 162 Double standard in women's studies, in Lorde, op. cit., pp. 117–118.

p. 162 Quote, in bell hooks, *Talking Back: Thinking Feminist, Thinking Black* (Boston: South End Press, 1989), p. 61.

p. 163 Rates of women working based on race and marital status, in Julianne Malveaux and Phyllis Wallace, "Minority Women in the Workplace," in Karen S. Koziara, Michael H. Moskow, and Lucretia D. Tanner (eds.), *Working Women: Past, Present, Future* (Washington, DC: Bureau of National Affairs, Inc., 1987), pp. 265–298, and from *U.S. Bureau of Labor Statistics,* Apr. 1986, Table 1, cited in Sara E. Rix (ed.), *The American Woman 1990–91: A Status Report* (New York: Norton, 1990), Table 11, p. 373.

p. 163 White women refusing to work beside Black women, in Gloria I. Joseph and Jill Lewis, *Common Differences: Conflicts in Black and White Feminist Perspectives* (Boston: South End Press, 1981), pp. 27–28.

p. 163 Black and White women in tobacco plants, in Beverly W. Jones, "Race, Sex, and Class: Black Female Tobacco Workers in Durham, North Carolina, 1920–1940, and the Development of Female Consciousness," *Feminist Studies,* vol. 10 (Fall 1984), pp. 441–451.

p. 163 Race segregation of jobs done by women, in Paula Giddings, *When and Where I Enter: The Impact of Black Women on Race and Sex in America* (New York: William Morrow & Co., 1984), pp. 143–144.

p. 164 Quote in Zora Neale Hurston, *Their Eyes Were Watching God* (Boston: Lippincott, 1937; reprint, Greenwich, Conn.: Fawcett, 1965), p. 16.

p. 164 Salaries for White and Black nurses, in Darlene Clark Hine, *Black Women in White: Racial Conflict and Cooperation in the Nursing Profession 1890–1950* (Bloomington: Indiana University Press, 1989), p. 93.

p. 164 Title VII of the 1964 Civil Rights Acts, in Alice Abel Kemp, *Women's Work: Degraded and Devalued* (Englewood Cliffs: Prentice Hall, 1994), pp. 308–310.

p. 164 Statistics on women in pink-collar jobs, in V. G. Nieva and B. A. Gutek, *Women and Work: A Psychological Perspective* (New York: Academic Press, 1981).

p. 164 Statistics on weekly earnings, U.S. Bureau of the Census from *U.S. Bureau of Labor Statistics,* Jan. 1989, Table 61, cited in Sara E. Rix (ed.), *The*

Notes

American Woman 1990–91: A Status Report (New York: Norton, 1990), Figure 11, p. 391.

p. 164 Shifts in White versus Black women's employment, in Vivian V. Gordon, *Black Women, Feminism, and Black Liberation: Which Way?* (Chicago: Third World Press, 1985), p. 39.

p. 164 Saying about careers versus jobs, in Julia Boyd *In the Company of My Sisters* (New York: Dutton, 1993), p. 115.

p. 165 Real liberation for Black women, in Benjamin Barber, *Liberating Feminism* (New York: Dell Publishing, 1975), p. 51.

p. 165 White women advancing at expense of Blacks, in Jacqueline Grant, *Black Women's Christ and Black Women's Jesus: Feminist Christology and Womanist Response* (Atlanta: Scholars Press, 1989), p. 98.

p. 165 Korn/Ferry International survey, in Ann M. Morrison and Mary Ann Von Glinow, "Women and Minorities in Management," *American Psychologist,* vol. 45 (Feb. 1990), pp. 200–209.

p. 165 "Glass ceiling," in Alice Abel Kemp, op. cit., pp. 220–221.

p. 165 Stories of Sandrya and Rebecca from telephone interviews, March 1993.

p. 166 Reference to Mallory and Esther in Bebe Moore Campbell, *Brothers and Sisters* (New York: G. P. Putnam's Sons, 1994).

p. 166 Quote by Esther, ibid., p. 306.

p. 166 Statistics on earning potential of Black female college graduates, *WAC Stats* (New York: Women's Action Coalition, 1993), p. 50.

p. 166 Interview research with Black women about White women and quote by one, in Letha A. Lee, "Tensions Between Black Women and White Women: A Study," *Affilia,* vol. 4 (1989), pp. 31–45.

p. 167 White female managers need to offset passive image, Althea Smith and Abigail J. Stewart, "Approaches to Studying Racism and Sexism in Black Women's Lives," *Journal of Social Issues*, vol. 39 (1983), pp. 1–15.

p. 167 Black female managers penalized for being aggressive, in Lee, op. cit., pp. 31–45.

p. 167 Stereotypes of Black women in workplace, in Janet R. Brice-Baker and Beverly Greene, "Quadruple Jeopardy: Black, Female, Professional, and in Charge," paper presented at the 18th annual Women in Psychology convention, Atlanta, March 11–14, 1993.

p. 167 Black women executives penalized if not nurturing, in Rhetaugh Dumas, "Dilemmas of Black Females in Leadership," in La Frances Rodgers-Rose (ed.), *The Black Woman* (Beverly Hills: Sage, 1980), pp. 203–215.

p. 168 Audrey Murrell's research refuting notion that Black women have advantage in their "double minority" status, in Steve Creedy, " 'Double Minority' No Help for Black Women," *Pittsburgh Post-Gazette,* sect. D., Aug. 8, 1993, p. 15.

p. 168 Statistics of managerial/executive positions, in Kemp, op. cit., p. 212.

p. 168 Race differences in group versus individual identities, in D. Merilee Clunis and G. Dorsey Green, *Lesbian Couples: Creating Healthy Relationships for the '90s* (Seattle: Seal Press, 1993), pp. 138–139.

p. 168 Story and quote by Black lawyer, in Ellis Cose, *The Rage of a Privileged Class* (New York: HarperCollins, 1993), p. 61.

p. 169 Quote by Esther about why affirmative action is necessary, in Campbell, op. cit., p. 307.

p. 169 Reference to Raquel, telephone interview, on June 11, 1994.

p. 169 Personal interview with Karen, March 16, 1994.

p. 170 Personal interview with Maureen, Nov. 22, 1993.

p. 170 Reference to research on self-protective strategies in Jennifer Crocker and Brenda Major, "Social Stigma and Self-Esteem: The Self-Protective Properties of Stigma," *Psychological Review,* vol. 96 (1989), pp. 608–630.

p. 171 Reference to White women receiving more affirmative action contracts, in Francine Knowles, "White Women Tally Biggest Gains in Contracts," *Chicago Sun Times,* March 26, 1995, Sunday news sect. p. 10.

p. 171 Reference to educational difference between White and Black women in workplace, in Aida Hurtado, "Relating to Privilege: Seduction and Rejection in the Subordination of White Women and Women of Color," *Journal of Women in Culture and Society,* vol. 14 (1989), pp. 833–855.

p. 171 Statistic of Black clerical workers, in Julianne Malveaux, "Current Economic Trends and Black Feminist Consciousness," *The Black Scholar,* vol. 16, March-April 1985, pp. 26–31.

p. 171 Percent of Black women who are registered nurses vs. nurses aides, in Kemp, op. cit., Table 7.4 on p. 219, and Table 7.7 on p. 245.

p. 171 Telephone interview with Ann L., May 1994.

p. 172 Personal interview with Anne Z., Aug. 20, 1994.

p. 172 Language skills necessary for pink-collar employment, in Virginia Shapiro, *Women in American Society,* 3rd ed. (Mountain View, CA: Mayfield Publishing, 1994), pp. 296–297.

p. 173 Personal interview with Darlene, May 1993.

p. 173 Black versus White modes of negotiating conflict, in Thomas

Kochman, *Black and White Styles in Conflict* (Chicago: University of Chicago Press, 1981), p. 18.

p. 173 Race differences among middle-class women in dispelling disagreements, in Stella Ting-Toomey, "Conflict Communication Styles in Black and White Subjective Cultures," in Young Yun Kim (ed.), *Interethnic Communication: Current Research* (Newbury Park: Sage Publications, 1986), *International and Intercultural Communication Annual,* vol. 10, pp. 75–88.

p. 174 Quote by Sharon A. from telephone interview, Aug. 26, 1994.

pp. 174–175 Quote by Nancy B. from personal interview, Dec. 15, 1993.

p. 175 Personal interview with Trish, Feb. 1992.

p. 175 Quote by Karen P. from personal interview, April 1994.

p. 176 White women acting like they deserve a medal for teaching at predominantly Black school, in April Sinclair, *Coffee Will Make You Black* (New York: Hyperion, 1994), p. 175.

p. 176 Quote by Jackie R. from personal interview, July 31, 1994.

p. 176 Reference to Frieda G. from telephone interview, Sept. 5, 1994.

p. 176 Two sayings about marshmallows and chocolate chips, in Laura B. Randolph, "Reverse Integration," *Ebony,* Jan. 1994, pp. 68–70, 72.

p. 177 Quotes by Louise Lindbolm and Carole Borgreen, ibid.

p. 177 Quote by Robin P. from personal interview, Jan. 1994.

p. 177 Quote by Shirley from telephone interview, conducted with her daughter Lavinia, in Nov. 1994.

p. 178 Workplace as where adults make new friends, in *Rocky Mountain News,* Spotlight sect., July 1, 1993, p. 7C.

p. 178 Quote by White secretary named Lucy from personal interview, Sept. 1994.

p. 178 Quote by Black woman named Keisha from personal interview, March 1994.

p. 178 Quote by anonymous Black accountant from personal interview, Aug. 1994.

p. 179 Quote by Raquel from telephone interview, June 11, 1994.

p. 179 Quote in Julia Boyd, "Ethnic and Cultural Diversity in Feminist Therapy: Keys to Power," in Evelyn C. White (ed.), *The Black Women's Health Book: Speaking to Ourselves* (Seattle, WA: Seal Press, 1990), pp. 226–234.

p. 180 Quote by anonymous Black woman complaining about having to escort White girlfriend, from personal interview, March 1994.

p. 180 Story and quote by Jill from telephone interview, March 1994.

p. 181 Story and quote by Cheryl from personal interview, June 17, 1994.

p. 181 Telephone interview with Crystal, June 1993.

p. 181 Telephone interview conducted with LaTisha, April 1994.

pp. 181–182 Quote by Lois from personal interview, Dec. 2, 1993.

p. 182 Friendship between Peggy and Betty Ann, in Bebe Moore Campbell, "Friendship in Black and White: Beyond the 'Some of My Best Friends Are . . .' Syndrome," *Ms.*, Aug. 1983, pp. 44–46, 95.

p. 182 Reference to Deana from personal interview, April 1994.

p. 183 Telephone interview with Carla, May 1993.

p. 183 TRIOS model, in James M. Jones, "Racism: A Cultural Analysis of the Problem," in J. F. Dovidio and S. L. Gaertner (eds.), *Prejudice, Discrimination, and Racism* (New York: Academic Press, 1986), pp. 279–311.

p. 183 Quote by Heather from personal interview, Sept. 15, 1994.

p. 184 Telephone interview with Karla, May 1993.

p. 184 Statistics about cross-race friendships and effect on attitudes, in Mary R. Jackman and Marie Crane, " 'Some of My Best Friends Are Black . . .' ": Interracial Friendship and Whites' Racial Attitudes," *Public Opinion Quarterly,* vol. 50 (1986), pp. 459–486.

p. 185 Interracial friendship and quote, in Althea Smith and Stephanie Nickerson, "Women's Interracial Friendships," *Women's Studies Quarterly,* vol. XIV (Spring–Summer 1986), pp. 15–16.

Chapter 6
Social Activism
Shared Agendas and Uneasy Alliances

p. 187 Audre Lorde quote, in *Sister Outsider* (Trumansburg, NY: Crossing Press, 1984), p. 60

p. 187 Robin Morgan quote from keynote address at the 18th Annual Women in Psychology Convention, Atlanta, March 11–14, 1993.

p. 188 Sue Purrington of Chicago NOW, in Kevin Johnson, "Illinois Democrat Is Overnight Sensation," *USA Today,* News section, March 19, 1992, p. 5A.

p. 188 Republican women voting for Braun, in Jon Margolis, "Upsets in Illinois Give Nation Food for Thought," *Chicago Tribune,* News sect., March 18, 1992, p. 1.

p. 188 Personal interview with Molly, March 17, 1993.

p. 189 Rosa Parks discussion, in Paula Giddings, *When and Where I Enter: The Impact of Black Women on Race and Sex in America* (New York: William Morrow & Co., 1984), pp. 261–265.

p. 189 Ella Baker and the SCLC discussion, in Paula Giddings, op. cit., pp. 268–269.

p. 189 Four students from North Carolina A & T, in Mary King, *Freedom Song: A Personal Story of the 1960s Civil Rights Movement* (New York: William Morrow & Co., Inc., 1987), p. 33.

p. 189 Sit-in movement, in Giddings, op. cit., pp. 273–274.

p. 190 Birth of SNCC, ibid., pp. 274–275.

p. 190 Diane Nash and Ruby Smith in SNCC, ibid., p. 278–279.

p. 190 The "mama," in Sara Evans, *Personal Politics: The Roots of Women's Liberation in the Civil Rights Movement and the New Left* (New York: Alfred A. Knopf, 1979) p. 51.

p. 190 Quote by Dorothy Burlage, ibid., p. 51.

p. 191 White women in field, ibid., p. 69.

p. 191 White women being good press, ibid., p. 44.

p. 191 White women sleeping with Black men, ibid., pp. 78–79.

p. 191 Black men's reactions to White women, in Giddings, op. cit., p. 301; in Evans, op. cit., p. 79.

p. 191 Reaction of White and Black female staff members to White female volunteers, in Mary King, op. cit., p. 464.

p. 191 Quote, in Evans, op. cit., p. 81.

p. 191 SNCC in state of disarray, in King, op. cit., pp. 437–438.

p. 192 Casey Hayden and Mary King, ibid., pp. 36, 42.

p. 192 Excerpt from King and Hayden's position paper, ibid., p. 445.

p. 192 Rosa Park's denial of rights due to Blackness not sex, in Gloria I. Joseph and Jill Lewis, *Common Differences: Conflicts in Black and White Feminist Perspectives* (Boston: South End Press, 1981), pp. 32–33.

p. 192 Black women believing only White women relegated to minor responsibilities in SNCC, in Giddings, op. cit., p. 302.

p. 192 Stokely Carmichael, King, op. cit., p. 452.

pp. 192–193 Manifesto paper, ibid., pp. 456–457.

p. 193 Lack of response from Black women to manifesto, ibid., p. 467.

p. 193 Values changing from feminine to masculine in Civil Rights Movement, in Evans, op. cit., p. 200.

p. 193 Black power and rising macho attitudes in SNCC, in Giddings, op. cit., pp. 315–316.

p. 193 Angela Davis quote, ibid., p. 316.

p. 193 Complaints of Kathleen Cleaver, ibid., pp. 316–317.

p. 194 Black nationalist pamphlet in Combahee River Collective, "A Black Feminist Statement" in Barbara Smith (ed.), *Home Girls: A Black Feminist Anthology* (New York: Kitchen Table, Women of Color Press, 1983), p. 278.

p. 194 Biological determinism applied to women, in Barbara Smith, "Some Home Truths on the Contemporary Black Feminist Movement," *The Black Scholar,* vol. 16, (March–April 1985), p. 5.

p. 194 Women giving up reproductive rights at 1976 Black Power Conference, in Giddings, op. cit., pp. 318–319.

p. 194 Regina Jennings, in Regina Jennings, "A Panther Remembers" *Essence,* Feb. 1991, p. 122.

p. 194 Barbara Sizemore, in Giddings, op. cit., p. 318.

p. 194 Mark Rudd and chicklib classes, in Evans, op. cit., p. 201.

p. 194 Sexist treatment of SDS White woman, in Giddings, op. cit., p. 303; in Joseph and Lewis, p. 53.

p. 195 Sex as protected category in Civil Rights Act and establishment of NOW, in Giddings, op. cit., p. 300.

p. 195 Founding of NOW, ibid.

p. 195 Sickness without a name, in Betty Friedan, *The Feminine Mystique* (New York: Norton, 1963), cited in Bernice Lott, *Women's Lives: Themes and Variations in Gender Learning,* 2nd ed. (Pacific Grove, CA: Brooks/Cole, 1994), p. 11.

p. 195 Working mothers, Betty Friedan, *The Feminine Mystique,* cited in Giddings, op. cit., p. 299.

p. 196 Black women having little sense of contradiction in their desire to model Victorian womanhood, in Michele Wallace, *Black Macho and the Myth of the Superwoman* (New York: Verso Press, 1991), p. 162.

p. 196 CR groups and White women discovering sisterhood and emerging from silence, in Joseph and Lewis, op. cit., p. 62–66.

p. 196 Black women objecting to "woman as slave" analogy, in bell hooks, *Ain't I a Woman* (Boston: South End Press, 1981), pp. 141–142.

p. 196 White women not realizing they are oppressed until later in life, Barbara Smith "Some Home Truths on the Contemporary Black Feminist Movement," pp. 4–13.

p. 196 Survival versus fulfillment, Brenda Eichelberger, "Voices of Black Feminism," *Quest: A Feminist Quarterly,* vol. III (Spring), pp. 16–28.

p. 197 White culture not encouraging sisterhood, in Joseph and Lewis, p. 66.

p. 197 Beauty parlor as space for consciousness raising for Black women, in bell hooks, "Straightening Our Hair," *Z Magazine,* Sept. 1988, pp. 33–37.

pp. 197–198 Poem, Willie M. Coleman, "Among Things That Used to Be," in Barbara Smith (ed.), *Home Girls: A Black Feminist Anthology,* pp. 221–222.

p. 199 Failure of Black CR groups, in Michele Wallace, *Invisibility Blues: From Pop to Theory* (London: Verso Press, 1990), p. 24.

p. 199 White women feeling and Black women doing, Audre Lorde, *Sister Outsider: Essays and Speeches,* p. 171.

p. 199 Protest at 1968 all-White Miss America pageant and Flo Kennedy, in Marcia Cohen, *The Sisterhood: The True Story of the Women Who Changed the World* (New York: Simon & Schuster, 1988), pp. 150–152.

p. 199 Handful of Black women in NOW, in Giddings, op. cit., p. 346.

p. 199 Black maid at Betty Friedan's apartment, in Marcia Cohen, op. cit., p. 188.

p. 199 Black women receiving approval from Black men for saying that they hated White women, in Wallace, op. cit., p. 23.

p. 200 Brownmiller quote, in Cohen, op. cit., p. 216.

p. 200 Friedan and women's strike for equality march, ibid., p. 273.

p. 200 Third World Women's Alliance and Frances Beal, in Giddings, op. cit., p. 305.

p. 201 Toni Morrison, *New York Times Magazine,* and her quote in Marcia Cohen, *The Sisterhood,* pp. 315–316.

p. 201 National Women's Political Caucus, in Cohen, op. cit., p. 315.

p. 201 National Black Feminist Organization, in Joseph and Lewis, op. cit., pp. 33–34.

p. 201 Norton quote, in Giddings, op. cit., p. 344.

pp. 201–202 Poem, Audre Lorde, "Who Said It Was Simple," *From a Land Where Other People Live* (Detroit: Broadside Press, 1973), cited in Joseph and Lewis, op. cit., p. 39.

p. 202 Louis Harris poll, in bell hooks, *Ain't I A Woman: Black Women and Feminism,* p. 148.

p. 202 1980 study, in Willa Mae Hemmons, "The Women's Liberation Movement: Understanding Black Women's Attitudes," in LaFrances Rodgers-Rose, *The Black Woman* (Beverly Hills: Sage Publications, 1980), pp. 285–299.

p. 202 Hernandez's growing discontent with NOW, in Giddings, op. cit., pp. 346–347.

p. 202 Sharon Parker, ibid., p. 346.

p. 203 "Failure of ERA due to racism in NOW," ibid., p. 347.

p. 203 Emergence of women's studies, in Sally Miller Gearhart, "If the Mortarboard Fits . . . Radical Feminism in Academia," in Charlotte Bunch and Sandra Pollack (eds.), *Learning Our Way: Essays in Feminist Education* (Trumansburg, NY: Cross Press, 1983), pp. 2–3.

p. 203 Black women annoyed at White women claiming male supremacy was root of oppression, Giddings, op. cit., p. 304; in bell hooks, *Talking Back: Thinking Feminist, Thinking Black* (Boston, MA: South End Press, 1989), p. 19.

p. 203 Absence of women in Black studies classes and Blacks in women's studies classes, Johnnetta B. Cole, *Conversations: Straight Talk With America's Sister President* (New York: Doubleday, 1993), p. 29.

p. 203 Black women's studies book, Gloria T. Hull, Patricia Bell Scott, and Barbara Smith, *All the Women Are White, All the Blacks Are Men, but Some of Us Are Brave: Black Women's Studies* (New York: Feminist Press, 1982).

p. 204 Analysis of class privilege, in bell hooks, *Ain't I A Woman: Black Women and Feminism,* pp. 145–146.

p. 204 Criticism of Black women forming feminist groups, ibid., pp. 150–151.

p. 204 Issue of being equal with which men, in bell hooks, *Feminist Theory: From Margin to Center,* p. 18.

p. 204 White women acting like they own women's movement, ibid., p. 53.

p. 204 Audre Lorde quote, Lorde, op. cit., p. 116.

pp. 204–205 White privilege, in Peggy McIntosh, "White Privilege and Male Privilege: A Personal Account of Coming to See Correspondences Through Work in Women's Studies," Margaret L. Andersen and Patricia Hill Collins (eds.), *Race, Class, and Gender: An Anthology* (Belmont, CA: Wadsworth Publishing Co., 1992), pp. 70–81.

p. 205 Womanism, Alice Walker, *In Search of Our Mother's Gardens: Womanist Prose* (New York: Harcourt Brace Jovanovich, 1983), p. xi.

p. 205 Womanism versus feminism, Cole, op. cit., p. 107.

p. 205 Objection to womanist, in bell hooks, *Talking Back: Thinking Feminist, Thinking Black,* pp. 181–182.

p. 205 Women shunning label *feminist,* in Bernice Lott, *Women's Lives:*

Themes and Variations in Gender Learning, 2nd ed. (Pacific Grove, CA: Brooks/Cole, 1994), p. 8.

p. 206 Midwives in South, in Linda Janet Holmes, "Thank You Jesus to Myself: The Life of a Traditional Black Midwife," in Evelyn C. White (ed.), *The Black Women's Health Book: Speaking for Ourselves* (Seattle, WA: Seal Press, 1990), pp. 98–106.

p. 206 Observed race and class differences in breast feeding in interview with Anne Zachman, RN, Dec. 18, 1993.

p. 206 Racial differences in incidence of breast feeding, in Jennifer D. Parker and Barbara Abrams, "Differences in Postpartum Weight Retention Between Black and White Mothers," *Obstetrics and Gynecology,* vol. 81 (1), May 1993, pp. 768–774.

p. 207 Women of means traveling to get abortions before *Roe* v. *Wade,* in Byllye Avery, "Breathing Life into Ourselves: The Evolution of the National Black Women's Health Project," in Evelyn C. White (ed.), *The Black Women's Health Book: Speaking for Ourselves* (Seattle, WA: Seal Press, 1990), pp. 4–10.

p. 207 Number of deaths caused by illegal abortions, in Angela Davis, *Women, Race, and Class* (New York: Vintage Books, 1983), p. 205.

p. 207 Sanger, ibid., p. 214.

p. 207 Sterilization abuse and eugenics movement, ibid., pp. 202–221.

p. 208 Hyde Amendment, in Bernice Lott, op. cit., p. 199.

p. 208 Government still paying for sterilization procedure for poor women, in Davis, op. cit., pp. 221.

p. 208 Quote, ibid.

p. 208 Differing abortion rates, in Table No. 111 "Abortions–Number, Rate, and Ratio, by Race: 1975–1992.," *Statistical Abstract of the United States* (114th ed.), (Washington, DC: U.S. Department of Commerce, 1994), p. 85.

pp. 208–9 NBWHP treating abortion as social problem, in Byllye Avery "Breathing Life into Ourselves," in Evelyn C. White (ed.), op. cit., pp. 4–10.

p. 209 Abortion rights rally, in Dorothy Gilliam, "Women of Color: 1 Voice" *Washington Post,* Metro sect., April 10, 1989, p. D3.

p. 209 Irene Esteves, in Barbara Brotman, "A Silent Minority: Whites Dominate the Debate—but not the passion—over the Abortion Issue" *Chicago Tribune,* Tempo sect., July 10, 1992, Zone: CN.

p. 209 Black Americans for Life and quote by Akua Furlow, in "Blacks 'No Longer Silent' on Abortion," *American Political Network,* Aug. 25, 1992, 11th story, Level 1.

p. 209 National Council of Negro Women survey, Barbara Brotman, op. cit.

p. 209 African American women being slow to embrace psychotherapy, in Deborah S. Pinkney, "Healing With Therapy," *Essence,* March 1993, pp. 45–46, 52, 54; in "negative attitude towards therapy," bell hooks, *Sisters of the Yam: Black Women and Self-Recovery* (Boston: South End Press, 1993), p. 73.

p. 209 Feminist psychotherapy, Bernice Lott, op. cit., pp. 305–306.

p. 209 Racial insensitivity of White therapists with Black patients, Julia A. Boyd, "Ethnic and Cultural Diversity in Feminist Therapy: Keys to Power" in Evelyn C. Whites (ed.), op. cit., pp. 226–234.

p. 210 Suicide viewed as a gesture of weakness, in bell hooks, *Sisters of the Yam,* p. 105.

p. 210 Suicide rates, in "Suicide Rates by Sex, Race, and Age Group: 1970 to 1989, Table No. 125, *Statistical Abstract of the United States,* 112th edition, U.S. Department of Commerce, Bureau of the Census, 1992.

pp. 210–211 Poem, Kate Rushin, in "In Answer to the Question: Have You Ever Considered Suicide?" in Evelyn C. White (ed.), op. cit., p. 3.

p. 211 Violence as main issue for Black women, Byllye Avery, "Breathing Life into Ourselves," pp. 4–10.

p. 211 Six out of ten Black women suffering from stress and quote about their silence, Julia Boyd, *In the Company of My Sisters* (New York: Dutton, 1993), p. 101.

p. 211 "Political is personal," Gloria Steinem, *Revolution From Within: A Book of Self-Esteem* (Boston: Little, Brown and Company, 1993).

p. 211 Julia Boyd telling Black women to better love themselves, in Boyd, op. cit.

p. 212 Black ministers rejecting feminist theology, in Pauli Murray, "Black Theology and Feminist Theology: A Comparative View," in James H. Cone and Gayraud S. Wilmore (eds.), *Black Theology: A Documentary History Volume One: 1966–1979* (Maryknoll, NY: Orbis Books, 1993, 2nd ed. rev.), p. 316.

p. 212 Paul's command about slaves and women, in James H. Cone and Gayraud S. Wilmore (eds.), ibid., p. 281.

p. 212 Church blocking feminist consciousness, in Pauline Terrelonge, "Feminist Consciousness and Black Women," in Jo Freeman (ed.), *Women: A Feminist Perspective* (Mountain View, CA: Mayfield Publishing, 1989), pp. 556–566.

pp. 212–213 Mary Daly and her two books *Beyond God the Father* and

Gyn/Ecology, in Jacqueline Grant, *Black Women's Christ and Black Women's Jesus: Feminist Christology and Womanist Response* (Atlanta: Scholars Press, 1989), pp. 151–172

p. 213 Criticisms of Daly, in Audre Lorde, "An Open Letter to Mary Daly," in Cherrie Moraga and Gloria Anzaldúa (eds.), *This Bridge Called My Back: Writings by Radical Women of Color* (NY: Kitchen Table, Women of Color Press, 1983), pp. 94–97.

p. 213 Criticisms of Theresa Hoover, in Theresa Hoover, "Black women and the Churches: Triple Jeopardy," in James H. Cone and Gayraud S. Wilmore (eds.), *Black Theology,* p. 302.

p. 213 Black women's feelings about church, in Alice Walker, *In Search of Our Mothers' Gardens* (San Diego: Harcourt Brace Jovanovich, 1983), p. 18; in Jacquelyn Grant, *White Women's Christ and Black Women's Jesus: Feminist Christology and Womanist Response* (Atlanta: Scholars Press, 1989).

p. 213 Barbara Harris as first African American Episcopal priest, in Hillary Lips, *Women, Men, and Power* (Mountain View, CA: Mayfield Publishing Co., 1991), p. 15.

p. 213 Summit of African American female pastors and statements by Bronson and Marrow, in Elizabeth Eisenstadt, "Women Tell of Struggle as Pastors," *Atlanta Constitution,* Nov. 6, 1993, sect. E., p. 6.

p. 214 White-supremacist forces at work in the Thomas hearings, in bell hooks, *Sisters of the Yam,* p. 3.

p. 214 Hill's refinement as a factor in White women's support of her by Julianne Malveaux, in M. P. Taylor, "A Call for Feminists to Mend Fences," *Dallas Morning News,* Aug. 4, 1993, Today sect., p. 5C.

pp. 214–215 Numbers of women in the House and Senate, Bernice Lott, op. cit., pp. 9–10.

pp. 214–215 Societal changes since Thomas hearings, including *Harris* v. *Forklift Systems* ruling, in Karen Branan, "Out for Blood: The Right's Vendetta Against Anita Hill's Supporters," *Ms.,* vol. IV, Jan.–Feb. 1994, pp. 82–87.

p. 215 Rebecca Walker, in Mariah Bear, "Feminist Flair for Flexibility: Young Activists Widen Approach," *Cleveland Plain Dealer* Dec. 13, 1992, Living Sect., p. 16.

p. 215 NOW and its involvement, *Warrior Marks* in Marie-Jose Ragab, "NOW Give New Visibility to Mutilation," *National NOW Times,* Nov. 1993, pp. 1, 2, col. 2.

p. 215 Reference to Mary Morten in personal interview, Nov. 16, 1991.

p. 215 Gillespie being new editor of *Ms.,* Ann Scales, "Black Women Face

Conflicts in Fight Against Racism, Sexism; Many Say Civil Rights, Feminist Movements Don't Fully Speak for Them," *Dallas Morning News,* Jul. 23, 1993, News sect. p. 1A.

p. 215 Efia Nwangaza, in Ann Scales and Judith Lynn Howard, "Black Women Face Conflicts in Fight Against Racism, Sexism: Many Say Civil Rights, Feminist Movements Don't Fully Speak for Them" *Dallas Morning News,* Jul. 23, 1993, p. 1A.

p. 216 Not necessary for Black women to identify with White women to give them credit for feminist influences, Joseph and Lewis, op. cit., pp. 57, 278.

p. 216 WAC, in Phoebe Hoban, "Big Wac Attack," *New York* magazine, Aug. 3, 1992, pp. 30–34, and to African American women being fastest-growing group in electoral politics in WAC Stats (115 Spring Street, NY: The Women's Action Coalition), p. 16.

p. 216 Carol Mosley Braun and United Daughters of the Confederacy, in Kevin Merida, " 'Sisters' Bring Change to Capitol Hill: Black Female Lawmakers are Working to Help Women and Children," *San Francisco Chronicle,* Aug. 5, 1993, Nation sect., p. A9.

Chapter 7
Relations on the Home Front

p. 217 Quote by Elinor Birney, in Susan Tucker, *Telling Memories Among Southern Women: Domestic Workers and Their Employers in the Segregated South* (New York: Schocken Books, 1988), p. 233.

p. 217 Quote, in Idella Parker, *Idella: Marjorie Rawlings' Perfect Maid* (Gainesville: University of Florida Press, 1992), pp. 128–129.

p. 218 Emancipation doesn't change Black women's lives, in Jacqueline Grant, *Black Women's Christ and Black Women's Jesus: Feminist Christology and Womanist Response* (Atlanta: Scholars Press, 1989), p. 197.

p. 218 Black women leave fields to become domestic servants, in Bonnie Thornton Dills, "Our Mothers' Grief: Racial Ethnic Women and the Maintenance of Families," in Margaret L. Andersen and Patricia Hill Collins (eds.), *Race, Class, and Gender: An Anthology* (Belmont, CA: Wadsworth Publishing Co., 1992), pp. 215–238; in Angela Y. Davis, *Women, Race, and Class* (New York: Vintage Books, 1983), p. 90.

p. 218 Caste system of South left intact, in David Katzman, *Seven Days a*

Week: Women and Domestic Service in Industrializing America (New York: Oxford University Press, 1978), p. 185.

pp. 218–219 Black domestics in North going back to colonial days, ibid., p. 203.

p. 219 1850 census figures, in Judith Rollins, *Between Women: Domestics and Their Employers* (Philadelphia: Temple University Press, 1985), p. 51.

p. 219 Black women unable to abandon domestic work after marriage, ibid., p. 54.

p. 219 Northward migration of Black women, in Tucker, op. cit., p. 46; in Katzman, op. cit., p. 203.

p. 219 Black women being turned away from factory jobs, in Grant, op. cit., p. 225.

p. 219 Changing demographics of domestic servants in North compared with South, in Rollins, op. cit., p. 54.

p. 219 Regional differences in status in having domestic servants, in Katzman, op. cit., p. 149.

p. 219 South referred to as "White housewives utopia," ibid., p. 185.

p. 219 60 percent of Black women employed as domestics in 1940, in Angela Y. Davis, *Women, Race, and Class* (New York: Vintage Books, 1983), p. 98.

p. 219 Number of women doing domestic work in 1940, in Rollins, op. cit., p. 56.

p. 220 Percent of women still doing domestic work in 1960 and 1970, ibid.

p. 220 1992 census figures on private household workers and their race, Table No. 664, "Employed Civilians by Occupation, Sex, Race, and Hispanic Origin: 1983 and 1992," *Statistical Abstract of the United States,* 113th ed. (Washington, DC: U.S. Department of Commerce, 1993), p. 407.

p. 220 Where domestic servants come from today, in Allyson S. Grossman, "Women in Domestic Work: Yesterday and Today," *Monthly Labor Review,* Aug. 1980, pp. 17–21.

p. 220 Quote, in Alice Childress, *Like One of the Family: Conversations from a Domestic's Life* (Boston: Beacon Press, 1956), pp. 36–37.

p. 220 Methodology, in Rollins, op. cit., pp. 8–10.

p. 221 Rationale for research, in Tucker, op. cit., p. 5.

p. 221 Regional differences in race relations, ibid., p. 13.

p. 221 Use of term "like one of the family," in Trudier Harris, Introduction, in Childress, op. cit., p. xviii.

p. 221 Black women knowing that White women delude themselves saying "like one of the family," in Nancie Caraway, *Segregated Sisterhood: Racism and the Politics of American Feminism* (Knoxville: The University of Tennessee Press, 1991), p. 101.

p. 221 White women singling out their own domestic servant as exceptional, in Tucker, op. cit., p. 227.

p. 221 Relationship between domestic servants and White employers flowing out of their roles as women, in Katzman, op. cit., p. 153.

p. 222 Blurred boundaries and devaluing of housework, in Rollins, op. cit., pp. 183–184.

p. 222 White women enjoying power over someone, in David Katzman, "Domestic Service: Women's Work," in Ann Strombery and Shirley Harkness (eds.), *Women Working* (Palo Alto, CA: Mayfield Publishing, 1978), p. 384.

p. 222 Comfortable hiring a woman of color as a domestic servant, in Rollins, op. cit., p. 184.

pp. 222–223 Telephone interview with Mike, in March 1994.

p. 223 Personal interview with Alice, April 15, 1994.

p. 223 Intimacy of home environment, in Rollins, op. cit., p. 91.

p. 223 Success of domestic arrangements measured in personal terms, ibid., p. 185.

p. 223 Karen Edwards quote, ibid.

p. 223 Elizabeth Roy quote, ibid.

p. 224 Zelda Greene quote, in Tucker, op. cit., p. 204.

p. 224 Quote, ibid., p. 147.

p. 224 White women confiding in Black women, in Tucker, op. cit., pp. 32, 190.

p. 224 Displaying deference, in Rollins, op. cit., p. 147.

pp. 224–225 Ruby Lee Daniels's quote, Nicholas Lemann, *The Promised Land: The Great Black Migration and How It Changed America* (New York: Alfred A. Knopf, Inc., 1991), p. 34.

p. 225 Black women bothered by being called by first names, in Katzman, op. cit., in p. 185; Rollins, op. cit., p. 176; in Susan Tucker, op. cit., p. 209.

p. 225 Wearing a uniform, in Patricia Hill Collins, *Black Feminist Thought: Knowledge, Consciousness, and the Politics of Empowerment* (Perspectives on Gender), vol. 2 (New York: Routledge, 1990), p. 57; in Katherine Boo, "Class Wear: Pride, Prejudice and the Not-So-Subtle Politics of the Working-Class Uniform," *Washington Post*, Feb. 7, 1993, Outlook sect., p. C1.

p. 225 Black women burdened by gifts, in Rollins, op. cit., pp. 189–190.

p. 225 Toting, in Tucker, op. cit., p. 146.

p. 225 Ellen Samuel, in Rollins, op. cit., p. 191.

p. 225 Maternalism, in Katzman, op. cit., p. 153.

p. 225 Southern Black domestics giving gifts back, Tucker, op. cit., p. 147.

p. 225 Quote by smug White female employer, ibid., p. 156.

p. 225 Quote by Joan Fox, in Rollins, op. cit., p. 214.

p. 226 White women view gift giving as positive gesture, in Tucker, op. cit., p. 149.

p. 226 Maternalism different in South, ibid., p. 146.

p. 226 Domestics giving the gift of time, ibid.

p. 226 Black domestics allowing White women to regress, in Adrienne Rich, "Disloyal to Civilization: Feminism, Racism, Gynephobia," in *On Lies, Secrets and Silence* (New York: Norton, 1979), p. 297.

p. 226 What White women call Blacks, ibid.

p. 226 Stealing, in Rollins, op. cit., p. 202.

p. 226 Flo Kennedy's mother, in Marcia Cohen, *The Sisterhood: The True Story of the Women Who Changed the World* (New York: Simon & Schuster, 1988), p. 161.

p. 227 Quote, in Bonnie Thornton Dills, "The Means to Put My Children Through: Child-Rearing Goals and Strategies Among Black Female Domestic Servants," in Lauren Richardson and Verta Taylor (eds.), *Feminist Frontiers III* (New York: McGraw-Hill, Inc., 1993), p. 110.

p. 228 Mattie Washington quote, ibid., pp. 109.

p. 229 Black domestics loving the White girl for no reason, in Jamacia Kincaid, "If Mammie Ruled the World," Geoffrey Stokes (ed.), *Village Voice Anthology, 1965–1980: Twenty-five Years of Writing from the Village Voice* (New York: Morrow & Co., 1982), p. 54.

p. 229 Personal interview with Tara, March 1994.

p. 229 Personal interview with Virginia, April 1994.

p. 229 Personal interview with Lynn, Dec. 1993.

pp. 229–230 Effects on Black children when mother takes care of White children, in Tucker, op. cit., p. 195.

p. 230 Excerpt about being raised to be tough, in April Sinclair, *Coffee Will Make You Black* (New York: Hyperion, 1994), p. 33.

p. 230 Excerpt about Pecola causing mess, in Toni Morrison, *The Bluest Eye* (New York: Washington Square Press, 1970), p. 87.

p. 231 Personal interview with Tara, March 1994.

p. 231 Excerpt about White and Black girls taking baths together, in Sinclair, op. cit., pp. 208–209.

p. 231 Willa Murray, in Bonnie Thornton Dills, op. cit., p. 107.

p. 232 Different parenting styles between White and Black women, ibid., pp. 100–110.

p. 232 Gloria Wade-Gayles quote, cited in Patricia Hill Collins, "The Meaning of Motherhood in Black Culture and Black Mother-Daughter Relationship," *Sage,* vol. 2 (1987), pp. 3–10.

p. 232 Othermothers, ibid.

pp. 232–233 Number of Black-White marriages in 1990 and 1970, in Jack Kroll, Vern E. Smith, and Andrew Murr, "Spiking a Fever," *Time* magazine, June 10, 1991, pp. 44–47.

p. 233 Number of Black-White biracial children, in Candy Mills, "The Biracial Baby Boom," *Interrace,* Feb. 1994, p. 19.

p. 233 Difficulty of getting accurate reporting of biracial children, in Nancy Nishimura Winn and Ronnie Priest, "Counseling Biracial Children: A Forgotten Component of Multicultural Counseling," *Family Therapy,* vol. 20 (Nov. 1993), pp. 29–36.

p. 233 Biraciality and measures of adjustment, in Raymond Vagas, "The Psychological and Social Functioning of Latency Age Black/White Biracial Girls From Intact Interracial Families," *Dissertation Abstracts International,* B 52/10 p. 5571, April 1992.

p. 233 Parenting strategies with biracial children, in Winn and Priest, op. cit., pp. 29–36.

p. 234 Different struggles of White versus Black mother, in telephone interview with Candy Mills, publisher and founding editor of *Interrace* and *Biracial Child* magazines, April 1994.

p. 234 One-drop rule of racial identity, in Kathy Russell, Midge Wilson, and Ron Hall, *The Color Complex: The Politics of Skin Color Among African Americans* (New York: Harcourt Brace Jovanovich, 1992), p. 14.

pp. 234–235 Quote about Gabriella from telephone interview with Candy Mills, publisher and founding editor of *Interrace* and *Biracial Child* magazines, April 1994.

p. 235 Gender differences in individuation from the primary caregiver, in Nancy Chodorow, *The Reproduction of Mothering* (Berkeley: University of California Press, 1978)

p. 235 Biracial children being successful, Francis Wardle, "Are Biracial Children Successful," *Biracial Child,* premier issue, Winter 1994, pp. 14–17.

pp. 235–236 Halle Berry quote, in Michelle Bennett, "Halle Berry: A Rising Star," *Interrace,* Jan.–Feb. 1994, p. 32.

p. 236 Mariah Carey quote, in Lynn Norment, "Mariah Carey," *Ebony,* April 1994, pp. 54–58, 60.

p. 236 Excerpt, in Lisa Jones, *Bulletproof Diva: Tales of Race, Sex and Hair* (New York: Doubleday, 1994), p. 29.

p. 237 White Mother Martyr Syndrome, in Russell, Wilson, and Hall, op. cit., p. 76.

p. 237 Problems of adjustment in biracial children, in Michael R. Lyles, Antronette Yancey, Candis Grace, and James H. Carter, "Racial Identity and Self-Esteem: Problems Peculiar to Biracial Children," *Journal of the American Academy of Child Psychiatry,* vol. 24 (1985), pp. 150–153.

p. 237 National Association of Black Social Workers, in Rita Simon and Howard Alstein, *Adoption, Race and Identity: From Infancy Through Adolescence* (New York: Praeger, 1992), p. 14; in Russell, Wilson, and Hall, op. cit., p. 100.

p. 237 Drop in transracial adoptions since 1975, in Simon and Alstein, op. cit., p. 12.

p. 238 Number of couples willing to adopt transracially, ibid., p. 13.

p. 238 Psychological adjustment of transracial children, in Christopher Bagley, *International and Transracial Adoptions: A Mental Health Perspective* (Brookfield, VT: Ashgate Publishing Co., 1993), pp. 80–81.

p. 238 Girls do well in transracial adoption situations, ibid., p. 16.

p. 238 Jessica Zang and her mother, in "Trans-Racial Adoption," WMAQ-Chicago (NBC) Channel Five News report, March 23, 1994.

p. 238 Carol Mosley Braun introducing bill in Congress, ibid.

p. 238 Illinois' new policy on transracial adoptions, in Jon Margolis, "Of Race and Reason in Adoption," *Chicago Tribune,* May 21, 1995, News sect., p. 2.

pp. 238–239 Lesbian couple granted transracial child, in James Warren, "D.C. Judge Grants Custody to Lesbian in Transracial Adoption Suit, *Chicago Tribune,* Feb. 20, 1994, Tempo section 5, p. 2.

p. 239 Types of surrogate motherhood, in Lori Andrews, *Between Stranger: Surrogate Mothers, Expectant Fathers, and Brave New Babies* (New York: Harper & Row, 1989).

p. 240 Number of surrogate births, in Martin Kasindorf, "And Baby Makes Four: Johnson vs. Calvert Illustrates Just About Everything That Can Go Wrong in Surrogate Births," *Los Angeles Times,* Jan. 20, 1991.

p. 240 Mary Beth Whitehead, in Lelia McDowell-Head, "On Surrogate Motherhood," *Essence,* July 1987, p. 136.

p. 240 Annie Johnson, in Martin Kasindorf, op. cit.

p. 240 Womb renting, in Lelia McDowell-Head, op. cit.

p. 241 White woman suing sperm bank, in Ronald Sullivan, "Mother Accuses Sperm Bank of a Mixup," *New York Times,* March 9, 1990, p. B1.

p. 241 Quotes, in Patricia Williams, *The Alchemy of Race and Rights* (Cambridge, MA: Harvard University Press, 1991), pp. 186–187.

Chapter 8
Pop Culture and the Media

p. 243 Whoopi Goldberg quote, in *Whoopi Goldberg Live* (Stamford, CT: Vestron Video, 1985).

p. 243 Madonna quote, in James Ledbetter, "Imitation of Life," *Vibe,* Sept. 1992, p. 113.

p. 244 Symbolism of Carrie Grace Battle's name from telephone interview with Kate Kane, Assistant Professor of Communication, DePaul University, Chicago, Nov. 10, 1994.

p. 245 Percent of literate nineteenth-century White women, in Glynis Carr, "The Female World of Love and Racism: Interracial Friendship in U.S. Women's Literature, 1840–1940. A dissertation submitted to Ohio State University, 1989 (Ann Arbor, MI: University Microfilms International, 1994), p. 44.

p. 245 Harriet Stowe and *Uncle Tom's Cabin,* in Patricia A. Turner, *Ceramic Uncles and Celluloid Mammies: Black Images and Their Influence on Culture* (New York: Anchor Books, 1994), pp. 48–49.

p. 245 Larger message about White women and Black women being friends, in Minrose C. Gwin, *Black and White Women of the Old South: The Peculiar Sisterhood in American Literature* (Knoxville: University of Tennessee Press, 1985), p. 27.

p. 245 Aunt Chloe is a mammy, in Turner, op. cit., p. 48.

p. 246 Mammy character stripped of sexual allure, in Elizabeth Schultz, "Out of the Woods and into the World: A Study of Interracial Friendships between Women in American Novels," in Marjorie Pryse and Hortense J. Spillers (eds.), *Conjuring: Black Women, Fiction, and Literary Tradition* (Bloomington: Indiana University Press, 1985), pp. 67–85.

p. 246 White women don't wish to hear truth about Black women's lives, in Turner, op. cit., p. 48.

p. 246 Harriet Wilson's *Our Nig,* in Henry Louis Gates, Jr., Introduction, Harriet E. Wilson, *Our Nig; or Sketches from the Life of a Free Black* (New York: Vintage Books, 1983), pp. xi–lv.

pp. 246–247 *Iola Leroy,* in "The Image of Black Women in Film," Marianna W. Davis (ed.), *Contributions of Black Women to America* (Columbia, SC: Kenday Press, 1982), p. 157.

p. 247 Tragic mulatto genre in White women's books, in Russell, Wilson, and Hall, op. cit., pp. 136–137.

p. 247 Black Renaissance, ibid., pp. 139–140.

p. 247 Larsen and Fauset, in Rita B. Dandridge, "On the Novels Written by Selected Black American Women: A Bibliographical Essay," in Gloria T. Hull, Patricia Bell Scott, and Barbara Smith (eds.), *All the Women Are White, All the Blacks Are Men, but Some of Us Are Brace* (New York: Feminist Press at The City University of New York, 1982), pp. 272–276.

p. 247 Late Renaissance authors writing for Black audiences, in Russell, Wilson, and Hall, op. cit., p. 142.

p. 248 Hurston working for Fannie Hurst, in Rita B. Dandridge, op. cit., p. 273.

p. 248 Hurst's book *Imitation of Life,* in Glynis Carr, op. cit., pp. 262–285.

p. 248 Hattie McDaniel in *Gone With the Wind,* in Langston Hughes and Milton Meltzer, *Black Magic* (Englewood Cliffs, NJ: Da Capo Press, 1967), pp. 298, 310.

p. 249 *Jezebel,* Richard Dyer, "White," *Screen,* vol. 29, Aug. 1988, pp. 44–64.

p. 249 Film *Imitation of Life,* in Bruce F. Kawin, *A Short History of the Movie,* 5th ed. (New York: Macmillan Publishing Co., 1992) pp. 312–315.

p. 250 Percentage of homes with TV sets, in the documentary *Color Adjustment* (San Francisco: California Newsreel, 1991).

p. 250 Sapphire stereotype in "Amos 'n' Andy," in Gloria Wade-Gayles, *No Crystal Stair: Visions of Race and Sex in Black Women's Fiction* (New York: The Pilgrim Press, 1984), p. 29.

p. 250 *Beulah,* in Turner, op. cit., p. 53.

p. 251 Vyry's forgiving gesture in *Jubilee,* in Minrose C. Gwin, "Jubilee: The Black Woman's Celebration of Human Community," in Marjorie Pryse and Hortense J. Spillers (eds.), *Conjuring: Black Women, Fiction, and Literary Tradition* (Bloomington: Indiana University Press, 1985), pp. 132–150.

p. 252 Growing militancy of maids in Black women's fiction, in Trudier

Harris, *From Mammies to Militants: Domestics in Black American Literature* (Philadelphia: Temple University Press, 1982); in Turner, op. cit., p. 56.

p. 252 Toni Morrison's *The Bluest Eye, Song of Solomon,* and *Tar Baby,* in Linda Buck Myers, "May As Well Be a Rainbow: The Fiction of Toni Morrison—A Story of Reading." A dissertation submitted to the University of Iowa, 1989 (Ann Arbor, MI: University Microfilms International, 1994).

p. 252 Conversation between Ondine and Margaret, in Toni Morrison, *Tar Baby* (New York: New American Library, 1981), p. 208.

p. 253 Alice Walker's *Meridian* suggesting new treatment of White women, in Wade-Gayles, op. cit., p. 240.

p. 253 Ellen Douglas's *Can't Quit You, Baby,* in Linda Kay Tate, op. cit., pp. 92–180.

p. 254 Gail Godwin's *A Mother and Two Daughters,* in Elizabeth Schultz, op. cit., pp. 67–85.

p. 254 Hollywood responding to political awakenings of Blacks and women, phone interview with Richard DeCordeva, Ph.D., Associate Professor of Communication, DePaul University, Chicago, Nov. 5, 1994.

pp. 255 Interracial male buddy genre, in Robyn Wiegman, "Negotiating America: Gender, Race, and the Ideology of the Interracial Male Bond," *Cultural Critique,* vol. 13, pp. 89–117.

p. 255–256 Spike Lee's treatment of women in film, in Julianne Malveaux, "Spike's Spite: Women at the Periphery," *Ms.,* Sept.–Oct. 1991, pp. 78–80.

p. 256 Goldberg's many maid roles, ESSENTIALS, "Maid to Order," *Essence,* Nov. 1992, p. 40; in *Ethnic Notions: Black People in White Minds* (San Francisco: California Newsreel, 1987).

p. 256 Goldberg's role in *Ghost,* in Lisa Jones, "The Defiant One: A Talk With Film Historian Donald Bogle," *Village Voice,* June 4, 1991, pp. 69, 88, cited in Judith Mayne, *Cinema and Spectatorship* (New York: Routledge, 1993), p. 142.

pp. 256–257 Frequency of Black actresses playing maids in film, in Wade-Gayles, op. cit., p. 28.

p. 257 Sixties activism forcing TV to change its images of Blacks, in *Ethnic Notions: Black People in White Minds* (San Francisco: California Newsreel, 1987).

p. 257 *Julia,* in Video Adjustment (San Francisco: California Newsreel, 1991).

p. 258 *Dynasty,* personal interview with Doreen Salina, Ph.D., director of clinical admissions, Northwestern University, Chicago, Nov. 10, 1994.

p. 259 Daytime television and Black viewership, Alan Carter, "All My Sisters," *Essence,* Aug. 1992, pp. 70–72, 114, 116.

p. 259 Aunt Jemima, in Marilyn Kern-Foxworth, *Aunt Jemima, Uncle Ben, and Rastus: Blacks in Advertising, Yesterday, Today, and Tomorrow* (Westport, CT: Greenwood Press, 1994), pp. 61–114.

pp. 259–260 Research by Carolyn West on advertising images of Black women being more sexualized, in paper entitled, "Developing an 'Oppositional Gaze': Black Women and Distorted Beauty Images," at the 18th Annual Women in Psychology Convention, Atlanta, March 11–14, 1993.

p. 260 Results of advertising survey and quote by respondent, "What Role Do Ads Play in Racial Tension," *Advertising Age,* vol. 63, Aug. 10, 1992, pp. 1, 35.

p. 261 Reference to WIC awards for Levi's for Women campaign and quote by Mimi Cook, copywriter, Foote, Cone, and Belding, telephone interview, Sept. 28, 1994.

p. 261 Racism in advertising report, in "Race Bias Seen in Magazine Ads," *Invisible Report,* New York City Department of Consumer Affairs, July 24, 1991.

p. 261 Preference for light-skinned models in advertising, Russell, Wilson, and Hall, op. cit., p. 156.

p. 262 Dark-skinned women in fashion modeling, in J. Clinton Brown, "Which Black Is Beautiful?" *Advertising Age,* vol. 64, Feb. 1, 1993, p. 19.

p. 262 Givenchy, in Sophfronia Scott, "It's a Small World After All: An Ethnic Rainbow Is Brightening Ads and Fashion Runways," *Time,* Sept. 25, 1989.

p. 262 Omission of Beverly Johnson from *Vogue* book and quote by her, *Kansas City Star,* Oct. 28, 1993, Stargazing sect., p. 1.

pp. 262–263 BGC, in Deborah Gregory and Patricia Jacobs, "The Ugly Side of the Modeling Business," *Essence,* Sept. 1993, pp. 89–90, 126, 128.

p. 263 Naomi Campbell quote, in Janet Ozzard, "Black Models Target Racism," *Toronto Star,* Dec. 26, 1992, Fashion sect., p. E6.

p. 263 Iman quote, in *Vancouver Sun,* Dec. 29, 1992, Vansun Style sect., p. C1.

p. 263 Black models asked to wear wigs, in Russell, Wilson, and Hall, op. cit., p. 154.

p. 263 History of Miss America pageant, in A. R. Riverol, *Live from Atlantic City: The History of the Miss America Pageant Before, After and in*

Spite of Television (Bowling Green, OH: Bowling Green State University Popular Press, 1992).

p. 263 First Black woman competing at national level, ibid., p. 103.

pp. 263–264 Controversy within Black community over Vanessa Williams winning Miss America, in Russell, Wilson, and Hall, op. cit., pp. 152–154.

p. 264 Runner-up Suzette Charles finishing Williams term, in K. Sue Jewell, *From Mammy to Miss America and Beyond: Cultural Images and the Shaping of US Social Policy* (London: Routledge, 1993), p. 53.

p. 264 Other Black Miss Americas, in Karima A. Haynes, "Miss America: From Vanessa Williams to Kimberly Aiken," *Ebony,* Jan. 1994, pp. 42–44, 46.

p. 264 Rockettes and Violet Holmes quote, in Patricia J. Williams, *The Alchemy of Race and Rights* (Cambridge, MA: Harvard University Press, 1991), p. 116.

pp. 264–265 Mere symmetry, ibid., pp. 116–117.

p. 265 Nontraditional casting, in Russell, Wilson, and Hall, op. cit., p. 150.

pp. 265–266 Telephone interview with Phylis Griffin, associate professor, Theater School, DePaul University, Chicago, Sept. 28, 1994.

p. 266 Janis Joplin's singing styles, in Ledbetter, op. cit., pp. 113–116.

p. 266 Manager in "Sandra's Blackness," ibid.

p. 267 Rare White performer in "Sandra's Blackness," ibid.

p. 267 Marketing of women singers' sexual appeal with the emergence of music videos, in Gillian G. Gaar, *She's a Rebel: The History of Women in Rock and Roll* (Seattle, WA: Seal Press, 1992), pp. 323–362.

p. 268 Women's sexuality hurting their image, in John Leland, "Our Bodies, Our Sales," *Newsweek,* Jan. 31, 1994, Arts sect., pp. 56–57.

p. 269 Comments made by Jamie Foster Brown, publisher, *Sister 2 Sister,* during panel discussion at the Speech, Equality, and Harm: Feminist Legal Perspectives on Pornography and Hate Propaganda Conference, Chicago, March 5–7, 1993.

p. 269 Quote by C. Delores Tucker in National Political Congress of Black Women, Inc., report, "Entertainment Commission Wages War on Gangster Lyrics and Misogyny in Rap: Is Anybody Listening? . . . Your Children Are!!!" issued on Nov. 2, 1993.

p. 269 Quote, in William Raspberry, "We Should Not Participate in Our Own Degradation," *Dallas Morning News,* Aug. 6, 1993, p. 27A.

p. 270 Quote by Euzhan Palcy, in Ally Acker, *Reel Women: Pioneers of the*

Cinema 1896 to the Present (New York: Continuum Publishing Co., 1991), p. 120.

Epilogue
Sisters Beneath the Skin

pp. 274–275 Telephone interview with Carmella Saraceno, Feb. 18, 1995.

Index

Jones, Lisa, 236–37
Jump roping, 45–46

Katzman, David, 225
Kegley, Michelle, 66
King, Mary, 192–93
Kistner, Janet, 50
Kochman, Thomas, 173
Korn/Ferry International survey, 165

Language skills, 172–73
Latino descent, 3, 220
Laurel School, the, 58
League of Women Voters (LWV), 34
Ledbetter, James, 267
Lee, Letha A., 166–67
Lee, Robinne, 100
Lee, Spike, 82, 255–56
Lesbian relationships, 7, 132–40
Levi's for Women ad campaign, 260–61
"Like one of the family," 221
Lindbolm, Louise, 176–77
Lips, size of, 93–95
Literature, 245–48, 251–54
"Long hair mystique," 82–83
Lorde, Audre, 131–32, 143, 147, 187,
    201–2, 204, 212
Lynching, 31–32, 33, 34

McDowell-Head, Lelia, 240
McIntosh, Peggy, 204–5
McLaughlin, Patricia, 88
Madonna (performer), 243
Madonna-whore dichotomy in sexual
    nature, 114–15
Malveaux, Julianne, 213–14, 255–56
"Mammy," 22
Manifesto, the (King and Hayden), 192–
    93
Marriage
  interracial, 8, 14, 124–32, 232–37
    backlash with, 131
    racial identity and, 6
Martineau, Harriet, 17
Mathabane, Gail, 111, 126
Media, 243–70
  advertising as, 259–61

early portrayals in, 245–51
film as, 254–57, 266–67, 270
literature as, 245–48, 251–54
modeling in, 261–63
music industry in, 267–70
performing arts in, 264–70
television as, 244, 250, 257–59
Medina, Venus, 137
Melanin, 77
Menstruation, 57
Mental health care, 209–11
Middle Eastern descent, 3
Midwives, 206
Mills, Candy, 233, 234–35
Misogyny, 268–69
Miss America Pageant, 99–100, 199, 263–
    64
Mitchell, Pamela, 87
Modeling, 261–63
Montgomery County NAACP
    (Washington State's), 65
Morgan, Robin, 187
Morrison, Toni, 43, 53, 76, 201, 230, 252
Morten, Mary, 133–34
Mosley, Kathleen, 40–41
Moss, Kate, 100
Motherhood, 232–40
  surrogate, 239–40
Mothers and daughters, 231–37
Mott, Lucretia, 24, 26, 27
"Mulatto hypothesis," 19, 74
"Mulattos," 14, 16, 19, 74
  as tragic characters, 247, 248
Mullins, Elizabeth, 125
Multiculturalism, 150, 214
Multiracial individuals, 14, 16, 19, 53–54,
    74, 232–37
  in literature, 246–48
Murrell, Audrey, 168
Murstein, Bernard, 129
Music industry, 267–70

NAACP (National Association for the
    Advancement of Colored People),
    195
  See also Montgomery County NAACP
National Association of Black Social

About the Authors

Midge Wilson is a professor of psychology at DePaul University in Chicago, where she also directs the women's studies program. **Kathy Russell** is a poet, scriptwriter, and former television insider who helped produce the nationally syndicated *Bertice Berry Show*. She also volunteers for the national civil rights organization Operation Push. They both live in Chicago. The authors' previous book *The Color Complex,* was widely acclaimed for its evaluation of color prejudices among African Americans.